Teaching Authority & Infallibility in the Church

Lutherans and Catholics in Dialogue VI

Edited by Paul C. Empie, T. Austin Murphy,
and Joseph A. Burgess

AUGSBURG Publishing House • Minneapolis

John Courtney Murray   (1904-1967)
Arthur Carl Piepkorn   (1907-1973)
Kent S. Knutson   (1924-1973)
Paul C. Empie   (1909-1979)
Warren A. Quanbeck   (1917-1979)

Ut Omnes Unum Sint

TEACHING AUTHORITY AND INFALLIBILITY
IN THE CHURCH

Copyright © 1978, 1980 Lutheran World Ministries and Bishops' Committee for Ecumenical and Interreligious Affairs

Library of Congress Catalog Card No. 79-54109
International Standard Book No. 0-8066-1733-0

Scripture quotations unless otherwise noted are from the Revised Standard Version of the Bible, copyright 1946, 1952, and 1971 by the Division of Christian Education of the National Council of Churches.

Citations: from *Theological Dictionary of the New Testament,* ed. by Gerhard Kittel and Gerhard Friedrich (Grand Rapids, Michigan: Wm. B. Eerdmans Publishing Company, 1964-1976), used by permission; from Paul Althaus, *The Theology of Martin Luther* (Philadelphia: copyright © 1966 by Fortress Press), reprinted by permission of Fortress Press; from Karl Rahner and Hans Küng, "A *Working Agreement* to Disagree," *America* 129 (July 7, 1973):9-12, used by permission.

MANUFACTURED IN THE UNITED STATES OF AMERICA

CONTENTS

ABBREVIATIONS

ACO = *Acta Conciliorum Oecumenicorum.* E. Schwartz, ed.
AP = *Apology of the Augsburg Confession*
BRHE = *Bibliothèque de la Revue d'Histoire ecclésiastique*
CA = *Confessio Augustana (Augsburg Confession)*
CIC = *Codex Iuris Canonici*
CBQ = *Catholic Biblical Quarterly*
Coll. Avell. = *Collectio Avellana*
CCL = *Corpus Christianorum.* Series latina.
CSEL = *Corpus Scriptorum Ecclesiasticorum Latinorum*
CT = C. Pharr, ed., *The Theodosian Code* (Princeton University Press, 1952).
DS = *Enchiridion Symbolorum.* H. Denzinger and A. Schönmetzer, eds. 33rd ed.
DTC = *Dictionnaire de Théologie Catholique*
Gasso = P. M. Gasso and C. M. Batlle, eds., *Pelagii I papa Epistulae quae supersunt* (Montserrat, 1956).
HNT = *Handbuch zum Neuen Testament*
JBC = *Jerome Biblical Commentary*
JBL = *Journal of Biblical Literature*
JK = Ph. Jaffé, *Regesta pontificum Romanorum.* 2nd ed., rev. by F. Kaltenbrunner.
LC = *Large Catechism*
LCL = *Loeb Classical Library*
LG = *Lumen Gentium*
L/RC = Lutherans and Catholics in Dialogue: 1. *The Status of the Nicene Creed as Dogma of the Church* (1965); 2. *One Baptism for the Remission of Sins* (1966); 3. *The Eucharist as Sacrifice* (1967); 4. *Eucharist and Ministry* (1970); 5. *Papal Primacy and the Universal Church* (Minneapolis: Augsburg, 1974); 6. *Teaching Authority and Infallibility in the Church* (Minneapolis: Augsburg, 1980). Volumes 1-4 were originally published by the Bishops' Committee for Ecumenical and Interreligious Affairs, 1312 Massachusetts Avenue, N.W., Washing-

ton, D.C. 20005 and the USA National Committee of
the Lutheran World Federation, Lutheran Center,
360 Park Avenue S., New York, N.Y. 10010. Volumes
1-3 have been reprinted together in one volume by
Augsburg Publishing House.

LW = Martin Luther. *Luther's Works*. J. Pelikan and H.
Lehmann, gen. eds.

M = *Sacrorum Conciliorum nova et amplissima* collectio.
J. D. Mansi, ed., continued by L. Petit and J. Martin.

MGH.Ep = *Monumenta Germaniae Historica. Epistulae.*

MGH.ES = *Monumenta Germaniae Historica. Epistulae
selectae.*

Mirbt-Aland = C. Mirbt and K. Aland, *Quellen zur Geschichte des Papsttums und des römischen Katholizmus.*
Vol. 1: *Von den Anfängen bis zum Tridentinum.*
6th ed.

MR = *Malta Report.* See "Common Statement," n. 12.

MT = Massoretic Text

NTD = *Das Neue Testament Deutsch*

NTS = *New Testament Studies*

PG = J. P. Migne, ed., *Patrologiae cursus completus, Series
graeca.*

PL = J. P. Migne, ed., *Patrologiae cursus completus, Series
latina.*

RGG³ = *Die Religion in Geschichte und Gegenwart.* 3rd
ed.

RB = *Revue Biblique*

SC = *Sources chrétiennes*

Schwartz = E. Schwartz, ed., *Publizistische Sammlungen
zum Acacianischen Schisma.* Abhandlungen der Bay-
erischen Akademie der Wissenschaften, Philos.-hist.
abt. n. f., fascicle 10 (Munich: 1934).

Sieben = H. J. Sieben, *Die Konzilsidee der Alten Kirche.*
Konziliengeschichte, Series B: Untersuchungen, vol.
1 (Paderborn: Schöningh, 1979).

SLH = *Scriptores Latini Hiberniae*

StT = *Studi e Testi*, Rome

Tappert = *The Book of Concord. The Confessions of the
Evangelical Lutheran Church,* T. Tappert, trans.
and ed. (Philadelphia: Fortress, 1959).

TDNT = *Theological Dictionary of the New Testament*

Thiel = *Epistolae Romanorum Pontificum Genuinae . . . a.
S. Hilaro usque ad Pelagium II.* Vol. 1, A. Thiel, ed.

ThLZ = *Theologische Literaturzeitung*

TS = *Theological Studies*

TWNT = *Theologisches Wörterbuch zum Neuen Testament.* G. Kittel and G. Friedrich, eds.

UR = *Unitatis Redintegratio*

WA = *D. Martin Luthers Werke.* Kritische Gesamtaus-
gabe. Weimar, 1883 to present.

ZNW = *Zeitschrift für die neutestamentliche Wissenschaft
und die Kunde der älteren Kirche*

PREFACE

Theological discussions between teams of scholars appointed respectively by the U. S. Roman Catholic Bishops' Committee for Ecumenical and Interreligious Affairs and the USA National Committee of the Lutheran World Federation (now called Lutheran World Ministries) began in July, 1964. The topic chosen was "The Status of the Nicene Creed as Dogma of the Church." Taken up in succession thereafter were the subjects "One Baptism for the Remission of Sins," "The Eucharist as Sacrifice," "Eucharist and Ministry," and "Papal Primacy and the Universal Church." The conversations were designed to proceed from areas of relatively extensive agreement to others in which historically disagreement had been substantial and divisive.

Only a single meeting was devoted to each of the first two topics and three meetings to the third. In contrast, the joint conclusions published in this volume on "Teaching Authority and Infallibility in the Church" required nine meetings over a span of five years!

There was good reason for this. The time spent on a subject was related less to its relative importance than to its complexity. It was necessary to view papal primacy in the perspective of the unity of the universal Church. In examining papal infallibility it was essential to study it in the context of teaching authority and the certitude of faith in the universal Church and particularly in the context of the Lutheran and Roman Catholic traditions. Biblical, historical, and doctrinal research provide illumination on aspects of the subject but do not by themselves provide final, universally acceptable answers.

The group concentrated on a common problem rather than striving to maintain rigid adversary positions of the past. Thus they achieved a degree of mutual understanding which hopefully will help to establish an approach and a climate for further progress toward resolving this difficult issue in the future. They regret that a greater measure of agreement was not reached in these talks. Nevertheless their work has served to elevate a long-standing debate from one of entrenched contradiction to one of open, mutual search for truth in a mood of respect, trust, and Christian love. We believe the Holy Spirit has guided and blessed this endeavor and that it will bear fruit.

As in previous volumes, we remind readers that the dialogue group and its individual members do not speak officially for the churches they represent. Nevertheless, as competent and responsible theologians their views merit serious attention and carry considerable weight.

In the past it has been the task of the staff members of the two sponsoring organizations to gather and edit the documents appearing in each volume, certification thereof being given by the undersigned. In this instance Dr. Joseph Burgess has done this arduous work; we express to him a special word of appreciation. To all of the participants who worked so long and gave so freely of their time and skills in this undertaking the whole Church will remain deeply indebted.

Co-Chairmen:

PAUL C. EMPIE
USA National Committee,
Lutheran World Federation

✠ T. AUSTIN MURPHY
Bishops' Committee for
Ecumenical and Interreligious Affairs

IN MEMORIAM

Dr. Paul C. Empie, co-chairman from 1965-1979 of the official dialogue sponsored by the USA National Committee of the Lutheran World Federation and the U.S.A. Catholic Bishops' Committee for Ecumenical and Interreligious Affairs, died September 1, 1979. At the meeting of the dialogue at Princeton, N.J., September 13-16, 1979, the members of the dialogue passed the following resolution:

We wish to express our sense of deep personal loss at the death of Paul Empie. He lived to serve, and he served in a multitude of ways—as pastor, as administrator, as participant in activities ranging from filmmaking to refugee resettlement and relief work to theological dialogue. Already in 1964 he suggested to Roman Catholics that the time had come for our two churches to begin theological dialogue. His enthusiasm continued after the dialogue actually started in 1965. He watched over the progress of the conversations with patience, care, and a steady hand. He appreciated the theologians' insistence on time for thorough discussion of difficult questions. At the same time he constantly pressed for progress and kept before the dialogue group the reality that their words and decisions must be communicated in an understandable way to all the people of the churches. His love for the Lord and his Church was a very evident part of his life among us. We miss him and we are thankful to the Lord for all that he has meant to us.

CHRONOLOGICAL LISTING
OF SESSIONS AND PAPERS

September, 1973, Allentown, Pennsylvania
Avery Dulles, "The Problem of Infallibility. Agenda for a Lutheran-Catholic Study" (unpublished).

February, 1974, Baltimore, Maryland
Avery Dulles, "Infallibility: The Terminology" (published in this volume).
George A. Lindbeck, "The Reformation and the Infallibility Debate" (published in this volume).

September, 1974, Princeton, New Jersey
Joseph A. Fitzmyer, "The Office of Teaching in the Christian Church According to the New Testament" (published in this volume).
John Reumann, "Teaching Office in the New Testament? A Response to Professor Fitzmyer's Paper" (published in this volume).
Karlfried Froehlich, "Fallibility Instead of Infallibility? A Brief History of the Interpretation of Galatians 2:11-14" (published in this volume).
Jerome D. Quinn, "Scriptural *Loci* on Infallibility" (unpublished).
Gerhard O. Forde, "Infallibility Language and the Early Lutheran Tradition" (published in this volume).
Warren A. Quanbeck, "Theses on Lutheran Counterparts to Infallibility" (unpublished).
Eric W. Gritsch, "Lutheran Teaching Authority: Past and Present" (published in this volume).
Avery Dulles, "Moderate Infallibilism" (published in this volume).
Carl J. Peter, "A Rahner-Küng Debate and Ecumenical Possibilities" (published in this volume).

February, 1975, St. Louis, Missouri
Joseph A. Burgess, "What Does It Mean for a Christian To Say, 'Christ Is the Truth'?" (unpublished).
Jerome D. Quinn, "On the Terminology for Faith, Truth, Teaching, and the Spirit in the Pastoral Epistles: A Summary" (published in this volume).
Warren A. Quanbeck, "The *Magisterium* in the Lutheran Church with Special Reference to Infallibility" (published in this volume).
Jared Wicks, "Papal Infallibility, 1350-1600" (unpublished).
George H. Tavard, "Infallibility: A Structural Analysis" (published in this volume).
George A. Lindbeck, "Theories of Language and Religion and the Permanence of Doctrine" (to be published as the *St. Michael's Lectures, 1974,* Gonzaga University, Spokane, Washington).

September, 1975, Washington, D.C.
Joseph A. Burgess, "The Historical Background of Vatican I" (published in this volume).
Fred Kramer, "Psycho-Social Factors in the Lutheran Opposition to Papal Infallibility" (unpublished).
Robert B. Eno, "The Roman Catholic View of the Authority of Ecumenical Councils: The Patristic Origins" (published under the title, "Pope and Council," *Science et Esprit* 28 [1976]:183-211).
Eamon R. Carroll, "Papal Infallibility and the Marian Definitions" (unpublished).
Karlfried Froehlich, "Remarks on Brian Tierney's Book, *Origins of Papal Infallibility, 1150-1350*" (unpublished).

February, 1976, Scottsdale, Arizona
Kilian McDonnell, "Infallibility as Charism at Vatican I" (published in this volume).

September, 1976, Gettysburg Pennsylvania
Robert B. Eno, "The Roman View of the Petrine Office in the Church, 366-461" (unpublished).

February, 1977, Washington, D.C.

September, 1977, Columbia, South Carolina
Robert B. Eno, "Some Elements in the Pre-History of Papal Infallibility" (published in this volume).

February, 1978, Lantana, Florida

September, 1978, Minneapolis, Minnesota

1

TEACHING AUTHORITY
AND INFALLIBILITY
IN THE CHURCH

I
Common Statement

INTRODUCTION

1. Lutherans and Roman Catholics in the United States
have been engaged since 1965 in a theological dialogue
dealing with the main issues which have divided their
churches since the 16th century.[1] The measure of consensus they were able to reach on the Eucharist and on
Ministry [2] was expressed in two joint statements that are
of major importance for continuing theological convergence. In approaching the topic of papal primacy, they
were aware of special difficulties, since this topic occasioned the most violent antagonisms of the past, and since
these antagonisms have left their mark on the mentalities
of contemporary Christians. Yet they were also able to
agree on many points in a joint statement in which papal
primacy is regarded as a Ministry to the universal Church.

Because papal infallibility is conceptually distinct from
primacy and has had its own, rather more recent, development, the agreed statement on primacy did not include
consideration of the question of infallibility. But, as had
been planned, the members of the dialogue began discussing this topic as soon as agreement had been reached on
the principle of a Ministry to the Church universal. The
present statement thus follows logically the previous discussions and joint statements of *Lutherans and Catholics
in Dialogue*.

In order to treat the subject adequately, this dialogue had to set the question of papal infallibility in a broad horizon. Papal infallibility is related to several wider questions: the authority of the gospel, the indefectibility of the Church, the infallibility of its belief and teaching, and the assurance or certainty which Christian believers have always associated with their faith. Furthermore, such a question cannot be examined in our day without referring to the contemporary crisis of authority, and without paying attention to the critical questions raised by linguistic analysis and philosophy regarding the use of language to express religious insights.

2. Discussion of papal infallibility on the Catholic side was given its focus by the First Vatican Council when the doctrine was defined in 1870. The Council taught that the bishop of Rome, as successor of Peter in the primacy, is divinely protected from error when he speaks *ex cathedra,* that is, when, "as pastor and doctor of all Christians" and by virtue of "his supreme apostolic authority," he "defines a doctrine concerning faith or morals" to be held "by the universal Church." In such an extraordinary case, the Council specified, the bishop of Rome proceeds with the infallibility with which "the divine Redeemer wanted his Church to be endowed in defining doctrine concerning faith or morals." [3] It was this infallibility which Pius XII invoked when he defined the doctrine of the Assumption of Mary in 1950.

Despite the careful delimitation of papal infallibility by Vatican I, this dogma was frequently understood more broadly in the period between the two Vatican Councils. Often for the popular mind, and also in theological manuals,[4] it was thought to imply that all papal utterances are somehow enhanced by infallibility. Encyclicals were sometimes interpreted as infallibly conveying the true doctrine even when they did not meet the conditions specified by Vatican I for *ex cathedra* definitions. Piux XII, indeed, pointed out that encyclical teaching may require the assent of Catholics, especially when it reiterates what is already settled Catholic doctrine or when the pope, even without appealing to his infallible teaching authority, expresses his intention of settling what was previously a controverted question.[5]

Following Vatican II and its treatment of infallibility in the Constitution *Lumen gentium*,[6] the climate of Catholic theology has favored reassessing popular assumptions and theological interpretations. The present common statement of *Lutherans and Catholics in Dialogue* is a contribution to this reassessment.

3. On the Lutheran side, there seems at first glance no room for reassessment. The Reformers' attitude toward papal infallibility was strongly negative.[7] They insisted that in proclaiming the Pauline teaching of justification of the sinner by grace through faith they had a biblical and catholic basis. Consequently they regarded the excommunication of Luther as an arbitrary act, an abuse of papal authority. They viewed the division in the Church as a tragic necessity, as the price they had to pay for fidelity to the Word of God. The promulgation of papal infallibility in 1870 appeared to Lutherans as the deepening of an already serious disagreement. The separation begun by the condemnation of Luther's teachings in *Exsurge Domine* [8] and later widened by the Council of Trent now seemed beyond hope of reconciliation. For while Lutherans share with Catholics the conviction that the Church of Christ is indefectible,[9] they regard the maintenance of this indefectibility as the sovereign work of God. It appeared to them that the dogma of infallibility was an attempt to usurp the Lordship which God has conferred on Christ alone.

Yet Lutherans need not exclude the possibility that papal primacy and teaching authority might be acceptable developments, at least in certain respects.[10] The Lutheran Reformers accepted the legitimacy of developments in the Church except where these denied or subverted the teaching of Scripture. Thus, they retained the liturgy of the Latin rite, making revisions where they judged its formulations to be contrary to the gospel; and they tried to preserve the episcopal structure of the Church and the traditional ecclesiastical discipline.[11] Theoretically, some aspects of the papacy could have been accepted in the same way. For while Lutherans see papal primacy as emerging over a long period of time, rather than something taught in the Scriptures, this function could, under proper conditions, be acknowledged as a legitimate development, maintaining unity, mediating disputes, and defending the Church's spiritual freedom.

This theoretical possibility of seeing papal teaching authority in a more favorable light is now being actualized. Roman Catholics are rethinking their position, and this suggests that Lutherans may well ask themselves whether the Roman Catholic doctrine of papal infallibility, even if not something which they would be able to affirm for themselves, need continue to be regarded by them as anti-Christian and therefore as a barrier to the unity of the churches. Catholics, on the other hand, must ask themselves whether their view of the papal teaching office and its infallibility can be so understood and presented as to meet the legitimate concerns of those Christians who have traditionally opposed the doctrine.

I
A FRESH LOOK AT DOCTRINAL AUTHORITY IN RELATION TO THE QUESTION OF INFALLIBILITY

4. Two areas of investigation have been especially helpful to us in examining infallibility afresh. First, the topic has been set in the broader horizon of doctrinal authority in the early Church, especially as examined in light of modern historical studies in Scripture and the Church Fathers. We set forth below not a complete historical survey but pertinent highlights from our discussions. Second, because of insights which arise when the question is examined in light of linguistic and cultural contexts, we have found ourselves able to think in ways which are different from earlier discussion. These influences have enabled us to view our mutual and individual concerns in new ways.

A) Gospel and Doctrinal Authority in the Early Church: Biblical and Patristic Roots

5. God, known to us above all through what he "has done for the salvation of the world in Jesus Christ," [12] is the source and ground of authority for the Church of Christ. The gospel, the proclaiming of this saving action of God in the person, life, death, and resurrection of Jesus and made present in the Holy Spirit, is an expression of this

authority. This gospel *(a)* was proclaimed by witnesses— apostles and others—in the early Church; *(b)* was recorded in the New Testament Scriptures, which have "a normative role for the entire later tradition of the Church";[13] *(c)* has been made living in the hearts of the believers by the Holy Spirit; *(d)* has been reflected in the "rule of faith" *(regula fidei)* and in the forms and exercise of church leadership; *(e)* has been served by Ministers.

1) Jesus Christ as Authority

6. In Jesus' day there were all sorts of authorities. For example, the political authority was that of the Roman Empire. Israel recognized the authority of the law (Torah), of the traditions (Mark 7:8) amplifying the law set forth by the teachers (Matt. 23:2), and of the temple and its cult administered by priests. In the New Testament authority is ascribed to Jesus Christ (John 17:2; 5:27; Rev. 12:10).

The New Testament pictures of Jesus are all influenced by the theologies of various writers reflecting on his earthly life in the light of the Easter event. Yet it is possible to discern, especially because of multiple attestation in our sources, that Jesus' contemporaries associated various kinds of authority with his words and deeds, even before his resurrection.

He was understood to be a prophet (Mark 6:2–4 and par.; Luke 7:39; 13:33–34), to speak and act as one of the prophets of old (Mark 8:28 and par.; Luke 7:16). Jesus was remembered as a man who taught with authority (Mark 1:22). He not only interpreted the law, as the rabbis did, but he did so with definitive authority (Matt. 7:28–29, with reference to the Sermon on the Mount). In the Gospel of Matthew he is depicted as speaking in his own name, in contrast to "the men of old": "But *I* say to you . . ." (Matt. 5:21–48).

Jesus was understood to have the authority of an exorcist because he cast out demons and worked cures (Mark 1:27; Matt. 12:27–28, par. Luke 11:19–20; cf. Luke 9:1 and 10:17). These wonders aroused hopes that he might be the expected King of Israel (John 6:14).

To him, as Son of man, the Gospels ascribe the authority on earth to forgive sins (Mark 2:5–10 and par.) and to interpret the Sabbath (Mark 2:23–28 and par.). In Jerusalem, in the context of his teaching (Mark 11:17) and the cleansing of the temple (Mark 11:15–17), he was asked specifically, "By what authority are you doing these things, or who gave you this authority?" (Mark 11:28).

Thus the New Testament authors see his authority, in various forms, as a feature of his ministry. Here was "something greater than the temple" (Matt. 12:6), greater than Jonah and Solomon (Matt. 12:41–42), and different from the power of "this world" (John 18:36).

7. After his death and resurrection, the authority in Jesus is seen in an entirely new dimension. He is now declared to be risen and enthroned at the right hand of God. He is acclaimed as the Lord, ruling with authority. He is designated Son of God "in power" . . . (Rom. 1:4). To him "all authority in heaven and on earth" is given (Matt. 28:18). He is exalted at God's right hand (Acts 2:34–36), acclaimed as Lord (*kyrios,* Phil. 2:9-11). Now the Holy Spirit is poured forth as the Spirit of Christ (Acts 2:33; Gal. 4:6).[14]

Faith as trust and obedience is the proper response to the Lord Jesus Christ (Rom. 1:5; 10:8–10; Phil. 2:12; 3:21). No one can confess him to be Lord without the Holy Spirit (1 Cor. 12:3). In the perspective of faith all creation is subject to him (Phil. 2:10): he has a role in creation (1 Cor. 8:6; John 1:3) and in the preservation of the world (Heb. 1:3); he will sit upon God's judgment seat (2 Cor. 5:10; cf. Rom. 14:10) as the one designated by God to judge the living and the dead (Acts 10:42). Past, present, and future are under the authority of Christ, in whom all God's promises are affirmed (2 Cor. 1:20).

2) *The Gospel as Authority*

8. The risen Lord's authority and power in the Christian community are expressed in the gospel, that message of Christ crucified and risen which his followers proclaimed (1 Cor. 1:21–23; 2:2; Rom. 1:16, 4:25; Matt. 26–28). It includes what Jesus himself had taught,[15] viewed in light of the Easter "good news" that "he is risen." This gospel, which is a word of power from God (Rom. 1:16; cf. 1 Cor. 2:5) and is truth (Gal. 2:5, 14; cf. Eph. 4:21), is expressed in various terms, as God's righteousness (Rom.

1:17, "justification"), reconciliation (2 Cor. 5:18–21), and forgiveness of sins (Col. 1:14; Matt. 9:2; Luke 4:18; Acts 10:43; 13:38). Indeed Christ is himself the gospel. This is true for Paul [16] and Mark [17] in particular. One can claim, indeed, that for the first two centuries of Christianity, "gospel" denoted "the revelation of Christ." [18]

3) The Gospel (a) Proclaimed by Witnesses

9. This gospel found expression in many ways, reflecting the church's needs and the diverse cultures and literary forms of the day.[19] It was proclaimed orally and later written down. It took the shape of credal formulas and confessions of faith (1 Cor. 12:3, "Jesus Christ is Lord"; 1 Cor. 15:3–5); hymns (Col. 1:15–20); letters (e.g., 1 Thessalonians); catechetical material (1 Cor. 6:9–11; Gal. 5:19–23; Matt. 5–7); miracle stories; narratives; and eventually gospel books and apocalypses large (Revelation) and small (Mark 13). It was proclaimed in Baptism (Matt. 28:19) and the Lord's Supper (1 Cor. 11:26). It was spoken, in the New Testament period, in Aramaic, Greek, Latin, and probably other languages. It employed images from the Hebrew Scriptures and from the cultures of the ancient Near East and the Hellenistic world. The gospel addressed needs of the Christian community in preaching, teaching, worship, and every aspect of daily life.

10. The witnesses who set forth this gospel shared in the authority of Jesus Christ. During his earthly ministry Jesus had sent forth disciples to carry on his mission by proclaiming the message about the kingdom of God (Mark 3:15; 6:7; Matt. 4:23; 9:35). After Easter the risen Lord commissioned followers with his authority to go forth into all the world, to the close of the age (Matt. 28:19–20), and promised them his presence in their corporate mission as his Church (Matt. 18:20). When they proclaimed his word, they shared in the authority of Jesus himself. Jesus said, "He who hears you hears me" (Luke 10:16; cf. Matt. 10:14, 40; John 17:18; 20:21). The witnesses to Jesus are enumerated in such groupings as apostles, prophets, teachers, evangelists, pastors, etc.,[20] and in lists of names such as those of "the Twelve." [21] Although those who exercised this apostolic Ministry are often anonymous and little is known about them, their boldness, confidence, and assur-

ance are striking.[22] They did not hesitate at times to assert that the Holy Spirit guided the decisions they had made (Acts 15:28, "It has seemed good to the Holy Spirit and to us"); they invoked anathemas on those who preached a false gospel (Gal. 1:6–9). Their statements reflect confidence that the truth of their message is ultimately anchored in God.[23]

4) *The Gospel* (b) *Recorded in Scripture*

11. In the period before the New Testament writings were composed and collected, the authoritative gospel about Christ was a spoken message transmitted by apostolic witnesses. Hence one can speak of "the Tradition of the Gospel (the *paradosis* of the *kerygma*)" by which Christians lived.[24] To be sure, the Christian community did have a Bible in what we term the Old Testament; these Scriptures were regularly interpreted in light of Jesus Christ and the good news about him (Luke 24:27, 45).

But to meet needs of their day and to offer their testimony in a more enduring form, the early witnesses wrote letters, Gospels, and other books, beginning about A.D. 50. Within the next 50 to 100 years all 27 books eventually designated as New Testament Scripture were composed,[25] and during the second, third, and fourth centuries these were assembled into the authoritative collection of books which we call the canonical New Testament. This collection provides a written precipitate of the primitive Church's faith. It witnesses to Christ, pointing to ways in which the gospel had been set forth. It was written "that you may believe that Jesus is the Christ, the Son of God, and that believing you may have life in his name" (John 20:31). The canonical collection,[26] which includes the Old and New Testaments, is normative and authoritative for all the Church's statements of faith and teaching.

5) *The Gospel* (c) *Made Living by the Spirit*

12. The Spirit of God has been at work in every stage of the transmission of the gospel. No one can confess Jesus as Lord (1 Cor. 12:3) or witness to him (John 15:26–27) apart from the Holy Spirit. Moreover, the Spirit is associated with Jesus' promise, "When the Spirit of truth comes, he will guide you into all the truth; for he will not speak on his own authority, but whatever he hears he will speak, and he will declare to you the things that are to come" (John 16:13). The Spirit is active not only in the inspiration of Scripture but also in the reception and further transmission of the message. The inscription of Scripture is to be understood within the setting of the early Christian community. It is a unique work of the same Spirit who through the ages enlivens Christ's people with his gifts and brings them to assurance of faith. The Spirit-filled community plays an authenticating role in the reception of Scripture and the gospel.

6) *The Gospel* (d) *Summarized in the* regula fidei

13. Brief summaries of the apostolic preaching were already developed in the first Christian generation. Some were in writing before that generation ended (cf. 1 Cor. 15:3ff.) and others were recorded in the second-generation Christian literature, including those documents that were later recognized as part of the canon of the New Testament (Titus 3:5–7; cf. 1 Clement 32:3–4). These summary statements, often used in the context of Baptism, were responses to the challenges of their day and guides to discerning the truth of the gospel. They continued to be fashioned in the second century, and the Church Fathers could describe such formulations as "the canon of the truth" (Irenaeus), "the rule of faith (*regula fidei*, esp. Tertullian). From such summary statements developed the Old Roman Symbol from which is derived the Apostles' Creed. In the third and fourth centuries these confessions of local churches grew into authoritative statements of faith, stressing central truths and affirming particular points that had become crucial. This development reached a climax in the conciliar creeds of Nicaea-Constantinople (A.D. 325, 381), which took up and reformulated credal statements of previous generations.[27]

7) *The Gospel* (e) *Served by Ministers*

14. Along with the emergence of Scriptures and credal statements in this period, forms of church leadership also developed. The apostles, prophets, teachers, *episkopoi*, deacons, presbyters, and evangelists [28] of the first century were succeeded by others who carried on their witness.

There developed an idea of "succession to the apostles," which has been interpreted as succession in doctrine, or as succession in office, or both.[29]

15. Of special relevance in the light of later developments is the "Petrine function" as delineated in the New Testament.[30] Among other texts, Matt. 16:18 has served to assure the faithful that "the powers of death shall not prevail" against the Church.[31] Peter, who is presented there as the "rock" on which the Church is to be founded, is the one for whom Jesus prayed that his faith might not fail (Luke 22:32); he has thus been associated with the notion of indefectibility.[32] Power and authority have also been associated with the image of Peter, to whom the "keys of the kingdom" are entrusted (Matt. 16:19) and who has, along with others (Matt. 18:18), the task of "binding and loosing." [33] Alongside of this, the Petrine function has been seen, in the light of Luke 22:32, as one of "strengthening the brethren," a responsibility which Peter also shares with others (Acts 15:32).[34]

However such passages are interpreted,[35] Peter's role should be understood in relation to Jesus' promise to remain with his disciples until "the close of the age" (Matt. 28:20). The extent to which this promise includes a guarantee of Christian preaching and teaching is a question which Scripture does not answer.

16. Infallibility is not a New Testament term. It is used neither of the gospel nor of its proclamation, let alone of books, doctrines, or persons. Yet the New Testament is concerned with many of the issues that arise in later theological discussions of the authority and infallibility of Scripture, Church, councils, and popes.

The Pastoral Epistles in particular display a special awareness of the problem of the faithful transmission of the gospel. The author directs Titus to "amend what is defective and appoint elders in every town" (Titus 1:5), and Timothy to "charge certain persons not to teach any different doctrine" (1 Timothy 1:3). Timothy is told, "guard what has been entrusted to you" (1 Timothy 6:20; cf. 2 Timothy 1:12, 14). The key virtue of the apostolic Ministry which Timothy and Titus share is faithfulness (Titus 1:7–9; 2 Timothy 2:2). From this faithfulness should flow their bold proclamation of the gospel (Titus

2:15; 1 Timothy 4:11–16). They share in and contribute to the solid assurance that belongs to "God's firm foundation" (2 Timothy 2:19; cf. 1 Timothy 3:15).[36]

B) Gospel and Doctrinal Authority in Subsequent Centuries

17. The concern for faithful transmission did not diminish during the following centuries. The Church Fathers emphasized the normative past and the Church's task of preserving the "deposit of faith." They trusted that the Holy Spirit would protect the gospel against false teaching. The earliest history of the appeal to an unbroken line of apostolic teaching is unclear. But in the late second century, especially in the struggle against Gnosticism, the Fathers linked the reliable transmission of apostolic teaching to episcopal sees regarded as founded by apostles. The doctrine transmitted in these sees became important for the councils, which endeavored to set forth authoritative interpretations of "the faith . . . delivered to the saints" (Jude 3).

18. Among these sees Rome gained special importance. At first the Roman bishops did not take much initiative in the doctrinal controversies, which took place mainly in the East. By the middle of the third century, however, they seem to have assumed special responsibility for preserving and interpreting the faith of "antiquity" because of the prerogatives of the See of Peter (*cathedra Petri*).[37] Some Roman emperors included the faith of the bishop of Rome in the official norm of orthodoxy, and the biblical image of the Church "without spot or wrinkle" (Eph. 5:27) began to be applied to the church of Rome. Rome became *the* apostolic see. As Pope Innocent I put it, from Rome "the other churches, like waters proceeding from their natal source . . . (like) pure streams from an uncorrupt head, should take up what they ought to enjoin." [38] As the Formula of Pope Hormisdas (A.D. 525) declared, in Rome "the catholic religion has always been preserved immaculate." [39] The conviction that Rome had always defended the purity of the faith continued on into the Middle Ages, and it found expression in such influential documents as the Pseudo-Isidorian Decretals, in statements by popes and theologians, and in collections of canon law.

19. There were, however, challenges to such claims, both in the East and in the West. Eastern Christians regarded Rome as one of several apostolic sees to which protection of the pure faith had been entrusted. The faithfulness of such popes as Liberius, Vigilius, and Honorius was questioned. Even in the early Middle Ages western metropolitans could see it as their duty to contradict papal decisions if necessary. Prophetic voices, from the 11th century on, warned that the pope might be an antichrist rather than the faithful preserver of the gospel.[40] It was readily admitted that individual popes of the past had been in error on specific points of doctrine, and the canonical tradition reckoned with the possibility that a pope might deviate from the faith.[41] Yet the formula that the Roman church "has never erred" survived, even though the expression *ecclesia Romana* was by no means ambiguous, particularly in its reference to the universal Church.

20. On the basis of the belief that Rome had never deviated from the truth, it came to be held that in the future Rome would be immune from error: the Roman church or the Roman bishop cannot err. While such a claim started appearing almost casually with Pope Gelasius (A.D. 492–496),[42] it did not imply that Rome could formulate "new doctrine," since novelty was the mark of heresy. Reformulations when attempted by bishops, synods, or councils were intended to affirm what had been handed down. Reception by the Church at large was undoubtedly a major factor in establishing the authoritativeness of such statements.[43] Roman bishops from the fourth century on regarded their "confirmation" of conciliar actions as an indispensable sign of authoritative teaching. Their own doctrinal decisions, however, needed to be accepted by secular authorities, councils, and fellow bishops in order to be enforced. With the growing practice of appealing to Rome, papal decisions came to be regarded in matters of faith as the last word, from which there could be no further appeal.[44] Popes since Siricius (A.D. 384–399) appealed to the Petrine function of "strengthening the brethren" (Luke 22:32) and to "solicitude for all the churches" (2 Cor. 11:28), in order to establish their teaching authority. The legal maxim that "the first see is judged by no one,"[45] which appeared first in the sixth century, was later interpreted as ensuring the pope's highest teaching authority in matters of faith and morals. It was restated in the era of the Gregorian Reform in terms of immunity from appeal and also on the basis of Christ's unfailing prayer for the faith of Peter (Luke 22:32). Shortly thereafter, Thomas Aquinas could describe the pope as the one to whose sole authority it belongs to "edit a new version of the creed," [46] and whose judgment in matters of faith must be followed because he represents the universal Church, which "cannot err." [47]

21. In this context the language of "infallibility" first came to be associated with the papal *magisterium*. According to some recent historical research, this usage was occasioned by the controversy over poverty in the Franciscan Order during the late 13th and early 14th centuries.[48] Advocates of a rigorist position used the word to defend the binding authority of statements by earlier popes against the decisions of their successors. A theologian of the 14th century, Guido Terreni, was the first to speak expressly of the "infallible" truth of the teaching of the Roman pontiff in matters of faith.[49]

22. To be sure, the term "infallible" had been used earlier with reference to God's truth, his revelation, the Church's normative teaching, and in similar contexts. It continued to be used with reference to the norm of the Word of God and Holy Scripture in the churches of the Reformation. But with the discussions of the 13th and 14th centuries it had taken on a new, highly technical meaning.

23. Whatever one may think about the appropriateness of the term "infallible," it points to the unavoidable issue of the faithful transmission of the gospel and its authoritative interpretation, guided by the Spirit.

C) Doctrine and the Cultural Context

24. Lutherans and Catholics share the confidence that the Spirit is present and guides Christian teaching not only in the first periods of church history but also in later developments. Both accept, for example, not only Scripture and the rule of faith *(regula fidei)* as formulated in the Apostles' Creed, but also solemn declarations by early ecumenical councils, such as the creeds of Nicaea-Constantinople, and statements of belief on a central point of doctrine, such as

the so-called Athanasian Creed, which focuses on the Trinitarian faith. Further, Lutherans have their confessional writings, and Catholics, various later dogmas. The churches have traditionally attached a high degree of authority to such formulations of their teaching, so that to deny the faith confessed in these documents has been seen as amounting to a rejection of the gospel.

25. By Christ's own commission, the gospel had to be preached in diverse civilizations and cultures, and to be transmitted from generation to generation to the close of the age. This communication of the gospel has implied that the Church has the obligation and the authority to formulate its faith in such a way that this faith can be recognized and believed. Such an authority is spiritual, for it is fundamentally the authority of the Spirit guiding the faithful. It is evangelical, for it is the authority of the gospel (the evangel) itself, knowledge of which is transmitted through the Church's preaching and teaching. It is apostolic, for it is rooted in the early apostolic commission and community. It is centered upon Christ, the Word of God Incarnate who is the one mediator (1 Tim. 2:5–7) of God's self-revelation to humankind.[50] It derives from God's gracious gift and not from any human work or merit. It is not a product of human culture or philosophy.

26. For our two traditions, the saving faith by which the gospel is received and believed has a noetic or intellectual aspect. Because human persons live in concrete cultural contexts, the gospel must be proclaimed in ways that speak to their culture. As cultures evolve, new emphases in the proclamation of the gospel may be needed, new conceptualizations may take shape, new formulations may become urgent. The formulation of the gospel, therefore, presents two aspects: the particular form in which the message is presented and understood, and the truth and certainty of the message itself. On the one hand, with respect to the form in which the message is presented, human language remains inadequate to the transcendent mystery of God and to the fulness of the paschal mystery of Jesus Christ. On the other hand, with respect to the truth and certainty of the message, Christians trust that through their Scriptures, their creeds, their conciliar definitions, and their confessional writings, they are led by the

Holy Spirit to the truth of the gospel and to an authentic life of faith.

27. The historical-cultural context of the Christian faith, which at times demands reformulation of the Church's teaching, makes it necessary for the Church to develop structures concerned with the task of reformulation. The members and leaders of the Church must listen carefully both to the diverse human cultures in order to be able to use their language, and to the Church's own past in order to maintain the proper continuity in the teaching of the Christian message. They must compare both the traditional understandings and contemporary reformulations of this message to the normative witness of the Scriptures.[51] Both Catholics and Lutherans believe that the Spirit will guide the process of reformulation so that the Church remains faithful to the gospel. They trust God's promise that the Church of the future will likewise be assisted by the Spirit in its missionary task.

28. This trust that the Holy Spirit guides the Church in transmitting the Christian message to new generations in fidelity to the gospel (cf. John 16:13) has given rise to the concept of the indefectibility of the Church, a term which is known to both the Lutheran and Catholic traditions. Indefectibility, like infallibility, has reference to the preservation of the Church thanks to the work of the Holy Spirit. But the two terms are not synonymous. Indefectibility refers to the continued existence of the Church in all its essential aspects, including its faith. Such fidelity is not an automatic quality of everything that the Church's leaders may say or endorse, but is the result of divine grace. It is recognized by testing the Church's faith and life by the standard of the Word of God. Infallibility has reference to an immunity from error in specific beliefs and teachings.[52] Even though protected by infallibility, such beliefs and teachings nonetheless reflect a merely partial understanding of the gospel, and may be inopportune or poorly expressed. Whatever their differences with regard to infallibility, the Lutheran and Catholic traditions share the certainty of Christian hope that the Church, established by Christ and led by his Spirit, will always remain in the truth fulfilling its mission to humanity for the sake of the gospel.

29. Thus both our communions hold that the gospel of

Christ is transmitted within the body of believers, the people of God. "The Spirit dwells in the Church and in the hearts of the faithful as in a temple." [53] Through the guidance of the Spirit, who distributes different gifts for the welfare of the Church, there is a unity of fellowship and service which is a sign that Christ is building up the Church as his own body. The gospel is transmitted in a special way in preaching and the sacraments, through which Christ unites his people to himself. Yet our two communions have sought to assure this transmission of the gospel along different lines.

II
CATHOLIC AND LUTHERAN EMPHASES

A) Catholic Emphases

30. In the contemporary Roman Catholic understanding of the Church, it is emphasized that the transmission of the gospel is the responsibility of the whole people of God. Within this people the college of bishops has a special role. Working together with priests, deacons, and laity, the bishop helps the believers to hear the Word of God in the preached word, in the sacraments, and in the life of the community.

The bishop, as a member of the episcopal college, has a responsibility not only to the local community but also to the Church universal. Each bishop represents his local Church, but all the bishops together in union with the pope represent the entire Church. [54] The episcopal college exercises its authority in a solemn way through an ecumenical council, and also in an ordinary way through the unity of the bishops dispersed throughout the world. [55]

31. Within the episcopal college the bishop of Rome has a unique function as head of the college. This function has many aspects. [56] One of these has been to supervise the transmission of doctrine in order that the faith of the people of God may be kept in its integrity and authenticity and may bear the fruit of a holy life. Teaching at the higher levels of authority has been exercised (1) through conciliar action, (2) in occasional papal statements, (3) through the guidance and supervision pro-

vided, under the pope, by the Roman congregations, sec-
retariats, and commissions.

32. The highest authority in the transmission of doctrine has been exercised in definitions of faith made by
councils or by the bishop of Rome speaking *ex cathedra*.
By virtue of divine assistance,[57] the bishop of Rome is
then acting with the infallibility with which the Church is
endowed. Such a definition depends on the guidance of
the Holy Spirit and is "irreformable." [58]

33. The Catholic belief that such definitions can be
made implies:

a) the confidence that, when the bishop of Rome is the
agent of the definition, he acts subject to conditions imposed by the Word of God and the faith of the Church,
with the careful investigation and study that the seriousness
of the action and the conditions of the time require and
permit;[59]

b) the recognition that the irreformability of definitions
does not rule out further research, interpretation through
the hermeneutical process, various applications to the life
of worship and piety, and new formulations that are called
for if fidelity to the Word of God expressed in previous
Catholic definitions is to be maintained, and if the needs
of new historical or cultural situations are to be met;

c) the acknowledgment that the exercise of infallibility
is open to historical investigation, that points of doctrine
that have been said to be infallibly proclaimed may in
fact not have been so proclaimed, and there is no official
list of *ex cathedra* definitions;

d) the trust that, thanks to the *sensus fidelium*, assent
to a definition of faith will not be lacking.[60]

B) Lutheran Emphases

34. In protest against what were viewed as distortions
of Christian truth, the Lutheran Reformers insisted on the
priority, objectivity, and authority of the address of God
to his creatures in his Word. The Word of God has priority: the initiative is God's. It has objectivity: God's Word
comes as his address to us; it is not a figment of our mind
or imagination. Authority resides ultimately in the power
of the proclaimed Word to convict of sin and convince of
grace. Given the depth of sin and the resultant human

capacity for self-deception, it is necessary that sinners look only to God and his promise for their hope of salvation. All things are created good, but their goodness has been rendered ambiguous by sin, and therefore not even the greatest of God's gifts in the realm of creation can be trusted apart from the promise of God in the gospel of Jesus Christ. Human reason, morality, religious experience, and church structures all have their value, but can all be deceptive guides apart from God's self-disclosure in Christ.

35. The Lutheran understanding of the way that the gospel is communicated in the Church is expressed concisely in the Smalcald Articles. ". . . the Gospel . . . offers counsel and help against sin in more than one way, for God is surpassingly rich in grace: First, through the spoken word, by which the forgiveness of sin (the peculiar [*eigentlich*] function of the Gospel) is preached to the whole world; second, through Baptism; third, through the holy Sacrament of the Altar; fourth, through the power of the keys; and finally, through the mutual conversation and consolation of brethren. . . ." [61]

The grace of God is thus made known and communicated in several distinct ways: proclamation, Baptism, Eucharist, confession and absolution, and the mutual edification of the life of the community. Luther emphasizes that proclamation is the oral announcement of God's love and mercy in Christ by one person to others. The Church, he stresses, is a "mouth-house" and not a "book-house." [62] In his speech to us God uses things he has created: human language, rites involving words and signs, human community, and the Church itself.

36. For the Lutheran Reformers, the signs of the apostolicity or genuineness of the Church are twofold: the actual proclamation of the gospel of God's love for sinners and the administration of the sacraments according to Christ's command. Where these two signs are present, one can be sure that Christ is at work, and where Christ is, there is the Church. Recognition of both signs depends upon the Spirit's illumination and guidance. Both signs, therefore, drive the community back to the Word of God, where God grants the decisive disclosure of his will. [63]

37. For the authentication of the Church's proclamation

of God's grace and love, the Lutheran Reformation looked primarily to the Word of God in Scripture. Even though modern historical study and the cultural relativity of all language complicate the process of interpretation, the Word of God as it is communicated to us in the Scriptures remains the final judge of all teaching in the Church.

38. The Reformers looked to tradition in the form of creeds and confessions as a secondary guide to the establishment of sound teaching. These texts, themselves the products of the Church's witness and often of theological controversy and struggle, show how the Scriptures were understood at certain critical periods in the life of the Church. The creeds and confessions also supply hermeneutical guidance for our reading of the Scriptures today.[64] Like the Scriptures, they too are expressed in human language, which is always relative to its culture and historical situation. They, therefore, are also in need of interpretation.

39. The traditional organs for continuing this process of interpretation were largely lost to the Lutheran churches at the time of the Reformation. The Reformers had a high regard for the authority of ecumenical councils and wished to maintain the historic ecclesiastical order, although they were unable to do so because of polemical conditions in the 16th century.[65] As a result, they were forced to rely heavily upon the princes and their theological advisers not only in the governance of the church but also in the formulation and acceptance of the Lutheran confessional writings. At present, Lutheran churches are organized in many different forms, episcopal, presbyterian, and congregational, depending upon the historical circumstances of their development. Doctrinal interpretation and discipline are accordingly exercised in a great variety of ways. These provisional arrangements have provided a platform, though not the most adequate, for Lutherans in the 20th century to confess together their faith as a worldwide communion. Lutheran communities, while rejoicing that these arrangements have helped to protect them from disintegration on the one hand and from excessive centralization and the sacralization of ecclesiastical power on the other, are increasingly sensitive to the shortcomings of their structures for teaching and mission in a worldwide ministry.

C) Common Ground and Divergences

40. There are notable differences in emphasis and in structure between Lutherans and Catholics. There is also a considerable common ground. Both communities have emphasized the authority of Christ, of the gospel, of Scripture, and of subsequent tradition, though in different ways and proportions. Lutherans have stressed Christ's presence and power in the Word proclaimed and also made visible in the sacraments. Catholics have, in addition, stressed his presence and power in the continuity of the Church as his body socially present and organized. There have been correlative differences in institutional structures, especially relating to authoritative teaching. Catholics have insisted on the authority of the Church's institutions, particularly of the structures of the Ministry of bishops and priests under the primacy of the bishop of Rome. But Lutherans have had to create other institutions, which, though intended to be provisional, have become part of the contemporary Lutheran patrimony. In both churches the structures are intended as means to promote the gospel. But as institutions become established, they tend to become ends rather than means. Each church has the responsibility of protecting its spiritual vitality against the weight of its institutions. And the two churches together have the responsibility of seeking ways of convergence, both at the level of doctrinal emphasis and at that of institutional structure.

III
CONVERGENCES

41. The context within which the Catholic doctrine of papal infallibility is understood has changed. Lutherans and Catholics now speak in increasingly similar ways about the gospel and its communication, about the authority of Christian truth, and about how to settle disputes concerning the understanding of the Christian message. One can truly speak of a convergence between our two traditions. The following instances of this convergence are significant. Our churches are agreed:

1) that Jesus Christ is the Lord of the Church, who discloses his gracious sovereignty through the proclamation

of the apostolic gospel and the administration of the sacraments;

2) that the Word of God in the Scriptures is normative for all proclamation and teaching in the Church;

3) that the apostolic Tradition in which the Word of God is transmitted, while normative for all other tradition in the Church, is interpreted within the family of God with the assistance of tradition in the form of creeds, liturgies, dogma, confessions, doctrines, forms of church government and discipline, and patterns of devotion and service;

4) that in accordance with the promises given in the Scriptures and because of the continued assistance of the risen Christ through the Holy Spirit, the Church will remain to the end of time;

5) that this perpetuity of the Church includes its indefectibility, i.e., its perseverance in the truth of the gospel, in its mission, and in its life of faith;

6) that among the means by which Christ preserves the Church in the truth of the gospel, there is the Ministry of Word and sacrament, which will never perish from the Church;

7) that there are Ministries and structures [66] charged with the teaching of Christian doctrine and with supervision and coordination of the ministry of the whole people of God, and that their task includes the mandate for bishops or other leaders to "judge doctrine and condemn doctrine that is contrary to the Gospel"; [67]

8) that there may appropriately be a Ministry in the universal Church charged with primary responsibility for the unity of the people of God in their mission to the world; [68]

9) that this Ministry to the universal Church includes responsibility for overseeing both the Church's proclamation and, where necessary, the reformulation of doctrine in fidelity to the Scriptures;

10) that in the Church universal the harmony between the teaching of the Ministers and its acceptance by the faithful constitutes a sign of the fidelity of that teaching to the gospel; [69]

11) that the Church in every age is able under the guidance of the Spirit to find language and other forms of witness which can communicate the gospel to persons liv-

ing in different cultures, that no human language succeeds in exhausting the diversity and richness of the gospel, and that no doctrinal definition can adequately address every historical or cultural situation.

In the light of these convergences, Catholics can better appreciate the significance of the Lutheran confession that the Church is indefectible. Specifically, the Lutheran trust that God will keep the Church in the truth of the gospel to the end has, in the context of Christian preaching and teaching, much in common with the Catholic concern for the Church's infallibility. Lutherans can recognize that Catholics affirm the supreme authority of the gospel and consider conciliar and papal infallibility as being subordinate to it.

42. This, to be sure, is not yet full agreement. Catholics, as well as many Lutherans, regret the absence in Lutheranism of a universal *magisterium* (i.e., of effective means of speaking to and for the whole Church), while Lutherans, as well as many Catholics, believe that the doctrine and practice of papal teaching authority and infallibility are not yet sufficiently protected against abuses. Catholics look upon the papacy, in view of its high responsibilities and the promises given to Peter, as especially assisted by the Holy Spirit. Lutherans think that Catholics have overconfidently identified the locus of the work of the Spirit with a particular person or office. Nevertheless, in the new context each side finds itself compelled to recognize that the other seeks to be faithful to the gospel. Further, given the convergence on the wider questions of authority and certainty in the Church, it becomes possible to hope that the two communions will be able to enter into further degrees of fellowship, while continuing to develop together their respective positions on infallibility.

43. These convergences, even though not complete, have concrete implications for the exercise of authority in the Church and for the method of settling disputes. The recognition of the primacy of the gospel enables us to see that Scripture, tradition, and church structures are means of transmission in the service of the gospel. While their subordination to the gospel message has never been actually denied, it has to some extent been overlooked in the past. Lutherans have a tendency to treat Scripture as if it were

identical with the gospel or the Word of God, while Catholics have shown a similar tendency with regard to tradition and church structures. We have now become more aware of the varied forms of oral and written proclamation, of practice, and of structure through which the gospel was and is handed on in the Church. The one message must often be presented in new ways in order to address specific audiences with reference to their particular problems. One cannot simply repeat Scripture and tradition in order to be faithful to the gospel, but one must be open to new ways of structuring its transmission in the Church. While this need has been recognized in the creative periods in the Church's life, it has often been ignored by theologians and church authorities, sometimes with unfortunate results.

44. Moreover, historical work has led to a better understanding of the relation of tradition and Scripture. Oral proclamation preceded the composition and collection of the writings of the New Testament.[70] Despite the polemics of the past, "Scripture can no longer be exclusively contrasted with tradition, because the New Testament itself is a product of primitive tradition." [71] Understood as the total process in which the gospel and Scripture itself are transmitted, tradition cannot be regarded as "merely human words." From this point of view Lutherans highly value liturgies, creeds, and confessions as embodiments of tradition.

45. In the Catholic Church there is a renewed appreciation of the privileged authority of Scripture. Scripture is the fount of virtually all we know of the founding Tradition, and is moreover the primary witness to the gospel. Catholic theologians now generally agree that there is no second source alongside Scripture which witnesses to the original revelation. Scripture is normative for all later tradition, and some Catholic theologians also find it possible to speak, as did the Reformers, of Scripture as the *norma normans non normata* and thus, in a certain sense, of *sola scriptura.*[72]

46. There is also a growing recognition of the need to restructure teaching authority in the Church. Although in the 16th century Lutheran churches spoke decisively on crucial doctrinal issues through the Confessions, they are

deficient in the dimension of universality today.[73] Lutherans, like other Christians in our present divided state, lack
the institutional means to participate with other Christian
traditions in doctrinal decision making. Thus they are confronted with the increasingly urgent need to develop new
structures or adapt old ones in a way that will do justice
to this universal aspect of their responsibility to the gospel.

47. Catholics increasingly recognize that all members
of the people of God share in principle the responsibility
for teaching and formulating doctrine. According to Vatican II, lay people "have the right and sometimes the duty
to make known their opinion on things which concern the
good of the Church." [74] The highest exercise of authority
is itself fundamentally ecclesial, since the bishop of Rome
acts in dependence on the faith of the Church.[75]

48. Moreover, structures can be developed that will
make reciprocal relationships more apparent on all levels.[76]
The laity should be enabled to participate in responsible
discussions of doctrine, since they must witness to the
faith. The clergy and theologians should be consulted, since
they have a teaching responsibility. Bishops have always
taken part in the consultations which have led to doctrinal
definitions, but further ways of participation of the episcopal college in the definition of doctrine should be de-
vised—for instance, through formal involvement of the
episcopal conferences and of the synod of bishops.

49. The understanding of infallibility is affected not
only by restructuring the process of defining doctrine but
also by the new context created by the modern science of
language. Whereas human languages have, at each moment, a recognizable structure, this structure does not remain stable through time. As the structure evolves, its
impermanence affects all the formulations of human language. The formulations of Scripture and of doctrine also
reflect the conditions prevailing at the moment when they
take shape. The interpretation of such statements must
accordingly take into account the historical circumstances
which have called forth the formulation, the intentions of
those who have drawn it up, and the religious and theological values they have attempted to assert or defend.
Therefore, no statement, whether biblical or doctrinal, can
be detached from its historical and cultural context if it is

to be adequately understood.[77] Because the questions and concerns of our period differ from those of the 19th century, it becomes necessary to reinterpret or reformulate the concept of infallibility so that its valid theological insight may become more persuasive.

50. We already find ourselves in growing agreement on the practice of doctrinal authority. "Neither the *sola scriptura* principle alone nor formal references to the authoritativeness of the magisterial office are sufficient." [78] It is through Scripture, tradition, and teaching authority that the Spirit enables the believing community to settle disputes about the gospel. The convergences we have outlined provide both the context and the beginning of a reinterpretation of infallibility.

IV

CONCLUSION

51. In light of the considerations mentioned above, it is clear that doctrinal definitions should be seen as decisive moments in the continuing pastoral and theological search for a deeper understanding of the mystery of Christ. They should not be viewed as bringing to an end all previous developments or as making all further discussion superfluous. The ultimate trust of Christians is in Christ and the gospel, not in a doctrine of infallibility, whether of Scripture, the Church, or the pope. Thus infallibility does not stand at the center of the Christian faith. Whatever infallibility is ascribed to Scripture, the Church, or the pope, it is wholly dependent on the power of God's Word in the gospel.

52. For Catholics, papal infallibility is now commonly discussed in the context of the infallibility of the Church and in relation to confidence in the faithful transmission of the gospel. As a consequence, the infallibility of the Church takes on greater importance than papal infallibility. Catholics, for whom the understanding of papal infallibility, though secondary, is important, should not therefore regard the Lutheran rejection of papal infallibility as equivalent to a denial of the central Christian message. What is more, the unresolved differences between Lutherans and

Catholics on this matter need not, of themselves, preclude a closer union than now exists between the two churches.

53. For Lutherans, the developments of the last two decades have given a new outlook on the dogma of papal infallibility. Historical and linguistic studies on the meaning of the dogma, the emphasis since Vatican II on the collegial relationship of the pope and the bishops in theology and practice, and the initiation of new styles of papal leadership by Pope John and Pope Paul can help Lutherans see that the pope is not an absolute monarch. The Ministry of the bishop of Rome should be seen as a service under the authority of the Word of God. The doctrine of infallibility is an expression of confidence that the Spirit of God abides in his Church and guides it in the truth.[79] This understanding should allay Lutheran fears that papal infallibility is a usurpation of the sovereign authority of Christ, and make clear that this dogma is not the central doctrine of the Catholic Church and that it does not displace Christ from his redemptive and mediatorial role.

54. For both Lutherans and Catholics, these convergences have implications for the exercise of teaching authority. In our discussions we have become aware of strengths and weaknesses in the existing structures of this Ministry in our churches. This leads us to ask practical questions of Catholics and Lutherans as we seek to bear witness to the gospel today, without implying that we would all answer them in the same way.

55. Has not the time come for our churches to take seriously the possibility of what we have come to call "magisterial mutuality"?[80] Should we not recognize the Spirit of Christ in each other's church and acknowledge each other's Ministers as partners in proclaiming the gospel in the unity of truth and love? Should we not listen to each other in formulating teaching, share each other's concerns, and ultimately develop a more unified voice for Christian witness in this world?

56. Specific questions are raised which Catholics ought to examine seriously:

1) What is their present understanding of the anathemas directed in the past at Luther and at Lutheran teaching? Are these condemnations relevant today? Since the trend of our times is to avoid anathemas—witness the

absence of any in Vatican Council II—should not the past anathemas against Lutheranism be reviewed? Could they possibly be "committed to oblivion" [81] or even rescinded?

2) Should not Catholic theology take a new look at the Lutheran Confessions, especially those—such as the Augsburg Confession—whose original purpose was irenic? Reinterpreted in a new context which would highlight their Catholic dimension, could these Confessions be recognized as valid expressions of the Church's teaching? Could such recognition serve as an instance of magisterial mutuality? [82]

3) Should not creative efforts be made to discover a form of institutional relationship between the Catholic and the Lutheran churches which would express magisterial mutuality and would correspond to the converging state of their traditions? The present Catholic authorization of some sacramental sharing with the Orthodox, who do not acknowledge papal infallibility, shows more flexibility in Catholic thought and practice than was anticipated a few decades ago. Should the current developments in our two churches lead to analogous authorizations regarding sacramental sharing between Catholics and Lutherans?

57. Specific questions are likewise raised which Lutherans ought to examine seriously:

1) Should not Lutherans be ready to acknowledge that the polemical language traditionally used to describe the papal office is inappropriate and offensive in the context of Catholic-Lutheran relationships today? [83]

2) Should not Lutherans, as participants in a movement toward a common Christian witness in our day, be willing to consult with Catholics in framing doctrinal and social-ethical statements?

3) Should not Lutherans move to develop closer institutional relationships with the Catholic Church in respect to teaching authority which would be expressive of the converging state of their traditions?

58. Our dialogue has thus completed another stage in a search for convergence between the Catholic and Lutheran traditions. Our dialogue began to bear fruit especially in 1967 with our agreed statement on "The Eucharist as Sacrifice." Since that date we have arrived at agreements on "Eucharist and Ministry" (1970) and on "Papal Primacy and the Universal Church" (1974). With the pres-

ent statement on questions raised by the Catholic doctrine of infallibility, we have found new areas of agreement in controversial matters which have for centuries separated Lutherans and Catholics. We are not in a position to state that all grounds for continuing division have been removed; we have not yet dealt at length with doctrinal issues such as justification; there are degrees of consensus which we have not yet been able to attain; there are reactions to our dialogue which we need to consider further; the agreements of theologians are not yet a consensus of the churches. It is our judgment, however, that the common grounds we have discovered in the doctrinal area point the way forward to significant changes in the lived relationships between our churches. We are convinced that our churches can overcome their past oppositions only as they become far more engaged, at all levels, through theological reflection, study of the Scriptures, worship, mission, and pastoral care, in a search for convergence along the lines developed in the work of this dialogue.

II

Roman Catholic Reflections

INTRODUCTION

1. The Roman Catholic participants are gratified by the convergence achieved in this dialogue on the questions of teaching authority and infallibility in the Church. Although the consensus is not complete, the discussion has unearthed elements in each tradition which, with cultivation, may eventually lead to an agreed ecumenical reinterpretation of these doctrines. We are pleased to have had a share in this process.

2. In what follows we intend to reflect more specifically on various aspects of the Common Statement in the light of traditional Catholic themes and to deal in greater detail with certain questions that have been put to us by the Lutherans at different times in this round of discussions.

3. The convergences with regard to the communication of the gospel, as summarized, for example, in paragraph

41 of the Common Statement, are noteworthy especially when taken in conjunction with the agreements noted in *Papal Primacy and the Universal Church*.[84] These convergences may be seen as compatible with a recognition of the universal teaching Ministry of popes and councils.[85] The most significant new agreements—partial though they are at the present stage—have to do with the emotionally laden and theologically complex question of infallibility.

4. The concept of infallibility is by no means free from difficulty. The Common Statement (16) calls attention to the fact that "infallibility is not a New Testament term." Absent also in patristic literature, it emerges only in the late medieval period. But we have to ask ourselves whether the concept and the term do not have a foundation in the data of the New Testament and in the faith of the first centuries. Examining the roots of the notion of infallibility, the Common Statement calls attention to the confidence of Christians, from the earliest times, that the Church could teach the truth of the gospel with assured authority.

5. The Common Statement (52-53) seeks to place the doctrine of infallibility in the theological categories of promise, trust, and hope rather than in the juridical categories of law, obligation, and obedience. Seen from this perspective, infallibility can be interpreted as a consequence of Christ's promise to be with the Church and to assist it "to the close of the age" (Matt. 28:20). That promise is regarded by Roman Catholics as the basis of their confidence and trust that all those who have doctrinal responsibility, and especially the pope and the episcopal college as servants of unity, will be assisted by the risen Christ.

6. It is the "gospel" that invites us as Christians to respond with faith and trust or confidence (Rom. 1:16). The Common Statement has accordingly set forth New Testament evidence about authority in doctrinal matters in terms of the gospel. The use of this term echoes the dynamism associated with *euangelion* by Paul (Rom. 1:16), its truth (Gal. 2:5, 14), and its relation to the Spirit (1 Thess. 1:5). It is to be understood as a brief way of referring to the proclamation of the saving revelation which comes to us in the person, message, and deeds of Jesus Christ. The term "gospel," understood in this inclusive manner, has a secure place in the Roman Catholic tradition [86] and is capable of summing up what Vatican II referred to as "the Word of God."

7. The Catholics in this dialogue understand that contemporary Lutheran thought, emphasizing the sinfulness of all human institutions and instruments, finds it difficult to recognize any episcopal see, church office, person, or officeholder as gifted with such unfailing assistance from the Spirit as to preclude error in teaching. Therefore, the Lutheran tradition does not tie to any institution the task of authentic reformulation of Christian doctrine, which Catholics assign preeminently to the episcopal college and the bishop of Rome. For the Catholic participants in these conversations, the doctrine of infallibility aims at safeguarding a basic Christian insight: that the Church, in view of its mission to preach the gospel faithfully to all nations, may be trusted to be guided by the Holy Spirit in proclaiming the original revelation and in reformulating it in new ways and languages whenever such reformulation is necessary. Such a trust, rooted in the sovereignty of God, is in our view inseparable from the Christian faith as understood and practiced in both our traditions.

8. In the following pages we propose to reflect more specifically on certain themes of the Common Statement: (1) the authority of the living Church; (2) the Catholic understanding of papal infallibility; (3) the biblical and historical background for the claim of papal infallibility; (4) noninfallible and doubtfully infallible papal teaching; (5) nonacceptance of infallible teaching; (6) conclusion.

I

THE AUTHORITY OF THE LIVING CHURCH

9. The Common Statement (28) calls attention to a major area of agreement between Lutherans and Catholics. Christ himself, who taught with the authority of the Son of God, by promising to be with his disciples to the end of the age and by bestowing the Holy Spirit, empowered the Church, as a community of faith, to abide forever in the truth of the gospel. Thanks to the divine assistance, the gospel will continue to be preached and believed, and thus

the Church will endure to the end. In other words, the Church is indefectible as a community of Christian faith and witness, even though all its members, including its pastors, continue to be subject to weakness and sin.

10. In more familiar Catholic terminology we may say, as did the medieval theologians, "The universal Church cannot err";[87] that is to say, its faith in the gospel of Jesus Christ is divinely protected against corruption. Thus Vatican II declared: "The body of the faithful as a whole, anointed as they are by the Holy One (cf. 1 John 2:20, 27), cannot err in matters of belief. Thanks to a supernatural sense of the faith which characterizes the people as a whole, it manifests this unerring quality when 'from the bishops down to the last member of the laity' it shows universal agreement in matters of faith and morals" (*LG* 12).

11. Going further, Catholics have felt entitled to assert that those charged with the Ministry to the universal Church, in their teaching of the revelation of Christ, will not be allowed to lead the Church astray, for Christ remains with the apostolic body which teaches in his name. Accordingly, Vatican I taught that the assent of Christian faith extends to all that is contained in the Word of God and taught by the universal teaching body as divinely revealed (DS 3011).

12. The infallibility of the total Church in teaching and in believing forms, in the Catholic understanding, the context of conciliar and papal infallibility. The infallibility of popes and that of bishops gathered at ecumenical councils are particular instances of expressions of the infallibility of the whole Church, for these organs are he'd to represent the whole Church. Thus Vatican I, in its definition of papal infallibility, ascribed to the pope no other infallibility than that with which Christ willed the entire Church to be endowed (DS 3074). Even though Lutherans do not recognize any particular office as gifted with infallibility, we do not think this would require them to deny that the whole body of pastors or the whole body of the faithful is protected against error.[88] Indeed, the Lutheran understanding of indefectibility implies the preservation of the Church, as a community of Christian faith and proclamation, in the truth of the gospel.

II
THE CATHOLIC UNDERSTANDING OF PAPAL INFALLIBILITY

13. The term "infallibility," especially when it is connected with some particular office, can easily give rise to confusion. It suggests to many that the office or officeholder is being somehow divinized and deprived of the capacity for error that is a mark of the human condition. Thus understood, the doctrine of infallibility seems to remove the official teachers from their subjection to Christ and the gospel and to put them, in the eyes of the faithful, on a par with the divine Persons. This, however, is not the Catholic teaching on the subject.

14. Vatican Council I did not state without qualification that the pope is infallible. Rather, it taught that when performing certain very narrowly specified acts, he is gifted with the same infallibility which Christ bestowed on his Church (DS 3074). In his explanation of the meaning of the definition, given to the Fathers two days before they voted on the draft, Bishop Vincenz Gasser clearly pointed out that absolute infallibility is proper to God alone and that the infallibility of the pope is limited and conditioned. "In fact," he went on to say, "the infallibility of the Roman pontiff is restricted in respect to the *subject*, when the pope speaks as teacher of the universal Church and as supreme judge seated on the chair of Peter, i.e., in the center. It is restricted in respect to the *object*, insofar as it concerns matters of faith and morals, and in respect to the *act*, when he defines what has to be believed or rejected by all the faithful" (M 52:1214).

15. Vatican I did not define the infallibility of the successors of Peter as a permanent property, definitely attached to the person of the pope. Though a personal infallibility is ascribed to a pope, it is present, as Gasser explained, "only when he exercises in reality and in act the function of supreme judge in the controversies of faith and doctrine of the universal Church" (M 52:1213). Here "act" must not be restricted too narrowly.

16. Admittedly, several misunderstandings have been occasioned by the expressions used in the Vatican I definition. Many difficulties have arisen from the sentence, "Such

definitions of the Roman pontiff are therefore irreformable by themselves *(ex sese)* and not by reason of the agreement of the Church *(non autem ex consensu ecclesiae)"* (DS 3074). This might seem to give the pope an authority independent of that of the Church, as though the pope were not a member of the Church but somehow above it.

17. Historical research, however, makes it clear that the final phrase, *non autem ex consensu ecclesiae,* was added for the purpose of excluding the tendency of some Gallicans and conciliarists, who regarded approval by the bishops as necessary in order to give infallibility to any papal definition.[89] Vatican I was here reacting against the kind of juridical language found in the fourth Gallican article of 1682, in which it was claimed that papal decrees are not irreformable until the assent of the Church *(ecclesiae consensus)* supervenes (DS 2284). Thus it is apparent that the term *consensus* at Vatican I is to be understood in the juridical sense of official approval and not in the more general sense of agreement or acceptance by the Church as a whole, which, according to Gasser, can never be lacking (M 52:1214). As Gasser also explains, the pope's infallibility is not "separate," for he is not protected against error except when he teaches as successor of Peter, and hence as representing the universal Church (1213). The same conclusion is supported by the statement of Vatican I that the assistance of the Holy Spirit is given to the successors of Peter not that they might manifest new doctrine but that they might safeguard and explain faithfully the revelation handed down through the apostles, the deposit of faith (DS 3070).

18. Another major difficulty arising from the text of Vatican I has to do with the term "irreformable," which is sometimes understood as though it excluded any further reformulation or reinterpretation. In order to dispel this impression, the Common Statement (49) emphasizes that the formulas of faith are historically conditioned and are therefore subject to revision according to circumstances of particular times and places. In that connection it asserts that the doctrine of infallibility itself may need to be reinterpreted and newly expressed, so that its enduringly valid theological insight may better appear.

19. Our Catholic reflections on papal primacy [90] have

already shown, with the help of the Declaration of the Congregation for the Doctrine of the Faith *Mysterium Ecclesiae* (1973), that definitions of doctrine are subject to a fourfold historical conditioning.[91] They are affected by the limited context of human knowledge in the situation in which they are framed, by the specific concerns that motivated the definitions, by the changeable conceptions (or thought categories) of a given epoch, and by "the expressive power of the language used at a certain point of time." [92] These four factors are critical for the proper interpretation of the Catholic teaching on papal infallibility. Application of the principles of *Mysterium Ecclesiae* to this question suggests the possibility of eventually finding new expressions faithful to the original intention and adapted to a changed cultural context. This process of reinterpretation was already at work in the way in which the doctrine of papal infallibility was treated at Vatican II, bringing new aspects to the fore. Seven factors in this reinterpretation seem noteworthy:

1) Vatican II made it clearer than had Vatican I that the infallibility of the pastors (pope and bishops) must be related to the *sensus fidelium* or the "sense of faith" possessed by the entire people of God. The popes and bishops are infallible insofar as they are assisted in giving official expression and formulation to what is already the faith of the Church as a whole.[93] This theme of Vatican II underscores what is implicit in the assertion of Vatican I that the pope has no other infallibility than that which Christ conferred upon the Church.

2) Vatican II saw the infallibility of the pope as closely connected with that of the college of bishops. Indeed, when it described the infallibility of the Roman pontiff, it referred to him as "head of the college of bishops," a phrase not used in the constitution *Pastor aeternus* of Vatican I. This suggests that normally, when he defines a matter of faith and morals, the pope should be expected to consult his fellow bishops and proceed in a collegial manner (*LG* 25, with footnote referring to Gasser in M 52:1213 AC).

3) Vatican II pointed out that while no antecedent or subsequent juridical approval by the Church is necessary for the exercise of infallibility, the assent of the Church can

never be wanting to an authentic definition "on account of the activity of that same Holy Spirit, whereby the whole flock of Christ is preserved and progresses in unity of faith" (*LG* 25). This observation, together with Vatican II's emphasis on the *sensus fidelium*, puts in proper context the assertion of Vatican I that papal definitions are irreformable *ex sese, non autem ex consensu ecclesiae* (DS 3074).

4) Vatican II placed the teaching of the pope in the context of a pilgrim church. His definitions of faith will reflect the situation of a church whose task is "to show forth the mystery of the Lord in a faithful though shadowed way, until at last it will be revealed in total splendor" (*LG* 8). In other words, such definitions will inevitably suffer from a certain obscurity.[94]

5) Vatican II recognized that the Church, insofar as it is an institution on earth, is always affected by human finitude and sinfulness (*UR* 6), failings that may leave their mark even on the most solemn acts of the highest magisterium. Even while true in the technical sense, a dogmatic statement may be ambiguous, untimely, overbearing, offensive, or otherwise deficient.[95]

6) By its ecumenical orientation, Vatican II gave rise to the question: Will infallibility be able to serve the purpose for which it is intended without far more consultation with Christian communities not in full union with Rome?[96]

7) Vatican II called attention to the fact that "in Catholic teaching there exists an order or 'hierarchy' of truths, since they vary in their relationship to the foundation of the Christian faith" (*UR* 11). This important principle suggests the possibility that authentic faith in the basic Christian message may exist without explicit belief in all defined dogmas—a question to be discussed below (Section V).

20. The state of the doctrine of papal infallibility at the end of Vatican II is not to be taken as the last word on the subject. The understanding of the doctrine will continue to be nuanced in various ways as the historical, cultural, and linguistic situations change. Recent debates may have been a factor contributing to the rather moderate statement of infallibility in the declaration *Mysterium Ecclesiae,* referred to at the beginning of paragraph 19 above.

III

BIBLICAL AND HISTORICAL BACKGROUND

21. With regard to the biblical and historical testimonies about teaching authority in the Church, no sharp differences between Lutherans and Catholics have emerged in this dialogue. Catholics have usually thought that there is a biblical and patristic basis for the doctrine of papal infallibility, but we would add that the doctrine cannot be found explicitly in these early sources, nor can it be strictly deduced from these sources by syllogistic argument.

22. The Common Statement, in our opinion, gives a satisfactory overall presentation of the testimony of the New Testament regarding authoritative teaching. Some of the texts mentioned in our Common Statement, however, have at times received greater emphasis in the Roman Catholic tradition.

23. The promise of the risen Jesus commissioning the Eleven to "make disciples of all nations, baptizing them . . . [and] teaching them to observe all that I have commanded you" (Matt. 28:19–20) has been understood as implying distinctions among Christ himself, those teaching, and those taught. While acknowledging that the function of the Eleven "represents Christ and his over-againstness to the community only insofar as it [the Ministerial office] gives expression to the gospel," [97] many Christians—correctly, in our view—have emphasized that the very commission given here is the basis of a teaching authority as a special Ministry within the Christian community, and one that is safeguarded by the assistance of Christ himself "to the close of the age."

24. Though this Matthean passage is not related literarily to the Pastoral Epistles, the Matthean commission to teach given by the risen Christ corresponds to the view of "the Church of the living God" and its apostolic Ministry spoken of in 1 Timothy 3:15. The phrase "the pillar and bulwark of the truth" in this text should not be heard anachronistically with jurisdictional overtones. Nevertheless, 1 Timothy 3:15 is a confident expression of the reliability of the Church—or at least of a Minister of the Church—to which the risen Christ has committed the preaching of the gospel. [98]

25. The Common Statement makes mention of the Petrine function and its relation to teaching authority in the Church. This function has to be understood with the explanations given in *Papal Primacy and the Universal Church* and in *Peter in the New Testament*.[99] As we move beyond the discussion of primacy presented there to the question of infallibility and the Petrine funciton, we see how limited are the New Testament data on this topic. In the course of the tradition the Petrine text of Luke 22:32 was given the major emphasis. Jesus' prayer for Simon, who would prove faithless in denying him, has to be understood as efficacious: "that your faith may not fail." In virtue of this assurance of Jesus, Simon is told that he, after being converted, would have a role of strengthening his brothers. Now it is obvious that the New Testament does not make the distinction of later theologians about *fides quae* (the faith which is believed) and *fides qua* (the faith by which one believes) and that Simon's "faith" here would have to be understood in a comprehensive sense; in any case, it cannot be restricted to faith in a content sense (*fides quae*).

26. Finally, it should be noted apropos of the Petrine texts in Matt. 16:18 and Luke 22:32, which are used in the Common Statement, that they have likewise been cited in the Dogmatic Constitution of Vatican I *Pastor aeternus* (DS 3066, 3070) and used in connection with papal infallibility. Some Roman Catholic theologians have at times regarded these biblical passages as officially interpreted, or even infallibly defined, by the Council.[100] However, Vatican I did not define the sense of these verses.[101] While we recognize that these Petrine texts have played an important role in the development of the doctrine of papal infallibility, we do not claim that these texts, taken exegetically, directly assert that doctrine.

27. As regards the patristic and medieval history of teaching authority in the Church, we have noted, as have the Lutheran participants, the gradual emergence of papal primacy in doctrinal decision making through a lengthy historical process briefly summarized in the Common Statement. The doctrine of papal infallibility was not formally taught until the end of the 13th century. It continued to be disputed within the Catholic Church, with many conciliarists and Gallicans denying it, until the definition of 1870. That definition was so restricted in scope and moderate in tone that it failed to satisfy the desires of ardent papalists, many of whom in the period after Vatican I went far beyond the letter of the Council in claiming infallibility for papal teaching that did not strictly meet the conditions for an *ex cathedra* pronouncement as set forth by Vatican I.

28. Lutherans and Catholics, of course, differ in their appraisal of the development they both recognize. However Lutherans evaluate this development, at very least they do not regard it as binding on all Christians. For Catholics, it represents an implication of the gospel or the Word of God as seen in the perspective of a long historical reflection, and as having developed in accordance with principles already present in the gospel from the beginning. Nevertheless, the doctrine has at times been too naively or rigidly understood by Catholics themselves and consequently stands in need of further nuancing. The concerns of Lutherans, as expressed in this dialogue, can help Catholics to understand papal infallibility in ways that better safeguard the primacy of the gospel and the freedom of the Christian believer.

29. It has sometimes been alleged that historical research can actually disprove the infallibility of the pope. Attention is called to various "papal errors," many of which were discussed at length both prior to and at Vatican I. There is no need, in these reflections, to review the evidence regarding the celebrated cases of Popes Liberius, Vigilius, and Honorius, which are discussed, to some degree, in our background papers.[102] In an earlier volume we published a background paper on Pope Boniface VIII and *Unam sanctam*.[103] Turning to yet another case, it need not be denied that Pope John XXII erred in his teaching regarding the beatific vision, which was corrected both by John XXII himself and by his successor Benedict XII.[104] No one doubts that popes can err in their teaching as private doctors. In none of the preceding cases can it be shown that the errors, or alleged errors, would have met the requirements specified by Vatican I for an *ex cathedra* pronouncement, and hence these historical difficulties prove nothing against the truth of the teaching of that Council

on infallibility. These historical difficulties, to which the Council fathers adverted, form part of the historical context within which the definition is to be understood.[105]

IV

NONINFALLIBLE AND DOUBTFULLY INFALLIBLE PAPAL TEACHING

30. The cases just mentioned illustrate the importance of distinguishing between two major categories of papal teaching: that which is, and that which is not, clearly infallible. Before discussing the obligatory force of the latter, it will be helpful to clarify certain questions concerning the former. The Lutherans in this dialogue have frequently pressed us to respond to the following two questions. First, how does one distinguish which papal statements are, or are not, to be considered infallible? Second, what obligatory force attaches to noninfallible papal teaching?

31. There are only two papal pronouncements which are generally acknowledged by Catholics as having engaged papal infallibility: the dogma of the Immaculate Conception (1854) and that of the Assumption of the Blessed Virgin (1950).[106] Several other types of papal pronouncement have, however, been thought by some to be infallible. With an eye to the teaching of 20th century theological manuals, several prominent examples may here be mentioned: the solemn canonizations of saints, the condemnation of certain doctrines, papal teaching concerning certain moral matters, and the decision concerning Anglican ordinations.

32. The theological manuals of recent generations rather commonly hold that solemn canonizations of saints, as contained in papal decretal letters, are infallible.[107] The tradition in favor of infallibility in the matter has been traced back at least to the time of Thomas Aquinas,[108] but there are genuine difficulties in seeing how canonizations fall within the object of papal infallibility as taught by Vatican I or Vatican II. Certainly, the virtues of particular persons of post-biblical times, and their present situation before God, can scarcely be reckoned as part of the apostolic deposit of faith. If one looks on revelation as having become

complete in Christ, holiness may reasonably be seen as a concrete way of living, in a given culture, the saving truth revealed in Christ. The Church has the power to recognize authentic Christian holiness, yet canonization would not seem of its nature to convey infallible certitude that the holiness in question was actually present in the life of this or that historical person.[109]

33. The condemnation of certain doctrinal errors—for example, those of the Jansenists or the Modernists—would seem to fall indirectly within the scope of papal infallibility, insofar as such errors deviate from basic Christian belief or previously defined doctrine. Whether a particular condemnation is an exercise of infallibility is always a factual question, and the affirmative answer to this question is not to be presumed. According to canon law, "Nothing is to be understood as dogmatically declared or defined unless this is clearly manifest" (*CIC*, can. 1323, #3). For the infallible character to be clearly manifest, the condemnation would have to claim infallibility for itself and would have to fall within the scope of papal infallibility as set forth by the two Vatican Councils. In point of fact, none of the papal documents condemning doctrinal errors evidently meets these two criteria. Whatever clearly infallible teachings are contained in such papal condemnations have this status because other more authoritative documents or the universal and constant teaching of the Church affirm the same points.

34. With regard to the Bull *Exsurge Domine* (1520), condemning certain views attributed to Luther, the Catholic members of this dialogue are convinced that there are no solid grounds for regarding it as an exercise of papal infallibility. It embodies propositions of unequal theological weight. If some of the teachings in this Bull are infallible, this is because other more authoritative documents, such as conciliar canons, affirm the same points.[110]

35. Some authors maintain that the pope has acted infallibly in issuing certain moral teachings, notably in the case of the statements about contraception in the encyclicals of Pius XI [111] and Paul VI.[112] The solution to this question depends in part on whether the Church's infallibility extends to questions of the natural moral law, to which these documents primarily appeal. But even granted

that it does so extend, there is the further point that the documents in question do not manifestly invoke infallibility. Moreover, Catholic commentators are not unanimous in regarding these teachings as infallible. Thus it seems that freedom to deny the infallibility of these documents must be allowed.

36. The principles just enunciated would hold likewise for the rejection of Anglican orders by Pope Leo XIII in the Letter *Apostolicae curae* (1896). Even granting that infallibility might extend to a "dogmatic fact" of this kind, the language of the Letter does not seem to demand that the decision be taken as infallible. In view of the lack of consensus among approved authors, the decision may be treated in practice as reformable.[113]

37. This brings us to the second question: the obligatory force of papal teaching which is not, or not evidently, infallible. Pius XII, in *Humani generis* (1950), pointed out that encyclicals, even when they do not engage the supreme teaching authority of the pope, have genuine doctrinal weight. More specifically, according to Pius XII, when the pope in such letters deliberately gives a decision on some previously controverted issue, the question may no longer be considered as one to be freely debated among theologians (DS 3885).[114]

38. *Lumen gentium* 25 restated and carried forward the essential teaching of Pius XII by its assertion:

Religious allegiance of the will and intellect should be given in an entirely special way to the authentic teaching authority of the Roman pontiff, even when he is not speaking *ex cathedra;* this should be done in such a way that his supreme teaching authority is respectfully acknowledged, while the judgments given by him are sincerely adhered to according to his manifest intention and desire, as this is made known by the nature of the documents, or by his frequent repetition of the same judgment, or by his way of speaking.[115]

As Karl Rahner points out in his commentary on this text, it may be significant that the Council did not reassert the doctrine of *Humani generis* forbidding further public discussion of matters settled by the pope, even though this doctrine appeared in the preliminary draft of November 10, 1962.[116]

39. There exists a vast literature dealing with the highly complex question of the authority of noninfallible papal teaching and the conditions under which this or that form of silent or vocal dissent may be permitted or required.[117] To illustrate one approach, we may refer to the collective Pastoral of the German bishops issued on September 22, 1967. Using an analogy which some have found helpful, this letter compares the noninfallible teaching of the magisterium to the decisions of a judge or statesman. "In such a case, the situation of the individual with regard to the Church is somewhat like that of a man who knows that he is bound to accept the decision of an expert, even though he knows that it is not infallible." [118]

40. As regards the legitimacy of dissent, the German bishops' Pastoral says that the contrary opinion may not be taught as Catholic doctrine, but that one may properly point out to the faithful the limited authority of such revisable pronouncements.

The Christian who believes that he has a right to his private opinion, and that he already knows what the Church will only come to grasp later, must ask himself in sober self-criticism before God and his conscience, whether he has the necessary depth and breadth to allow his private theory and practice to depart from the present doctrine of the ecclesiastical authorities.[119]

41. As this quotation illustrates, there is a very important difference between the assent of faith which is called for by infallible teaching and the religious allegiance or submission which is per se expected in the case of ordinary but noninfallible papal teaching.

V

NONACCEPTANCE OF INFALLIBLE TEACHING

42. Much of our discussion in the present round of dialogues has focused on three undoubted instances in which infallibility has been invoked: the conciliar dogma of papal infallibility itself (1870) and the two papal dogmas of the Immaculate Conception (1854) and the Assumption (1950). Questions have been raised about the implications of these three dogmas for the continuing relations between Catholics and Lutherans. To what extent does nonacceptance of these teachings preclude communion and unity?

43. First of all, the Catholic members of this dialogue must record their conviction that these dogmas refer to realities and values that are important for the Christian's response to God's word of revelation in Christ, even though they do not stand at the very center of Christian faith and teaching. In accordance with Vatican II, which presented these doctrines in a way calculated to show their relation to the mystery of the Church,[120] we are persuaded that these doctrines ought not to be viewed in isolation but in relationship to the entire Christian vision of God's saving work. We recognize, however, that the Lutherans represented in this dialogue consider that their Christian faith does not oblige them to affirm these teachings.

44. Second, we acknowledge that the community of those who accept these dogmas is not coextensive with the full number of individuals and groups that are rightly called Christian. Catholics do not hold that membership in Christ's Church is restricted to persons who formally and explicitly accept the three dogmas in question. For example, there are some Catholics today who belong to the Church even though they accept these teachings only implicitly.[121]

45. Third, the question arises about persons and groups who, after considering these doctrines, decide not to accept or even to reject them. Here it may be well to recall that each of the teachings in question was accompanied by an anathema (DS 3075) or its equivalent (DS 2804, 3904). Canonically, an anathema involves an excommunication (*CIC*, can. 2257, #2), which, however, is not incurred except by persons whose disbelief is culpable, obstinate, and externally manifested. The language of the anathemas in the instances that here concern us seems to reflect the presumption that only in rare and exceptional situations could a Christian in good faith deny these dogmas once they had been defined. However necessary presumptions are, they are understood in church law to yield to facts and to be open to change when facts so indicate. In our day it seems evident that many sincere Christians are unable to profess these dogmas with personal faith. And yet these same individuals wish very much to belong to Christ's Church; they gather together in his name to announce his death until he comes; they confess his Lordship; they accept his message as reflected in the Bible and the early Christian creeds; and they bear witness to him in their lives of service to his brothers and sisters. The questioning or denial of these dogmas should not be regarded, at least today, as presumptive evidence of a lapse from Christian faith.

46. A step in this direction was taken by Vatican II, which permitted *limited* Eucharistic sharing between Catholics and Orthodox,[122] even though the latter do not normally accept (and even at times explicitly reject at least one or more of) the dogmas in question. The situation of the Orthodox and Lutherans, though different in many ways, is similar at least in the following: both find themselves for the most part unable to accept one or more of these teachings as part of the deposit of faith. If this inability on the part of the Orthodox does not preclude all Eucharistic sharing with Catholics, the same inability on the part of Lutherans should not of itself do so either. Lack of Christian faith would and should so preclude. But the operative presumption is that Christian faith sufficient for Eucharistic sharing exists in the case of Catholics and Orthodox despite the inability of the latter to accept all these particular dogmas. We believe that this presumption regarding Christian faith should be extended also to Lutherans. If so, it would not thereby follow that limited Eucharistic sharing was justified in their case too. But it would follow that such sharing ought not to be ruled out because of Lutheran failure to accept these three teachings.

47. In this connection it should be mentioned that some Catholics are at times unable to accept one or other or even all these dogmas with personal faith. We are not here considering the hypothetically possible case of someone who would claim to be a Catholic and yet believe only what he or she would find personally appealing. We restrict our remarks to the refusal to accept the three dogmas with which we are here concerned. Given the information explosion, its impact on religious communication, and the widespread influence of mass media, it is understandable that the beliefs of many Catholics have been affected.

Could it be that, in their questioning or denial of these three dogmas, not a few Catholics are reacting more against the inadequacy, incompleteness, limited expressive power, and historically-conditioned character of the official formulations than against the Word of God to which these dogmas bear witness? Would not this be especially indicated if such persons adhere to, and seek to live, their Catholic faith in other matters? We think our church leaders ought to consider whether a presumption to this effect may not be called for in our day. We do not concede that one can be a Roman Catholic Christian by simply wanting to and without thereby being committed to the acceptance of any specific teachings. We admit that at times the rejection of the three dogmas we are considering may be a sign that one has separated oneself from Catholic tradition and faith, but we think this ought not to be presumed. Indeed, a good case can be made for the opposite presumption.

48. Finally, we must say something about the question of lifting the anathemas themselves. Since the anathemas do not refer directly to the truth of the dogmas but rather to the canonical effects of their denial, they could be withdrawn without altering the truth of the dogmas or the obligation to believe them. The removal of these anathemas has in fact been suggested.[123] Such an action would serve to highlight the imperfect ecclesial communion that exists between Catholics and Lutherans despite the latter's nonacceptance of these three dogmas.

49. Nevertheless, there are grounds for hesitation in view of the historic nexus that exists between the anathema and the truth of the dogma. Given that nexus, the formal removal of the anathema might well contribute to the "take your pick among the dogmas" mentality that is already found among some Catholics (and other Christians). That anathemas were attached to such teachings in the past is something over which we, the living, have no control; past history cannot be undone. To judge the consciences of those, whether Lutheran or Catholic, who leveled anathemas at their opponents is best left to God. True, anathemas from the past might be lifted in the present. Indeed, the lifting in the case of these three dogmas might be a sign pointing to the ecclesial communion

already in existence and contributing to the growth of that communion. But could this be accomplished without giving the impression that the Catholic Church no longer holds and teaches these dogmas? This is far from sure. On the question, then, whether the anathemas should be lifted, there is need for further discussion within the Catholic community. In this connection it is worth noting that Vatican II, true to its general style of teaching, reaffirmed these dogmas, in a new context, without restating the anathemas.

50. However this discussion may be resolved, we wish to stress here two important points. First, whether the anathemas are lifted or not, the differences between Catholics and Lutherans regarding these dogmas do not of themselves exclude all Eucharistic sharing between the churches.[124] Second, the truth-implications of these dogmas must not be overlooked. We aim at mutual communion one day with Lutherans without requiring either side to give up the fundamental evangelical convictions and values of its tradition. Even if there were a mutual recognition of Ministries and limited Eucharistic sharing, we would feel that we owed it to evangelical truth, as we are given by the Spirit to understand it, to continue to pray and study with Lutherans about these questions. It would still be important to preserve a mutuality of discussion regarding the meaning of these three dogmas, their place in this hierarchy of truths, and their roles in the effective transmission of the Word of God. If our discussions were to lead one day to such recognition and such limited sharing, there would still be a task incumbent on both traditions: to search for a more shared understanding of the Word of God as it applies to Mary and to the one who continues in a unique way the Petrine office among the disciples of Jesus today.

VI

CONCLUSION

51. Considering both the progress already achieved and the task that still remains before us, we are both saddened by our inability to announce full agreement between Lutherans and Catholics regarding the infallible character

of certain teaching and encouraged by the large measure of agreement that does exist regarding the nature and importance of teaching authority. Even with regard to infallibility, we have found it increasingly difficult, as our dialogue has proceeded, to specify the exact point at which, in fidelity to our respective traditions, we are bound to disagree.

52. There are certain understandings of infallibility which Lutherans, according to their own principles, would evidently have to reject. For example, if Catholics were to teach that any papal statement issued with certain juridical formalities, regardless of its basis in Scripture and tradition and its consonance with the faith of the Church, could be imposed as a matter of faith, Lutherans would legitimately protest that the primacy of the gospel was being imperiled. But as we have sought to show, such an understanding of infallibility would be a misinterpretation of the Catholic doctrine.

53. Again, if irreformability meant that the solemn teaching of popes and councils had to be accepted forever as it was understood and stated when originally promulgated, with the result that it could not be reconceptualized and reformulated according to the needs and possibilities of different times and cultures, Lutherans would have good reason to reject irreformability. But, as we have explained, irreformability does not preclude further reinterpretation, reconceptualization, or rephrasing.

54. Because of the nuanced understanding of infallibility in much contemporary Catholic theology, we find that some Lutherans, even while denying what they recognize as infallibility, come very close to affirming what some Catholics understand by that term. They can in fidelity to their own tradition accept a certain presumption in favor of the evangelical truth of the preaching of duly constituted pastors, especially when this preaching resonates with the faith of the Christian community and is seen, upon examination, to be consonant with Scripture and early tradition. This kind of presumption could tell in favor of the pope as a bishop specially charged with the Ministry of universal supervision in matters of doctrine.

55. The denial of infallibility from the Lutheran side might seem to Catholics, at first sight, to open the path

to radical questioning of the inherited affirmations of faith, but we do not hear the Lutherans in this dialogue so questioning Christian tradition. They do not hold that a contemporary Christian would be entitled to interpret the Bible in a sense patently contrary to the ancient creeds and confessions which, in their estimation, reliably express the teaching of Scripture and the faith of the Church. Drawing upon this shared heritage of Christian belief, and working in the light of a new will to overcome our past divisions, this dialogue has been able to achieve a convergence about teaching authority and infallibility which could scarcely have been thought possible even a few years ago.

56. The attempt to express papal infallibility in terms of promise, trust, and hope has already brought us a long way toward agreement. As to the limits that do remain in our present agreement on teaching authority, their source may lie in other issues that have been long debated by Catholics and Lutherans. Some of our remaining differences may be rooted in the content of certain dogmas and their basis in Christian revelation (e.g., the Immaculate Conception of Mary and her Assumption). Moreover, our theologies may still differ about the way the Scriptures are normative for faith.[125] Furthermore, Lutherans and Catholics could well direct further attention to the effects of grace and sin on individuals and institutions, including the teaching Church. We, therefore, need to discuss the doctrine of justification, a doctrine at the very root of the Reformation itself.

57. There remains an important ecumenical task incumbent on Catholics: infallibility has to be further examined in the light of the primacy of the gospel and of Christ's saving act; but it is also important to show how infallibility can render a service to God's people by giving expression to that primacy.

58. To promote a more ecumenical dimension in our Church's teaching function, we recommend:

a) that Catholics, particularly writers and teachers, observe an evangelical discretion in the titles bestowed on the papacy, avoiding that exaggerated language which tends to obscure the radical distinction between Christ or his Spirit and all other teachers within the Church, including the pope;

b) that Catholic leaders invite Lutheran church authorities to participate in the formulation of Catholic doctrine in a consultative capacity, seeking to follow and even to go beyond the precedent set by the participation of non-Catholic observers at Vatican Council II;

c) that Catholic bishops and their Lutheran counterparts seek to give joint witness (e.g., in pastoral letters) to emphasize and further Christian unity;

d) that Catholic theologians and religious educators make greater use of statements issued by Lutherans, especially when this will demonstrate and strengthen the unity of Christian faith.

The recommendations we have made refer to the Lutheran churches, because it is with them that we have been in dialogue. We trust that these recommendations offer a positive contribution to the efforts Christians are making toward greater unity in faith.

III

Lutheran Reflections

1. As is true of previous topics in this dialogue series, there is much that the Lutheran participants need to say to their fellow Lutherans about the question of infallibility beyond what is contained in the Common Statement. We need to explain from a Lutheran perspective the nature and reasons for both our growing agreements and our remaining disagreements with our Roman Catholic fellow Christians.

2. That we can speak of even partial agreement may seem extraordinary in view of the divisiveness of this issue in the past. The Lutheran participants were prepared for disappointments as they approached this round of the dialogue. The issue of papal infallibility seemed to be an inner-Catholic problem to which Lutherans had little to contribute. Yet we recognized the inescapability of the theme. While not identical with papal primacy, the concept of papal infallibility is closely related to the exercise of the universal teaching office in the Roman Catholic

Church and thus had to be discussed after the completion of our work on papal primacy and the universal Church. During the course of our conversations, however, we have become aware that the issues at stake in this particular doctrine are anything but a solely Roman Catholic problem. The very nature and truth of the gospel, the verification and authority of its proclamation and interpretation, and the credibility of the Church's preaching and teaching Ministry are involved in this question. Our partners in dialogue have pressed us hard on many of these points, and we are deeply grateful to them. We discovered that, as Lutherans, we were not as clear as we have traditionally supposed about how to give account of our confidence in the truth of the gospel and in the authority of a teaching office. We have also discovered that the Roman Catholics with whom we are in conversation are as concerned as we are about the Lordship of Christ and the truth of the gospel. We have been led to examine afresh some of our most fundamental assumptions and cherished emphases in the course of trying to understand what Roman Catholics mean today when they affirm the infallibility of the papal magisterium. Some of the results of our reflections must be spelled out here.

3. It seems best to start where we started as a group. Thus we shall first treat of Lutheran problems with traditional infallibility claims and language. This will provide us with the viewpoint from which, in the second and third places, Roman Catholic and Lutheran convergences and continuing difficulties in this area can be assessed. Finally, we shall discuss the possibilities and hopes for the future opened up by our growing though by no means complete agreement on the nature and function of teaching authority in the Christian churches.

I

4. Ever since its definition in 1870, the dogma of papal infallibility has been widely seen as both theologically and emotionally the most divisive of all the issues separating the Roman Catholic communion from the churches of the Reformation. To be sure, Lutherans have difficulties not only with papal infallibility but with the ascription of

infallibility to any of the Church's teaching offices (including ecumenical councils). Before turning to the theological core of these difficulties, however, we need to remind ourselves of the history of objections to the notion of an infallible pope.

5. From the 16th century on, Lutherans rejected what they regarded as exaggerated claims by the late medieval papacy, among them the claim to teach truth inerrantly. "Nor should that be transferred to the popes which is the prerogative of the true Church: that they are pillars of the truth and that they do not err." [126] Following an older tradition, they even called the pope the "antichrist," [127] in part because they saw him arrogating to himself the sole authority to interpret scriptural truth without fail. Thus antipapal polemics have remained a major part of the Lutheran stance. The First Vatican Council seemed to confirm all former suspicions. Its definition of infallibility was seen by many as the final step in the direction of papal absolutism, widening the gap between Roman and Reformation churches and making the break irreparable. The attempts at reconciliation and unification which occurred before the 19th century now seemed fruitless. While much of the emotion over Vatican I had national and political overtones, Lutherans reacted against the terminology of papal infallibility primarily because they thought it contradicted their basic conviction of the fallibility of all ecclesiastical institutions and orders. To speak of the pope or any of his pronouncements as infallible suggested to them the usurpation of the place which only Christ and the Word of God could occupy in the Church's teaching Ministry.[128] Infallibility language thus became the clearest proof, in the popular Lutheran perception of the decades since 1870, of what was regarded as the autocratic, oppressive, and anti-Christian character of the Roman Catholic Church. The definition of the Marian dogma of the Assumption[129] hardened this attitude even in irenic circles.[130] Lutherans objected not only to the claim of infallibility for this dogma but also to the very notion that the Assumption of Mary could in any sense be proclaimed a doctrine of the Church. It did not serve, they believed, to protect the gospel, nor did it have the scriptural basis which is necessary for authoritative teaching.

6. It next needs to be noted, however, that the theological difficulty many Lutherans today have with infallibility language and claims is much broader and more fundamental than the specifically interconfessional problems raised by the dialogue between Lutherans and Roman Catholics. The critique of such language and claims in recent history has been directed in the first instance against certain aspects of the Lutheran tradition itself, especially against claims made about the infallibility or inerrancy of Scripture.[131] In defense of their normative scriptural principle, the fathers of the second Lutheran generation[132] used the late medieval language of inerrancy for Holy Scripture as the Word of God and developed a doctrine of scriptural infallibility which was elaborated in ever greater detail during the period of Lutheran orthodoxy.[133] Some Lutherans even today regard the doctrine of the "inerrancy of Scripture" as the true touchstone of faithfulness to the Lutheran Confessions.

7. Others, however, have come to hold that such an emphasis on the letter of Scripture is not compatible with the doctrine of justification by faith, the article by which "the Church stands and falls."[134] Put most simply, this doctrine affirms that because God justifies the ungodly, forgiving sinners for Christ's sake, nothing else can be trusted for salvation. Neither scriptural inerrancy nor, even less, the infallibility of the Church's teachers, teaching offices, and doctrines is the basis of the Christian's confidence. All these may err, but not the gospel of God's unconditional mercy in Jesus Christ to which the biblical writings are the primary witness.

8. In the light of this, Lutherans believe that the transcendence which the gospel enjoys over human truth claims consists precisely in the fact that through the gospel God declares sinners righteous for Jesus' sake. The gospel, so to speak, establishes its own transcendence. Its truth becomes known and its authority acknowledged only upon being heard through the Word, received in the sacraments, and believed through the power of the Spirit. The authority of the Church's teachings and teaching office is dependent on the degree to which these further the proclamation of the gospel in accordance with Scripture.

9. One corollary of this emphasis on the self-authenti-cating character of the gospel is that questions about its authority can be answered ultimately only in its proclamation and celebration in preaching and sacraments when the Word of God genuinely encounters human beings in judgment and grace. Thus the Lutheran Confessions' use of something akin to infallibility language is in connection with the promises of God, i.e., "God does not lie" in such promises.[135] This, in turn, is inseparable from the conviction that the promises of God can be received only by faith, and that faith, by definition, is trust in such promises.

10. This understanding of faith has important consequences for the Lutheran view of church doctrine. It becomes necessary to make a careful distinction between faith as trust in the divine promises and those aspects of the faith of the Church which are responses to the divine promise through confession, action, teaching, and doctrinal formulations. These responses are necessary: the gospel (the promise of God) does indeed have a specifiable "knowledge" content. But the authority of this content, Lutherans believe, is established by its power to convict of sin and convince of grace through the work of the Holy Spirit and is not enhanced by saying that the teaching office or doctrinal formulations are themselves infallible.

11. Thus doctrinal formulations for Lutherans are, on the one hand, confessions and doxologies rather than promulgations of infallible dogma; and, on the other, they function as guides for the proper proclamation of the gospel, the administration of the sacraments, and the right praise of God rather than as statements which are themselves objects of faith. Furthermore, the scriptural witness to the gospel remains the ultimate norm for such formulations. Yet this does not exclude a high regard for their authority. Although they are the result of human responses to the word of forgiveness, church doctrines when rightly used are vitally important in order to foster, insofar as possible in changing historical contexts, the proper proclamation of the Word and the transmission of that Word in its purity. Lutherans should be supremely conscious in all this that "we have this treasure in earthen vessels, to show that the transcendent power belongs to God and not to us"

(2 Cor. 4:7). The Church abides and its teachings are authoritative, yet both remain *in via* until the day of Jesus Christ.

II

12. Although Lutherans have used this view of doctrinal authority in recent times largely as a critique of aspects of their own tradition, it is natural for them to apply it also in their interconfessional discussions with Roman Catholics. This leads them, on the one hand, to resist any suggestion that attributing infallibility to persons, institutions, doctrinal formulations, or even the Church as a whole could enhance the authority of the gospel; on the other hand, they welcome the assurance of the Roman Catholics that infallibility language is not intended to add anything to the authority of the gospel, but rather to let that authority be recognized without ambiguity. They rejoice in the increasing emphasis among Catholics on the supremely normative status of the gospel as witnessed to in Scripture, and on the importance of understanding infallibility in terms of trust, confidence, and hope in God's promises.

13. Roman Catholics, like Lutherans, have been impelled by historical research, the philosophical critique of language, and the contemporary experiences of change and pluralism to recognize the culturally conditioned character of all doctrinal formulations, though without surrendering convictions regarding their dimensions of abiding validity and truth. Further, changes in the understanding of the Church at Vatican II have begun to transform the monarchical features of papal infallibility into something more communal and collegial. As is made clear in both the Common Statement and the Catholic Reflections, infallibilist claims take on a very different appearance in this new context of thought and life. From the Lutheran perspective, it is now much clearer than before that Catholics also wish to place their ultimate reliance not in the teaching of popes, councils, or the Church but in God's promises in Jesus Christ.

14. One consequence of this is that Lutherans can no longer simply repeat their traditional objections to infallibility. What many Roman Catholics, including those who

regard as important the acceptance of this doctrine, now affirm is not what Lutherans have in the past rejected. Our partners in dialogue deny that there is any automatic guarantee of the truth of dogmatic pronouncements. They seem to us to hold that assurance of the truth of a doctrinal pronouncement does not ultimately depend on promulgation by pope or council but on the Word of God witnessed in Scripture and interpreted in the community of faith under the unfailing guidance of the Holy Spirit. We have come to recognize that it is for them often difficult to determine whether a particular teaching is to be numbered among infallible doctrines and that there is no official list of such doctrines. We hear them saying that their confidence in the abiding truth of, for example, the ancient Trinitarian and Christological creeds (which Lutherans also accept) is ultimately based on trust in God and his promised guidance of the Church, not in juridically conceived authority. Their acceptance of infallibility sometimes seems to us little different from the affirmation which we share, that God will not permit the Church to err definitively on any issue vital to the faith: "the gates of hell shall not prevail against it" (Matt. 16:18 KJV).

15. As Lutheran theologians, we find it difficult to object to such a position. Lutherans also have a confidence, rooted in God's mercy, that the early ecumenical creeds, not to mention the Reformation decision on justification, are of abiding validity and value. As a result, it has sometimes seemed in these discussions that our disagreements over the possibility of infallible doctrines are more verbal than real.

16. Verbal disagreements, to be sure, can be important. The language of infallibility continues to seem dangerously misleading to most of us even when applied to the Bible, and to all of us when used in reference to popes, councils, or doctrinal formulations. It can too easily be abused to detract from the primacy of God's justifying act in Jesus Christ. Nevertheless, we must record our conviction that this is not the way this language is understood by the Catholic theologians with whom we have discussed these issues. There is, we are persuaded, increasing agreement between us on the centrality of the gospel and of trust in God and his promises. This has the consequence that we

often find it difficult to pinpoint exactly where or how we differ from each other on the question of infallibility.[136] Yet this is an embarrassment in which we rejoice, because it grows from the convergence of Catholic concerns with those which spring from the Reformation.

17. Much, to be sure, remains to be done. Even if the difference on infallibility were overcome, there would still remain divergences between Catholics and Lutherans on specific doctrinal questions. The most manifest of those doctrinal divergences which we have not yet dealt with are the Marian dogmas of 1854 and 1950. Yet, given the convergence on the primacy of the gospel evident in our past and present discussions, it is our hope and prayer that even these need not be church-dividing.

III

18. Convergence, however, has taken place not only from the Catholic side. While Catholics are rethinking the meaning of infallibility, many Lutherans are reawakening to the importance of an ecumenical or universal teaching Ministry within the Church. This has been our experience in this dialogue. Our Catholic partners have stimulated us to consider how vital it is for the churches to speak, when occasion demands, with one voice in the world and how a universal teaching office such as that of the pope could exercise a Ministry of unity which is liberating and empowering rather than restrictive or repressive.

19. This convergence, propelled by the Lutheran confessional commitment to the cause of Christian unity,[137] occurs in the midst of conflicting claims to authority in the modern world. Lutherans, like Catholics, are called to move in creative, ecumenical ways toward an effective expression of universal teaching authority. We share the conviction that decisions about the truth of the gospel have to be made for the sake of the gospel's life in the world. Consequently, we affirm a Ministry which has the responsibility of reformulating doctrine in fidelity to the Scripture when circumstances require.[138] In order to fulfil this responsibility, we need to overcome our past difficulties in organizing an effective *magisterium* which can articulate the doctrinal concerns of Lutherans around the globe. It should

be the explicit purpose of such a magisterium to break through parochial, national, and denominational barriers and share in the ecumenical responsibility of witnessing in the world.[139] Ecumenical councils in conjunction with the papacy could thus become once again the instrument through which the unity and mission of the Church are affirmed and realized. Lutherans have always recognized that, though not guaranteed against error, the doctrinal decisions of free and universal councils are, when accepted by the churches, the highest exercise of the teaching office.[140]

20. To be sure, the Lutheran characterization of such a Ministry remains distinct from the Catholic one. As has been repeatedly emphasized, we continue to question the appropriateness of speaking of the Church's teaching office or doctrines as "infallible."[141] Infallibility suggests something above and beyond that indefectibility of the Church which we also accept. For us, there is no special gift (charism) of infallibility to the *magisterium*, although there is a preaching and teaching authority which exists to serve the proclamation of the Word and for the sake of order and discipline in the Church. Such order and discipline are, in part, the responsibility of the Ministry, which exists to ensure that the gospel is transmitted and preserved. The only guarantee of this transmission is the Holy Spirit, "who works faith, when and where he pleases."[142] Doctrinal decisions of the Church are to be taken with utmost seriousness, but this means that they are to be constantly reexamined and reinterpreted in the light of God's Word. We thus return to the emphasis on God's promises, which is expressed in the affirmation that only the Word of God found in Scripture is "infallible and unalterable."[143]

IV

21. Yet, although our accord on infallibility is not complete, the convergences we have traced are of great significance. To agree on the primacy of the gospel is more than a change of climate. It calls, as the Common Statement has already noted, for "magisterial mutuality," for cooperation with Catholics in the teaching function of the Church. Concrete steps need to be taken to right old wrongs and to

prepare for new directions at this crucial point in the history of our churches. Thus we recommend to our churches:

a) that they officially declare that the Lutheran commitment to the Confessions does not involve the assertion that the pope or the papacy in our day is the antichrist; [144] in this way our churches would publicly affirm that antipapal polemics should be replaced by an attitude of respect and love;

b) that they undertake an examination, with the participation of Catholics, of catechetical and other teaching materials, in order to identify and eliminate distorted accounts of historic and contemporary Roman Catholicism;

c) that in the presentation of our common Christian faith they encourage the greater use of Roman Catholic doctrinal, theological, catechetical, pastoral, and liturgical materials;

d) that they facilitate Catholic contributions to the process of formulating Lutheran positions on doctrinal and ethical issues; this might include Catholic participation in Lutheran conventions and assemblies;

e) that they develop structures for regular consultation with Catholic bishops on the local and national levels regarding matters of mutual concern;

f) that they declare their willingness to participate in a worldwide and ecumenically-based *magisterium;* this participation might take many forms, from representation in synods of bishops to joining in a fully ecumenical council.

We are aware that these recommendations are difficult to implement. They are in some respects ahead of what is at present possible. Yet, if our two traditions have indeed drawn as close in their understanding of the primacy of the gospel of Jesus Christ in relation to the Church's teaching authority as our work indicates, then it is incumbent on Lutherans to take concrete steps to bring the insights of our encounter to fruition. Only thus can Lutheranism become what it originally claimed to be: a reformation movement under the gospel within the Church catholic. We belong together with our Roman Catholic brothers and sisters in sharing the sufferings, joys, and tasks to which our common Lord calls us in God's world.

2

INFALLIBILITY:
THE TERMINOLOGY

Avery Dulles, S.J.

The following essay, commissioned for the February 1974 meeting of the Lutheran-Catholic Dialogue, is here presented with only slight revisions. The intention is to provide a basic glossary for an ecumenical discussion of infallibility. The terminology is explained in accordance with standard Roman Catholic usage as found in the documents of Vatican Councils I and II and in manuals and commentaries growing out of those councils. The present memorandum is not intended to prove anything about infallibility but rather to elucidate what has been claimed by the Catholic Church, particularly at Vatican I. For the bilateral conversation it will be helpful if all participants can agree about the meaning of the terms or, failing that, at least understand one another's usage, so that they will not simply talk past one another.

A. Underlying Concepts

When terms such as *infallibility* are used, the speakers generally presuppose certain more basic notions, such as *truth, falsity, error,* and *fallibility*. The discussion will be facilitated if these prior notions are first clarified.

1. *Truth.* It is extremely difficult to say what truth means when applied to revelation and dogma. Creedal and dog-

matic statements function in various ways, not always clearly separable from one another. Five key functions may here be enumerated:

(a) to praise God by expressing and evoking adoration, gratitude, and similar responses;

(b) to give witness to the gospel, inviting others to accept it in faith;

(c) to elucidate the contents and implications of revelation in answer to the questions of critical intelligence;

(d) to condemn false interpretations and warn against heresy;

(e) to regulate the use of language in the Church.

These five functions may be labeled respectively as the *doxological,* the *confessional,* the *explicative,* the *normative,* and the *linguistic-regulative.*

Creedal and dogmatic utterances are appropriate ways of giving praise to God, bearing faithful witness to Christ, clarifying the meaning of God's Word, guarding against heresy, and facilitating communication among Christians.

When referring to the "truth" of creedal and dogmatic statements, people generally have in mind their "logical" truth. This concept of truth is somewhat narrower than the biblical or Semitic concept of truth, which includes the "rightness" of a statement as leading to fullness of life and to salvation.

Logical truth exists first of all in the mind judging. It is the conformity of the mind, in its act of affirming, and the real order, to which the affirmation refers. A statement is true if its meaning corresponds to the reality referred to.

Propositions or statements about God create a particular problem. We cannot speak of God (whether in himself or in his self-communication to creatures) either positively or negatively except by using concepts derived from the created order. For this reason all our affirmations about God are necessarily deficient. God is not wise, loving, powerful, personal, etc., except in a manner far surpassing our power to imagine or conceive.

In the classical tradition all human affirmations about God are held to be *analogous.* Analogy is not the same as figurative language or metaphor, for it purports to affirm what is true in the proper sense of the word (e.g., "God is love") rather than improperly (e.g., "God is a rock"). Because of the transcendent factor in analogous predications, creedal and dogmatic statements have a peculiar kind of logical truth which differs from the truth of univocal statements, especially those of a merely factual character.

2. *Falsity, error.* These terms may be, and here will be, used as synonyms, to designate the opposite of truth. Within the genus of meaningful propositions, truth and falsity are contradictorily opposed. If not true, false; if not false, true.

When a distinction is drawn between falsity and error, error is held to refer to the act of the mind judging; falsity, to the statement made. Falsity does not by itself imply any intention to deceive.

3. *Fallibility.* This term means the state of being subject to error, though not necessarily erroneous. It is derived from the Latin term *fallere*, to deceive. Fallibility is therefore the possibility of deception. One may distinguish between active deception (deceiving another) and passive deception (being deceived).

B. Infallibility and Its Divisions

With these preliminaries we may now proceed to the definition of *infallibility.* The term means immunity from error, i.e. protection against either passive or active deception. Persons or agencies are infallible to the extent that they can neither deceive nor be deceived.

Infallibility is a negative term, but in Christian theological usage it refers by implication to something positive. The Church (and various persons and organs of the Church) is said to be infallible insofar as it is assured of abiding in the truth of the gospel. (The term "gospel" is here used as a synonym for Christian revelation, i.e., the divine revelation communicated in, or certified by, Jesus Christ.)

Since infallibility is essentially the gift of not falling away from the truth already given, it does not by itself imply the capacity to define new doctrines. Even if the pope could never define any new doctrines, he might be infallible in the sense that he would continue to believe and teach according to the gospel.

To avoid confusion about infallibility, it is important to

keep in mind some of the traditional distinctions or sub-divisions:

1. *In believing/In teaching*. Infallibility in believing means exemption from error in one's inner convictions, even though these remain unexpressed or badly expressed. Such infallibility in believing is commonly held to be the goal or purpose of infallibility in teaching. Many Christian theologians hold that the Church as a whole is infallible in be· lieving and that anything that manifests the belief of the whole people of God is therefore normative.[1]

Infallibility in teaching refers to the exemption of certain authoritative persons or organs in the Church from error in their doctrinal formulations. This, as we shall see (Section D), is often attributed to the bishops as a group, to ecumenical councils, and to popes.

Infallibility in defining (discussed under E2 below) is a special case of infallibility in teaching.

Some authors call infallibility in believing "passive infallibility" and infallibility in teaching "active infallibility." The term "passive infallibility" is unfortunate inasmuch as it suggests that belief is passive or that it simply mirrors what one's teacher has said.

2. *Habitual/Transitory*. Habitual infallibility is a relatively permanent capacity to be able to believe or teach infallibly. Transitory infallibility is such a capacity given only on certain occasions, e.g to a prophet when the prophetic afflatus is upon him. Vatican Councils I and II apparently attributed to the pope a habitual infallibility in the sense that he is *always* secured against teaching error in his *ex cathedra* statements. But that habitual infallibility can proceed into act only when certain conditions are verified; thus the exercise of infallibility is only transient.

3. *Absolute (unlimited)/Conditioned (limited)*. Absolute infallibility (in all respects, without dependence on another) is proper to God, of whom it is often said that he can neither deceive nor be deceived. All other infallibility is derivative and limited in scope.

The infallibility attributed to the Church, its organs and officers, is derivative from God, and its scope is proportioned to the purpose for which it is given, namely, to preserve the Church in the truth of Christian revelation and to enable it to communicate the revelation according to the needs of particular times and circumstances.

The extent and conditions of the church's infallibility will be further discussed below (Section E).

4. *A priori/A posteriori.* The term *infallibility* is generally understood to designate a logically antecedent immunity from error; in that sense all infallibility is *a priori*. Where conditional, the infallibility depends on the conditions being verified. In asserting the infallibility of popes and councils, theologians mean that if (antecedently) all the conditions are verified, then (consequently) these popes and councils cannot teach error.

Some recent authors have used the term "*a priori* infallibility" to describe the position (rejected by them) that for a statement to be infallible, it is sufficient that certain publicly verifiable conditions of a formal or juridical nature be antecedently fulfilled.[2] This position has undoubtedly been held by some authors, but it may be doubted whether this is in fact the teaching of either Vatican I or Vatican II.

C. Related Terms

For the sake of clarity, infallibility should be distinguished from *inerrancy*, *indefectibility*, and *irreformability*.

1. *Inerrancy*, unlike infallibility, implies nothing about the possibility or impossibility of error. It means a *de facto*, rather than a *de iure*, absence of error and thus an *a posteriori*, rather than an *a priori*, reliability.

In classical Christian theology, both Protestant and Catholic, Scripture is generally held to be inerrant. Since the 19th century many theologians, both Protestant and Catholic, have preferred to affirm only a qualified inerrancy of Scripture. Vatican II, in *Dei Verbum*, art. 11, apparently attributed inerrancy to the Bible only in the sense that whatever errors it contains do not corrupt the authenticity of its witness to divine revelation. The inerrancy of Scripture (whether total or limited) is generally seen as flowing from inspiration, a charism given to the prophets, apostles, and other biblical authors. Biblical inspiration is held to preclude error *a priori* and thus is understood as a charism somewhat similar to infallibility. In fact the Bible itself has occasionally been called infallible both by Catholics and by Protestants, especially in the late 16th and 17th centuries.[3]

In the later Middle Ages some authors used the term *inerrabilitas* to mean what is commonly called infallibility today. Thus Peter John Olivi (d. 1298), usually cited as one of the early witnesses to the doctrine of papal infallibility, maintained that the pope was to be believed as an *inerrabilis regula* in matters of faith and morals.

2. *Indefectibility,* a term derived from *deficere* ("to fail," "to defect"), means the impossibility of ceasing to exist, or, in other words, antecedently guaranteed continuation in being. Many Christians believe that, thanks to the promises of Christ and his continued presence in the power of the Holy Spirit, the church is indefectible. Some Scripture texts are adduced as evidence for this (e.g., Matt. 16:18; 28:20).

If the Church is understood as being essentially a community of Christian faith and proclamation, its indefectibility would seem to involve a certain infallibility in belief and in preaching, at least in the sense that God will see to it that the gospel is preached and believed in its purity somewhere. In preserving the Church as Church, God preserves it in the truth of the gospel. Whether minor or temporary lapses in faith or doctrine would be incompatible with indefectibility is a matter discussed among theologians.

3. *Irreformability.* The councils do not speak of infallible statements, but only of "irreformable" statements. The irreformability of the statements is seen as the immediate consequence of the speaker's infallibility.

The term *irreformable,* as used in Vatican I, comes out of the Gallican controversy. It had been disputed in the 17th century whether a decision of the pope was subject to approval or amendment by the various national hierarchies or by a general council of the whole Church. The last of the Four Articles of the Gallican Clergy (1682) held that papal statements were not irreformable unless accepted by the "consent of the Church" (DS 2284). Vatican I directly denied this. Thus irreformability in the usage of Vatican I apparently refers in the first instance to juridical finality or irreversibility. Nevertheless the Council fathers made it

clear that the reason for the irreformability of papal definitions was that their truth was protected by the infallibility
of the pope in the act of defining.

The irreformability of dogma implies that it cannot
be reversed or cancelled out by future developments, as
some Hegelians and Modernists apparently held that it
could be (cf. DS 3020, 3458, 3541, etc.). What is infallibly
taught is therefore irreformable in the sense of irreversible.

The question of reformability should not be confused
with that of *reformulation*. Reformability has to do with the
content or meaning of statements; reformulation, with the
mode of expression. The two are of course intimately related, since changes of language generally involve at least
minor changes in meaning. Sometimes, however, reformulation is called for precisely *in order to retain* the meaning of
an old formula in a situation in which the terms have
changed their meaning. Infallibility therefore does not
preclude reformulation; in fact, it may positively call for
this.

A more subtle question, which cannot be pursued here,
is the extent to which irreformability allows for *reconceptualization*, that is to say, the reaffirmation of the same
truth in new conceptual categories. To the extent that the
meaning of a proposition is separable from the conceptual
structure, the substitution of new concepts would seem to
be compatible with irreformability.

D. The Subject of Infallibility

The meaning of infallibility is differently nuanced according to the various subjects of which it is predicated.

1. *The Church as a whole.* The idea that the Church as a
whole is providentially protected against falling away from
the truth of the gospel may, as we have seen, claim some
biblical foundation. In the patristic period this idea formed
part of the justification for the authority of ecumenical
councils, which were deemed to be representative of the
faith of the whole Church. In the Middle Ages, authors
such as Thomas Aquinas repeatedly asserted that the
Church as a whole cannot err in its faith. This idea was
preserved not only in Eastern Orthodoxy but also in early

Protestantism. Luther, Melanchthon, Calvin, and Zwingli all held that the Church, as a community of faith and witness, is in some sense infallible.[4]

2. *The Roman Church.* Some ancient authors looked upon the Roman Church as the touchstone of orthodoxy. Irenaeus, for instance, held that the traditions of that church were commended by a richer apostolic inheritance than those of other churches (*Adv. haer.* III.3.2). Cyprian, relying on Rom. 1:8, asserted that infidelity can have no access to the Roman Church (*Ep.* 59,14). (Other testimonies to the purity of the Roman tradition are cited by Robert Eno in his essay for the present volume.)

3. *Official teachers*

(a) The *apostles* as prime witnesses to the revelation of Christ are often thought to have spoken with infallible authority, at least in their preaching of the faith. Luther, for example, called the apostles *infallibiles doctores.*[5]

(b) *Peter* as head and spokesman of the apostolic college has been thought to have been infallible in an eminent degree. The biblical texts used in this connection are well known.

(c) The *magisterium*, i.e., those who have the office of teaching in the Church. They are often thought to be infallible in their teaching of the faith because if they were not, the Church as a whole would inevitably be led into error.

(d) The *bishops* collectively, insofar as they have the fullness of the *magisterium* (in episcopally ordered churches). In modern Roman Catholic thought the bishops collectively are held to be infallible both in their ordinary teaching and in their extraordinary teaching. By the ordinary teaching of the bishops is meant that which all of them teach as a matter of faith in their own dioceses. Their extraordinary teaching is their action of defining truths of faith and morals when they act in unison, e.g., at an ecumenical council. The conditions for an ecumenical council, it may here be noted, have never been precisely determined. There is no officially approved list of ecumenical councils, still less of the infallible definitions of ecumenical councils.

(e) The *pope,* by reason of his succession to Peter and his responsibility for the universal faith of the Church, is held to be infallible (as are general councils) in the act of defining.

Is the pope *personally* infallible? The response requires a distinction. The pope is not infallible as a private person. On the other hand, it would not be acceptable to say that the papal office alone is infallible, for this would open the way to the Gallican distinction between the office and the officeholder, between the *sedes* and the *sedens,* a distinction rejected by Vatican Council I. Thus the pope is held to be infallible as a *public* person. Infallibility may also be attributed to the papal office insofar as possession of the office is a source or condition of the pope's infallibility.

4. *Statements of the Church and its officeholders.* As noted above (C3), the councils do not apply the term *infallibility* to the statements of church authorities who make the statements. The statements themselves are called true, obligatory, and irreformable. In a wider sense it seems permissible to use the term *infallible statement* to designate a statement made by a person or organ acting infallibly, just as a person speaking truly may be said to make a "true statement." But in view of the analogous character of religious language, dogmatic statements are especially difficult to interpret, and the danger of objectifying the truth is correspondingly greater.

E. Conditions of Infallibility in Defining

Councils and popes, as noted above, are held to be infallible in the act of defining. Their infallibility is conditioned by reason of the object and the act itself.

1. *The object.* The primary or direct object of infallibility is held to be any truth contained explicitly or implicitly in the deposit of divine revelation committed to the apostles. (We may prescind here from the debate about whether the "virtually implicit" can be dogmatically defined.) Under the secondary or indirect object, theologians generally include truths intimately connected with revelation—i.e., those without which the revelation would be unintelligible, unrecognizable, or incredible, or those which evidently follow from revelation, so that to reject them would be tantamount to rejecting the revelation itself. (Vatican I and

II never defined that popes and councils are infallible with regard to the secondary object. That they are is an agreed opinion of the bishops and theologians who spoke at Vatican I and II and is regarded as theologically certain.)

2. *The act*. Whereas the infallibility of the Church as a whole, the episcopate, councils, and popes is the same with respect to its object, the acts by which the infallibility of these agencies is exercised differ from one another. With regard to the Church as a whole and the bishops in their ordinary teaching, no special acts are designated. In other words, the acts may be anything that sufficiently manifests their faith and doctrine. The acts by which general councils or popes exercise their infallibility are known as "definitions." A definition, in the technical meaning here used, is the act of imposing on all the faithful a precisely formulated truth in the name of fidelity to divine revelation. Some speak of *solemn* definitions, but the adjective *solemn* adds nothing to the force of the definition. No particular external solemnities are required for validity.

Since the technical distinction between general conciliar teaching and dogmatic definitions is a modern one, it is not easy to establish precisely what teachings of councils prior to Vatican I are to be reckoned as definitions. Sometimes this appears from the language or acts of the council; sometimes it does not. With regard to Vatican I, the definitions generally occur in the canons to which anathemas are attached, but the chapters also contain definitions, since the canons for the most part reaffirm what is taught as Catholic faith in the chapters. At Vatican II the Theological Commission stated that nothing was to be understood as a definition unless the Council openly declared its intention of defining.[6] Theologians generally agree that Vatican II did not impose any new definitions.[7]

For a papal definition, it is necessary that the pope be speaking *ex cathedra (Petri)*. This is a technical term summarizing the following four conditions recognized by Vatican I (cf. DS 3074):

(i) in fulfillment of his office as supreme pastor and teacher of all Christians;

(ii) in virtue of his supreme apostolic authority, i.e., as successor of Peter;

(iii) determining a doctrine of faith and morals, i.e., a doctrine expressing divine revelation;

(iv) imposing a doctrine to be held definitively by all. Vatican I firmly rejected one condition which the Gallicans had regarded as necessary for infallibility, namely, the consent of the whole church. This is the meaning of the famous phrase *ex sese, non ex consensu Ecclesiae* (DS 3074). The Council here denied that the *reason* for the irreformability of papal definitions is the consent of the Church; it did not deny that the consent of the Church will be present or even that such consent is necessary as a condition for recognizing an authentic exercise of the infallible *magisterium*.

F. Sources of Infallibility

The infallibility of the Church and its teaching authorities is generally attributed, at least primarily, to the promised assistance of the Holy Spirit. The Holy Spirit is thus the principal efficient cause. Christ is said to be the impetrative cause insofar as his prayer brings about this assistance (cf. Luke 22:32; John 17:14-26). Teaching is listed by Paul as one of the *charismata* of the Holy Spirit (Rom. 12:6-7). According to the Fourth Gospel the Holy Spirit assists the disciples by enabling them to recall and rightly understand the revelation given in Christ (cf. John 14:26). The Pastoral Letters connect reliable teaching in a special way with office and ordination (1 Timothy 4:14; 2 Timothy 1:6; 2:1-2). It is thus a charism linked with an office; it is a "grace of office."

Infallibility in teaching is not a distinct entity, but rather a modality of the assistance given to teachers in the Church. Since the formal effect of infallibility is negative (the prevention of error), infallibility does not by its nature demand any positive illumination. In practice, however, the Holy Spirit presumably prevents error by guiding into the truth (cf. John 16:13).

As instrumental causes of infallibility one may point to created means such as the canonical Scriptures, the monuments of tradition, the living faith of the pastors and faithful, theological scholarship and discussion. The assistance of the Holy Spirit, as understood in Catholic theology, does not exempt church authorities from using these created aids, but rather it prompts them to do so. It is normally only after a considerable period of study, deliberation, and consultation that a pope or council feels authorized to commit the Church definitively.

3

MODERATE INFALLIBILISM

Avery Dulles, S.J.

The term "moderate infallibilism" is taken from George Lindbeck's Père Marquette Lecture, *Infallibility*,[1] and from his February 1974 paper, "The Reformation and the Infallibility Debate."[2] In the following pages I shall try to set forth a certain understanding of infallibility which I regard as valid and defensible and which fits better into the category of "moderate infallibilism" than into Lindbeck's other two categories, "absolutistic infallibilism" and "fallibilism." Instead of commenting on the work of Rahner and Kasper, whom Lindbeck takes as representative of the moderate position, I shall present my own ideas, which I believe to be in line with the Vatican I Constitution, *Pastor aeternus*, with the Vatican II Constitution, *Lumen gentium*, and with the 1973 Declaration of the Congregation for the Doctrine of the Faith, *Mysterium Ecclesiae*.

For the sake of precision I shall center my remarks on papal infallibility, i.e., on the infallibility of the pope in teaching and, more specifically, in defining. I shall not here deal directly with either the infallibility of the entire episcopal body in teaching or that of the Church as a whole in believing and in bearing witness to the gospel.

The moderate infallibilist position includes two traits. In the first place, it affirms that the pope is infallible or at least that he has on certain occasions a charism that may

81

not too deceptively be called infallibility. Second, the position asserts that papal infallibility, being limited, is subject to inherent conditions which provide critical principles for assessing the force and meaning of allegedly infallible statements.

Moderate infallibilism is contrasted with a kind of infallibilism which is described as "traditional" or, in more pejorative terms, as "absolutistic," "extreme," "fundamentalistic," or "hypertrophic." More neutrally, this other infallibilism is one that questions or denies the limitations and conditions emphasized by moderate infallibilists. An infallibilism of this second type may be found in the pre-Vatican I writings of William G. Ward, H. E. Manning, and Louis Veuillot, and in the post-Vatican I writings of J. M. A. Vacant, J. C. Fenton, and I. Salaverri.[3] Moderate and extreme are, to be sure, matters of degree. Moderate infallibilism is not necessarily minimalist, nor is extreme infallibilism necessarily maximalist.

The relevance of moderate infallibilism to the Lutheran-Roman Catholic Dialogue at the present stage of its discussions should be evident. George Lindbeck asserts that it is the position that "has the best chance of uniting the exigencies of the Reformation and of *Romanitas*." [4] A position that repudiated papal infallibility would be difficult to recognize as Catholic; one that was not moderate could scarcely hope to handle the difficulties that would be raised from within the Roman Catholic community, let alone those arising from the Protestant side.

Moderate infallibilism, although it may not be fully acceptable to Christians outside the Roman Catholic tradition, may nevertheless hold some interest for those who are convinced that the gospel cannot stand in the absence of all propositional truth (according to the famous dictum of Luther, "Take away assertions and you take away Christianity" *[Tolle assertiones et christianismum tulisti]*) [5] and who are concerned with maintaining what Lindbeck calls "the objective particularities which constitute the essence of distinctive Christian identity." [6] This kind of concern may be presumed to have existed in the group that issued, several years ago, the statement, "The Status of the Nicene Creed as Dogma in the Church." [7]

The Case for Moderate Infallibilism

Like many other confessional assertions, papal infallibility depends on testimony and cannot be rigorously deduced from other beliefs used as logical premises. It simply declares how the papal office understands its teaching authority and how that authority is understood in the Roman Catholic Church. As a faith claim, infallibility has a certain plausibility for Christians who accept certain other beliefs, such as the following:

1. God provides for the Church effective means by which it may and will in fact remain in the truth of the gospel till the end of time.

2. Among these means are not only the canonical Scriptures but also, as an essential counterpart to the Scriptures, the pastoral office. Without such a pastoral office the Christian community would not be adequately protected against corruptions of the gospel.

3. The pastoral office is exercised for the universal Church by the bearer of the Petrine office (which means, for Catholics, by the pope). It is therefore reasonable to suppose that the pope is equipped by God with a special charism (or grace of office) for correctly interpreting the gospel to the universal Church, as circumstances may require.

4. In order that the papacy may adequately discharge its function of preserving unity in the faith and exposing dangerous errors, the papal charism must include the power to assert the truth of the gospel and to condemn contrary errors in a decisive and obligatory manner. Authoritative pronouncements from the Petrine office that are seriously binding on all the faithful must have adequately certified truth, for there could be no obligation to believe what could probably be error.

These speculative arguments for infallibility are reinforced by certain biblical and historical arguments. *Pastor aeternus,* chapter IV, refers to the well-known texts Matt. 16:18 and Luke 22:32 as they have been interpreted in the Catholic tradition, and to conciliar texts from Constantinople IV, Lyons II, and Florence. It appeals also to the time-honored practice of the Holy See in issuing definitive judgments on doctrinal questions since ancient times.

The case for moderate, rather than extreme, infallibilism

rests, at least partly, on the limited character of the claims made for the infallibility of the pope in the official documents to which we have referred. On general speculative grounds it would seem unreasonable to presume that the popes or other officeholders in the Church would be miraculously enabled to speak the truth on all questions, regardless of the effects of human historicity and sinfulness. Hence discernment is needed on the part of the faithful to determine whether a given statement is protected by the charism of infallibility and if so, how its infallible content is to be understood at a given time and place. Extreme or fundamentalistic infallibilism tends to ignore the limits imposed by the creaturely condition of all human teachers.

The Limitations Acknowledged by Vatican I

When the definition of Vatican I is compared with the claims made for the pope by neo-Ultramontanists such as Veuillot, Manning, and Ward, it becomes apparent why Newman felt entitled to say that divine Providence gained a victory: "Pius has been overruled—I believe that he wished a much more stringent dogma than he has got." [8] Hans Küng, no ardent champion of infallibility, writes:

All too often outside the Church the Vatican definition is considered as the high point, unmatchable, of the concentration of teaching authority of the pope and as the establishment of an unlimited papal infallibility. At the same time it is a fact that this very definition signifies a very clear *limitation vis-à-vis* all that which frequently has been asserted about the infallibility of the pope in the Catholic Church before the council. One could rightly view it as a victory for the council minority. . . . [9]

As a first step in our exposition of moderate infallibilism, therefore, we may properly undertake some analysis of the Vatican I definition, especially in the light of the quasi-official *relatio* given at the Council by Bishop Vincenz Gasser, who laid down the basic principles of interpretation which were presumably in the minds of the bishops when they voted on the decree. He unequivocally asserted:

Absolute infallibility belongs only to God, the first and essential truth who can never in any way deceive or be deceived. All other infallibility, by the fact that it is communicated for a certain end, has limits within which and conditions under which it is judged to be present. This is true likewise of the infallibility of the Roman pontiff.[10]

Among the conditions recognized by the Council one may distinguish between certain general or fundamental conditions that were mentioned in the debates on the Council floor and properly theological conditions that were written into the definition itself. As a general condition, for instance, it was acknowledged that the pope, in defining, must be performing a free human act. Considerable attention was devoted to the question of coercion. Monsignor J. Cardoni, Archbishop of Edessa, in his *votum* prepared for the Theological Commission in 1869, held that the pope, in making an *ex cathedra* pronouncement, must be free from violence, coercion, or fear.[11] A "shotgun" definition would therefore have no dogmatic force. In view of this principle it seems proper to say that a definition would be invalidated by any circumstances that would deprive the pope of his freedom and rationality—e.g., a severe mental illness.

Another general condition recognized by commentators is that it must be clear that the act in question meets all the conditions of infallibility. According to the Code of Canon Law, "Nothing is deemed to be dogmatically declared or defined unless this manifestly appears" (CIC 1323 #3).

The theological conditions spelled out by the Council are familiar to all students of Roman Catholic dogmatics and may be rather briefly summarized here. Some commentators, following the very language of the definition (DS 3074), specify the following four conditions:

(a) The pope must be speaking not as a private person but as a public person and more specifically in his capacity as "supreme pastor and teacher of all Christians." He is not infallible as a private theologian, as a bishop of the diocese of Rome, as metropolitan of the Roman Province, as Patriarch of the West, or in any other capacity than as primate of the universal episcopate.

(b) He must appeal to his supreme apostolic authority, i.e., that which pertains to him as successor of Peter.

(c) He must be teaching within the sphere of "faith and

morals." The expression *res fidei et morum,* as used at Vatican I, is not easy to interpret.[12] The Council used *mores* in a narrower sense than did Trent, for which Council the term apparently included matters of custom and ecclesiastical discipline. Vatican I in several texts (DS 3060, 3064) drew a contrast between "faith and morals" on the one hand and matters "which pertain to discipline and to church government" on the other. The sphere of infallibility, therefore, is considered to extend to doctrine rather than to precepts and practices.

On the other hand the Council did not say that the pope is infallible only when he defines the contents of revelation. As appears from the records of the debates both in the Deputation of Faith and on the Council floor, there was general agreement that the sphere of infallibility extends to two classes of object:

(i) revealed doctrines (the primary object of infallibility)

(ii) doctrines necessary to maintain, preach, or defend the content of revelation (the secondary object)

In the Deputation on Faith it was agreed that it is a dogma of faith that the pope is infallible with reference to divinely revealed truth; it is theologically certain that he is infallible with regard to things necessarily connected with revelation.[13] Because of some unclarity about how far the secondary object extends—e.g., whether it includes what is merely *useful* for explaining or justifying revealed truth—Vatican I refrained from saying anything about the secondary object.

The distinction between the two classes of object was alluded to by Vatican II, which stated: "This infallibility with which the divine Redeemer willed his Church to be endowed in defining a doctrine of faith and morals extends as far as the deposit of divine revelation, which must be religiously guarded and faithfully expounded" (*Lumen gentium* 25). The final clause is intended to refer to the secondary object of infallibility.

(d) The pope must be proposing the doctrine as something to be held by the whole Church, that is to say, as a doctrine having universal obligatory force. The term "held" (*tenenda*) was consciously selected as an alternative to "believed" (*credenda*), a term which would have implied that the infallible teaching is to be accepted on a motive of divine faith. Had this latter expression been used, the Council would have been restricting the sphere of infallibility to strictly revealed doctrine, and this it did not wish to do.

Since the Council did not explicitly teach that infallibility extends to the secondary object, this extension is not considered to have been defined. Anyone limiting infallibility to the primary object would not be contradicting the clear teaching of Vatican I or, for that matter, of Vatican II; but he would be opposing what was the common opinion at both Councils.

Further Properties of Infallible Statements

The two general conditions and the four theological conditions just mentioned are not here proposed as exhaustive. From the official sources on which we are commenting it is possible to gather up certain other properties or attributes of infallible statements, which might also be regarded as conditions. We shall here enumerate four.

(a) Agreement with Scripture and Tradition

Vatican I clearly alluded to this requirement in its discussion of the goal of papal infallibility: "For the Holy Spirit was not promised to the successors of Peter that by his revelation they might make known new doctrine, but that by his assistance they might inviolably guard and faithfully expound the revelation or deposit of faith delivered through the apostles" (DS 3070). It is evident that a valid definition could not be in violation of the true meaning of the Scriptures or contrary to previous infallible pronouncements.

At Vatican II, Paul VI proposed to insert into *Lumen gentium* 22 a statement to the effect that the pope is "answerable to the Lord alone" in his actions as a vicar of Christ. The Theological Commission rejected this proposal and stated: "The Roman Pontiff is also bound to revelation itself, to the fundamental structure of the Church, to the sacraments, to the definitions of earlier councils, and other obligations too numerous to mention." [14]

(b) Agreement with the Present Faith of the Church

Vatican I ruled out the consent of the Church as the source of irreformability in papal teaching. The source, it said, is the Holy Spirit, who assists the pope by special charisms attached to the papal office. The Council, however, did not deny that the consent of the church will be present or even that such consent is necessary as a condition for recognizing an authentic exercise of the infallible magisterium. Hence Vatican II deemed it proper to add the explanation:

Therefore his definitions, of themselves, and not from the consent of the Church, are justly styled irreformable, for they are pronounced with the assistance of the Holy Spirit, an assistance promised to him in blessed Peter. . . . To the resultant definitions the assent of the Church can never be wanting, on account of the activity of that same Holy Spirit, whereby the whole flock of Christ is preserved and progresses in unity of faith *(Lumen gentium* 25).

According to the *relatio* of the Theological Commission, infallible definitions of popes and councils "are irreformable of themselves and do not require the approbation of the people, as many in the East have erroneously held, but they carry with them and express the consensus of the whole community." [15] Bishop B. C. Butler remarks in this connection that while the consent of the Church does not make a definition infallible, it may be necessary to make sure that an alleged definition is in fact infallible.[16] In a similar vein, George Tavard writes: "In his definitions, encyclicals, instructions and actions, [the pope] must embody the Church's unanimity, which is not reached by obedience to one man's opinions and decisions but by free and mutual consultation and discussion in the spirit of the Gospel. Papal encyclicals which do not embody this unanimity are theological documents with no claim on the allegiance of the Church's members." [17]

It would not be proper to regard the pope as a mere mouthpiece for voicing what had previously been explicitly agreed to by the whole Church. As supreme pastor and teacher he has a special responsibility and charism for doctrine.[18] But, for the reasons given above, it seems evident that definitions, if they authentically correspond to the charism of the papal office, will find an echo in the faith of the Church and will therefore evoke assent, at least eventually. If in a given instance the assent of the Church were evidently not forthcoming, this could be interpreted as a signal that the pope had perhaps exceeded his competence and that some necessary condition for an infallible act had not been fulfilled.[19]

(c) Agreement with the Universal Episcopate

It is clear from the teaching of Vatican I, repeated at Vatican II, that the pope in his infallible teaching is not juridically dependent on any prior, concomitant, or subsequent assent of the body of bishops as a condition for the validity of his acts. On the other hand both councils recognize that the bishops, as the highest body of official teachers in the Church, enjoy a certain corporate infallibility. Vatican I's Constitution on Faith, *Dei Filius,* asserted that the ordinary and universal teaching of the bishops, even when dispersed, as well as their solemn teaching when united in council, is to be accepted on a motive of divine and catholic faith (DS 3011). In *Pastor aeternus* Vatican I taught that the infallibility of the pope is not something altogether peculiar to himself, but is identical with the charism with which the divine Redeemer willed his Church to be endowed in defining doctrines of faith and morals (DS 3074). Vatican II, after setting forth the doctrine of episcopal collegiality, spoke even more explicitly of the infallibility of the whole episcopal body, both when dispersed around the world and when gathered in council (*Lumen gentium* 25). The same doctrine is repeated in *Mysterium Ecclesiae,* no. 3.

Because the assistance of the Holy Spirit is promised both to the pope and to the bishops as a corporate body, it seems clear that they would not fail to assent to any valid papal definition of the faith. If the bishops with moral unanimity held the contrary, one would be put on notice that the conditions for a genuinely infallible act on the part of the pope might not have been fulfilled.

(d) Sufficient Investigation

Bishop Cardoni, in his *votum* on infallibility at Vatican I, made the point that the pope is seriously obliged, under pain of sin, to take the necessary means to ascertain that his definition in fact conforms with the Christian revelation.[20] Some Council fathers, such as Bishop Moriarty, wished to insert into the definition the specification that prudent investigation on the part of the pope would be a condition *sine qua non* for the validity of an infallible pronouncement.[21] The majority, however, were disinclined to impose any such restrictions on the pope as conditions for the validity of his act.

Vatican II, in *Lumen gentium* 25, asserted that the pope "strives painstakingly and by appropriate means to inquire into that revelation and to give apt expression to its contents." *Mysterium Ecclesiae* is still more specific. It states that since the charism of infallibility "does not come from new revelations . . . it does not dispense them (the pope and the bishops) from studying with appropriate means the treasure of divine revelation contained both in Sacred Scripture which teaches us intact the truth that God willed to be written down for our salvation and in the living tradition that comes from the Apostles." [22]

Reflecting theologically on the texts of Vatican I and Vatican II, George Wilson observes:

Because the Church has been given the gift of infallibility, the promise of infallible guidance, this by no means frees the human agents of the need to act and respond *as* human agents. We must restore the gift of infallibility to a whole economy of means-to-end. If God promises the end, He also promises the means, but this implies that suitable means will be taken and we simply cannot think of the end in isolation. Though one could not maintain that Vatican I formally teaches that the gift of infallibility guarantees not only the truth of the definition but also that it will be arrived at in a humanly valid manner, its exclusion of inspiration or new revelation for the definer and its mention of the means supplied by divine providence ["aliis, quae divina suppeditabat providentia, adhibitis auxiliis" (DS 3069)] would seem to imply that in accepting a definition the believer is really assenting to the validity of the process by which the Church makes its way from the original data of faith to the contemporary formulation of the definition.[23]

The inseparability of the definition from the process raises questions as to whether we are here confronted, in effect, with a new condition. What if it were evident that in a given case the pope did not have access to certain essential data or did not take the requisite measures to ascertain what was in Scripture or tradition? Are we to assume that a miracle would supply for the diligence lacking to the pope?

In response to questions such as these, many appeal to divine providence as assuring that the pope will not abuse his powers as supreme teacher in cases involving infallibility. Gasser in his *relatio* put the matter as follows:

> There is no reason to fear that the universal Church will be led into error concerning faith by the bad faith or negligence of the pope. For the protection of Christ and the divine assistance promised to the successors of Peter are a cause so efficacious that, if the judgment of the supreme pontiff were erroneous and destructive of the faith, it would be impeded, or if the pope did actually define, it would be infallibly true.[24]

Although accepted by many theologians from Joseph Kleutgen to Karl Rahner, this argument from divine providence has some weaknesses. In general, it is hazardous to appeal to what God in his providence would or would not permit. He has permitted doubts and disagreements to persist for some time about who is the true pope, and this would seem to be an evil at least as great as a particular error in papal teaching. Further, the argument appears to assume too hastily that an erroneous papal teaching under the claim of infallibility would destroy the faith of the universal Church. Why could not the faithful find ways of recognizing the error through theological criticism being brought to bear on the pronouncement, through the unfavorable reaction of bishops and other pastors, and through the inward teaching of the Holy Spirit which, according to Vatican II, gives a certain inerrancy to the faith of the entire people of God (*Lumen gentium* 12)?

Perhaps in our day, thanks to a greater appreciation of the many ways in which the Spirit instructs the Church, we should recognize that adequate investigation of the sources of revelation is a true condition for an infallible teaching. This view, proposed by the minority at Vatican I, could, I believe, be integrated into a moderate infallibilism.[25]

The position here proposed will be resisted on the ground that it might give rise to doubts as to whether a given definition enjoys the prerogative of infallibility. For some, the very essence of infallibility consists in the *a priori* assurance that if certain easily verifiable conditions are fulfilled, the definition may be regarded as unquestionably true. This, however, is to my mind an oversimplification. At Vatican I, it will be recalled, it was acknowledged that if the pope lacked freedom, his definition would not enjoy the guarantee of infallibility. At this point a host of possible doubts come into view. Was the fear of certain bad consequences for the Church a factor in this or that definition? Was the pope, in seeking to meet a certain crisis in the life of the Church, really free in his action? What was his inner state of mind and what was the degree of his true psychological freedom?

Again, Vatican I did not rule out the view of most theologians since the Middle Ages that it is possible for a pope to fall into heresy or schism.[26] If he did so, he would presumably be incapable of validly exercising his office (since heresy and schism, if externally manifested, automatically excommunicate from the Church). Thus any alleged definitions issued by a schismatical or heretical pope would be invalid. But it is not always easy to determine what deviations amount to heresy or schism. Hence in some cases it could be doubtful whether the pope were validly defining.

In the majority of cases, the validity of a definition will not be a problem for the Church at large. But if grave and widespread doubts were to arise among committed Christians who are orthodox on other points, the definition would have to be treated as dubious and hence as not canonically binding. This consequence does not appear to me to be disastrous to the whole concept of infallibility.[27]

Reinterpretation of the Vatican I Definition

Much of the discussion of infallibility has been hampered by a rather fundamentalistic understanding of the teaching of Vatican I. Thanks to the principles set forth in *Mysterium Ecclesiae,* no. 5, it is at present possible to justify a reinterpretation that better corresponds to the exigencies of our time. *Mysterium Ecclesiae* recognized two crucial limiting factors: the transcendence of divine revelation and the historicity of human formulations.

As regards the first of these principles, the Sacred Congregation quotes *Dei Filius* to the effect that the hidden mysteries of God "by their nature so far transcend the human intellect that even after they are revealed to us and accepted by faith, they remain concealed by the veil of faith itself and are as it were wrapped in darkness" (DS 3016). In a similar vein, Vatican II pointed out that the pilgrim Church is able to show forth the mystery of the Lord "in a faithful though shadowed way, until at last it will be revealed in total splendor" (*Lumen gentium* 8). Thus the formulations of faith will always fall short of expressing the full richness of the divine mystery to which they refer.

In view of the transcendence of the content of faith, one may properly hesitate to employ expressions such as "revealed doctrines," although such expressions appear in some church documents (e.g., DS 3803, defining the Immaculate Conception). It must be recognized that the categories used in ecclesiastical definitions are human and that the definitions therefore fall short of adequately expressing the content of revelation itself. Dogmas must be seen as human formulations of the Word of God, formulations not undialectically identified with the revelation they transmit. Thus it is possible that one and the same faith may be expressed in formulas that stand in tension with one another and, indeed, that seem contradictorily opposed. Hence the fact that some seem to be contradicting a definition of faith does not necessarily mean that they have "made shipwreck of the faith," as the expression has it (cf. DS 2804). One must explore very carefully what they mean by their statements and see whether they are at variance with the mystery of revelation itself.

These observations cast some light on the situation of Christians who declare that they cannot accept the doctrine of papal infallibility. The doctrine, as formulated by the Councils, is a limping human effort to articulate a mystery that defies clear expression. The believer who has difficulties with the formulas may be more keenly conscious than some others are of complementary facets of the revealed mystery.

Second, *Mysterium Ecclesiae* acknowledges the historical conditioning of statements of faith. It states, in effect, that such pronouncements are influenced by the presuppositions (i.e., the "context of faith or human knowledge"), the concerns (i.e., "the intention of solving certain questions"), the thought categories (i.e., "the changeable conceptions of the given epoch"), and the available vocabulary (i.e., the "expressive power of the language used at a certain point of time").

1. As regards presuppositions, there can be no doubt that Vatican I moved in a universe of thought far different from our own, and it may be questioned whether even Vatican II, in *Lumen gentium* 25, sufficiently allowed for the difference. Questions such as the following must be squarely faced:

(a) Did Vatican I assume, in its statement on infallibility, that revelation could be directly and adequately embodied in human propositions? Today we are more conscious than Vatican I seems to have been of the desirability of pluralism in formulations. Appeal is often made to the tolerance exercised by the Council of Florence, in its Decree of Union with the Greeks, regarding the term *filioque*.[28]

(b) Did Vatican I assume that every doctrine deemed requisite for an adequate profession of faith at any one time must always remain requisite? Do we assume this? If not, can we not consider that a proposition taught at one period under anathema need not be so taught at another period? [29]

(c) Did Vatican I assume that the Christian Church was fully and adequately present in Roman Catholicism? Is this a position we wish to share? Or should we build into the notion of infallibility an added dimension of "ecumenicity," as proposed by Lindbeck? [30] According to this view a doctrine would not be recognized as infallible unless a serious attempt had been made to speak not only to and for Roman Catholics, but to and for Christians of all churches.

(d) Did Vatican I assume too easily that faith is a collection of divinely guaranteed propositions, so that a mistake about these would involve the destruction of faith itself? Do we think today that Christian faith can coexist with serious speculative errors about what God revealed in Christ? If so, should the area of infallibility be narrowed to propositions that express the very core of Christian faith or that seem necessary, in a given situation, to protect that core?

(e) Did Vatican I assume too rapidly that the faithful

were abjectly dependent for the content of their faith on the authoritative teaching of the pope, so that if he erred they would all be led inevitably into the same errors? Do we today count more, as suggested above, on the *many* ways in which the Holy Spirit teaches the faithful and on their capacity, thanks to these resources, to detect the errors even of a pope? If so, can we not admit more conditions to infallible teaching than were explicitly recognized by Vatican I?

2. With regard to the concerns of Vatican I, it may be important to note that the main target of *Pastor aeternus*, in all four chapters, was that remnant of "Gallicanism" still represented in the thought of theologians such as Ignaz von Döllinger, Lord Acton, and Bishop H. Maret. The central question therefore was not infallibility or even irreformability. All the parties to the discussion simply assumed that the supreme *magisterium* in its definitive pronouncements was preserved from error. The question was rather: What is the locus of the supreme teaching authority? Is the pope by himself capable of speaking definitively, so that his statements are irreformable "of themselves," or do they first acquire irreformability when the consent of the entire Church (i.e., of the universal episcopate) accrues? The latter was the classical Gallican position as expressed in the "Four Articles" of 1682 (cf. DS 2284). Vatican I's *ex sese, non autem ex consensu Ecclesiae* must be interpreted as an echo of the language in the Gallican articles and thus in relationship to the position being repudiated.[31]

On the basis of these considerations it could be argued that Vatican I did not thematically address itself to the question of infallibility. Instead of describing what infallibility means, the Council contented itself with stating that the pope, under certain conditions, enjoys that infallibility with which the divine Redeemer was pleased to endow his Church. This statement leaves open the tremendous question of what kind and measure of infallibility God did choose to confer upon the Church.

Some therefore find it possible to maintain that one could be in substantial accord with the teaching and intention of Vatican I if one accepted the supreme teaching authority of the pope, quite independently of any formal or juridical approval by the bishops, but denied that this teaching power could properly be called infallible. This seems to be the position of Küng, who points out that the bishops and theologians at Vatican I simply presupposed that the promises given to the Church necessarily implied infallible propositions. In this respect, Küng argues, the Council "was blind in regard to the basic problematic" and left the hard work on the nature of infallibility to be done by subsequent generations.[32]

I would not myself go so far as to say that one could be faithful to Vatican I while denying that the pope has any kind of infallibility under any circumstances, but I do think that the vagueness of the Council gives very large scope for interpreting what is really involved when "infallibility" is referred to. One might reasonably question some of the presuppositions that were accepted by both the majority and the minority in 1870.

3. Regarding the concepts and terms in use at Vatican I, it may be sufficient to point out that these depended very much on the presuppositions and perspectives just examined. The fathers at that Council had a highly authoritarian mentality; they saw truth as descending from above, that is to say, from the highest pastors in the Church, through subordinate or local pastors, to the simple faithful in the pews. They had a relatively static view of the universe and operated more easily with juridical and metaphysical than with historical or psychological methodologies. These factors must be borne in mind when the contemporary reader, from the standpoint of a more dynamic and empirical approach to reality, reads in the conciliar texts terms such as *ex cathedra*, "irreformable," "definition," and "infallibility."

In discussing the problems raised by the use of terminology that bears traces of "the changeable conceptions of the given epoch," *Mysterium Ecclesiae* mentions two possible courses to be followed. In some cases theologians of a later generation continue to use the same terms but make "suitable expository and explanatory additions" to clarify what has become obsolete. In other cases the formulas themselves give way to new expressions which convey more clearly to a new generation what the older expressions really intended. Applying these principles to the present discussion, one may maintain that terms such as *infallibility*, if they continue to be employed, should be carefully explained so as not to carry with them the world view *(Weltanschauung)* of an earlier time. It may happen that these terms will eventually be rejected as being excessively burdened with the conceptuality and polemics of a bygone era. Several contemporary Catholic theologians have maintained that *infallible* should be regarded as an expendable *term*.[33] Although this is true, I should add that in my opinion the term is still salvageable. In the interests of the historical continuity and the identity of the Roman Catholic communion, I believe that the key terms of Vatican I should be salvaged if possible. I therefore prefer the less radical course, that of using the old terminology with suitable additional expository comments.

The Obligatory Force of the Dogma of Infallibility

Thus far we have concentrated our attention on the correct interpretation of the doctrine of infallibility. Something more should be said about the force to be attributed to the tenet of infallibility and to statements that have been issued with the warrant of papal infallibility. Up to the present it has been rather widely assumed by official Catholic spokesmen, including the approved theologians, that to question or deny any such statement would be to "make shipwreck of the faith" and to merit expulsion from the Roman Catholic communion or perhaps even from the Church of Christ.

As an intra-Roman Catholic policy, this principle is becoming increasingly difficult to apply. Many practicing Catholics, especially in the under-40 age bracket, feel grave misgivings about the only three doctrines that have, in recent centuries, been formally promulgated as divinely revealed—the Immaculate Conception, the Assumption of the Blessed Virgin, and papal infallibility itself.

At least five attitudes toward these three dogmas appear to be current in the Roman Catholic body.

1. Some accept these dogmas at face value as unquestionably true and as obligatory upon all under pain of excommunication.

2. Some accept the dogmas as true and necessary but reinterpret them in ways that would probably have sur-

prised those who worked for the definitions. They might say, for instance, that the pope is indeed infallible when he proposes the contents or implications of the deposit of faith but that the individual remains free to question whether in a given instance the pope has gone beyond his proper competence and thus beyond his powers. With reference to the Immaculate Conception they might say that, thanks to the redemptive grace of Christ, all human persons—and not Mary alone—are conceived without actually contracting original sin. Or they might say, regarding the Assumption, that all the blessed—and not Mary alone—at their death enter into a fully human (and therefore corporeal) life of union with God and that therefore Mary is but one among the "assumed."

3. Some, while accepting these three dogmas as true and universally binding, do not feel confident that any particular interpretation is the right one. They therefore assent with a kind of formal or implicit faith, acknowledging that the *magisterium* did not err but not attaching any determinate meaning to what the *magisterium* said.

4. Some say that these three dogmas, although certainly true in some sense, are too unclear in their meaning and too peripheral in importance to be of decisive moment for good standing in the Church. They would argue, therefore, that Christians who fail to accept these dogmas are not for that reason alone to be considered outside the Roman Catholic communion, still less outside the Church of Christ.

5. Some say that the pope, in the case of the two Marian dogmas, and the Council, in the case of the infallibility definition, exceeded their rightful powers and hence that these dogmas, even if true, have no binding force. They would add that some essential condition for a valid definition was lacking, e.g., sufficient grounding in Scripture or tradition, free and frank discussion in the whole Church, or ecumenicity (as discussed above).

Limiting myself for present purposes to the dogma of papal infallibility, I would think that it does not have the value of providing an easy and sure access to the truth in matters that are otherwise obscure. But I would judge that the dogma is a meaningful one, since it focuses attention on the real importance of the papacy not simply as an organ of government or jurisdiction but as a center of doctrinal leadership for the whole Church. I am convinced that the occupants of the papal office do enjoy special assistance from the Holy Spirit and privileged means of access to the tradition of the whole Catholic communion of churches. Hence I acknowledge that the infallibility of the universal Church and of the worldwide body of pastors comes to expression in a singular way in the definitive teaching of the Roman pontiffs. I believe that, prudently and moderately interpreted, the definition of *Pastor aeternus,* chapter IV, should be accepted. Although Vatican I may have lacked something by way of ecumenicity, I am hopeful that this can be supplied by subsequent discussion with other Christian bodies and that the value of the papal office in overseeing the faith of the universal Church may in time become more apparent both to Roman Catholics and to Christians of other traditions. Roman Catholics, concurrently, should strive to become more appreciative of the gains to be achieved by drawing upon the insights of other Christian bodies.

I separate myself, therefore, from the first and fifth of the attitudes described above. With regard to the second and third attitudes, I can accept them if they do not mean that the definitions are meaningless or that purely arbitrary interpretations, not justifiable by reasonable hermeneutical principles, are to be indulged. The recent dogmas allow for a certain latitude of theological interpretations, and only time will tell which interpretations are most faithful to the true intent of the dogmas.

The fourth position is on the whole the one that I find most satisfactory. Papal infallibility is unquestionably a problematical doctrine, even for many Catholics, and is rather remote from the core of the gospel. Vatican II, in my opinion, implicitly conceded that Christians who in good faith fail to accept this dogma are not thereby excluded from eucharistic and ecclesial communion with Roman Catholics. In several texts the Council taught that there is today no dogmatic obstacle to what might be called "limited open communion" (to employ the Lund terminology) with the separated Eastern Churches, who have never accepted the dogma of 1870.[34] Heribert Mühlen, who notes this fact in his perceptive essay on the "hierarchy of truths" (*hierarchia veritatum*), justifies the Council's liberality on the ground that infallibility, though true, does not pertain to the substance of the faith but rather protects the latter.[35]

Mühlen, in the article just cited, makes an impressive case for lifting the anathema attached by Vatican I to the dogma of papal infallibility (DS 3075) and to the two Marian dogmas proclaimed by the pope with the claim of infallibility. In principle he appears to be correct. There is no reason why every teaching that is true and certain, even though it emanates from the highest organs of the *magisterium,* should be backed by an anathema. The anathema, I suggest, should be reserved to those teachings which, in a given situation, are incompatible with and are destructive of the basic stance of Christian faith. The fact that the Roman Catholic church was able to exist and prosper for many centuries without the dogma of papal infallibility and that all other Christian churches and communities flourish without it makes one wonder whether the anathema of 1870 was not imposed to meet a passing crisis within the Roman Catholic community and has not outlived its usefulness. The lifting of the excommunications attached to the dogma of infallibility and to the two recent Marian dogmas would require a great deal of pastoral preparation if it were not to be misunderstood by the Catholic people and by others as a change in official doctrine. But such an action, if it could be carried out with full pastoral responsibility, would be a gesture of major significance both for Catholics who have difficulty understanding the three dogmas here in question and for other Christians who have never been able to accept them. One could hardly imagine any step that would contribute more to the ecumenical reconciliation for which we are obliged to work and pray.[36]

4

THE REFORMATION AND
THE INFALLIBILITY DEBATE

George A. Lindbeck

This essay is an attempt to evaluate from a Reformation perspective the debate now going on in Roman Catholic circles over the doctrine of infallibility.[1] It distinguishes two major trends or positions, "fallibilism" and "moderate infallibilism," and argues that the second has greater potential than the first for becoming a (or the) standard way of understanding the infallibility of the teaching office within Roman Catholicism. In a way this is ecumenically unfortunate: fallibilism is *prima facie* more congenial from a Reformation perspective. Yet on the other hand, so I shall argue, moderate infallibilism need not be church-dividing. While churches faithful to the Reformation could not adopt it as their own position in the form in which it is presented by contemporary Roman Catholics, it nevertheless is not, from a Reformation perspective, unchristian or antichristian. It can be seen as a legitimate expression of Christian faith and is compatible with mutual doctrinal recognition between Lutherans and Catholics. It need not, therefore, be a barrier to full communion between the churches (providing one agrees that pluralism rather than uniformity of doctrinal formulations is possible or desirable within the one Church).

An essay such as this clearly represents a sharp departure from our usual procedure in these Catholic-Lutheran dialogues. We have, on the whole, stayed out of each other's intramural controversies. Each side has limited itself to expounding its own doctrinal positions. In the case of infallibility, however, this seems impossible. In order to give a Reformation response to the doctrine of infallibility, it is necessary first to decide how to interpret that doctrine, but this is currently a matter of major dispute among Roman Catholics. As a non-Catholic I have no alternative but to try to make up my own mind on which of the proposed options in this area is both sufficiently Roman Catholic to be worth taking seriously and also provides possibilities for ecumenical *rapprochement*.

This approach, however, is an uncomfortable one. First, it sounds presumptuous: it is as if a non-Catholic were telling Roman Catholics what they should hold. It is worth emphasizing, therefore, that this is far from my intention. This essay should be read as an extended question to our Catholic partners in dialogue. Does this Lutheran evaluation of the current debate over infallibility make sense to them, and how should it be amplified, changed, or corrected? The mood is interrogatory rather than assertoric—even if the rhetoric of what follows often makes this less than self-evident.

The second difficulty is that my argument is critical of fallibilism even though this is the position with which Lutherans are most nearly in agreement. Hans Küng's attack on infallibility, for example, is one with which a non-Catholic such as myself is bound to be in sympathy, and yet his case seems to me defective both for general theological reasons and because it is so destructive of Roman Catholic identity that it is not a serious possibility for that church. Such a critique of his view, however, is likely to appear as a betrayal by a Protestant of a friend in the Roman camp. It is therefore important to stress that the moderate infallibility which seems to me more viable than Küng's fallibilism would allow or require full freedom for the discussion of Küng's theses. It would be opposed, if I understand it rightly, to the exclusion from the church of a position such as Küng's by disciplinary action.

Turning now to the substance of this discussion, I must first say a few words about the relatively simple nature of the traditional Protestant-Catholic disagreement over infallibility before noting the reasons it has in recent times become bewilderingly complex. In the past, both sides understood—or thought they understood—much the same thing by the word *infallibility*. The disagreement between them was over the realities to which the word applies. Both parties affirmed the infallibility of the Bible (and, of course, also the infallibility of God), but Roman Catholics in addition asserted magisterial infallibility, that is, the infallibility of the Church *in docendo:* in exercising its ultimate teaching authority through ecumenical councils and through popes. On a third possible application of the word the situation was more ambiguous. The Reformers did at least in part agree with Catholics that the Church is infallible *in credendo;* it could not as a whole fall into ultimately serious error in matters of faith. Luther, for example, argued for the validity of infant Baptism on these grounds. If infant Baptism were invalid, then in view of its universal acceptance and practice during long centuries the Church would have ceased to exist. Since this is impossible (because the Church is indefectible), infant Baptism cannot be invalid, but is infallibly valid.[2] Because of polemical relations to Rome, this kind of appeal to tradition became unpopular in later Protestantism, and infallibility was increasingly ascribed exclusively to Scripture. Nevertheless, from the point of view of the Reformation itself the dispute was basically over magisterial infallibility. Catholics affirmed the infallibility of councils and (after 1870) popes when defining dogma, while Protestants denied it.

The situation has now become much more complex. Medieval and early modern theories of truth shared by both Catholics and Protestants have become problematic, and thus the meaning of the word *infallible* has been put in question. Advances in biblical studies have made use of the term in its older meanings inapplicable to Scripture, and most Protestant theologians now refuse to speak of the infallibility of the Bible. This, as we all know, has produced immense difficulties. If the Bible is not infallible, how can it be authoritative, and if it is not authoritative, what is?

It is an analogous though not identical problem which Roman Catholicism is now confronting. Past theories of truth and of the meaning of infallibility have disintegrated for most theologians, and they cannot, therefore, give the same interpretation of the infallibility of the Bible, dogmas, and the teaching office as previously. For Catholics, however, the crux is not so much biblical as magisterial infallibility. If popes and councils are not infallible in the old ways, how can they be genuinely authoritative, and if they are not, what is?

The current phase of the debate of interest here has been over the retention of the doctrine. Fallibilists, led by Hans Küng, are in favor of dropping it entirely, while the moderate infallibilists, who for the purposes of this essay are represented chiefly by Karl Rahner and Walter Kasper,[3] wish to reinterpret it. The controversy, it will be observed, is not between progressives and traditionalists. Those who adhere to older views of truth and of infallibility have for the most part stayed outside of the discussion. Rather, both the opponents and the proponents of magisterial infallibility in the present dispute are progressives in the sense that they agree the standard positions of the past on this subject are no longer tenable.

The complexity of the discussion arises from the extraordinarily large number of factors involved. Some are technical and theoretical, while others are intensely practical and emotional. On the technical side, there are divergent philosophical theories of truth, of propositions, of language, and of religious meaning, as well as sophisticated theological reflections on the nature of faith, Christianity, dogma, and the Church. Historical considerations are also important, as are sociological and psychosocial inquiries into the character of human communities in general and religious ones in particular. What kind of authority do such communities need in order to maintain identity, continuity, and unity?

In order to understand the passionate intensity with which these discussions are pursued, we must, needless to say, refer to their practical and, indeed, church-political dimensions. Both major parties agree that the renewal of the Church requires that it become less authoritarian and less papalist. The principles of subsidiarity and conciliarity enunciated at Vatican II must become structurally effective. This is necessary for the Christian authenticity and contemporary relevance of the Roman Catholic communion. The debate is not over the importance of these general objectives, but over the question of how they can be best pursued. Hans Küng vociferously insists that anything in the least reminiscent of traditional infallibility, especially papal infallibility, must be eliminated. This applies even to the term.[4] Its connotations are incurably absolutistic, i.e., ineradicably supportive of ecclesiastical authoritarianism and exaggerated papalism. Those who, like Rahner, wish to retain the concept while reinterpreting it are in effect compromising with reactionary traditionalism. This is true even when the reinterpretations do not theoretically legitimate authoritarianism. The very retention of the word confuses the public and plays into the hands of the conservatives. The moderate infallibilists, to be sure, are often willing to let the word fall into disuse (for they agree that it is overburdened with misleading connotations), but even this is not enough. The term and the doctrines for which it stands must, according to Küng, be repudiated. Anything less than this will give aid and comfort to the enemy by allowing old patterns of ecclesiastical governance and action to persist, and they are dangerous to the welfare of the Church and the authenticity of its Christian witness.

Küng's case for eliminating rather than simply reinterpreting the doctrine of infallibility is, to be sure, not only practical or church-political, but also intellectual and theological. He does not believe the reinterpretations proposed by the moderates are in fact what they claim to be. They equivocate. They replace infallibility with what is really a new concept and doctrine and are thus fundamentally confused or dishonest, whether they know it or not, when they claim to be reinterpreting.

Such accusations are not always explicit, but they are unmistakably implicit in Küng's writings.[5] They help account for the vigor of the reaction. Those opposed to Küng on this issue are in general convinced that claims to infallibility are too deeply interwoven with Catholic life and faith simply to be excised. That would unravel the fabric. It is necessary for the sake of Roman Catholic identity to reinterpret, not repudiate. Küng, most seem willing to grant, may be personally a good Catholic, but his position does not do justice to the specifically Roman elements in the Roman Catholic tradition. He lacks what a non-Catholic such as myself is inclined to call *Romanitas* (using this word in a descriptive and nonpejorative sense rather different from the one in which it is often employed). Even some other fallibilists seem to think this is true. Gregory Baum, for example, considers it advisable to continue to use the word *infallible* even though he is further removed from the traditional concept, as far as I can see, than is Küng.[6] In short, this debate involves not only a theological discussion but a political confrontation. The fallibilists are suspected of being bad Roman Catholics, indifferent to the welfare (i.e., the continuity and unity) of the Church,[7] while the moderates, in turn, are charged with equivocation and lack of courage.

When seen in these terms, the two sides are powerful in their criticism of each other but vulnerable to attack. Küng is persuasive when he argues that the fight against an archaic and unchristian authoritarianism requires the elimination of infallibility, but he is weak in maintaining Roman Catholic identity. The moderates seem to be right that the continuity and unity of Roman Catholicism require the reinterpretation of the dogma, not its rejection, but they have difficulty showing that they are not equivocating and that they are in *effect* (not simply in intention) opposed to papal absolutism. The viability of the two positions depends essentially on their success in answering criticism. Therefore in the remainder of this discussion I shall concentrate on their ability to counter criticism rather than on the positive arguments in their favor. My conclusion will be that the moderate infallibilists can better answer the charge of equivocation than the fallibilists can deal with the suspicion that they lack *Romanitas*.

Starting with the fallibilists, I will look at two of the ways they can argue that their position is an authentic part of the tradition and therefore not destructive to Roman Catholic identity, and then turn to a somewhat longer discussion of the difficulties of equivocation which bedevil the moderates.

The first of the fallibilist defenses is dependent on recent historical work and is illustrated, though in rather different ways, by Francis Oakley and Brian Tierney.[8] On the basis of their research they contend that the tradition is either opposed or uncommitted to papal infallibility and that therefore there is nothing un-Catholic or un-Roman in rejecting it. Oakley points out that historians who have worked on the relevant material are now virtually unanimous that *Haec sancta* from the Council of Constance (1415), which affirms that councils are in certain circumstances superior to the pope, has as good a claim to dogmatic status as *Pastor aeternus* from Vatican I (1870), which appears to maintain the contrary. While it might be theoretically possible to reconcile the pronouncements of the two councils, their concrete, historically ascertainable meanings (so Oakley argues) are clearly in contradiction. One must thus choose between papal and conciliar infallibility (unless one rejects both—an option Oakley does not consider).

Tierney's studies add further historical difficulties. He shows that the origin of explicit claims to papal infallibility (though not to papal primacy) date from the 14th century and arose from a desire to limit the power of a contemporary pope to change the decrees of previous popes. The originators of the doctrine intended to say that the pope can do nothing new, whereas now, so Küng argues, papal infallibility implies that the pope can do anything he pleases.[9] Tierney believes that any doctrine with such questionable roots in tradition is of doubtful status within Roman Catholicism, and he apparently assumes that it can therefore be abandoned without threatening the Roman Catholic Church's identity.

These are powerful arguments and must play an important role in any future serious consideration of the doctrine, but it seems to me that only born-and-bred historians for whom the past is as real as the present would think they show papal infallibility can be simply dropped without traumatic consequences. The devout laity, who are the fundamental bearers of the communal tradition, would be hard to persuade on this point, and the difficulties would be no less, to put it mildly, among bishops and popes. Systematic theologians are also likely to find these historical arguments unconvincing. Even according to Roman Catholic tradition, a dogma does not depend on the arguments adduced in its favor. The exegetical or historical reasons originally advanced may prove faulty, but it is always possible that the basic convictions which undergird a given doctrine may be deeper and stronger than any which have yet been successfully articulated. In any case, the possibility of harmonizing apparently contradictory historical data is so refined and the complexities and ambiguities of doctrinal development are so immense that it is difficult to imagine any historical discovery in this area which theologians would not be able to absorb into their systems. In summary, neither the masses, nor the authorities, nor the systematic theologians are likely to find credible a defense of the authentically Roman Catholic character of a rejection of papal infallibility based on such historical considerations.

A second defense of fallibilism invokes theoretical and conceptual considerations rather than historical ones. Both Küng and Baum argue, although in different ways, that the traditional notion of infallibility as applied to dogmas is in effect meaningless. It cannot be coherently affirmed, and it is neither true nor false. It is a "non-dogma." Thus one denies or contradicts nothing which the church has asserted in the past (for a meaningless statement can assert nothing) if one simply drops it.

The form which this argument takes in Hans Küng's work is that of appealing to modern views of the historicity and relativity of all propositionally statable truths, whether dogmatic or nondogmatic. Because no propositional meanings are unchanging, all propositions must be said to be, at best, both true and false. None can be permanently true, and therefore none can be infallible.[10] Baum's argument is less sweeping. He does not contend that no propositions can be permanently or infallibly true, but rather that religiously significant utterances, including dogmatic ones, are not characterized by propositional truth but rather by what he calls "symbolic truth." A symbolic truth can involve or be accompanied by false propositions, and therefore to say that the teachings of the church are infallible (as Baum wishes to continue to do) says nothing about their propositional truth or lack thereof.[11] The two lines of argument, while different, reach basically the same conclusion. Because the kind of propositional infallibility which the bishops at Vatican I had in mind is a meaningless nonentity, this dogma can be dropped without actually denying anything which the church has ever succeeded in defining.

As a non-Catholic, I see two major difficulties in these approaches. First, they depend on highly technical theories about propositions, truth, and the meaning of religious language, which, although widespread, are by no means universally accepted by those philosophically competent to assess them either inside or outside the Catholic Church. Indeed, my impression is that in English-speaking lands, especially under the influence of ordinary language and analytic philosophy, Küng's and Baum's philosophical presuppositions are unacceptable to more non-Catholics than Catholics.[12] So rarified and debatable a defense of the falliblist position is by its very nature not likely to be widely persuasive.

A second and theologically more telling difficulty is that it is by no means clear that these theories are compatible with historic Christian convictions regarding the final and unsurpassable character of God's revelation in Jesus Christ. From the point of view of faith there seems to be something objectively, propositionally, and infallibly true about, for example, the affirmation that "Jesus is Lord" (1 Cor. 12:3), or "God was in Christ reconciling the world to himself" (2 Cor. 5:19). One way of putting this point is to say that such affirmations, as well as many others, cannot be false within any recognizably Christian language system. They are "intrasystematically" infallible, that is, they are infallible within the circle of faith. This kind of infallibility, it should be observed, does not characterize only Christian affirmations, but it is also an attribute of the central assertions of non-Christian religions and of comprehensively articulated philosophical positions. Such assertions are guaranteed to be true by the whole language system or faith perspective of which they are a part. Their truth, in other words, is inescapable for those who employ the language in which a given faith is articulated. I doubt that Küng wants to deny this, but his way of attacking the meaningfulness of dogmatic infallibility seems to make such a denial logically necessary.

Thus the second defensive tactic is even weaker than the first. It in a sense saves *Romanitas* (for infallibility is merely meaningless, not actually false), but at the cost of imperiling *Christianitas*. Luther certainly would consider the cure worse than the disease: *Tolle assertiones et Chris-*

tianum tulisti ("Take away assertions and you take away Christianity").[13] For moderates also, the denial of the possibility of permanently and infallibly true propositions is Küng's weakness, and it is the main focus of the German Catholic bishops' critique of his book.[14]

Turning now to the difficulties of moderate infallibilism, it needs to be remembered that the weaknesses of the fallibilist position are no guarantee that the opposition is any stronger. In this debate, as in many others, there may be no winners. If there are none, however, the results would be serious. It would mean the failure of theological efforts to provide help in the Roman Catholic version of the authority crisis which is now a major problem within all Christian churches as well as society at large. The alternatives to moderate infallibilism may well be either rigid traditionalism, on the one hand, or chaos on the other.

The major problem with moderates, as I have already suggested, is their apparent equivocation. They claim to reinterpret the traditional dogma, but many think that they reject it. The question is therefore whether they have succeeded in formulating a tenable alternative to the positions of traditional infallibilism and fallibilism.

The moderate infallibilism proposed by, for example, Rahner and Kasper, holds, first of all, that the infallibility of the teaching office does not guarantee a dogma against all kinds of error, but only against the ultimately serious kind which would "definitely separate the Church from Christ and his truth." [15] A dogmatic pronouncement may be poorly formulated and badly abused, but it can be, and in the long run will be, reinterpreted in a way which is harmonious with Christian truth. Its deficiencies are reparable rather than irreparable, and it can therefore be irrevocable, or in the language of *Pastor aeternus* at Vatican I, "irreformable." [16]

It would seem possible on such a view for Catholics to share most of the standard Protestant objections to, for example, the Marian and papal dogmas and yet hold that they are infallible. They could agree that these doctrines have been widely used for unchristian or antichristian purposes and were promulgated for questionable reasons, and yet believe that they are not so irremediably harmful that they cannot be understood and utilized in ways consistent with the gospel. The difference between such a Catholic infallibilist and a Protestant fallibilist might then simply be that the Catholic believes these doctrines are susceptible to an evangelical interpretation and use, while the Protestant can at most hope they are. None of the moderates have expressed themselves in quite these terms, but this appears to me to be implied by their position.

A second limitation of the traditional view is that an infallible exercise of the teaching authority must not only be formally or canonically universal (ecumenical) but really and substantially universal. This condition casts doubt on the infallibility of a good many conciliar and papal dogmas. *Pastor aeternus* and the Marian definitions, for example, were formulated without awareness of or interest in the concerns of large bodies of Christians which now, since Vatican II, are recognized as churches or ecclesial communities. It can thus be argued, as Richard McBrien among others has done,[17] that they were not genuinely ecumenical in intent, and therefore it is not clear that they are infallible even in the qualified sense indicated in the first point.

Third, it can be maintained that another condition which must be met before a doctrinal definition can be recognized as clearly infallible is reception by the Church as a whole. This excludes that kind of *a priori* infallibility which is a main focus of Küng's attack.[18] It excludes, in other words, the assumption that infallibility is assured, apart from considerations of content, by the fulfillment of purely formal and canonically specifiable conditions, such as being an *ex cathedra* pronouncement. Further, if one interprets the church which receives the teaching broadly enough, the status of all specifically Western and Roman dogmas becomes questionable. The Eastern churches have not even had the *opportunity* to receive them, for they have not been effectively submitted to them for consideration.

The theory of infallibility outlined in these three points would be acceptable to many non-Catholics. The emphasis on substantial ecumenicity and on reception would meet with the approval of the Eastern Orthodox and of many Anglicans, and when one adds the insistence that only ultimately serious errors are excluded, it might even be compatible with a Reformation position. More will be said about this possibility later. Moreover, it is not clear that most Catholic fallibilists actually deny anything which this view affirms. It does, to be sure, assert that dogmatic decisions are irreformable in the sense of being irrevocable, and thus it goes beyond the insistence on the indefectibility of the Church—its "remaining in the truth in spite of all possible errors" [19]—with which Küng wants to stop. Yet Küng does not clearly deny that this may involve the immunity of some dogmas from ultimately serious error. The question he would raise, as suggested in his controversy with Rahner,[20] is whether this attenuated notion of infallibility does not represent so radical a reinterpretation of the traditional view that it is meaningless to continue to use the same word.

Whatever the merits of this objection, it must first be said that it does not imply that moderate infallibilism contradicts the official formulations of the doctrine in *Pastor aeternus*. These formulations do not specifically exclude any of the three points we have listed. On the first point, the bishops at Vatican I clearly did not mean to say an infallible dogma is immune from error of every kind. They were well aware that God alone is absolutely infallible.[21] Presumably they would have been scandalized at the suggestion that only ultimately serious errors are excluded, but in failing to define the degree of exemption from error which infallibility involves, they left their formulations open to this minimalistic interpretation. Similarly, in reference to the second and third points (ecumenicity and reception), they not only failed to exclude the possibility that these are necessary conditions for the infallible exercise of the Church's teaching authority, but left room for them by never suggesting that they had enumerated all the conditions which must be met. Further, they deliberately refrained from broaching the long-disputed questions of whether a pope can fall into heresy in his official teaching role, and thus it can be argued that they deliberately left open the question whether reception is necessary in order finally to authenticate such teaching (for in view of the Church's infallibility *in credendo*, the Church would reject heresy).[22] Thus there is no logical impossibility in construing *Pastor aeternus* in a moderately infallibilist way.

Such a logically possible construal, however, might be wholly discontinuous with or contradictory to older inter-

pretations of infallibility. It can be argued that these interpretations understood infallibility within a partly scholastic and partly modern, rationalistic framework, according
to which the meanings of words and propositions can be
permanently specified in the context of a *philosophia
perennis.* If so, an infallible dogma is not simply an unre-
pealable yet indefinitely reinterpretable decision. It is rather
an enduringly adequate statement of revealed truth. The
proper attitude toward it is simply acceptance and obedience. The practical effect of attributing the power to
define such doctrines to the pope was to encourage authoritarian absolutism.[23]

Modern infallibilism, in contrast, opposes such absolutism. Although it holds that conciliar and papal dogmas
are preserved by God's grace from irretrievable error, it
also insists that they may be so gravely defective that it is
the duty of Christians to object, criticize, and reinterpret.
Given the absolutistic connotations which are intrinsic to
infallibility in ordinary usage, it does indeed seem less than
candid for proponents of this view to cast themselves in
the role of defenders of the doctrine.

Yet, as I have already noted, there seems to be no viable
alternative. Magisterial infallibility, whether of the conciliar
or papal variety, cannot be simply repudiated by Roman
Catholics who are concerned about the continuity and
unity of their church. It is too deeply embedded in the
tradition, and its symbolic importance is too great. Those
who reject it are bound to have their credentials as good
Roman Catholics questioned, while those theologians who
claim to accept it are more likely to influence those whose
sense of specifically Roman Catholic identity is strong, and
it is on these that the transmission of the tradition chiefly
depends. Given the nature of human communities, whether
religious or nonreligious, it does not seem that fallibilism
can have much of a future within the Roman communion.
The choice is between rigid traditionalism and moderate
infallibilism.

If the moderates triumph, the problem of equivocation
will vanish. Nothing is more common both outside and inside the church than major shifts in the meanings of concepts. For example, in this post-Einsteinian era we are now
accustomed to the idea that a straight line is not the short-

est distance between two points. The very notion of what constitutes reason varies enormously from epoch to epoch. There is no reason, in other words, why a new understanding of the doctrine of infallibility should not eventual'y become established and seem quite ordinary and common-sensical.

In the meantime it is important to note that the new meaning is by no means wholly discontinuous with the old. If one does not think so much in terms of abstract concepts but of functions, it becomes evident that both traditional and moderate infallibilism have to do with maintaining the unity of the Church. The first legitimates authoritarian ways of maintaining that unity, while the second favors less authoritarian ones. Both, however, give the teaching office a unifying role which cannot easily be matched by other views of the Church's *magisterium*.

It can be further argued that the more absolutistic version of infallibility, however unfortunate, did have a relative historical justification. It was perhaps inevitable that the procedures for maintaining unity became authoritarian in a social context which was itself authoritarian and in which Catholicism was the established religion of many nations and whole cultures. This authoritarianism was reinforced by the defensive position into which the Roman Church was pushed by its failure to respond positively to the Reformation and to adapt to modern developments. It was further strengthened by the intellectual climate of the times. Various forms of rationalism reigned through most of the post-Reformation era and were certainly dominant at Vatican I. The models for understanding all reality, including meaning, propositions, and dogma tended to incorporate Cartesian, Euclidean, and Newtonian emphases on clear and distinct ideas, and to involve naive correspondence theories of truth. It was assumed that, for those trained to understand them, dogmatic definitions were as pellucid and unchanging in meaning as geometric theorems, and as isomorphic with revealed realities and prescriptive for the life of faith as Euclid was supposed to be for space and time.

Social and intellectual changes, however, have destroyed this context within which traditional infallibilism may have had a certain limited justification. Yet while authoritarianism must be abandoned, authority continues to be necessary for unity; and this authority, so the Roman Catholic could argue, needs to be legitimated by the functional equivalent of the old doctrine of infallibility. What is now needed is a *nonauthoritarian authority*, an authority with which one can disagree and debate, but which nevertheless must be listened to and taken seriously. It is this requirement to listen to and take seriously what a central authority says which generates a community of discourse; and discourse, when it involves genuine communication, is the fundamental unifying activity. The possibility of disagreement, furthermore, is what makes the community a free and creative one.

Yet there must be limits to disagreement if unity is to be preserved. Discord cannot take the form of breaking off communication, of leaving the Church. Criticism, though allowable and sometimes mandatory, must remain loyal. The truly obedient sons and daughters of the Church, in this interpretation, are those who know that their role is sometimes to be the loyal opposition.

It is this attitude of loyal opposition which moderate infallibilism authorizes. There is nothing in the Church's life and teaching which is exempt from error and may not need to be actively opposed, but yet (so the moderates seem to say) one must trust God that these errors are not definitive, and consequently one is never at liberty voluntarily to withdraw from the Church. Even with reference to the Church's dogmatic definitions, one may be compelled to actively object and vigorously seek to improve them, but one may never simply reject them or stop listening.

The argument, then, is that if one looks at infallibility functionally and historically in terms of the promotion of unity and community, older and newer versions of the doctrine can be meaningfully said to be in substantial continuity—even though, on another level, they are dramatically different.

Karl Rahner has developed this way of looking at the function of infallibility in reference to its implications for theological methodology. He has suggested that for him the chief problem with Küng's position is that it makes a Catholic way of doing theology impossible.[24] The right procedure, he says, is to assume the truth of what the magisterium teaches and then subject these teachings to rigorous examination in the light of Scripture, history, logic, and philosophy. This will help distinguish the propositionally specifiable affirmations from the conceptual and symbolic frameworks in which these are embedded, thus helping to determine the range of possible interpretations, including many new ones, to which they are susceptible in new situations and contexts. The procedure reminds one of a lawyer's search for loopholes in the laws of the land,[25] and in both cases the search always succeeds. The reason is that neither a law nor a dogma can be so framed as to anticipate more than a small fraction of the ever-new problems, questions, and demands which multiply in the course of time. The Church's dogmas are thus genuinely relativized while yet retaining a propositionally identifiable continuity. They come to resemble a limiting yet open framework which excludes certain options permanently, yet still leaves freedom in searching for new answers to new questions in the light of Scripture, tradition, and the present experience of the Church.

This is not simply a methodological concern. For Rahner, the Church itself would suffer if this method were abandoned. The community of theological discourse constituted by the common acceptance of a common dogmatic framework is an indispensable, though far from sufficient, aid in developing and sustaining communication and unity throughout the community of faith. Thus it is ecclesiologically important that theologians regard the *magisterium's* dogmas as true, in a fashion analogous to the way in which lawyers accept legislative acts as binding simply because they have been legitimately enacted by properly constituted authorities.

The case for such an approach is strengthened by a consideration of communal intellectual enterprises, especially in the natural sciences. As Thomas Kuhn has argued in *The Structure of Scientific Revolutions,*[26] the exact sciences are in their normal state the most dogmatic of intellectual disciplines. Neophytes are rigorously drilled in an elaborate set of theories and investigative procedures, and only after they have thoroughly mastered these do they begin devising experiments of their own. Only rarely, and only if a scientist is what is usually called a scientific genius, does he or she move on to question established positions and formulate new basic theories. Furthermore, this happens in a fundamental sense only when an older scientific outlook—the Newtonian, for example—begins to prove untenable and unfruitful under the accumulating weight of exceptions and contrary evidence. It is precisely this methodological *a priori* dogmatism of the exact sciences which makes them to be communal activities *par excellence* and to be cumulative and progressive in a way that humanistic studies rarely are.

There is, to be sure, a crucial difference between the methodological dogmas of theology and those of either science or law. Theological dogmas have to do with matters of faith which engage the whole human being. It would be blasphemous for Christians to treat as *a priori* true, even for methodological purposes, what they regard as possibly opposed to Jesus Christ himself. In the theological realm, therefore, acceptance of certain starting points or premises requires an assurance that, at the very least, these are not irremediably opposed to the gospel, that they are exempt from ultimately serious error, that they are in this sense infallible.

Turning finally to a brief comparison of this moderate infallibilism with a Reformation view, I will note certain resemblances and differences between both these positions and the prophetic attitude in the Old Testament. If the moderates are right, then Rome and the Reformation are agreed that the official leaders of the people of God under the new government may be as radically unfaithful (even in their teaching) as they were under the old. Prophetic protest to the point of persecution or excommunication may at times be obligatory. Yet within this shared conviction, the Reformers were closer to the prophets in one respect, and Roman Catholics are closer in another. The Reformers, like the prophets and unlike the Catholics, set no limits to the possible unfaithfulness of leaders. The latter's teaching may at times be in irreconcilable conflict with Yahweh, with Christ. On the other hand, moderate Catholics—like the prophets and unlike the Reformers—do not envision the possibility, if expelled by the authorities, of establishing alternate ecclesiastical orders or new churches. This unshakable Roman Catholic loyalty to a concrete and empirically specifiable people of God, even when it is unfaithful, is similar to that of the biblical prophets; the Reformers, on their side, shared the prophets' refusal to set any limits to the possible errors of the leadership of the people of God.

The convergence is great, but the remaining differences are far from trivial. The moderates, however much they may have qualified the traditional view of magisterial infallibility, retain the historic Roman conviction that only the communion united around the Petrine See is indefectibly the visible body within which the Church of Christ subsists. That Church of Christ subsists also in other communions, but not indefectibly, and their teaching offices are therefore not infallible, not exempt from ultimately serious error. Lutherans cannot accept such a view of any concretely identifiable church, including their own, without repudiating the Reformation. God has promised indefectibly to uphold the Church as a whole, not any one of its divided parts, and therefore no specific teaching authority within the divided church can act with the infallibility which Christ desires his Church to have. This disagreement does not require either side to view the other as opposed to the truth which is in Christ, but it does mean that while Roman Catholics believe their church will forever be preserved from such errors, the heirs of the Reformation can only hope and pray that this will be true of their own churches—and also of that of Rome.

These differences in degree of assurance are not trivial. They lead, for example, to contrasting views on the legitimacy of the separate church orders set up by the Reformers after the break with Rome became definitive. Yet there seems to be no reason why they should now prevent full communion. In the contemporary situation, providing other questions are resolved, Roman Catholics and Lutherans can live together in one church even though the first believe, and the second simply hope and pray, that the *magisterium* of the united communion will be preserved from irretrievable error. What Catholics assert in this respect, Lutherans need not deny, although they cannot themselves affirm it. Both sides can recognize the Christian authenticity, even if not the full adequacy, of each other's positions on infallibility, and this is enough for full communion.

Thus the conclusion of this Lutheran evaluation is that a moderate infallibilism can maintain a nonauthoritarian version of the traditional Roman Catholic claim of magisterial infallibility, while at the same time allowing for full communion with churches which make no similar claims. Whether this is in fact the case, however, is a question for Roman Catholics, and not Lutherans, to answer.[27]

5

INFALLIBILITY LANGUAGE
AND THE EARLY
LUTHERAN TRADITION

Gerhard O. Forde

Assertions about infallibility in early Lutheran theology arose almost entirely in the context of the polemical situation of the times. Lutheran theologians were concerned on the one hand to question the right of human persons and institutions to claim infallibility and on the other hand to accord that right only to the Word of God.[1] A perusal of the literature gives one the impression, which I leave unsubstantiated for the moment, that infallibility language was not integral to the positive theology of early Lutherans. It appeared for the most part in polemical instances where the concern was to negate then-current views on papal or conciliar infallibility. Direct positive assertions about infallibility, even the infallibility of the Word of God, were quite rare. In speaking positively, early Lutherans and especially Luther seemed to prefer assertions of a different sort. They spoke of an "authority" which establishes and interprets itself, of the "power, (Macht, potestas) or "clarity" and "sufficiency" of the Word or the gospel which claims or binds the believer and the Church, and like expressions. The use of infallibility language was thus governed by a no and a yes: a no to certain applications of such language, and a yes—a particular affirmation of the nature, source, and ground of authority in the Church which determines where infallibility language may be used, if it is to be used at all. It is important to see that the no was grounded in the yes if misunderstanding is to be avoided.[2] What follows is an attempt to indicate, all too sketchily, I am afraid, the manner in which infallibility language was handled in early Lutheran theology, especially by Luther himself, in both a negative and positive manner. I shall deal first with the no and second with the yes, although it is difficult to make such a division absolutely. No attempt will be made to trace the development of Luther's ideas or to enter into the complex discussion about the historical sources or correct interpretation of Luther's views prior to 1520. Rather what I shall attempt is a more "systematic" exposition of the position of early Lutheranism after 1520, when it achieved a more or less stable form.

I

It is well known that Luther and the early Lutherans denied the right of the papacy to claim infallibility and to be the final court of appeal in interpreting Scripture.[3] This denial received final form in Luther's *Address to the Christian Nobility of Germany* in June of 1520:

They (the Romanists) want to be the only masters of Holy Scripture, although they never learn a thing from the Bible all their lives long. They assume the sole authority for themselves, and, quite unashamed, they play about with words before our very eyes, trying to persuade us that the pope cannot err in matters of faith, regardless of whether he is righteous or wicked. Yet they cannot point to a single letter (of Scripture).[4]

and confessional status in Melanchthon's *Apology to the Augsburg Confession* (7-8:27):

Nor should that be transferred to the popes which is the prerogative of the true church: that they are pillars of the truth and that they do not err.[5]

and the *Treatise on the Power and Primacy of the Pope* (58):

The errors of the pope are manifest, and they are not trifling.[6]

It is equally well known that early Lutherans denied infallibility to the councils of the Church. The views of the mature Luther are expressed in his disputation *De potes-*

tate concilii (1536), from which the following theses are taken:

11. Where therefore those succeeding do not follow or hold the apostolic foundation, they are heretics or antichristians—as ones outside the foundation and lost.

12. Therefore a council of the bishops can err, just as other humans, either in office or privately without office.

13. Where, however, they do not err, that occurs either by chance or by virtue of some holy and pious person who happens to be present or of the church of common believers and not by the power and authority of the assembly.

14. Thus the Council of Nicea averted error due to the power of the single man Paphnutius because Christ was so beneficial to his Church.

15. For the Holy Spirit is bound by no promise to assemblies of bishops or councils; this can in no way be proven.

17. For who will assure or make certain to us or them that the Holy Spirit is necessarily so obligated and bound to their assemblies?

18. One can easily make assemblies. But to assemble in the Holy Spirit is not possible except to those who follow the apostolic foundation and not their own thoughts but rather operate according to the standard or manner of faith.

19. They are right in saying that they represent the Church of common believers; for they are not the Church but at most only represent the Church.

20. And when they only represent the Church they are the Church only as a painting of a man is a man, that is, only represented.

21. Where, however, they are something more and are the true Church, that happens (as stated above) by chance and not by the inherent power of the Church being represented: only because they represent the Church of common believers.

22. To speak rightly, the council is always the representation of the Church of common believers to itself. Only by chance, however, is it perhaps a right or true assembly or Church.[7]

Commenting on these theses and the disputation following, Paul Althaus has this to say:

A council as such does not possess unconditional spiritual authority any more than the church and its tradition do. The councils have constantly claimed that they assemble in "the name of Christ" and thus that they are not able to err—according to Christ's promise in Matthew 18:20 ("Where two or three are gathered together in my name . . . "). Luther points out that the mere claim to have gathered in the name of Christ does not yet mean that a council really has done so and possesses Christ's authority. "If they have come together in the name of Christ, they will show that by acting according to Christ and not contrary to the gospel." Thus the content of the council's decrees will determine whether a council has actually gathered in the name of Christ. "Even though saints are present at the council, even though there are many saints and even though angels are there, still we do not trust personalities but only God's word, since even saints can make mistakes. There is nc excuse for saying that a man was a saint and is therefore to be believed. Most certainly not; Christ says just the opposite, believe him only if he speaks correctly about me." This is not a majority decision; rather, "if I see someone who thinks correctly about Christ I ought to kiss him, throw my arms around his neck, and let all the others who think falsely alone." Thus the pure truth of the gospel gives genuine authority to the men of the church who witness to Christ. Luther asserts the same thing when he says that only those have assembled in the Holy Spirit who bring the "analogy of faith" and not their own thoughts (WA 39 I, 186).

When a council does not err but bears witness to the truth, we should not take it for granted. Such a council does not necessarily witness to the truth because it is ecumenical or because of its formal authority; when a council does so, that is an empirical and "accidental" fact (in distinction from that which can be taken for granted). Each such instance is a particular sign of Christ's grace toward his church, whether he uses an individual saint in the council or the voice of the entire church. As has been said, this is a particular grace and does not simply follow from the council's authority. Truth is not guaranteed by the authority of the council, but Christ's free gift of the truth in a specific instance gives a council its authority. The mere fact that a council "represents" the church also does not mean that it itself is the church, the true church. This is, as has been said, not something to be taken for granted and not simply given with the assembling of the council, but is a purely empirical and "accidental" fact.

Luther recognizes that the Holy Spirit has been promised to the church of Christ. But this is not necessarily promised to the gathering of the bishops or the council. This means that no council can cite the promise of the Holy Spirit to prove its decrees and derive binding authority for its canons from the promise of the Holy Spirit. The ecclesiastical legitimacy of such a gathering does not necessarily include its spiritual legitimacy.

This latter depends completely on the apostolicity of its doctrines and resolutions.[8]

Underlying this denial of the right to claim infallibility to pope and council is not merely an empirical judgment or the common assumption that "to err is human," but also a theological judgment: all human institutions are subject to sin and by that fact cannot claim infallibility for themselves. Thus the denial of infallibility affects not only pope and council, but also the institutional church itself and its traditions. Luther himself realized full well that this was not a judgment one can make easily or lightly. Nevertheless, this is a judgment that *must* be made when something contrary to God's Word is taught:

But "the church is holy, the fathers are holy!" Granted. Nevertheless, even though the church is holy, it still has to pray (Matt. 6:12): "Forgive us our debts." Similarly, even though the fathers are holy, they are still obliged to believe in the forgiveness of sins. Therefore if we teach anything contrary to the Word of God, neither I nor the church nor the fathers nor the apostles nor even an angel from heaven should be believed. But let the Word of the Lord abide forever (I Peter 1:25), for without it this argumentation of the false apostles would have prevailed altogether against Paul's doctrine. For it was really something tremendous to line up the whole church and all the company of the apostles on one side before the Galatians, and on the other side just Paul, a newcomer with very little authority. Thus this was a cogent and nearly conclusive argument. *For no one likes to say that the church is in error;* and yet, if the church teaches anything in addition or contrary to the Word of God, one *must* say that it is in error.[9]

Thus the denial of infallibility to human institutions rests ultimately on the doctrine of sin and the commandment to pray, "Forgive us our sins." Not only must individual Christians pray thus but also the Church as a whole, in spite of the fact that it is called holy.[10] For early Lutheran theology therefore, infallibility language is out of place when applied to human institutions: to pope, to council, to the institutional church and its traditions. Whatever authority they possess can only be derived authority and not an unconditional authority; it is relative to and dependent on the Word of God.

II

We turn now to an indication of those instances where infallibility language was apparently judged to be applicable in early Lutheran theology and to the structure of thought which informs such use of the language. Luther himself was of course acutely aware that the denial of infallibility and unconditional authority to the institutional church opened him to the charge of subjective caprice. That charge occasioned in him some of his most severe *Anfechtungen*.[11] Luther interpreters insist, however, that it is a gross misunderstanding of Luther and early Lutheran theology to claim that the objective authority of the Church was dismantled in order to put subjective caprice in its place.

It would be a mistake to understand Luther's battle from this perspective as

a battle against every form of teaching office *(Lehramt)* and teaching authority *(Lehrgewalt)*. The subjectivistic interpretation of the Reformation which sets the individuality of conscience absolutely against that which is objectively binding, so that there is a denial of obligatory dogma on the part of the individual awakened to independence, is and remains a misunderstanding resting on profound misinterpretation, even if such misinterpretation has persisted into the present. Luther did not fight against every form of teaching authority and binding doctrine in general, but only against the kind of and manner in which teaching authority in his time confronted him. Otherwise put, he disputed the false claims of teaching authority exactly in the name and for the sake of its genuine claim. One cannot understand his battle when one overlooks the basis *(Standort)* from which it is waged.[12]

If one asks for the basis from which Luther's struggle was conducted, one would have to say that it was that of one who sought only to be a faithful and obedient hearer of the Word of God. That is to say that for Luther and early Lutheran theology the charge of subjectivism could be overcome not by introducing at that point obedience to church institutions but only by being grasped by and becoming subject to the Word of God in faith, to what it commands and proclaims, and to those institutions and traditions properly derived from and dependent on the

Word of God, or at least not contrary to it. That is to say, individual subjectivism could not be overcome simply by appealing to the collective subjectivity of human institutions. For Luther subjectivism is overcome only when one is grasped by that which comes truly "from without," the address of God in the gospel promise, in such fashion that one in turn gives sole authority and honor to that address, to its actual content. Thus Luther could be comforted in his *Anfechtungen* in this regard by Staupitz' words that his (Luther's) doctrine gave all honor to God and not to human beings.[13] And for Luther this doctrine itself was not something arbitrarily established, but one based on Scripture. One who hears the gospel promise—who is grasped, judged, and redeemed by the content of the Word of God— could not place himself above that Word, but only under it. In Luther's view, to say that Scripture in its basic intent and content is obscure or ambiguous to the extent that an authoritative teaching office must be placed above it to clarify it would itself be evidence that one has not been grasped by its content, or at least not thought through the implications of being so grasped. This is especially evident in Luther's argument with Erasmus over the clarity of Scripture.[14] Thus, to Luther's mind, both the claims of "spiritualists" to possess an authority from the Holy Spirit over and above Scripture and the claims of the Roman See to possess such authority were of the same basic sort: both were subjective.

For we shall not prove the spirits by arguments about learning, life, talent, numbers, dignity, ignorance, crudity, rarity, and lowliness. Nor do I approve of those who have recourse to boasting of the Spirit; for I have had this year (1525) and am still having a sharp enough fight with those fanatics who subject the Scriptures to the interpretation of their own spirit. It is on this account also that I have hitherto attacked the pope, in whose kingdom nothing is more commonly stated or more generally accepted than the idea that the Scriptures are obscure and ambiguous, so that the spirit to interpret them must be sought from the Apostolic See of Rome. Nothing more pernicious could be said than this, for it has led ungodly men to set themselves above the scripture and to fabricate whatever they pleased. . . .[15]

This understanding—or perhaps better, experience—of being

grasped by the content of God's Word, the gospel, established for Luther his *primum principium*, that which governs all:

The first principle of Christianity is therefore nothing other than the divine Word; all human words, moreover, are conclusions therefrom and are to be in turn tested and checked by it. This primary principle must be most firmly and universally noted, not as something taught and established by persons, but as that by which persons are judged.[16]

Against this background I will attempt to indicate some of the major instances and the manner in which infallibility language was used positively in early Lutheran theology. This account cannot pretend to be exhaustive—that would be a much greater undertaking—but it should help to outline the basic position of early Lutheranism, i.e. to clarify and pinpoint what was meant by its appeal to the "Word of God." In general it can be stated, and I think accurately, that infallibility language was used very rarely and then only in specific contexts.

To begin with, infallibility language was applied to the Holy Scriptures as such. The word *infallible*, however, was used very rarely. The only unquestionable instance I have been able to discover in Luther's own utterances where infallibility was attributed to the Holy Scriptures was in the debate with Eck (again a polemical context!):

Moreover as to the argument from the example of Augustine: "If one were to admit error in a council, the universal authority of councils would be shaken"—that is an inappropriate comparison. Augustine argues concerning Holy Scripture, which is the infallible Word of God (*verbum dei infallibile*), whereas the council is subordinate to that Word. One does injury to the Word of God by such comparison if one concedes that it is possible for councils to err. . . . [17]

The preface to *The Book of Concord* speaks of the "Word of God" as being "pure, infallible, and unalterable." [18] There is some debate among Lutherans as well as among Reformation scholars, however, as to whether Luther and the early Lutherans consistently attributed formal infallibility to the Holy Scriptures as such. The majority are inclined to view that they did not.[19] Luther's writings abound, of course, with references to the inspiration of Holy Scriptures and to the authorship, words, phrases, thoughts, and sometimes even linguistic irregularities being the work of the Holy Spirit.[20] However, what one is to infer from that as far as formal infallibility is concerned, especially in light of passages which seem to indicate otherwise, is a debatable question. In any case for our purposes here I think it is correct to say that early Lutheran theology refrained, especially because of its battle with "left wing" factions in the Reformation, from using scriptural infallibility as a formalistic principle in the derivation of Christian dogma or ethical practice.[21] That was a development which occurred in later Lutheranism. For the most part infallibility language seemed to be applied to the Word of God in its function as gospel in order to back up the trustworthiness of the promises of God. Thus Luther in the *Large Catechism* said in the section on Baptism:

We bring the child with the purpose and hope that he may believe, and we pray God to grant him faith. But we do not baptize him on that account, but solely on the command of God. Why? Because we know that God does not lie. My neighbor and I—in short, all men—may err and deceive, but God's Word cannot err.[22]

And on the Lord's Supper (on whether one should feel distress and hunger and thirst for the sacrament):

If you cannot feel the need, therefore, at least believe the Scripture. They will not lie to you, and they know your flesh better than you yourself do.[23]

Melanchthon, in the *Apology to the Augsburg Confession*, again in the context of the promise of the sacrament, wrote:

Because this is a sacrament of the New Testament, as Christ clearly says (I Cor. 11:25), the communicant should be certain that the free forgiveness of sins, promised in the New Testament, is being offered to him. He should accept this by faith, comfort his troubled conscience, and believe that the testimonies are not false but as certain as though God, by a new miracle, promised his will to forgive.[24]

In the *Formula of Concord* as well, infallibility language is used solely in connection with the promises of God in the sacraments and in divine election. In discussing the grounds on which Lutherans stand in the controversy over the sacrament, the *Formula* says:

The third ground is that God's Word is not false nor does it lie.[25]

and in connection with election:

And we should not regard this call of God which takes place through the preaching of the Word as a deception, but should know certainly that God reveals his will in this way, and that in those whom he thus calls he will be efficaciously active through the Word so that they may be illuminated, converted, and saved.[26]

These citations from Luther and the confessional writings indicate that with rare exceptions infallibility language is used positively only in a gospel context. It is used to assert that the promises of God in his Word are trustworthy and that they apply to the hearers of that Word.

The question which naturally arises at this point is: What is the Word of God to which this kind of infallibility is ascribed? A formal legalistic biblicism is clearly not what Luther and early Lutherans had in mind. In the controversy with the peasants especially, and with other sectarians of the times as well, such biblicism was encountered and rejected. "Luther's ultimate authority and standard was not the book of the Bible and the canon as such but that scripture which interpreted itself and also criticized itself from its own center, from Christ and from the radically understood gospel." [27] For Luther, the authority of Scripture was Christ-centered and therefore gospel-centered. Scripture bears testimony to all the articles about Christ and is on that account to be so highly valued.[28] One who does not find Christ in the Scriptures engages in superfluous reading, even if he or she reads it carefully.[29] One should "refer the Bible to Christ . . . nothing but Christ should be proclaimed." [30] Luther can even go so far as to say: "If adversaries use scripture against Christ, then we put Christ against the scriptures." [31] The Word of God therefore is ultimately Christ and the proclamation of the gospel.

It is not strange, therefore, that infallibility language can sometimes be used of Christ himself:

Here it is to no avail to cry "Church and the Fathers," because as we have said, human deeds and speeches outside of and without God's word do not matter to us in such high matters, even if it were an angel from heaven. . . . We must have the man of whom alone it is written: "He has never sinned nor spoken falsely." [32]

This kind of statement indicates that Luther and early Lutherans took the "infallibility" of Christ for granted as the true and ultimate mediator of God's Word. It seems, however, that not a great deal was made of such an assumption. One encounters direct assertions of Christ's infallibility only rarely, and again the weight rests more on Christ's authority, might, honor, etc., as the mediator of the gospel. This is due, no doubt, to the fact that early Lutherans did not look to Christ predominantly as a "teacher" or bringer of a "new law" but rather as one who brought the gospel to light.

In sum, infallibility language was applied in early Lutheranism to the Word of God as the highest and only true source of authority in the Church. That authority ultimately rests, however, not on the ascription of infallibility to it by human institutions but on the content of the Word itself, on the promises of God, on Christ, and on the Word of the gospel. ". . . For Luther the content of scripture and the proof of its authority coincide as do the content and basis of faith." [33] That is to say that the Word of God authenticates itself in grasping and claiming believers through faith. It was impossible, for early Lutheranism, to appeal to any authority beyond that.

This understanding of the authority of the gospel of course raises the question of who has the right to claim to be the proper interpreter or proclaimer of this Word of God. This is a question which is not strictly speaking the subject of this paper and will, I trust, be dealt with in other papers. It is in place, however, at least to raise the question here, since it leads to the problem of the authority or infallibility of the Church and its teaching office. Is there no sense in which early Lutheranism could apply infallibility language to the Church? Here one must take account of the fact that infallibility language *was* used of the Church, but only of the *true* or hidden Church, and not of the empirical church or its institutions. Luther's reply to Erasmus in *The*

Bondage of the Will is perhaps the *locus classicus* for this kind of assertion. Erasmus charged that it was incredible that God should have tolerated error in his Church in the points at issue for so long. Luther replied:

This is my answer to your statements that it is incredible that God should have concealed an error in his church for so many centuries, and should not have revealed to any of his saints what we claim to be the chief doctrine of the gospel. First we do not say that this error has been tolerated by God or in any of his saints. For the Church is ruled by the Spirit of God and the saints are led by the Spirit of God (Rom. 8:14). And Christ remains with his church even to the end of the world (Matt. 28:20); and the church of God is the pillar and ground of the truth (I Tim. 3:15). These things, I say, we know; for the creed that we all hold affirms, "I believe in the holy Catholic church;" so that it is impossible for the church to err, even in the smallest article. And even if we grant that some of the elect are bound in error all their lives, yet they must necessarily return to the right way before they die, since Christ says in John 10 (:28): "No one shall snatch them out of my hand."

But here is the task, here is the toil, to determine whether those whom you call the church are the church. . . . For it does not immediately follow that if God has permitted all those whom you quote . . . to be in error, therefore he has permitted his church to err.[34]

After recounting the manifest errors of the Church (both in the Old Testament as well as in the New Testament times!) Luther continued:

The church of God is not as commonplace a thing, my dear Erasmus, as the phrase "the Church of God;" nor are the "saints of God." They are a pearl and precious jewels, which the Spirit does not cast before swine (Matt. 7:6) but keeps hidden, as scripture says (Matt. 11:25), lest the ungodly should see the glory of God. Otherwise, if they were plainly recognized by all, how could they possibly be as harassed and afflicted in the world as they are? As Paul says: "If they had known, they would not have crucified the Lord of glory." (I Cor. 2:8).

Thus infallibility language was used of the *true* Church, the *communio sanctorum,* the hearers of the Word of God. But it is an article of *faith* that the true Church cannot err, not a claim that could be made the object of sight in "this age." For the true Church cannot claim infallibility for itself or its institutions as though that could be an openly recognized fact or accomplishment which should compel obedience. Luther's *theologia crucis* governed also his view of the Church. The true Church lives under the sign of the cross and can assert its authority in no other way than that of its Lord: revelation under the form of opposites, humility, service, suffering, death. That true, hidden Church becomes visible or revealed in this world, therefore, only through the proclamation of its Lord and his gospel, the administration of the sacraments, and the bearing of the cross.

But if the true Church is hidden, how then is one to judge when a dispute arises? Luther introduced at this point his idea of two kinds of judgment corresponding to two kinds of scriptural clarity, the internal and the external.[35] The internal is made by virtue of the witness of the Holy Spirit within believers: it is a judgment, we might say, "from within" because believers have been made "insiders" by the Spirit. This corresponds to the "internal clarity" of Scripture, its own internal perspicuity and consistency. That is to say that for Luther, the problem people have in facing Scripture is not that Scripture is unclear, but that *we*, as human beings, are "unclear" and internally confused. We are "outsiders" and without the Holy Spirit will not understand a word of Scripture.[36] To say that Scripture is unclear and in need of an infallible teaching office would be, for Luther, a fundamental misreading of our sinful predicament.

However, Luther realized the judgment made from the inside, i.e., through the Spirit, is a purely individual matter and *could not* as such be used institutionally. Luther was supremely aware of how appeals to the Spirit could lead to caprice. Thus in the public office of preaching and teaching in the Church, appeal can be made only to the *external* clarity of the Word, the *literal* word of Scripture. It is only on the basis of this external clarity that debate about doctrinal matters can be conducted.[37] But what is to be noted, of course, is that the debate can proceed *only* on the premise of the *clarity* and sufficiency of Scripture, *not* on the assumption of its unclarity or ambiguity so that appeal must be made to figurative interpretations or extra-scriptural institutions.[38] Thus in the debate with Erasmus Luther appealed to the external clarity of the literal Word as a completely clear, sufficient "law" or arbiter in the dispute, and refused to accept allegations of unclarity, ambiguity, or insufficiency (apart, of course, from minor historical, linguistic, and grammatical matters).

Luther's meaning in this seems to be that anyone claimed by the Spirit through the Word—and who is thus grasped by its "internal clarity"—can in turn never attribute unclarity, ambiguity, or insufficiency to that Word, nor will he or she claim special authority on the Spirit's account, but will move instead to grant all authority and honor to the external, literal Word of Scripture as the means through which the Holy Spirit works—however lowly, strange, or offensive that literal Word may seem to men. This, I believe, is the point of Luther's insistence on the Holy Spirit as author of Scripture. The Word, too, stands under the *theologia crucis;* indeed, it *is* the Word of the cross.

For early Lutheranism, therefore, questions about who has the right to interpret and proclaim the Word of God will lead one to what I suppose, in logical terms, is a circle. But that circle is designed to protect the freedom of the gospel. Those persons have the right to preach and teach who through being grasped by the Word give the Word the right and honor which it claims for itself, letting the Word be what it is, establish itself, and interpret itself. Infallibility language, therefore, if it is to be used at all cannot be extended beyond that circle: the Word of God and the true Church which hears and proclaims that Word. The Church confesses itself to be generated by the Word and can only for its part accord that Word the honor due it. The Church, consequently, cannot claim for itself any authority in establishing or proving articles of faith:

1. The Church of God does not have the power to set its own articles of faith; it has never done so and can never do so.

3. All articles of faith are set sufficiently by the Holy Scriptures so that no one may set any more.

5. The Church of God has no power as judge and ruler to attest or prove articles of faith or morals or the Holy Scriptures; it has never done so and never will do so.

6. Rather the Church is to be attested and judged by the Holy Scriptures or the gospel, as by a judge and Lord.

7. The Church attests to the gospel and the Holy Scriptures

as a subject witness and confesses, just as a servant wears his master's seal and colors.

8. For this is certain: whoever has no power to promise and grant either future or present life has no power to prescribe articles of faith.[39]

The impression stated at the outset of this paper can perhaps now be restated more in the form of a conclusion (however tentatively!): infallibility language, even though it was occasionally used, was not integral to the stance of early Lutheran theology. One finds such language only rarely, and when used it functions not to reinforce the teaching office of the Church directly, but rather to add weight to claims of the gospel and the sacraments. Perhaps one can say that infallibility language belongs to an understanding of the truth claims of the Church which is different from that of early Lutherans. Luther, for instance, could find no real function for such language in reinforcing the gospel:

Who is then certain about where the gospel is? Answer: and who is certain whether there is a gospel even if the Church authoritatively attests it a hundred times over? For it is not believed because the Church attests it but because one senses (*sentitur*) it is God's Word, as the Thessalonians did (Acts 17:11 and 1 Thess. 1:5).

Still more: who is certain whether there is a Church at all on earth if one does not beforehand believe the gospel which teaches of the Church? For we do not first have the Church and from it the gospel, but first the gospel and from it the Church, as St. Augustine says and Paul in 1 Cor. 4:15: "I became your father in Christ Jesus through the gospel;" also James 1:18: "he brought us forth by the word of truth. . . . " The gospel is certain to all who have in themselves the witness of the Holy Spirit that this is the gospel . . . whoever believes, believes and whoever does not believe, does not believe. The believer is certain, the unbeliever remains uncertain. The Lord, however, gathers the believers together that there might be a Church.[40]

The Church is established by the gospel and not *vice versa*. Thus infallibility language in its usual function is rendered virtually pointless. The warrant from Scripture which one encounters repeatedly in early Lutheranism in this regard is John 10:5, 27:

A stranger they will not follow, but they will flee from him, for they do not know the voice of strangers. . . . My sheep hear my voice, and I know them, and they follow me.[41]

Whether this attitude toward infallibility language can be maintained in later Lutheranism or whether it provides a sufficient basis for establishing the preaching and teaching office of the Church is a subject for subsequent papers.

Appendix

The puzzling question about the status of propositional truth *vis á vis* infallibility in Luther's thought raised in the current discussion would have to be handled, it seems to me, in the light of the development of Luther's hermeneutics and the distinction between law and gospel and between the "Word of God" and "human teachings" (*Gotteswort* and *Menschenlehre*). It is well known that Luther insisted, in the argument against Erasmus, on the place of assertions in the Christian faith ("Take away assertions and you take away Christianity"),[42] and that "doctrine must be straight as a plumb line, sure and without sin."[43] How can this be maintained in the face of denials of infallibility and perhaps seeming unconcern about the status of propositional truth? Luther's disparate assertions here can be held together, it seems to me, only if one takes into account his fundamental distinction between law and gospel as it develops out of his hermeneutics (see the several studies by Gerhard Ebeling in this regard). Perhaps it can be stated briefly as follows: The Word of God impinges on us as law and as gospel. This means first that it takes up residence in human discourse in the form of propositions, i.e. as literal word, in the form of law, subject to the canons of human discourse. But the ultimate purpose of the letter or law is not to call attention to itself, but to point to another who is its end and *telos*. That is to say that the important question (*a la* Ebeling) is not merely what the words signify, perhaps infallibly, but what they do and how they do it. The important question for Luther, is how the words are used. Indeed, one must say that the purpose of the letter, the law, is to "destroy all confidence in the flesh," all attempts to base faith on human forms of legitimation. The law kills the "old Adam" according to the flesh so that the new person may be raised in the Spirit. The gospel heard through the power of the Spirit is precisely that word of liberation from God which frees from the tyranny of the law, i.e. from dependence on "the flesh" and its forms of legitimation (which bind us to the tyranny of the law). The gospel is therefore the true and ultimate Word of God which authorizes itself and stands above all human forms of legitimation.

The Church is the body of believers that has been called into being *by the gospel*. Its primal doctrinal *datum* is thus precisely the difference between law and gospel. The Church knows this difference and has as its primary doctrinal responsibility the custodianship of this difference. Indeed, this is the canon by which purity and rectitude in doctrine is to be measured. Whatever position the Church may take on the truth or infallibility of propositions, it would be guilty of confusing law and gospel were it to invoke such truthfulness or infallibility as legitimation for its claims. At the same time, however, the Church as the custodian of both law and gospel is concerned about the letter, the law, through which the gospel comes and the Spirit does his work. That is to say that the Church is concerned about propositional truth, about assertions, and about the "external clarity" of the Scriptures. The Word of God has taken residence in such propositions and the Church is concerned to preserve, guard, and protect them.

Since, however, revelation occurs *sub contrario*, under the form of opposites (through the letter which kills that the Spirit may give life), the movement from propositional truth to faith is not a direct one. Faith occurs in the freedom of the Spirit through the hearing of the gospel when the law has done its work. Therefore it seems to me questionable whether one can simply link infallibility *in docendo* with infallibility *in credendo* and infer forwards or backwards from one to the other. Faith is called forth by the gospel and has its own form of legitimation apart from the rectitude of the teachings. The "assertions" which *faith* makes (in which it delights, and without which the Church would cease to exist) are, for Luther, *confessions*, assertions "of conscience" placed on believers' lips by the Holy Spirit. Indeed, the ultimate subject of those assertions is the Holy

Spirit. Thus the section in the debate with Erasmus where such assertions are at issue closes with the famous words: "The Holy Spirit is no skeptic, and it is not doubts or mere opinions that he has written on our hearts, but assertions more sure and certain than life itself and all experience." [44]

The manner in which the assent of faith is worked, therefore, is not through the insistence on the infallibility of propositions as such but through the proper *use* of the words in the preaching of the Word. Thus Luther says that one need not pray for forgiveness if one has *preached* correctly and truly about God.[45] The doctrine, indeed, must be "straight" and "pure." Doctrine for Luther, however, is primarily a summary of the Church's preaching. The concern of Luther and even later Lutheranism was for "pure" doctrine rather than "infallible" doctrine. *Purity*, it would seem, indicates a concern somewhat different from *infallibility*. Doctrine should not be "mixed with" or "contaminated by" the opinions of human beings, and, perhaps one can also say, their systems of legitimation. And the critical measure for this is the proper distinction between law and gospel so that the affirmations of faith are made in the freedom of, and bondage to, the Spirit.

6

LUTHERAN TEACHING AUTHORITY: PAST AND PRESENT

Eric W. Gritsch

Normative Lutheran assertions about the "teaching ministry" of the Church focus on the lordship of Christ and the means by which his lordship is known: the Holy Spirit, the gospel in Word and sacrament, Holy Scripture and its interpretation, the three ecumenical creeds (Apostolic, Nicene, Athanasian), and the Lutheran Confessions (in the *Book of Concord* of 1580).[1] Although 16th century Lutherans tried to preserve existing ecclesiastical order, such as the liturgy, general councils, and bishops, their insistence that such order represented "human tradition" rather than "divine institution" was officially judged by the Roman Catholic Church to be false teaching.[2] The distinction between that which is "according to the gospel" and that which is not was at issue in the Reformation. Lutherans labeled all the items that fall under the heading of "church law" (*ius ecclesiasticum*) "adiaphora," that is, "things that make no difference," or "things neither commanded nor forbidden."[3] Since the *form* of any specific juridical arrangement of ecclesiastical functions, such as the episcopal office, falls under the category of *ius ecclesiasticum*, any definition of "office" (*Amt*) in terms of a juridical arrangement is of necessity adiaphoristic. While Lutherans have always affirmed the *function* of teaching authority in the Church, the specific *form* of this function is an *adiaphoron*. "The

Church knows no absolute adiaphora just as it knows no absolute form." [4]

Lutheranism has lived through various adiaphoristic controversies since the 16th century. The chief issue in these controversies has been the question whether or not Christian liberty under the gospel can be preserved by ecclesiastical government. This essay presents an historical sketch of Lutheran theological reflection on that issue in the context of Lutheran attempts to exercise ecclesiastical teaching authority in a variety of ways.

Luther and the Lutheran Confessions

For Luther the "Word of God" is the highest authority in the Church. He gained his understanding of the "Word" as God's revelatory instrument through personal struggle *(Anfechtung)*, exegetical work (especially on Psalms and Paul), and an enduring historical critical encounter with the tradition of the Fathers (especially those of the first five centuries, including Augustine).[5] The Word of God is revealed as *law* in God's created order (his "strange work—*opus alienum*) and as *gospel* in the story of Jesus Christ (God's "real work"—*eigentliches Werk*). Consequently God is both "hidden and revealed" *(absconditus et revelatus)* in his creation and redemption; while in the masks of law and order he discloses the sin of the human race, he reveals his unconditional love for his creatures in the death and resurrection of Jesus of Israel. The Church, therefore, as the people of God in the new covenant of Christ, must properly distinguish between law and gospel; and since the gospel is God's real work, it is the Word which communicates salvation through Christ *(was Christum treibet)*. Here then is the root function of teaching authority for Luther: the Word of God (audible in preaching and visible in the sacrament, according to Augustine) is a hermeneutical reality which comes alive in the communication event of Word and sacrament, disclosing God's unconditional promise of righteousness "by faith alone apart from works of law," that is, by a relationship without the condition of human merit. "Justification by faith alone" is for Luther the doctrine (based upon the prophetic and apostolic authority in Scripture) which is the *raison-d'être* for Christian existence and the *sine qua non* for Christian unity, i.e., "the article by which the Church stands and falls" *(articulus stantis et cadentis ecclesiae).*[6]

The function of Lutheran teaching authority is to engage in a hermeneutical process whereby the purity of the gospel (always understood in terms of the principal article of faith as the promise of salvation without human merit) is maintained in the Church and impurities are removed. Thus the teaching office *(magisterium)* is essentially a preaching office *(Predigtamt).* Luther and the Lutheran Confessions assert that God instituted "the ministry of teaching the Gospel and administering the sacraments."[7] Office *(Amt)* in this context is an ordered *function* on the part of persons. Persons may be charged with a variety of such functions or offices. Clergy tend the gospel Word, princes are instituted to govern by the law of the sword. Luther regarded *both* estates *(Stand, ordo)* as Christian, united by the sacrament of Baptism.[8] Ministry carries out the order of God, the Redeemer; government *(Obrigkeit)* carries out the order of God, the Creator. The Church lives by the Word; the state lives by the sword. Both realms overlap in the interim between Christ's first and second coming. Both offices, that of the Word and that of the sword, are divinely instituted. But their particular *forms* (episcopal, monarchic, etc.) are not.[9] When German Diets (especially at Speyer in 1526 and Augsburg in 1555) legislated the "law for reform" *(ius reformandi)* as the responsibility of secular princes and territories, Lutherans cooperated with their princes to create territorial churches led by bishops called "superintendents."[10] Thus the *Augsburg Confession* of 1530 makes careful distinctions between the teaching authority of bishops (essentially limited to Word and sacrament) and the governing authority of princes. Since all human beings and whatever they arrange in terms of authority are subject to error, princes may become "emergency bishops" of the Church when regular bishops teach anything which is contrary to the gospel.[11]

Territorial ecclesiastical constitutions and church orders in the 16th century clearly show that the criteria for what is true or false teaching are usually conditioned by prevailing historical circumstances.[12] Doctrinal controversies between Lutheran factions after Luther's death in 1546 also reveal some variety.[13] The *Formula of Concord* of 1577 developed three basic norms for the proper exercise of teaching authority: (1) Scripture, (2) the first three ecumenical creeds, and (3) the *Augsburg Confession* and its appropriate interpretation through other symbolical books in the *Book of Concord* of 1580.[14] *Orthodoxy* must be defined in terms of what is and what is not "according to the gospel" at a given time. But the hermeneutical process of definition must be guided by the prophetic and apostolic writings in Scripture as the only "rule and norm" *(regula et norma)* and "touchstone" *(Probierstein, lapis Lydius)*. In short, the teaching office is essentially an instrument to guard the preaching office which was instituted by God to evoke faith in the promise that human beings are saved without human merit.[15] The authors of the *Formula of Concord* insisted that detailed magisterial work is to be done in the face of doctrinal controversy; there must be proper distinctions made between needless contentions which destroy rather than edify the Church and necessary controversies which preserve the truth of the gospel.[16] The teaching office not only settles conflict but participates in it. For as long as the Church is on earth it is a body of conflict, consisting of believers and saints as well as false Christians and hypocrites.[17]

Once territories had implemented the law for reform *(ius reformandi)*, especially after the Peace of Augsburg in 1555, the superintendent, general superintendent, dean *(Propst)*, and bishop—the various titles of ecclesiastical leaders varied widely in German territories after 1580 [18]— became the guardians and executors of doctrine, together with the territorial prince. Consistories (since 1539 the judicial agencies of Lutheran territories) assumed more and more power with the increase of the authority of princes, who had become the highest overseers *(summus episcopus)* in their territories.[19] This political development also cemented the relationship between territorial power and the university. Lutheran bishops and princes were not eager to institute new laws for the protection of Lutheranism. Whenever possible they adhered to existing legal practice. Thus candidates for the Doctor of Theology at Wittenberg University continued to take the medieval oath to teach what they had learned since 1546 as the body of Lutheran doctrine; the practice of taking such an oath had been instituted in 1508. Lutheran ordinands had to take a similar oath in certain territories when they were awarded prebends by a prince (in Ansbach-Bayreuth, for example, after 1529). Usually this was demanded because of anti-Calvinist feelings.[20] The theological generation after the *Book of Concord* of 1580 was eager to create a territorial Lutheranism which combined pure doctrine *(die reine Lehre)* with loyalty to the state.

Lutheran Orthodoxy and Pietism

The alliance between Church and state on the one hand and Church and university on the other created a Lutheran Orthodoxy which was to be a bulwark against the Roman Counter Reformation and Calvinism. Luther's preaching office was transformed into a dogmatic teaching office. The universities of Jena and Wittenberg became centers of dogmatic systems which used Aristotelian logic to demonstrate the purity of doctrine. Theologians like John Gerhard (1582-1637) saw ministry in exclusively juridical terms; the power of jurisdiction *(potestas iurisdictionis)* of the ecclesiastical office included the power to ordain and to guard public morals.[21] This meant that the teaching office, particularly in its function of judging doctrine and of exercising the power of the keys to forgive and to retain sin, was separated from local congregations, that is, from the common priesthood of all believers.[22] The theologian David Hollatz (1648-1713) saw the teaching office within an intricate system of ecclesiastical authority culminating in the doctrine of synods: [23] (1) there was the *ecclesia synthetica*, consisting of those who preach and hear the gospel —the phenomenon of *ecclesia* in its fundamental function; and (2) there was the *ecclesia repraesentativa*, consisting of ecclesiastical representatives assembled in councils and synods. They were the judges of what is orthodox in faith, morals, and worship on the basis of the canonical Scripture. These synods and councils were chaired by a *praeses ecclesiasticus* (the equivalent of a bishop) and a *praeses politicus*, usually the prince of the territory or his representative.

Together they constituted the "office for correct doctrine" *(magistratus orthodoxus)* in charge of the religion of the land. Although the ecclesiastical and secular powers were seen as separated in theory, they tended to be united in practice; pure doctrine was enforced by secular police authority. Occasionally convents of theologians or a religious collegium *(Religionskollegium)* of 10 to 12 orthodox university teachers assisted the synods in making decisions during controversies.[24] This entire process of exercising the teaching Ministry of the Church was regarded as an extension of Luther's idea that ecumenical councils could constitute the highest juridical authority of the Church.[25]

Lutheran Pietism, originating with Philipp J. Spener in 1675, opposed Lutheran territorial orthodoxy on the grounds that the Holy Spirit is not bound to convents of theologians, princes, and synods. Instead the Holy Spirit might be found more abundantly in the conventicles of Bible-studying lay people. The "religion of the heart" is more orthodox than the "religion of the mind." Some pietist groups, such as the Moravian Brethren, combined Lutheran doctrine with the doctrine of apostolic succession; under the leadership of the Lutheran Count Nikolaus von Zinzendorf at the community of Herrnhut, they accepted the *Augsburg Confession;* the Moravian bishop Daniel Jablonski consecrated Zinzendorf as their bishop in 1737, thus linking him to the ancient Hussite tradition. But although the Archbishop of Canterbury acknowledged the consecration as valid, German Lutherans rejected it as contrary to the Lutheran Confessions.[26]

Lutheran Orthodoxy and Pietism reflected in an extreme fashion the vicissitudes of a theology based on the distinction of law and gospel. Lutheran Orthodoxy could teach the verbal inspiration of Scripture as the highest doctrinal authority guarded by a legalistic conception of the teaching office; Lutheran Pietism could reject scholastic and juridical expressions of faith altogether in favor of a spiritualistic personal piety as the highest authority in the Church. That both of these options became historical realities (and still are in some Lutheran circles) only supports the point that the Lutheran teaching office deserves careful consideration in the systematic reflections of Lutheran theologians.

From the 19th Century to the Present

An intensive debate in the 19th century over the nature and authority of the ecclesiastical office drove Lutheran theologians to consider the juridical location of the teaching office in the structure of the Church.[27] Sparked by the revival of confessionalism in the wake of the third centennial of the Reformation in 1817 and by the revolutions of 1848, the debate explored the theological foundations of ecclesiastical law and order. The chief issue was whether or not Christ had instituted an office *(Amt)* in a juridical sense. Wilhelm Löhe and his disciples argued for a divinely instituted sacramental office climaxing in the episcopacy as the teaching office of the Church (without the doctrine of apostolic succession). Johann Höfling and his disciples saw in the common priesthood of all baptized believers the foundation of all official structure in the Church. Both groups based their arguments on New Testament research and the Lutheran Confessions. Since Löhe had missionary connections with American Lutherans, the debate was extended to the United States, where the Missouri and Buffalo Synods quarreled over the same issue. Carl F. W. Walther, the founder of the Missouri Synod, tried to mediate between both parties in Germany as well as in America by asserting the interdependence of Luther's "common" and "special" priesthoods.[28] The most elaborate reflections about the teaching office came from Theodor Kliefoth (1810-1895), the Mecklenburg theologian and churchman who advocated the most radical reconception of the early Lutheran confessional position of ministry.[29] Kliefoth held that all order is divinely instituted and distinguished three offices in the Church: (1) the office of the means of grace *(Gnadenmittelamt)*, which was instituted by Christ, continued in the Apostles who instituted a presbyterate (the ordained clergy), and will be exercised fully again by Christ when he returns in glory; (2) the office of the congregation *(Gemeindeamt)*, which is the common priesthood of all baptized Christians; and (3) the ruling office of the Church *(Kirchenregieramt)*, which is established to create organic unity in the Church on earth. This was Kliefoth's teaching office. Its specific task was to guard the Church in a *juridical* way against the sin of disunity and immo-

rality. Grace and its means, Word and sacraments, needs
law in order to be effective. The order of salvation and the
order of human interrelationships are both divinely instituted. "God deals with human beings through the ruling
office of the Church as well as through the preaching office.
Through the preaching office he offers all people his saving
grace; through the ruling office he mandates order for all
those who have accepted his offer of grace." [30] There is a
definite tendency in Kliefoth's argumentation to view the
"ruling office" as the highest office in the Church since it
ultimately facilitates all other life in the Church. Since he
was adamantly opposed to the revolutionary democratic
ideals of 1848, Kliefoth returned to a hierarchically conceived order of the Church.

Although Kliefoth was able to put his theological reflections on ecclesiastical law and order into practice in the
territorial church of Mecklenburg (his hierarchical reorga-
nization lasted until 1918), his conception of the teaching
office as a divine institution remained a highly controversial
minority opinion in 19th century Lutheranism.

But the issue of the relationship between the preaching
and the teaching offices remained. "There is no end to the
writing and quarreling about the Church, the ecclesiastical
office, and church regiment," complained one of the participants in the controversy in 1862; and a modern authority on church law, Johannes Heckel, after reviewing the
10th century controversy, notes: "Very little has changed
since." [31] Although no 19th century theologian endorsed
one specific form of the teaching office, such as the papacy,
most pleaded that the Lutheran church should have a
teaching office for the sake of unity. Only Rudolf Sohm, a
jurist rather than a theologian, argued at the turn of the
century that law is totally contradictory to the nature of the
Church.[32] But Lutheran theologians by and large agreed
with the sober contention of the Lutheran jurist Günther
Holstein that law and order belong to God's creation and
thus also to the realm of the new creation, the Church.[33]

Episcopal teaching authority, already prevalent in the
Lutheran tradition, became the subject of discussion in pan-
Lutheran and ecumenical relations during and after World
War II. In Germany the *Kirchenkampf* between the "Ger-
man Christians" (*Deutsche Christen*) under the leadership

of a *Reichsbishof* appointed by the Nazi government and the "Confessing Church" *(Bekennende Kirche)* produced a sharp controversy over the interpretation of the separation between "spiritual" and "temporal" power in the territorial churches. The *Barmen Declaration* of 1934 ardently reaffirmed the typically Lutheran trinity of authority: the gospel of Jesus Christ, Holy Scripture, and the creeds of the Reformation.[34] At the same time the *Declaration* rejected as false teaching any view which holds that the Church is subject to "special leaders *(Führer)* with powers to rule." [35] Clergy and laity were brought together in their exercise of teaching authority during the Nazi period. As a result, the postwar constitutions of the Lutheran territorial churches in Germany emphasized the interrelationship of Ministry and common priesthood. Both exercise the authority of the gospel as the priestly people of God who are mature *(mündige)* servants in the world. Bishops therefore are only first among equals *(primi inter pares)* rather than special spiritual officers. In this connection the *Declaration (Erklärung)* of the United Evangelical Church in Germany in 1954 rejected the idea of an apostolic succession of bishops. Instead it reaffirmed the Reformation view that apostolic succession, properly understood, encompasses the Church in its entirety with all its members, and therefore cannot be bound to a single distinguishing mark or to a special group of persons occupying the office of Ministry.[36]

Scandinavian Lutheran churches took similar positions with regard to the question of episcopal authority. When the Anglican Lambeth Conference acknowledged the preservation of apostolic succession in the Church of Sweden, the Swedish Bishops' Assembly of 1922 found it necessary to explain that, according to their understanding, the ecclesiastical office existed not *iure divino* but *iure humano*. The Church of Finland followed suit in 1934.[37] Gustaf Wingren's definition of ecclesiastical authority was widely accepted as a reaffirmation of Reformation principles: "The authority lies primarily in the means of grace themselves. The means of grace do not receive any authority because they are administered by those who have the office, but they possess authority in themselves, because Christ has bound his own presence to them." [38]

Lutheran churches in the United States have only recently begun to concern themselves with theological and practical considerations of teaching authority in terms of a *magisterium*.[39] American Lutherans could not develop territorial churches because of the political principle of the separation of Church and state. With a sense of nonchalant pragmatism, synodical and congregational structures were adopted by immigrant Lutherans who distrusted Anglican episcopalianism. The laconic statement of the Swedish Lutheran leader Lars P. Esbjörn in 1852 is typical of 19th century Lutheran attitudes: "The Lutheran Church has based its hope of salvation and eternal life entirely upon Jesus' passion and death and his atonement, and not upon high ecclesiastical offices."[40]

The highest Lutheran ecclesiastical authority in America is usually located in a biennial convention consisting of an equal number of clerical and lay delegates. The Lutheran Church in America is fairly typical here. Its convention is chaired by the president of the church, who is "leader and counselor in matters spiritual and temporal;"[41] the "confession of faith" in Article II of the Constitution assigns the highest authority to Jesus Christ as the Lord of the Church, with the Holy Scriptures as the norm for the faith and life of the Church; the Unaltered *Augsburg Confession* and Luther's *Small Catechism* are accepted as true witnesses to the gospel.[42] It may be assumed that teaching authority in the various Lutheran churches of the United States is closely tied to the office of president or bishop, i.e., leaders of synods and national communities.

A survey of confessional subscription among the members of the Lutheran World Federation indicates that Luther's definition of authority as a hermeneutical process in terms of the interaction between Word and faith seems prevalent.[43] While some churches express this hermeneutical process in terms of a dynamic of Scripture and tradition, other churches emphasize the verbal inspiration of Scripture, thus moving in the direction of what one could call hermeneutical infallibility.[44] Both positions reflect the shift in the definition of teaching authority which occurred during the 16th century doctrinal controversies leading to the *Formula of Concord*. While the *Augsburg Confession assumes* that tradition is judged by Scripture, the *Formula of Concord asserts* that this must be so.[45] How such assumptions and assertions should be interpreted is to be seen in the light of ongoing discussion within the Lutheran World Federation.[46]

Conclusion

Recent Lutheran systematic reflection on the *magisterium* of the Church has been stimulated by ecumenical dialogue, be it bilateral or along general scholarly lines (for example, as "polemical theology" *[Kontroverstheologie]* in Germany). Some theologians have made pioneering attempts to build bridges to other traditions, especially Roman Catholicism.[47] Others have made urgent appeals to discuss the teaching office in the context of a "hermeneutic of doctrine" *(Dogmenhermeneutik)*.[48] The mutual recognition of ministry between the various churches should lead to *magisterial mutuality:* the sharing of significant doctrinal insights and decisions for the sake of an effective communication of the gospel without mutual condemnation.[49] Lutherans have insisted that doctrinal decisions are essentially confessional: they are the witness of the Church to the gospel at a given place and time. This means that the *magisterium* of the Church safeguards the eschatological nature of the infallibility of the gospel rather than the infallibility of a particular structure of the Church on earth. To this extent, Lutheran teaching authority functions as a demythologizer of the Church—a process also demanded by some Roman Catholic theologians today.[50]

It remains to be seen how far Lutheran theology can extend the insights of biblical hermeneutics and ecumenical encounters between communions into the whole *realm* of doctrinal formulation in the postbiblical tradition. If progress is made at this point, ecumenical discussions about the strengths and weaknesses of past conceptions of the *magisterium* should be quite rewarding and help to find unified ways to tell the world that Christians should believe with authority.

7

THE *MAGISTERIUM*
IN THE LUTHERAN CHURCH
WITH SPECIAL REFERENCE
TO INFALLIBILITY

Warren A. Quanbeck

At the time of the Reformation the structures of the Lutheran churches were provisional, and in certain important respects they have remained so until the present. From 1517 until the Council of Trent most leaders of the Reformation hoped for the reestablishment of unity among the churches of the West, looking to an ecumenical council as the agency for accomplishing it.[1] Even after the Council of Trent many ardent spirits continued to hope for reunion on terms that would recognize the consonance of Lutheran doctrine and practice with traditional catholic positions. The *Augsburg Confession* of 1530 is an attempt to show that the faith and practice of the Lutheran Reformers is truly catholic and should not be condemned as heretical. In this confession, and in its *Apology* written in reply to the Roman Catholic *Confutation,* Melanchthon appealed to the Scriptures, to the Fathers, and to many church leaders of later times to show that the Reformers were in accord with generally accepted standards of catholic teaching and practice. He invoked the Fathers, especially Augustine,[2] Cyprian,[3] Jerome,[4] Ambrose,[5] Chrysostom,[6] Irenaeus,[7] and Gregory the Great,[8] as well as many medieval theologians such as Thomas,[9] Duns Scotus,[10] Peter Lombard,[11] Gabriel Biel,[12] John Gerson [13] and Bernard of Clairvaux [14] in support of the Reformers' position, and contended that the authorities were wrong to condemn positions sanctioned by the Scriptures, the Fathers, and many saints and theologians of the Middle Ages.

The *Smalcald Articles* of 1538 were prepared by Luther himself as guides to Lutheran participants in a hoped-for general council. The Articles delineated what the Reformers regarded as essential to a theological position in agreement with the gospel. Luther regarded Christian unity as a necessity, but saw the papal party as a virtually insurmountable barrier to its recovery in his lifetime.[15] The loss of Christian unity and the difficulties set in the way of its recovery seemed to him apocalyptic indications of the end of the world.[16]

Luther's pessimism on the matter of Christian unity in 1538 is somewhat difficult for us to understand. We tend to fault him for insufficient concern for unity or else see his attitude as justification for a contemporary indifference to the issue. We may be helped in understanding his attitude if we recall that he had opposed Tetzel's peddling of indulgences on pastoral and theological grounds, and in obedience to his vow as Doctor of Theology to defend the truth of the Scriptures in the church. He was genuinely shocked that his protest received no real hearing. The bishops to whom he submitted his protest took no action.[17] The haste and irregularity of the examination procedures by the Roman authorities and the shabby theological argumentation of the papal condemnation convinced him that the pope and his supporters were more concerned about papal rights and power than they were with the truth of the gospel or the welfare of the congregation.[18] Lacking modern perspectives on the interpretation of prophecy and apocalyptic material, Luther interpreted these events in the spirit of popular medieval apocalyptic expectation and saw them as fulfillment of prophecies concerning the "man of sin" (2 Thess. 2), the "abomination of desolation" (Mark 13 and parallels), and the "antichrist," (Revelation 12 and 13), and as indications of the approaching end of the age.

This foreshortened eschatology not only made Luther pessimistic about the recovery of unity but has had considerable influence on the Lutheran Church's subsequent understanding of Christian unity, the task of missions, and the connection between justification and ethics. The exploration of these relationships both in Luther and in Lutheran theology remains an important task today.

The Lutheran Reformers wanted to stand in continuity with the Catholic tradition in the West, not only in doctrine but also in maintaining traditional episcopal polity and discipline.[19] Their inability to find bishops who would ordain priests for evangelical congregations compelled them to find alternative church structures. They did so in various ways, usually adapting existing administrative arrangements in city or territorial government.[20] Sometimes a prince served as emergency bishop *(Notbischof);* sometimes civic authorities or former cathedral canons became leaders in the new church administration. Only in Sweden were the Reformers able to carry out their intention of maintaining traditional episcopal polity and discipline. Elsewhere a variety of church structures arose. This seemed in keeping with the teaching of Augustana VII that agreement in the proclamation of the gospel and administration of the sacraments was sufficient for unity in the Church. Any form of administration that served effectively in the proclamation of the gospel and administration of the sacraments was therefore regarded as acceptable. This has given rise to great variety in the administration of Lutheran churches to the present day. One can find the whole range of traditional polities among Lutheran churches: episcopal polity in Sweden, Finland, and the missionary churches founded by them; modified episcopal polity in Denmark, Norway, and parts of Germany; modified presbyterian polity in eastern Europe; and modifications of congregationalism in the United States and Canada.

In one respect the Lutheran churches preserved a feature of medieval practice more completely than the Roman Catholic Church has done. From the early Middle Ages the theological faculties of universities served as consultants in theological disputes. Had not the controversy about indulgences touched so nearly on matters relating to the financing of the new basilica of St. Peter in Rome and the closely related pluralistic episcopal ambitions of Albert of Brandenburg, perhaps more time could have been found to let the theological faculties examine Luther's cause. At the time, however, it was apparently more urgent to silence the troublesome monk from Wittenberg than to inquire into the pastoral and theological merits of his case.[21] The theological faculties were divided on the issues of the Reformation and thereafter lost the role they had played in settling theological controversies. The churches of the Reformation, however, continued the medieval practice and referred theological questions to the faculties of universities and seminaries. At various times in the history of Lutheran churches theological faculties have exercised even more influence than they did in the Middle Ages.[22]

The provisional character of church government in the churches of the Lutheran Reformation is shown by the fact that to this day there is no central administrative agency for these churches. The Lutheran Confessions assert the importance of the unity of the Church and the Reformers desired to maintain it. Melanchthon asserted his willingness to grant a unifying role to the pope under proper conditions: that it be recognized as of human right, and that the Reformers' understanding of the gospel be recognized as catholic.[23] Yet for more than four centuries Lutherans have continued to exist as separate churches held together only by a common subscription to the ecumenical creeds and the Lutheran Confessions of the 16th century.

Not until 1947 did Lutherans even have access to a centralized service agency, although attempts were made as early as 1925 to establish a Lutheran World Convention as a kind of occasional meeting place for Lutherans of the world.[24] The establishment of the Lutheran World Federation at Lund, Sweden in 1947 has appeared to many outside the Lutheran church, and even to some within it, as a move toward centralized authority. An examination of the performance of the Federation should quickly dispel such an idea. The Federation has served chiefly as a service agency for the Lutheran churches of the world in two main areas: 1) coordination of the mission operations of the churches and especially in relation to mission churches deprived of support because of World War II and its aftermath; 2) administration of relief and emergency funds to churches suffering damage to institutions or personnel because of war or other natural or political disasters. Funds have been used, for example, to aid in rebuilding church buildings and institutions in Norway, Finland, Germany, and France, and for assistance to refugees in Hong Kong, Taiwan, Jordan and Bangladesh.

The agencies now grouped within the Department of Studies (Theology, Worship, Stewardship, and Evangelism, etc.) were never intended to serve magisterial functions among Lutheran churches, nor indeed have they done so. The staff involved has been minimal (usually one staff person for each department, and three at most). The tasks assigned have usually pointed to preparation for Assemblies or the assistance of younger churches.[25] The influence of these departments has been precisely the persuasive power of their materials. The member churches can (and frequently do) ignore, receive, study, or adopt them. Throughout the work of the Federation it is plain that LWF is a servant of the member churches and has just as much authority and power as is granted by member churches through action of Assemblies or of the executive committee. In its quarter century of operation the Federation has not presumed to display much initiative in such matters.

It can be maintained nevertheless that Lutheran churches have a *magisterium,* although compared to the Roman Catholic exercise of teaching authority it seems fluid, variable, and well-dispersed.

A. At the level of doctrinal definition Lutheran churches have been extremely reluctant to act. Here again the provisional character of the Reformation can be noted as well as a characteristically Lutheran attitude toward doctrine. The Lutheran churches have never made provision for doctrinal definition, apparently assuming that the definitions contained in the ecumenical creeds and the Lutheran Confessions are sufficient for any foreseeable future. Attempts have been made to add doctrinal definitions to the confessional corpus, but have never found general acceptance by Lutheran churches. As examples we can cite the following:

1. The *Barmen Declaration,* drawn up by "confessing" theologians in Nazi Germany, asserted the freedom of the gospel and the Church over against a totalitarian regime. Some supporters of this document have claimed confessional status for it, but Lutheran churches have not understood it in this light.[26]

2. *A Brief Statement,* a document setting forth the doctrinal position of the Lutheran Church—Missouri Synod. In

1959 the San Francisco convention of the LCMS passed a resolution which at least seemed to give confessional status to this document,[27] an action rescinded at the next convention of the Synod at Cleveland.[28] The New Orleans convention of the LCMS in 1974 adopted a statement on the interpretation of Scripture which has caused controversy within the Synod, some affirming it as not an addition to the Lutheran confessions but a necessary implement for doctrinal discipline within the synod.[29] Others oppose it on the ground that it is in addition to the Lutheran Confessions and an attempt to infringe the freedom of pastors and theologians by insisting on one interpretation of the Lutheran Confessions to the exclusion of others.

3. Many conservative Lutherans, and not only within the Missouri Synod, have contended over the years that the question of biblical authority is sufficiently important in our time to deserve special treatment in authoritative doctrinal definitions. Many series of theses have been drawn up as bases for intersynodical agreement among Lutherans on the question of biblical authority as well as on other questions in dispute, such as election, predestination, and conversion. Most theologians have not regarded these documents as having confessional status but rather as tertiary authorities expounding contemporary understandings of the Scriptures and Lutheran Confessions.[30]

The attitude of the great majority of Lutheran churches and theologians has been that the ecumenical creeds and Lutheran Confessions provide adequate testimony to an evangelical understanding of the New Testament message and that contemporary declarations or theses are not to be seen as having the same level of authority.

B. *At the level of ethical interpretation Lutheran churches have been quite active in modern times.* The social changes of the past century have been extensive and rapid enough to raise questions as to how traditional Lutheran moral counsel relates to contemporary situations. In this area one can observe the operation of a Lutheran *magisterium* or rather a congeries of Lutheran magisterial structures. Each church body has its own way of offering counsel to its members on the kind of action which is considered appropriate in today's situations. Occasionally church bodies will band together in a common approach to such problems. The Lutheran churches of Germany have sometimes used such a cooperative approach, as have also the Lutheran churches of the Scandinavian countries. In the United States Lutheran churches sometimes approach such questions individually, but sometimes they work cooperatively through agencies such as the National Lutheran Council or the Lutheran Council in the USA.[31] It should be noted, however, that these agencies are instruments of the churches, and no document produced by such an agency becomes effective until it is adopted by the individual church bodies. As in the case of the LWF, the cooperative agencies operate with as much initiative and freedom as is granted them by the member churches and are never in a position of authority over against them.

As an example of the fluidity of the Lutheran exercise of magisterial authority one can look at the way the American Lutheran Church operates.[32] The decision-making body in the ALC is the church convention, which meets biennially for about a week. It consists of about one thousand delegates, half clergy and half laity, elected as delegates by the 18 districts of the church. It elects national officers, members of national boards, sets budgets, makes decisions for the church on questions such as the ordination of women, decides questions of synodical and ecumenical relationships, passes on memorials submitted through district conventions, and issues statements on current ethical questions ranging from problems of church and state to war and peace, divorce and remarriage, and abortion.[33]

Most of the matter which comes before the convention has been discussed and prepared by the church council of the ALC, consisting of the national officers (president, vice-president, and secretary of the church) and three representatives of each district: a pastor, a lay member, and the district president (who has voice but no vote).[34] Financial matters are handled in a somewhat more complicated way, but they do not concern us here. Some of the materials on the agenda come from operational divisions of the church (missions, congregational services, etc.), some from districts. Matters relating to ethical decisions may come from district memorials or may have originated with the church council through assignment of questions to a commission on church and society. Matters which are considered complex or controversial may be routed through one of the theological faculties [35] or through subcommittees including district officials, theologians, pastors, lay persons, and individuals regarded as having special expertise on the question. Such questions may then be referred to the districts for discussion before they are sent on to the church convention. Alternatively they may be sent in to the Lutheran Council in the USA for discussion by a committee involving representatives of all four member churches. This ensures a wider base in theological reflection and also provides the possibility of common Lutheran action on a problem. If a problem involves international issues, the work of committees of the LWF or World Council of Churches may be consulted. The work of other church bodies or of committees of the National Council of Churches may also be consulted.

The decision-making procedure of the ALC thus involves many persons and agencies and is perhaps more fluid and variable than that of most other Lutherans, a fact some would attribute to the high incidence of persons of Norwegian descent in its membership. But other Lutherans have similar, if less complex, procedures for arriving at decisions on questions of a doctrinal or an ethical nature. Most would involve synodical leaders, theologians, pastors, and lay persons, and many would look for persons with competence in the human sciences as an assurance that the decision-making process confront issues as they actually are today.

Lutheran Equivalents of Infallibility

As we have already noted, the *Augsburg Confession* asserts that "one holy Christian church will be and remain forever." [36] In the apologetic context of the *Augsburg Confession* this is an attempt to identify with classical catholic ecclesiology. To most theologians of the period the statement would have had both epistemological and ontological implications. The Church that continues forever is the same Church that is preserved in the truth of the gospel. The indefectibility of the Church is seen as a consequence of the faithfulness of God, who through his Word and gracious presence among his people preserves them in the truth. This is not because of any qualities in the community or its Ministry but because of God's sovereign faithfulness.

The postconfessional development in Lutheranism showed two distinct theological lines.[37] The first is the scholastic line which reinterprets Luther in scholastic categories (in spite of his vehement attack upon scholasticism as an Aristotelian distortion of the gospel). In their polemic against Roman Catholic theology these Lutheran scholastics met the claim of magisterial infallibility with an attempt to relocate infallibility in the Church, in the Word of God, or in the Scriptures. The traditional doctrine of inspiration was heightened in the direction of a dictation theory of inspiration: [38] God has given us the assurance of the truth of the Scriptures by the Spirit's activity in providing the writers of the sacred books not only the general idea of what they are to write, but the very words. Thus Calov affirmed that "all the particulars contained in the Holy Scriptures" have been given "by the special dictation, inspiration and suggestion of the Holy Spirit." [39] Hollaz declared that the Holy Spirit has preserved the writers from all error in the writing of the divine word.[40] Hutter went on to say: "Although God did not directly write the Scriptures, but used prophets and apostles as his pen and instrument, yet the Scripture is not, on that account, of any the less authority. For it is God, and indeed God alone, who inspired the prophets and apostles, not only as they spoke, but also as they wrote; and he made use of their lips, their tongues, their hands, their pen. Therefore, or in this respect, the Scriptures, as they are, were written by God himself. For the prophets and apostles were merely instruments." [41]

It is interesting to note that these same theologians treated the doctrine of the Word of God in a somewhat different way in another context in their theology.[42] The statements above are drawn from their theological prolegomena, in which they sought to establish the authority of the Word of God in the Scriptures. In their discussion of the means of grace they were closer to Luther, and spoke of the Word of God in the dialectic of law and gospel, thus fending off the danger of literalism and legalism which stalks their theory of inspiration.

A second line of Lutheran theology is found in the salvation-history tradition, flowing from Luther to A. Bengel,

J. T. Beck, J. C. K. von Hofmann, and Sören Kierkegaard.[43] These theologians stress the historical, existentialist, and christological accents in Luther's theology. They see the element of infallibility not in the Scriptures but rather in the Word of God, which must of course be seen in relation to Scripture but also is to be distinguished from it. This approach follows Luther's emphasis on the Church as a "mouth-house" rather than a "book-house," [44] a community which lives by the living proclamation of the Word of God, i.e. the communication of the crucified and risen Christ in sermon and sacrament.

These theologians can speak of an indefectibility of the Church because the Church is God's creation and the object of his care. But this infallibility is not negotiable by members of the Church; it always resides in the sovereign lordship of God. Where the Lutheran scholastics can speak of the truth of theological propositions and of propositional truths, the salvation-history theologians think of truth as truth in Christ, truth which transcends the propositions but which is witnessed to by the propositions.

We can honor the Lutheran scholastics for their valiant defense of the Reformation cause under extremely difficult conditions, but most of us find it impossible to follow them in their attempt to establish the infallibility of Scripture. The rock on which this theology ultimately founders is Scripture itself. Scripture has little interest in the doctrine of inspiration and less in infallibility and inerrancy as these terms are used by the Lutheran scholastic tradition. Scripture and the language in which it is written share in the relativity of the cultures from which they rise far more deeply than these theologians recognize. The Lutheran theological future lies much more along the lines of Hofmann and Kierkegaard, who saw the historical relativity of the Scriptures, the ecumenical creeds, and the Lutheran Confessions, and also penetrated more deeply into the problems of language. Developments in the human sciences and in the study of language require that we push on even beyond these positions.

8

A RAHNER-KUNG DEBATE
AND ECUMENICAL
POSSIBILITIES

Carl J. Peter

Not a few Roman Catholics react in an embarrassed fashion when there is mention of papal infallibility. They seem to regard the dogma in question as an albatross around their church's neck. In recent years a number of historians and theologians have tried to lighten this burden. In the case of Hans Küng, the effort has led to a denial of magisterial infallibility. On the other hand, Karl Rahner and others have criticized Küng's position sharply. They have proposed not the rejection but rather a reinterpretation of the dogmatic decree *Pastor aeternus*, in which the definition of papal infallibility was promulgated by the First Vatican Council in 1870. It is to some ecumenical implications of this dispute among Roman Catholic theologians that this essay will address itself. In the process the author will argue that:

a) the resolution of this theological debate among Roman Catholics about the meaning and grounds for the dogma of papal infallibility is not within sight;

b) this lack of consensus among Roman Catholics poses problems for ecumenical efforts aimed at bringing the two traditions represented in this bilateral consultation closer together;

c) progress may nevertheless be made toward greater unity if theologians in the traditions of Trent and Augsburg can arrive at a consensus about the degree of confidence Christians can have regarding their belief in the final and unsurpassable character of God's revelation in Jesus Christ.

A Moment of Clarification

The month of May in 1973 saw a significant exchange of letters between Karl Rahner and Hans Küng about infallibility. After the publication of this correspondence, one thing stood out very clearly. Neither of the two had given up the position he had taken earlier. Küng had argued against infallibility; Rahner had defended the dogma. This remained true after they entered into their working agreement to disagree. Neither wished the cold war between them to continue; both thought détente was desirable. It may help to cite their own words.

Küng described the dispute with Rahner in the following way:

In the concrete aspects of our theology (as distinct from methods), even the differences are often extremely slight and scarcely perceptible to the non-specialist. Is it surprising, then, that some of our mutual friends are wondering what we were really fighting about? Nevertheless it was not an idle skirmish between theologians. For with all our readiness—I hope, on both sides—to make concessions, you presumably will not be able any more now than formerly to admit that even a solemn papal or conciliar definition could (though not necessarily "must") in principle be not merely "historically" restricted, limited, inadequate, dangerous, one-sided, mingled with error and therefore open to correction, but—measured by the Gospel itself—downright erroneous. Here then would lie the persistent slight difference.[1]

Küng continued by noting that very likely both participants had said as much as they could profitably at that point. If so, he suggested, then the time had come to let the question rest and leave the judgment to history. If it turns out that the power to produce infallible propositions is in fact given to persons with the assistance of the Holy Spirit, why, he asks, should he be disturbed? Peace between the two means that Rahner should allow his (Küng's) view to stand as Catholic; he (Küng) seeks acceptance as the

Catholic theologian he would like to be.[2] In short Küng does *not* accept as adequate Rahner's reinterpretation of the teaching of Vatican I on papal infallibility. But neither does he hold that compromise or peaceful coexistence with that position is excluded by the Word of God revealed in Jesus Christ.

Rahner for his part replied:

You are right when you say I shall presumably not admit that even a solemn papal or conciliar definition could (though not necessarily "must") in principle be not merely historically restricted, limited, open to correction, but measured against the Gospel itself—downright erroneous.[3]

As to the supremacy of conscience, Rahner said his conscience forbids him in such cases to be a higher authority than the Church and therefore able to reject such propositions as mistaken.[4] With regard to describing Küng as a liberal Protestant, he pleaded innocent and claimed that he:

. . . merely said that on this one question I could only argue as if I were dealing with a liberal Protestant, for whom a council and Scripture are not absolutely binding forces, particularly not in the sense of a presupposed inerrancy—which the nonliberal Protestant claims at least for Scripture.[5]

Rahner did not think that the question of whether Küng's view may be regarded as Catholic needed to be decided in the immediate future merely by a Roman verdict. For his own part he (Rahner) saw no solution other than that contained in the definition of Vatican I, correctly interpreted and at the same time applied to the present situation. He hoped that such an interpretation and Küng's view—"better expressed and given a more Catholic stamp"—could be made to coincide.

In other words, neither participant in the debate about infallibility withdrew his objections to the other's position. The consequence was that both were at odds, agreed to disagree, and urged something of a wait-and-see policy.

A word of interpretation may be appropriate at this point. In the dispute between Küng and Rahner, each seemed to regard the other's position as at least a possible threat to the gospel. That this is the case can be shown by posing the same question to both.

Can solemn papal or conciliar definitions be mistaken or

erroneous when measured against the gospel? Küng answered this question affirmatively while Rahner said he
had to reply negatively, not merely as a Roman Catholic
but as a Christian and theologian conscious of the Church's
nature. Christian commitment and conscience required of
the one what they did not in the case of the other, although
each asserted his identity as a Roman Catholic theologian.
Put in this context, the issue between them was indeed—
to repeat Küng's words—no idle skirmish. What the gospel
does or does not require absolutely in instances of solemn
papal or conciliar definitions makes the difference between
Rahner and Küng one of concern to each—because to that
same gospel both cling in hope of salvation. Yet the threat
each sees in the position of the other is not of such a
magnitude (in the opinion of either) as to throw the Roman
Catholic community into a state of urgent crisis or peril.

An Official Reaction

Shortly thereafter, in June of 1973, the Roman Congregation for the Doctrine of the Faith issued a document
entitled *Mysterium Ecclesiae;* this had been ratified, confirmed, and ordered published by Pope Paul VI on May
11th of that same year.[6] The form was that of a declaration made in defense of the Catholic doctrine of the
Church against certain errors of the present day. The
content unequivocally reasserted magisterial infallibility,
primarily by means of references to papal and conciliar
documents. Given the unmistakable intent of the document—to react negatively to Küng's position—it may be
helpful to offer the following observations.

In the first place, *Mysterium Ecclesiae* affirms, in the
face of denials, that the Church and its magisterium can
indeed teach the Word of God infallibly. Despite this
frankness the tone is not harsh. Roman Catholic theologians had argued publicly and loudly over this subject.
They had not always observed the same moderation in
criticizing one another's positions. Indeed they had re-
sorted to name-calling. In the letter cited at the beginning
of this paper, Küng said he heartily wished Rahner would
stop describing him—to the joy of their common opponents—as a liberal Protestant. Rahner retorted by distin-

guishing between Küng and this one position held by Küng
—which still needed "a more Catholic stamp." He in turn
spoke of Küng's letter as conciliatory and ". . . not at all
like some of the observations directed at me in *Fallible?*" [7]
A bitter criticism emanating from Roman authorities in
such circumstances would not have been without precedent. Fortunately any temptation to react in this fashion
was resisted. The meaning of *Mysterium Ecclesiae* is clear
enough to make it unwelcome and unacceptable to many
Christians.[8] There is however an admirable restraint manifested in its tone. To Lutherans who look in hope for signs
of a papacy renewed in the light of the gospel, this ought
to be of some significance.

Second, it is important to call attention to the attitude
the document manifests toward Roman Catholic theologians.
That attitude is not one of antagonism. To be sure, readers
are reminded that theologians remain subordinate to the
living *magisterium* of the Church. To the latter, however,
theologians can be of considerable assistance in dealing
with the historical conditioning of the human words in
which God's Word has been expressed over the centuries.[9]
This admission is an important one. Theology arises from
the faith of believers; by a critical and honest inquiry into
the meaning and grounds of that same faith, theologians
can make a real contribution to the believing community
to which they belong. They have, to be sure, often enough
in the past lacked the freedom their discipline requires if
such service is to be rendered. Be that as it may, a reminder that wanting to be of assistance to the faith of
believers is not always the same as actually being of such
assistance was still timely. Theologians need to be reminded of how complex the needs of believers are. It is
not really fair then to object to *Mysterium Ecclesiae* for
such a warning, which it undeniably contains.

Third, *Mysterium Ecclesiae* has ecumenical implications in what it has to say about infallibility. Here the
document relies heavily on the teaching of the Second
Vatican Council and calls attention to what had been a
matter of public record for the better part of a decade. It
emphasizes the hierarchical nature of the people of God,
as had the Council in the third chapter of the *Constitution
on the Church*. Bishops and the pope have a unique role in

the Church; in teaching they have been promised divine
protection from error in certain circumstances. The same
Council, to be sure, had also enunciated principles of subsidiarity and collegiality, which clearly introduce relationships affecting the exercise of papal and episcopal teaching.
It also spoke of the confession and witness that are to be
expected from all members of God's people because of
Baptism. These other teachings of Vatican II are not
stressed by *Mysterium Ecclesiae* as much as the ability of
bishops and the pope to teach infallibly in certain circumstances and under certain conditions. (The opposite
has been the case with quite a few theologians.) Such a
phenomenon of different emphasis or even selective reading
has precedent in the history of earlier conciliar decrees. To
cite but one example: it takes real care to give equal emphasis to the two natures and one person of Jesus Christ.
History bears witness that such care has not always been
taken by those who subscribe to the Chalcedonian formula.
This is not a criticism either of the theologians or of
Mysterium Ecclesiae. Care to strike a delicate balance
between various aspects of a mystery is not the only legitimate motivation for the publication of research by a
theologian or for a public statement by the magisterium
of the Church. Each may think a particular point needs
special emphasis and proceed accordingly. That clearly
was the case with *Mysterium Ecclesiae*. When an issue
cannot be resolved on theological grounds to the satisfac-
tion of the participants, when the dispute is not an idle
skirmish or when Christian values are at stake in the view
of all involved, one has no right to demand silence from
the church's teaching office. If in such circumstances the
magisterium reasserts an official doctrine, Lutherans have
a right to object if the doctrine in question is in their view
clearly at odds with the gospel. In their exchange of letters neither Küng nor Rahner said this is the case with
papal infallibility. In *Mysterium Ecclesiae* one finds a re-
assertion of what was already the teaching of Vatican II
about infallibility. The publication of such a document is
not ecumenical perfidy; it is rather an indication that official Roman Catholic doctrine on this issue remains what it
was said to be by the Council, notwithstanding unresolved
and serious theological questions. Ecumenical progress may

well be fostered by such a candid statement of Catholic convictions.

As to the explanations that *Mysterium Ecclesiae* gives for the position it takes on infallibility, there is something left to be desired. At times being convinced is simply not enough; a teacher has to try to be convincing, especially when offering supposed grounds for a conviction. If the Congregation for the Doctrine of the Faith felt it should reassert the teaching of Vatican Councils I and II, it might well have tried harder to be convincing. To be sure, that would not have been easy with an audience scattered throughout the world and characterized by such cultural diversity. What one actually finds in *Mysterium Ecclesiae* is the expression of the conviction that in certain circumstances the Church is by God's grace infallible in believing and teaching. I share that conviction and understand it in much the same way Karl Rahner does.[10] That means accepting the corresponding teaching of Vatican I and II with the proviso that both need to be interpreted to see how they help express the gospel in the situation of the present day. Transcendental method appears, at least in my opinion, to be the most promising philosophical theory to warrant the conviction that time-conditioned language can express infallible truth. I know many find that theory and indeed that conviction about infallibility very questionable. But does the Roman Catholic Church have to wait to take a stand, wait, that is, until all philosophical difficulties have been dealt with adequately? I do not think so. But I am also of the mind that it is important to recognize the questioning of the dogma of infallibility by serious scholars; their objections are far from frivolous. My strongest argument is that the objections to the dogma in question on the grounds of the impossibility of infallible propositions strike equally against the confession of Jesus Christ as the unique and final revealer of God. Nevertheless, *Mysterium Ecclesiae* would have had a better chance of helping people in doubt if it had faced up to those objections more effectively. When grounds are offered for a dogma, it is important (at least today) that they manifest full cognizance of the difficulties involved. *Mysterium Ecclesiae* might have done much better on this score. Of course by admitting some historical conditioning of dogmatic expressions, it left room for further investigation of what the infallibility asserted by Vatican Councils I and II may mean in a broadened cultural and Christian horizon. As to the *theological* dispute regarding infallibility, it may be around for a good while, especially since Roman Catholics can and do live their faith in a way that is directly affected very little by this controversy.[11]

Consequent Ecumenical Problems

If the Lutheran-Roman Catholic Dialogue in the United States had not long ago placed the question of magisterial infallibility on its agenda, room would likely have to be made for the topic at present. The reason is that what may appear to be a purely Catholic dispute has implications that affect other Christians as well.

This is due to the fact that at least those Roman Catholics who work in the rarefied atmosphere where such issues are heatedly debated are seriously divided as to what the implications of God's Word are in some instances they regard as crucial. As late as May of 1973 Karl Rahner, when asked by Küng to state whether his (Küng's) opinion was Roman Catholic, did not choose to do so without qualification. On the major point of difference between them Rahner said his own reaction came as a Christian and theologian, one conscious of the Church's nature. He hoped his own interpretation of Vatican I and Küng's opinion would coincide in the future. But it was Küng's position that needed further clarification and a more Catholic stamp. From the other side, even in his "conciliatory" letter when contrasting his method with that of Rahner, Küng described his colleague's approach as speculative and transcendental while his own was evangelical. One Catholic in this dispute holds that accepting as infallible some propositions that were formulated in the past (however unlikely it may be that new definitions will be made in the future) is sometimes required by the gospel. The other does not. It would be surprising if Lutherans did not find this of more than peripheral interest in their concern for the well-being of all churches, the Roman Catholic included. Even if there were no questions on the part of Lutheran pastors and their congregations as to what has happened to Roman

Catholic claims regarding infallibility, the controversy could hardly be dismissed as insignificant in a consideration of closer union between Lutheran churches and those of the Roman Catholic confession. Lutherans ought to be able to appreciate the importance of what to many must appear to be an idle skirmish.

Can Lutherans help in this situation? Quite possibly! They might request that the terminology of the participants in the dispute be clarified. Perhaps a question will show how this request could prove to be of assistance.

Is there an ambiguity present in the positions taken by Küng and *Mysterium Ecclesiae?* Rahner thinks there may be. Is the error that Küng will not exclude as impossible in solemn dogmatic definitions all that different from that historical incompleteness which even *Mysterium Ecclesiae* admits in some dogmas? Rahner is not sure.[12] Neither Küng nor Rome has said, he continues, what is meant by an erroneous proposition as distinguished from a true one whose historical conditioning and incompleteness call for future rearticulation. And this is not splitting hairs; the positions may not be incompatible if the dispute involves different usages of the word *erroneous*. The Lutheran members of this dialogue might at the very least expect of their Catholic counterparts efforts corresponding to those taken earlier to define the meaning of the *Petrine function,* but this time applied to the term *erroneous*.

Along the same line, it will be recalled that in giving his description of the historical conditioning possible even in solemn papal or conciliar definitions, Küng included the phrase "mingled with error." In his reply Rahner left those words out. Prescinding from the inclusion and omission, the Lutheran members of this dialogue might ask the Catholic members whether a solemn papal or conciliar definition may be mingled with error even if, when measured by the gospel, it would not be downright erroneous.[13]

Rahner maintains that there have been no solemn definitions that when measured by the gospel are downright erroneous. Do the Lutheran and Catholic members of the dialogue agree on this? Especially in view of the permanent truth ascribed to dogmatic definitions in a statement issued by members of the International Pontifical Commission of Theologians, such a question seems to call for an answer.[14]

Both traditions represented in this dialogue look to the eschaton for the final validation and perfection of faith. From this perspective all confessional formulae are provisional, even the infallible definitions of Roman Catholics.[15] But it is also true that both traditions regard doctrinal differences as obstacles that must not be ignored in efforts to achieve closer union between Christian churches that have been seriously divided for centuries. However provisional the formulations of dogma may be in relation to eternity, differences about infallibility between Lutherans and Roman Catholics are too significant to be brushed aside as inconsequential—this in the name of the unity that already exists between the two confessions.

A Suggestion for the Dialogue

What then can this dialogue do as it attempts to clarify the issues and reduce the differences? It might look to christology while continuing its work in ecclesiology. Perhaps the following will help to explain what this might involve.

". . . I shall argue that probably every religion, and certainly Christianity, is committed to affirming the infallibility of at least some of its central affirmations." [16] This has been described as "intrasystematic infallibility." [17] That in Jesus Christ God has revealed himself in a final and unsurpassable way is a prime example of such an infallible affirmation. With regard to the unswerving confidence Christians should have in this conviction, the members of this dialogue should be able to reach genuine agreement. If that is so, they might try to give joint witness to this shared conviction and to render an account of their hope in as credible a way as possible. The very effort to do so might put into proper context the differences about infallibility that have yet to be resolved.

9

INFALLIBILITY:
A STRUCTURAL ANALYSIS

George H. Tavard

Contemporary linguistics is an explosive science which goes in many directions. Several major currents have been left out of the present essay, notably the one deriving from the philosophy of Ludwig Wittgenstein (to be treated by Prof. George Lindbeck) and American structuralism, which itself has many aspects, from Edward Sapir's anthropological approach to language and Leonard Bloomfield's mechanistic postulates to Noam Chomsky's transformational-generative grammar (used in theology by Erhardt Güttgemanns). My work will be limited to the European structuralism deriving from Ferdinand de Saussure.[1]

I

In keeping with the definitions of Vatican Councils I and II, infallibility is a predicate with four possible subjects:[2]

    (a) the speaker of a discourse (e.g. the pope);
    (b) a discourse (a definition of faith);
    (c) the office of a speaker of a discourse (the papacy);
    (d) the context in which a discourse is pronounced (the conditions for *ex cathedra* definitions).

Thus infallibility raises problems of a linguistic order, in "a" and "b"; of an institutional order, in "c"; of a contextual order, in "d." "A" and "b" are closely related, since according to Vatican I and II it is not anyone, but rather the bishop of Rome, who makes infallible discourses. (For clarity's sake I will not consider the question of the infallibility of councils, or bishops teaching doctrine with the unanimity of the episcopal college, and of the Church in general). 'A" and "c" imply each other, since the speaker "a" is the holder of the office "c." "B" and "d" imply each other, since by definition the discourse "b" takes place only in the context of the conditions "d."

We may obtain a first approximation of the problem by looking at the articulation of action in A. J. Greimas' analysis: [3]

addressor ————▶   OBJECT ————▶   addressee

ally —————▶   SUBJECT ————▶   adversary

This diagram reads: a subject, assisted by an ally and opposed by an adversary, catches an object sent by an addressor to an addressee. Such is the basic structure of action-reporting stories.

This structure can be applied to Vatican I's account of the infallibility of the pope:

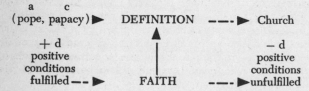

This diagram reads: Faith accepts as infallible a discourse addressed by the pope to the Church when it sees certain positive conditions fulfilled; it does not accept such a discourse as infallible when it does not see these conditions fulfilled.

Infallibility was examined at Vatican I and II in relation to "a, c," the addressor, and "d," the conditions for *ex cathedra* definitions. A preliminary question relating to "b," the subject/object, or the relationship between *faith* and *definition* (or, *dogma*), was left unexamined, being presumably taken for granted. Yet this question is basic to the whole infallibility construct: Can a discourse ever be recognized as infallible? It would be rash to assume that the answer to this question must necessarily be affirmative. For faith can recognize a discourse as infallible only if infallibility is compatible with the inner structure of human discourse.

I will address myself to this question by briefly examining (II) the elementary structure of signification in the light of Greimas' analysis, (III) and (IV) theology as language in the light of Hjelmslev's glossematics, (V) the doctrine of infallibility in the light of the structure of myth. This will lead to (VI) some suggestions for a reinterpretation of the doctrine of infallibility.

II

The notion of infallibility is a complex notion which involves at least two elements: the notion of truth (the infallible discourse is true), and that of obligation (the infallible discourse must be accepted by faith, as implied in the anathemas of Vatican I against those who would deny the doctrine). I will examine a third element later.

These two elements may be viewed in relation to the quadrilateral of meaning.[4] Meaning implies that four terms can be placed in correlation, namely a term, its contradictory or antithesis or negation, its opposite (in the sense of opposite but not antithetic), and the contradictory of its opposite. Applying this to something (doctrine, injunction, or whatever) which could be true and obligatory, we obtain the following quadrilateral:

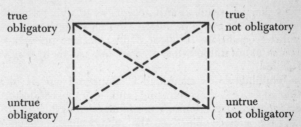

true obligatory		true not obligatory
untrue obligatory		untrue not obligatory

It appears immediately that, if the truth of a discourse is intrinsic to it and can be verified with appropriate rules of verification, the obligation to believe it for membership in a church is not intrinsic to it; the obligation to believe it can be verified only by reference to something which is outside the discourse itself, namely the rules of adhesion to the church. A discourse is true or untrue in itself. Its legally binding value for the members of the church depends, not on the discourse as such, but on the rules of the church. This corresponds to the distinction between theological truth and canonical obligation. Analysis of a discourse may possibly verify its truth; it cannot verify the legal system of the church.

Thus the scope of my investigation is restricted to what may be said about the language of discourse. That a certain discourse is used in a further "game" to define church membership raises problems of another order, which I will not examine here.

III

Theological statements (to which I will assimilate dogmatic definitions, which are one kind of theological statements) are samples of a language usually called *theology*. Theologies are technical languages using the resources of natural languages. We know that the natural language used (English, French, German, Latin, Greek, etc.) is not indifferent to the sort of theology one elaborates. What is not realized so often is: first, that as a language every theology necessarily follows the basic structure of all language; second, that as a technical language each theology creates its own rules in the light of its basic axioms.

In Hjelmslev's analysis, the basic structure of language contains five characteristics: [5]

a) A language has two levels, expression and content.

b) A language is structured along two axes, that of discourse (process, text), which may be imaginatively represented as horizontal, and that of system (represented as vertical), according to which the component elements of discourse are related to one another.

c) Expression and content are related; and relationship can be discovered and verified by commutation (as when the content changes with changes in the expression).

d) A language is made of units of meaning related to

one another by "rection" (necessary implication, which may be unilateral or bilateral) and combination (nonnecessary implication).

e) There is nonconformity between expression and content: although closely related, these are not related by necessary implication.

This analysis suggests a preliminary reflection. Since a theological discourse (for example, the Constitution *Pastor aeternus* of Vatican I) depends on the theological system in which it is composed, it can be properly understood only within that system. Criticism made in the context of another system is not a useful exercise. Criticism ought to be made either within the same system (showing, as it may happen, that the language has been used improperly) or in the light of a metalanguage applicable to the discourse which is being examined.

Languages function through the use of certain numbers of units of meaning. Sense emerges when units of meaning are combined according to certain rules or conventions. In classical grammar, the units of meaning correspond to semantics, the rules of combination to syntax. The units of meaning are signs whose meaning is elicited by their combination according to the syntax of the language. A basic principle of the structural analysis of language defines the sign as including two aspects, that which signifies (the expression) and that which is signified (the content).[6] This distinguishes the linguistic sign from chemical and mathematical symbols, from esthetic symbols, and from philosophical and theological differentiations between signal, sign, and symbol (as in Paul Tillich's theology). A linguistic sign does not point to something else. That which it points to is part of it. The levels of expression and of content are distinct but inseparable.

Following Hjelmslev, one may analyze this further.[7] In a sign there is, striking first the eye (in reading) or the ear (in hearing), *the form of the expression;* we perceive sounds or their written equivalents. This form of the expression conveys *the substance of the expression;* sounds or written alphabetic symbols are perceived as units of meaning combined in a certain way. This substance of the expression conveys *the form of the content;* each language has its own ways of combining units of meaning so that sense will emerge. The form of the content elicits the meaning intended by the form of the expression; this meaning is *the substance of the content*. Thus the linguistic sign has four interrelated components. The form of the expression is the (audible, readable) form of the syntactic form of the content. The substance of the content is the (intelligible) substance of the (intended) substance of the expression. The form of the expression conveys the substance of the content by means of the substance of the expression organized as the form of the content.

This analysis suggests some reflections on the famous distinction between the substance of the faith and its formulation, a distinction promoted by John XXIII and widely accepted since Vatican Council II:

The substance of the ancient doctrine of the deposit of faith is one thing, and the way in which it is presented is another.[8]

In this quotation the distinction between substance and formulation is carried to the point of separation. But the previous analysis of a linguistic sign makes such a separation unacceptable. Expression and content are not so exterior to each other that several expressions (signs in the banal sense of the word) can cover one content indifferently. "Son of God," "Word of God," "Second Person," and "Lord" are not interchangeable expressions equally applicable to the same divine reality. They are expressions of different aspects of the same reality, covering different contents. The linguistic status of a doctrine ties together the formulation and the substance within the framework of a given theology. The formulation (the form of the expression) and the substance of the doctrine (the substance of the content) are joined together by two mediating levels, the substance of the expression and the form of the content. The substance of the expression may be identified as the theological categories (paradigms) used. The form of the content corresponds to the construction of these categories according to the relevant theological syntax into a recognizable pattern of meaning.

Thus it is not sufficient to say, with Hans Küng, that papal infallibility is a clumsy formulation of the indefectibility of the Church. It is indeed legitimate to attempt to restate the substance of the content (*e.g.* the notion of papal infallibility) in the vocabulary and syntax of another theology. But this, successful or not, does not tell against the unique relationship of formulation and substance in the discourse of Vatican I. This points up the problem of theological translation, which is strictly parallel to that of translation from one natural language into another. No two languages are exactly isotopic.[9] "I do not know" may be translated as, but does not equal *Je re sais pas;* it can also be translated as *Je ne connais pas* and as *J'ignore,* and these expressions convey differences of meaning. If a French speaker understands "I do not know" as meaning *Je ne sais pas,* this is not because the substance of the two contents are identical (they are not), but because they are mutually recognizable. The two somewhat different senses convey, besides their special connotations, a denotation which evokes one metasense, namely the common experience of not knowing.

These remarks throw some light on the problem, debated since the Middle Ages, of the object of faith. For Thomas Aquinas, followed by all modern theology, the act of faith has as its object God's self-revelation.[10] The *enuntiabile* or formulated doctrine about God's self-revelation is only the instrument by which God revealing himself claims the attention of our intellect by entering our epistemic field. It is obvious, however, that God reveals himself through linguistic signs (the Scriptures, the Word of God). These signs must themselves be the object of faith if indeed a linguistic sign includes not only the exterior instrument of communication but also the intended and grasped meaning. Meaning is an integral part of the sign. Within the oneness of a theological sign, therefore, the *enuntiabile* and God must constitute one joint object of faith. Applying this to the notion of infallibility, we should say either that infallibility is properly (not necessarily, fully, or exhaustively) formulated as an object of faith by its definition, or that the definition, being unfaithful to the syntax of its theological language, is a nondefinition conveying no recognizable meaning. To these alternatives we should also add two others: the notion thus properly defined is verified as nonexistent, or it is nonverifiable. The former alternatives depend on the linguistic analysis of theology; the latter do not, but refer to theology as epistemology.

Since de Saussure, structural analysis has insisted on the arbitrariness (nonnecessity) of both semantics and syntax.[11] If this is the case, then the definition of infallibility can be accepted as true only by those who admit the arbitrary aspects of its theological language. For instance, in the definition of Vatican I, there can be papal infallibility only if infallibility has been bestowed by God upon the Church, and if the bishop of Rome, under certain conditions, is the instrument of it: infallibility of the Church is a metalinguistic principle expressed by a given theology in the form of papal infallibility. The same metalinguistic principle may conceivably be expressed differently by other theological languages. We then face again, however, the problem of translation. *Expressed* differently, one metalinguistic principle will be *understood* differently. If no doctrine keeps exactly the same meaning when it is translated into other *natural* languages, all the more will its meaning be bent by translation into other *theological* languages. This of course raises a much more radical question than that of infallibility; the notion of doctrinal orthodoxy is involved.

IV

Once the content of a discourse has been perceived, one may verify its truth or untruth: by way of empirical verification in the case of empirical statements, by way of metaphysical reasoning in the case of metaphysical statements, by way of comparison with the sources of theological certainty (revelation, Scripture, tradition, reason, or a combination thereof) in the case of theological statements. Usually such verification will be made after the expression of the doctrine has been understood and systematically examined.

The hypothesis of papal infallibility, however, posits a special difficulty in that the theological discourse considered to be infallible (e.g. the definition of Mary's Assumption) would not only convey something true, the truth of which would be verifiable by theological research; it would also be known as conveying something true antecedently to the perception of its content. This is the third element in the notion of infallibility. An observer could draw conclusions about the infallibility of a doctrine by investigating the circumstances of its formulation. After examining who spoke, concerning what kind of question, in what capacity, with what intent, one would verify if the four conditions of *ex cathedra* parlance as listed by Vatican I have been met. In other words, the complex of signs constituting a presumably infallible definition would contain more than the four levels that are constitutive of a linguistic sign. There would also be some sort of nonlinguistic (belonging to other categories than those of language) and extralinguistic (not expressed in language) form subsuming the form of the expression and its content. Clearly, the structural analysis of language can say nothing for or against the existence of such nonlinguistic and extralinguistic conditioning of discourse, which would, by definition, escape its analytical methods.

Since, however, the content of a sign is part of the sign, the meaning of a doctrinal definition is part of the definition. Anyone who analyzes and tests it according to the criteria of the language in which it is couched should be able to assess its truth or falsity. Obviously truth is not taken here in the thomist sense of *adequatio intellectus et rei*. The truth of a sign is its meaning. To judge that this meaning is true in the thomist sense must be done by the verification proceedings which are valid in the context of the theology in use. Analysis of a doctrine may lead to a conclusion regarding its meaning as sign and to another regarding its truth as *adequatio intellectus et rei*. But there is no way in which the analysis of a doctrine can make an antecedent judgment as required by the notion of infallibility. We face the peculiar situation that a doctrine preached, let us say by Father Joe Smith, may be judged to be correct though not infallible, while the same doctrine proclaimed by Pius XII in the proper *ex cathedra* conditions would be judged to be both true and infallible. The meaning of a formulation of doctrine may be discerned in its language; its truth may be verified with the proper criteria. But infallibility would belong to another order. It cannot pertain to the language, natural or theological, which is the vehicle of the doctrine. If infallibility is affirmed, it must be predicated of something other than the formula in which a doctrine is expressed. But as there is no doctrine apart from its formulation, infallibility cannot logically be predicated of any doctrine. So far, therefore, it would seem that of the four possibilities listed above as to the status of the discourse of Vatican I, the second one applies: it is a nondefinition, conveying no recognizable meaning, because it postulates the existence of a nonexistent, namely the recognizability of the truth of a discourse before that discourse has been formulated.

In linguistic parlance, infallibility therefore cannot belong to the denotation or denotative meaning of the terms used, but, in certain circumstances, to their connotation.[12] It belongs to the connotation of terms which are used within the recognizable constellation constituted by the conditions for *ex cathedra* definitions. We would say that infallibility attaches to a statement *in obliquo,* not *in recto.* We could also say, in Hjelmslev's language, that it is not expressed in the language used but is one of the elements of an overarching "connotative semiotic": "A connotative semiotic is a semiotic which is not a language and whose level of expression is constituted by the levels of content and of expression of a denotative semiotic." [13] In this case one should try to discover the nature of the connotation and the structure of its recognizability. But this takes us outside of linguistic analysis in the strict sense.

V

Yet another type of structural analysis may be appropriate. The doctrine of papal infallibility reveals a certain structure within the Roman Catholic Church. This structure has to do with the relationships of various segments of the Church with the doctrines which, as objects of faith, bind the Church together: when certain conditions are met, a positive relationship between a doctrinal formulation and the Church may be asserted antecedently to the emergence of the intrinsic meaning of the doctrine involved. More specifically, one may gather the following propositions from Vatican Councils I and II:

1. There exists an undetermined infallibility of the Church. (Undetermined means that the nature and conditions of it have not been clearly ascertained).

2. This infallibility of the Church comes to determination in the bishop of Rome speaking *ex cathedra.*

3. Other bishops, when in ecumenical councils or in the consensus of their teaching, also share in determining the infallibility of the Church; yet the modes of this sharing themselves remain largely undetermined.

4. Other church members share in determining the infallibility of the Church by their *sensus fidelium;* this also remains undetermined except when seen simply as assent to the infallibility of the Church in general and papal infallibility in particular.

5. The *sensus fidelium* may remain dormant, and this assent may be withheld by individual believers without ruining their effectiveness among church members in general.

The same points may be expressed differently:

1. The bishop of Rome has a positive, determined, antecedent relationship to the definition of doctrine.

2. The bishops as a college have a positive, undetermined, nonantecedent relationship to the definition of doctrine. (It is nonantecedent insofar as no conditions have been agreed upon by which its antecedence may be asserted; one might say that it is antecedently presumed but not certain.)

3. All members of the Church as people of God have a positive, undetermined, nonantecedent relationship to the definition of doctrine, which becomes determined in its assent to papal infallibility and less strictly determined in its assent to episcopal-conciliar infallibility.

4. All members (which includes bishops) individually have a negative, undetermined, nonantecedent relationship to the definition of doctrine, which becomes positive and determined in its assent to papal infallibility and to a lesser degree in its assent to episcopal-conciliar infallibility.

5. Unbelievers have a negative, determined, nonantecedent relationship to the definition of doctrine. (Yet there may also be antecedent unbelief, which will reject any defined doctrine as a matter of principle).

	formulation	determination	antecedence	*assensus*
Rome	+	+	+	+
College	+	−	−	+
sensus fidelium	+	−	−	+
individuals	−	−	−	+
unbelievers	−	+	+ or −	−

This may be translated into the basic structure of myth. For clarity's sake I will reduce the schema to four terms, dropping the Episcopal College as redundant since its infallibility functions "with and under" *(cum et sub)* the infallibility of the Roman Pontiff. I will also reduce the four points (formulation, determination, antecedence, and assent) to assent, since the negatives which appear in the first three columns are corrected by the positives of the fourth, except in the case of unbelievers, where negativity as to *assensus* is reinforced by the previous negatives and positives.

We obtain the formula:

$$\frac{\text{Rome}}{\text{unbeliever}} \quad \sim \quad \frac{\text{sensus fidelium}}{\text{believer}}$$

which derives from the quadrilateral:

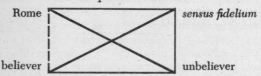

Rome   *sensus fidelium*

believer   unbeliever

The mythical content of the formula emerges when we replace each of these four terms by its equivalent in terms of relationship (kinship):

$$\frac{\text{relationship asserted}}{\text{relationship refused}} \quad \sim \quad \frac{\text{relationship presumed}}{\text{relationship accepted.}}$$

This corresponds well to the more theological terms:

$$\frac{\text{definition}}{\text{denial}} \quad \sim \quad \frac{\text{implicit acceptance}}{\text{explicit acceptance.}}$$

This analysis illustrates the problem of infallibility.

As analyzed by Claude Lévi-Strauss, *myth* constitutes, besides the two dimensions detected by de Saussure *(langue,* or the linguistic systems of semantics and syntax having synchronic consistency; *parole,* or the spoken flow of phonemes in which *la langue* comes to life in diachronic sequence), the third dimension of language.[14] Myth participates in both the fluency of *la parole* and the permanence of *la langue,* and in both the irreversibility of *la parole* and the reversibility of *la langue.* Its function is to provide language with an overall meaning in relation to human destiny; it acts as a metalanguage of all that we say. Furthermore, myth has been analyzed as illustrating relationships between power, forces of domination over human beings and nature, and ties of kinship. Kinship is the datum of human life, the nature with which one starts in society. Power is the ineluctable vocation of human life in its struggle for survival, the means by which nature is transformed by culture.[15]

Now the structure of salvation in Christianity subordinates the appropriation of the power of salvation to certain relationships to the Savior. The notion of papal infallibility subordinates the appropriation of the power of salvation (as formulated in doctrine) to kinship, not only with the Savior, but also with the bishop of Rome. Aspirants to salvation become recipients of it by assent through entering a positive kinship with the bishop of Rome speaking *ex cathedra.* The bishop of Rome alone has a twofold relationship to salvation as both recipient and formulator of saving doctrine. (Admittedly, nuances would be needed to give a complete picture; but the present streamlining usefully pinpoints the problem). We thus obtain a mythical structure of the Church, where the myth is built in terms of relationships to the saving doctrine which are positive or negative, or, in Lévi-Strauss's terms, overestimated ($+$) or underestimated($-$).

The basic structure of myth suggests that the notion of papal infallibility derives from a fundamental structure of language which emerges when language is used to delve into the deeper questions of human destiny. The theological language in which it appears has incorporated the third dimension of language, thus showing at the same time the linguistic status of infallibility and its correlation with the great religious myths of humankind. There is of course no suggestion that the mythical form of Christianity had to take this particular shape. One can then wonder why the mythical dimension of language has taken the form of papal infallibility in Roman Catholicism and what forms this mythical dimension has adopted in other Christian traditions.

Be that as it may, that papal infallibility partakes of the structure of myth points to the value it may still have as a positive element in theology.

Where does infallibility reside? I see three possibilities. One has often spoken of it as residing in the dogmatic definitions. But this should be ruled out. For if papal infallibility is antecedent, it cannot reside in the defined doctrine which results from it. Second, does it then reside in the bishop of Rome? If so, it would itself be an object of faith independently of any doctrinal definitions that may derive from it. It would then be a pure form with no other content than itself. But a faith without content cannot be the medium through which we receive God's self-revelation. This should also be ruled out.

A third hypothesis remains. Belief in a positive, determined, antecedent infallibility presupposes a prospective tension toward the future. If myth symbolically translates an eagerness to overcome the anguish of humankind before the ambiguities of existence, the infallibility myth expresses the hope that the diachronic unfolding of the Christian faith prepares positively for the ultimate unveiling of human destiny. Faith does not assent to the form of the myth but to its substance, to what it intends. It looks forward to an event when whoever embodies God's self-revelation in formulated doctrines will do so with the ultimate concern to express the truth under the unfailing guidance of the Spirit of God. The conditions for *ex cathedra* definitions may thus be seen as minimal tests assuring us that the bishop of Rome intends no other thing than to follow the Spirit. In this case, however, papal infallibility resides neither in the definition nor in the bishop of Rome intending to define it or defining it, but in the hope of the people of God that the Church will not be misled.

It would therefore seem that the *anathema sit* which follows the definition of papal infallibility at Vatican I was overoptimistic in seeing infallibility at the level of faith. It should have looked at it in the perspective of hope.

VI

Structural analysis should, at its best, provide some elements of a model for the point under study. Our analysis so far has led us to the conclusion that the definition of papal infallibility rests on the basic assumption that behind the Christian doctrines believed to be revealed by God in Christ, God's own Word to the faithful acts as a metalanguage. Being utterly true, like God himself who is, by hypothesis, the absolute Truth, this metalanguage leaves its imprint on the human formulation of what has been grasped of the revelation. Theoretically several possibilities could be open at this point:

1. The transcendent metalanguage is detected *a posteriori* through the analysis of formulations of doctrine.

2. It is detected at the very moment when doctrine is formulated: e.g. when we read the Scriptures or recite the Creed or listen to the proclaimed Word, this transcendent metalanguage is perceived as activating our language.

3. This metalanguage is foreseen even before a doctrine is formulated.

Thus the detection of God as the metalanguage of our faith language could be posterior to, simultaneous with, or anticipatory of the formulation of doctrine. The third hypothesis was selected by Vatican I as correct with respect to the infallibility of the bishop of Rome. Since, however, according to the same Council, papal infallibility depends on the convergence of four conditions which are considered necessary to the existence of an *ex cathedra* definition of doctrine, the element of anteriority is considerably attenuated. The Council assumed that one may have advance notice that a papal proclamation will be *ex cathedra*. But since we have no such previous certainty of a future event, the judgment that a papal pronouncement is infallible can only be made *a posteriori*, after the conditions under which the statement was made have been examined. In any case the condition relating to the revealed character of a doctrine can hardly appear before this doctrine has been examined carefully. Thus the third option (anteriority) presupposes the first (posteriority). But the notion of antecedent certainty of doctrine appears then to be absurd, since anteriority cannot depend on posteriority. The judgment that a doctrine is infallibly true can only be a retroactive judgment.

This allows us to discern several features of a satisfactory model for infallibility. (1) God is the metalanguage behind all doctrines considered to be infallible. (2) The judgment that a doctrine is imprinted with this metalanguage so that it may be called infallible is a temporal judgment, related to the doctrine by relationships of posteriority or anteriority. (3) An anteriority judgment of infallibility cannot bear on the doctrine itself, which is yet inexistent since it has not yet been formulated. It can bear, however, on the person who is likely to attempt to formulate it. In this case, the bishop of Rome is seen by anticipation as likely to proclaim a doctrine in the near or the distant future. Thus the judgment of infallibility belongs to the domain of hope and eschatology.

The structural analysis of myth allows us to go further in model-building. As the third dimension of language, myth becomes operative when language attempts to formulate insights into the ultimate destiny of humankind. As applied both to the pope as formulator and to the doctrine as formulated, infallibility suggests that such formulations belong to the very essence of the Christian faith as it touches on ultimate human destiny. But such a tie between the formulation of doctrine and ultimate human destiny cannot be restricted to occasional solemn pronouncements made by the bishop of Rome. The concept of infallibility should therefore be extended further than envisioned by Vatican I. One should add at least two points:

1. All Christian doctrines, insofar as they participate in the structure of myth, share the infallibility with which God, as metalanguage, marks the human expression of the divine self-revelation.

2. All persons who, in one capacity or another, formulate those Christian doctrines which relate to ultimate human destiny share the infallibility with which God, as metalan-

guage, marks those who formulate his self-revelation in human language.

Thus infallibility should be understood as a term expressing a believer's threefold attitude. *Knowing* that God is the absolute truth, a believer *hopes,* antecedently, that those who will formulate the Church's apprehension of revelation will do so with infallible certainty; when so satisfied, concommitantly or posteriorly, that they do so, the believer *assents* to the doctrines thus enunciated. Accordingly infallibility expresses both a horizontal and an eschatological relationship to God's revelatory epiphany by way of faith. It should be understood as an analogical participation in God which is effective in all Christian faith, is experienced by all Christian believers, and is expressed in all Christian discourse.

10

THE OFFICE OF TEACHING IN THE CHRISTIAN CHURCH ACCORDING TO THE NEW TESTAMENT

Joseph A. Fitzmyer

The discussion of infallibility as a characteristic of teaching within the Christian Church must ultimately rest on a consideration of what the New Testament (NT) contains about the role of teaching within the early Christian community, whose heritage guides the later church. But just as the function of papal primacy and the Ministry of the universal Church had to be recast in terms of the NT description of the Petrine function in that community, lest unwarranted anachronisms were to be foisted on the texts that bear in some way on the function,[1] so too the question of infallibility has to be approached. In this case the problem is even more delicate because, if NT data were found to provide some points on a trajectory—if only inceptive—of the Petrine function, the points in the issue of infallibility are decidedly less numerous and less unambiguous, if existent at all. *Infallibility*, as its etymology shows, emerged from a later, Latin theological tradition, and it is not a NT concept. For this reason the NT has to be interrogated in another, more basic way to see whether data found in it may describe the function of teaching within the early Christian community and its character.

I hope to show that, even if infallibility in preaching and teaching is not a NT concept, there is in the NT a concern for authoritative teaching, a teaching function, and even traces of a Ministry of authoritative teaching. But before I try to assemble and order what such data may be, a few preliminary remarks are in order explaining the objective of this paper and its mode of procedure.

First there is the question whether *teaching* differs from *preaching*. Are they adequately distinct, or do they overlap? When we approach the NT data we find distinct terms for these functions in the early Christian community: on the one hand, *kērygma* (and *kēryssein*), *euangelion* (and *euangelizesthai*), even *logos* [2] are words used to express the essential Christian message or proclamation; on the other, *didachē* or *didaskalia* (and *didaskein*)[3] are words that sometimes seem to describe a distinct function. Moreover it is difficult to single out not only what may be the crucial difference between these word-groups but also the nuances that they sometimes have, e.g. whether they connote the content or object of the preaching/teaching or the activity itself. For instance, *kērygma* may at times mean what is proclaimed, and at times the activity of proclaiming itself; that would have to be said of *didachē* too. Consequently in interrogating the NT data about teaching, we shall have to try to determine its nuances.

Second, there will be little dissent about the NT data concerning what the early Christian Church preached, namely the kerygma or gospel, the basic message of Christ crucified and raised, or about its relation to the preaching of Jesus Christ himself—even though that relation was being viewed with the eyes of Easter faith. Similarly one recognizes with Paul that the assistance and guidance of the Spirit is needed for a person to confess this crucified and raised Jesus as Lord (1 Cor. 12:3). That is, acceptance of the preached Word in faith is only done with the help of the Spirit of God. But if the teaching of the early community is to be understood as a development of its preaching, as something somehow distinct from the latter, then the question might be raised about the relation of it to the preaching of Jesus himself. For although, as will be seen, the evangelists present Jesus as teaching, a distinction between his preaching and teaching makes little sense. But the distinction begins to emerge in the early community, and it presents a problem about its character or quality. Is it authoritative? Is it official? What is its relation to false teaching?

If one concedes that the commission of Jesus to his apostles to preach the gospel carried with it or implied an office or Ministry of preaching within the community of believers, can one argue similarly for an office or Ministry of teaching? The *Malta Report* of the international study commission established by the Lutheran World Federation and the Vatican Secretariat for Promoting Christian Unity sought the basis of a "special office in the church" for gospel Ministry precisely in the *Gegenüber* implied in Jesus' commission to bear witness to the gospel, i.e. in the distinction between the preacher and those preached to: "Both [Lutherans and Catholics] agree that the office stands over against the community as well as within the community. Further, they agree that the office represents Christ and his overagainstness to the community only insofar as it gives expression to the gospel." [4] An *office (Amt)* was implied in the *mission (Auftrag)*. The *Malta Report,* however, did not raise the question about an office of teaching; but one may ask whether, when the Christian Church teaches something not limited to an expression of the gospel, it shares in any function found in the NT writings.

The fourth statement issued by the United States dialogue, *Eucharist and Ministry,* found agreement in the understanding of a "special Ministry," which "has the twofold task of proclaiming the gospel to the world—evangelizing, witnessing, serving—and of building up in Christ those who already believe—teaching, exhorting, reproving, and sanctifying." [5] In this statement "teaching" is seen as part of the twofold task of the special Ministry within the Christian Church. Hence the question can be posed: Does the commission to proclaim the gospel imply not only a Ministry of proclamation, but also a function of teaching, even a Ministry of teaching with authority within the Christian community *(Lehramt)*? To what extent is there anything in the NT bearing on such questions?

Third, intimately connected with the two preceding aspects of the problem is the character of the gospel itself. Again, whereas there would be little dissent about its kerygmatic character, its normative character might raise different questions. Yet the gospel is recognized as a norm for

Christian faith, life, and conduct; but can that normative character of the gospel be ascribed to a function of teaching within the Christian community, to a teaching office, and even to official teaching? Or to put it another way, does the normative character of the gospel itself call forth a teaching function or office within the Christian community?

Fourth, the question about the teaching office in the NT has to be asked with all the reservations that were set forth in *Peter in the New Testament* (Augsburg, 1973) with regard to the Petrine function, i.e. with a respect for source criticism, form criticism, and redaction criticism (where applicable), with a respect for the authenticity and chronology of various NT writings, and with a respect for the differing "theologies" in these writings—in short, with a respect for the historical and critical study of the NT books, as this has been developed in the currently recognized discipline of this part of the Christian theological inquiry.

My approach to the NT data bearing on teaching in the Christian Church will follow more or less that of *Peter in the New Testament*,[6] inquiring of various books or groups of books what data may be pertinent to this discussion. It should be realized at the outset, however, that the question is not so well-defined as it was for the Petrine function, where one was more or less directed to those passages in which Peter was mentioned or possibly hinted at. In this case the question is more nebulous, and the net has to be cast more widely. It is hoped that at least the major passages that bear on the question will thus be covered in this consideration. I propose to interrogate the NT data in the following order: (I) the genuine letters of Paul (1 Thessalonians, Galatians, Philippians, 1 and 2 Corinthians, Romans, Philemon); (II) doubtfully genuine letters of Paul (2 Thessalonians, Colossians, Ephesians);[7] (III) the Synoptic Gospels (Mark, Matthew, and Luke); (IV) Acts; (V) the Deuteropauline Letters (1 Timothy, Titus, 2 Timothy); (VI) James; and (VII) the Johannine literature (John, 1, 2, 3 John). The data in the other Catholic Epistles (1 and 2 Peter, Jude), Hebrews, and the Apocalypse[8] are so meagre that the isolated items that occur in them will simply be introduced into the discussion at appropriate places.

I. Teaching in the Genuine Pauline Letters

The aim here is to see what Paul, the first Christian theologian, recorded in his genuine letters (1 Thessalonians, Galatians, Philippians, 1 and 2 Corinthians, Romans, and Philemon) on the function of teaching in the Christian community.

(1) Only rarely did Paul describe his own role as that of a teacher.[9] For reasons that need not detain us here, he insisted rather on his title of "apostle" (Gal. 1:1; 1 Cor. 1:1; 9:1-2; 2 Cor. 1:1; 12:11; Rom. 1:1; 11:13) [10] and thought of himself more as a preacher *(kēryssōn)* or a herald, even though he never used the term *kēryx* of himself.[11] The latter is, however, implied in Rom. 10:8, 14 *(ho kēryssōn, chōris kēryssontos).*[12] He was certainly explicit when he said of himself: "Christ did not send me to baptize but to preach the gospel *(euangelizesthai)* and not with eloquent wisdom, lest the cross of Christ be emptied of its power" (1 Cor. 1:17).[13] Yet that was a gospel that tolerated no rival (Gal. 1:6-9), carrying within it its own authority and "truth" (Gal. 2:5, 14), and eliciting from human beings the confession that "Jesus Christ is Lord," a confession that could only be made with the guidance and assistance of the Spirit of God himself (1 Cor. 12:3). It is clear from Paul's letters that he considered his gospel preaching authoritative and normative for Christian conduct and based on a God-given revelation (Gal. 2:15-16); for he was preaching with the authority of Christ himself.

But despite such insistence on his task as a gospel-preacher, Paul did on one occasion describe himself as having taught and implicitly applied the same function to Timothy's activity as well: "I sent to you Timothy . . . to remind you of my ways in Christ, as I teach them everywhere in every church" (1 Cor. 4:17). Here the object of Paul's teaching is *tas hodous mou tas en Christō,* and in the context they seem to be something broader than the gospel, though based on it and derived from it. For in vv. 15-16 he admitted to the Corinthians that he had become their "father in Christ Jesus through the gospel" and consequently demanded of them: "Be imitators of me." This notion of imitation is found elsewhere in Paul's letters (1 Thess. 1:6; 2:14; Phil. 3:17; 1 Cor. 1:11 [cf. 2 Thess. 3:7, 9; Eph.

5:1])[14] and though it may seem *prima facie* to be implied in his "teaching," it really involves much more. In any case, both the teaching of "my ways in Christ" and imitation of Paul seem to involve something more than merely faith in the preached gospel. They appear to be an application of "the gospel" to newly emerging problems in Christian living.

(2) Paul insisted that the gospel he was preaching was not received from any human being nor was it "taught" to him *(oute edidachthēn,* Gal. 1:12). Perhaps in this statement we find a distinction between what he preached and what he taught. His gospel came "through a revelation of Jesus Christ" (Gal. 1:12); for God "was pleased to reveal his Son to me (or "in me"), in order that I might preach him among the Gentiles" (v. 16). To his gospel Paul clearly related the response of faith: a hearing *(akoē,* Rom. 10:14-17) that had to result in a personal commitment to God in Christ Jesus (what he calls the *hypakoē pisteōs,* Rom. 1:5; 16:26). Faith as the essential element of Christian life and conduct was the response to his preached gospel, and he did not normally speak of it in a context of teaching.

Linked to it crucially is "the truth of the gospel" (Gal. 2:5, 14), a phrase that seems to express for him a normative character of the gospel rather than carry with it some of the other nuances of biblical "truth," which have often been discussed in recent times.[15] For it was the criterion that he used in rebuking Cephas' *conduct* (Gal. 2:14),[16] and an aspect of the gospel that had to be preserved because of its relation to the "freedom which we have in Christ Jesus" (2:4). In other words the matter of dietary regulations, which was certainly not part of the Christian kerygma or gospel, came under scrutiny when the norm of the gospel was applied. The matter of dietary regulations was never spoken of by Paul in terms of teaching; but it shows that matters outside the realm of faith have to stand the scrutiny of the gospel, the guarantee of Christian freedom. In this incident perhaps we find a reason why Paul emphasized his role as a preacher more than that of a teacher, but it also reveals a Pauline stance about a matter indifferent in itself that had to be normed by the gospel, and his (implied) teaching about it was certainly intended to be authoritative.

(3) Paul is, moreover, aware of the function of the teacher (*didaskalos* or *ho didaskōn*) in the Christian community. In enumerating seven charisms bestowed on the one body that Christians form in Christ, Paul explicitly mentioned in the third place the teacher (*ho didaskōn*, Rom. 12:7),[17] along with the prophecy (*prophēteia*), service (*diakonia*), the exhorter (*ho parakalōn*), the contributor (*ho metadidous*), the superior (*ho proistamenos*),[18] and the one who does acts of mercy (*ho eleōn*). Again, the charism of teaching occurs in the third place in the list of eight gifts bestowed diversely by the one Spirit within the unity of the body of Christ (1 Cor. 12:28): "first apostles (*apostolous*), second prophets (*prophētas*), third teachers (*didaskalous*), then workers of miracles (*dynameis*), then gifts of healing (*charismata iamatōn*), helpers (*antilēmpseis*), administrators (*kybernēseis*), (speakers in various) kinds of tongues (*genē glōssōn*)." In both these passages the distinction of some Christians who are teachers is recognized; Paul listed their role as a charisma diverse from others and considered their role at least as a separate function, if not a separate *office*.[19] Yet in these passages he hinted neither at the object of the teaching nor at its relation to the gospel. It is a Spirit-guided function, but it does not differ in this regard from other functions. K. H. Rengstorf thinks the difference between the prophets and the teachers in such a list is that the former are " 'pneumatics' (and he refers to 1 Cor. 14:29ff.), whereas the latter are 'nonpneumatics' who edify the congregation by means of their own clearer understanding." [20] That seems to be an unwarranted distinction, scarcely corresponding to either the immediate context of 1 Cor. 12:28 or to the larger understanding of the *pneumatikoi* in Paul's letters. Two queries rise at this point: (1) Why is there no mention of the preacher in these charismatic functions (*ho kēryssōn* or *ho kēryx*)? This function, indeed, is almost certainly implied in that of the *apostolos*, but the distinction of functions does emerge later and will be noted below (see pp. 203-204); (2) Is there any significance in the occurrence of the teacher in the third place in both of these lists? Is it a mere coincidence, or does it reflect some emergent order of classification? [21]

(4) Paul also seemed to be aware of some sort of official teaching when in Romans 6, after his discussion of Baptism and the new life into which it introduces Christians, who are now dead to sin and self, he exhorted them: "But thanks be to God, that you who were once slaves of sin have become obedient from the heart to the standard of teaching *(typon didachēs)* to which you were committed" (6:17). The passage is not uniformly interpreted by commentators because of an ambiguous relative pronoun.[22] By some the *typos didachēs* has been understood as a baptismal catechesis,[23] by others as a more generic mold or norm which should shape the conduct of a person who is delivered over to it and has become obedient to it, in becoming a Christian.[24] Whatever the exact designation may be, it seems to suggest that Paul was aware of some sort of official teaching that is to shape Christian conduct. It is not the same as the content of the gospel, but probably represents a formulation guided by it for the conduct of Christian life. It is thus authentic teaching with the Christian community.

(5) Paul was likewise aware that some Christian community [25] has persons in it "who create dissensions and difficulties, in opposition to the doctrine *(didachē)*" which has been learned *(hēn hymeis emathete,* Rom. 16:17), and he counseled avoidance of them. In this context the doctrine can scarcely be limited to the gospel or even to faith in a content sense; Paul seemed to relate it to a form of wisdom (v. 19), which suggests a reference to more practical matters. Yet he called it "doctrine" and implied that it may not tolerate dissent.

References in the genuine Pauline letters to teaching are not elaborate. Rengstorf has noted the "comparative paucity in Paul" of the use of *didaskein*.[26] Of the 95 occurrences of the verb in the NT, "there are only 10 instances in Paul (including Eph.)." [27] Part of the reason for this is the hellenistic context of Paul's apostolate and part of it is the recognized Jewish content of *didaskein* in a religious sense, with its connotation of exposition of the Torah, a connotation that is manifest in numerous places in the NT outside the Pauline corpus. Rengstorf maintains that "we can . . . see that the emphatic use of the term is among the first followers and in the early Church rather than in the Gentile congregations of Asia Minor or Greece." [28]

Though Paul did not often describe himself as a teacher (perhaps because of his personal insistence and struggle to be recognized as an Apostle), he was aware of the function of teaching and of a special group of persons engaged in it. He recognized it as Spirit-guided. It is difficult to specify the content of it, and it would be wrong to identify it solely with the gospel, although it is clearly based on the gospel and stands under it. And he was aware that there was some sort of official or correct doctrine that was meeting with some opposition.

II. Teaching in the Doubtfully Genuine Pauline Letters

In turning to the letters of the Pauline corpus that are not considered authentic by some NT commentators today (2 Thessalonians, Colossians, Ephesians), we find data that are a little more explicit about the role of teaching in the early church.

In 2 Thessalonians the author insists on the obligation to "stand firm and hold to the traditions which you were taught by us, either by word of mouth or by letter" (2:15). The crucial phrase is *paradoseis has edidachthēte*. The word *paradoseis* is in the plural and may seem to imply something more than the essential Christian *paradosis*,[29] which Paul otherwise related to his gospel (see 1 Cor. 15:1-2) and which he traces to the *Kyrios* (1 Cor. 11:1-2, 23), or it may simply suggest details of the essential tradition. If the former, then perhaps it reflects an understanding later than Paul's, one clearly associated with the activity of teaching, but one to which a crucial term could be applied at least in an analagous sense. But if it denotes details of the gospel-tradition and the meaning is that these have become the object of teaching, then there is a significant advance over the gospel that was not taught to Paul (Gal. 1:12), but that could now be described as taught. For Rengstorf the traditions are no more than "instruction of the communities at the time of their foundation." [30] In any case, in this passage the emphasis seems to be on the normative aspect of it; the author calls for fidelity to such "traditions."

Moreover, the lack of a clear distinction between teaching and preaching is found in some of these letters. Thus in Col. 1:28, where the author, having spoken of the wealth of the mystery of Christ that has been made known among the Gentiles, the mystery being "Christ in you, the hope of glory," continues, "Him we proclaim *(hon hēmeis katangellomen)*, warning every man and teaching *(didaskontes)* every man in all wisdom, that we may present every man mature in Christ." Though the gospel is here described as mystery, emphasizing its relation to salvation history, it is proclaimed, as might be expected. But closely related to that activity are two others, warning (or correcting, *nouthetountes)* and teaching. And the question rises whether in this instance the object of the latter is the gospel or a newly formulated theological understanding of Christ's role. Rengstorf insists on a "pastoral and ethical sense" of *didaskein* "as a function of Christians in their mutual dealings." [31] This may be so, but it may also reflect an extension of the function of proclaiming to teaching.

Again, in Colossians we find teaching related to the activity of the gospel-tradition. In a context in which the author counsels the Colossians and Laodiceans about proper understanding, wisdom, and knowledge and warns them against being deluded by beguiling speech, the author rejoices at their "good order and the firmness" or their faith in Christ (2:5); "As therefore you received *(paralabete)* Christ Jesus the Lord, so live in him, rooted and built up in him and established in faith, just as you were taught *(bebaioumenoi tē pistei kathōs edidachthēte)"* (2:6). *Paralambanein* is a technical NT term for the reception of kerygmatic tradition (see 1 Cor. 15:1-3); it connotes a tradition about Christ Jesus, and the reception is precisely that of faith, as the end of the verse also indicates. Though the establishment in faith probably means something more than the content-sense of faith, an aspect of the faith-process is here linked to an activity of teaching.

The relation of teaching to wisdom, detected earlier (Col. 1:28), is again met in 3:16, where the author may be distinguishing the Christian message ("the word of Christ") from other aspects of Christian life. As part of a series of hortatory counsels, the author says, "Let the word of Christ dwell in you richly, teach *(didaskontes)* and admonish *(nouthetountes)* one another in all wisdom, and sing psalms and hymns and spiritual songs with thankfulness in your hearts to God." In this case, however, the context does not suggest that the dwelling of Christ's word in the Colossians is simply another expression for the response of faith. The line-up of counsels refers to less substantial matters, and to these the activity of teaching is related, to be carried out with "all wisdom."

In Eph. 4:11 another list of functions within the Christian community is found, similar to those of Rom. 12:7 and 1 Cor. 12:28. Among the gifts *(domata)* that the exalted Christ bestowed on the community are these: "that some should be apostles *(tous men apostolous)*, some prophets *(tous de prophētas)*, some evangelists *(tous de euangelistas)*, some pastors and teachers *(tous de poimenas kai didaskalous)*, to equip the saints for the work of ministry, for building up the body of Christ. . . . " These functions are cited in a context in which the author warns against "every wind of doctrine, the cunning of men, by craftiness in deceitful wiles" (4:14). In this instance the teachers are in the fourth place, behind the apostles and prophets (as in 1 Cor. 12:28), but also behind the evangelists, now explicitly accorded a place in the list of gifts. Furthermore they seem to be identified with or at least related to the shepherds (pastors), being linked by one definite article.[32] As in 1 Corinthians and Romans, the function is recognized and regarded as a gift of the exalted Christ; and the general context is again that of the unity of the Christian Church ("one body and one Spirit . . . one Lord, one faith, one baptism, one God and Father of us all," 4:4-6). The difference in Ephesians, however, seems to be not merely that the diversity of gifts should not militate against the unity (as in 1 Corinthians and Romans), but that the gifts are destined *eis ergon diakonias*, "for the work of ministry" (v. 12), and as distinct offices should be used to offset every wind of (different) doctrine, the cunning of men, craftiness, and deceitful wiles (4:14). And what is more, four of the last five charisms of 1 Cor. 12:28, if not all five, have completely disappeared. Though the author of Ephesians, with all his insistence on unity, never brings himself to speak of *mia ekklēsia,* "one church," nevertheless the function of the apostles, prophets, evangelists, and pastor-teachers is aimed at unity and the upbuilding of the saints. Their functions are Christ-bestowed and imply authority of some sort.

Finally, a relation of teaching and truth is expressed in Eph. 4:21. Counseling the Ephesians against the futility of the ignorance of God, licentiousness, greed, and uncleanness, the author exclaims, "You did not so learn Christ!— assuming that you have heard about him and were taught in him *(en autō edidachthēte),* as the truth is in Jesus." Truth is here related to conduct, as in Gal. 2:5, 14, but it is no longer the "truth of the gospel." It is a truth acquired by being in Christ, which may connote something more.

In these doubtfully genuine Pauline letters, then, we see a greater emphasis on the role of teaching than we found in Paul's genuine letters. The function of the teacher is again recognized and regarded as a charismatic role; teaching is also normative for conduct. In one instance at least it is associated with preaching, but it is not easy to specify either the exact relationship of the two or their specific objects.

III. Teaching in the Synoptic Gospels

As we move from the Pauline literature to other NT writings, especially the Gospels and Acts, our task becomes more complicated because these writings purport to narrate what Jesus did and said and how the early Christian community developed. But these accounts were written with hindsight and experience, born of faith, and the extent to which they actually reflect the *Sitz im Leben Jesu* for any particular teaching or the *Sitz im Leben der Kirche* for the actual function in the early community rather than a given writer's view of such teachings or functions has to be scrutinized.

In the Synoptic Gospels, the function of teaching is clearly attributed to Jesus himself; he is not only hailed as *didaskale, epistate,* or *rabbi,*[33] and regarded as a *didaskalos,*[34] but he is clearly depicted as teaching *(edidasken)*;[35] he says or implies that he is *didaskalos.*[36] In most instances we are simply told that "he taught" (with various locales being indicated: frequently in synagogues,[37] sometimes in the Temple,[38] and even in a boat [39]), and only rarely do we find the object of that teaching expressed. For example, in Mark 12:14 // Matt. 22:16 // Luke 20:21 Jesus is said to teach "the way of God" because he personally either "is true" (Mark, Matthew) or "speaks rightly" (*orthōs*, Luke). Or he teaches in their synagogues and preaches "the gospel of the kingdom" (Matt. 4:23); or he teaches "that the Son of man must suffer" (Mark 8:31; 9:31); or he teaches some interpretation of OT passages (Mark 11:17; 12:35; Luke 4:16-22).[40]

As has often been noted, the teaching of Jesus himself has to be understood against the background of the Palestinian Jewish teaching of his time. The absolute sense of the verb *edidasken* that is met so frequently (Mark 1:21; 6:2; Matt. 4:23; 9:35; Luke 4:15; 6:6; 13:10, etc.) makes sense only when it is understood as a reflection of Hebrew *limmēd*,[41] and the *didaskalos* is "one who indicates the way of God from the Torah." [42] But Jesus

rejects the absolutising of the Law historically presupposed by the word *[didaskein]* in view of its Semitic equivalent *limmēd*. This rejection is to be viewed simply as the repudiation of an aberration. In opposition to it, Jesus resumes the true line of *limmēd* in the *didaskein* attributed to Him. For He is again advancing the claim of God to the whole man in a way which does not allow either contradiction or theoretical reflection.[43]

One also detects in this background to the absolute use of *didaskein* attributed to Jesus, with its implied relationship of disciple-teacher, the difference between the Pauline use of *didaskein* (which knows not a discipleship) [44] and the Synoptic use of it. In any case, Jesus' teaching is not restricted to an exposition of the Torah.[45]

Occasionally, the quality or mode of his teaching is indicated: with authority (Mark 1:22//Matt. 7:29//Luke 4:32); or in parables (Mark 4:2). Indeed, his teaching with authority has to be understood as only one manifestation of his authoritative ministry described in the Gospels. He interpreted the OT, but not as the scribes and Pharisees. And Matthew depicts his pitting his authoritative teaching over against that of what was said of old (5:21-48).

These are, however, three points in the Synoptic material

that call for special comment, because they have a bearing on the function of teaching in the early Christian community.

(1) There is first the Lucan emphasis on teaching, a point that is related to what is found about teaching in Acts. As a matter of fact the number of references to Jesus being hailed as a teacher or depicted as teaching is almost as great in Mark as in Luke. But there are Lucan verses that give a special emphasis to the activity. For instance, Luke depicts the child Jesus "sitting among the teachers, listening to them and asking them questions; and all who heard him were astonished at his understanding and his answers" (2:46-47). As in a number of other details in the Lucan infancy narrative, a chord is being struck that will be orchestrated later in the gospel or in Acts. Not only is John the Baptist hailed as *didaskale* (only in Luke, 3:12), but Jesus is asked to teach his disciples to pray, "as John taught his" (11:1).[46] Not only is the parallelism of John and Jesus, clearly foreshadowed in the infancy narrative, now echoed in a specific way, but it all serves the Lucan identification of Jesus and his movement with forms of Judaism. Among the Synoptics it is only Luke who introduces the Spirit into a relation with the teaching role: "for the Holy Spirit will teach you in that very hour what you ought to say" (12:12), when disciples are haled before synagogues, rulers, and authorities.[47] All these details find a climax in one way or another in Acts; in the Lucan Gospel they are introduced by way of foreshadowing. They serve to bear out the purpose of the Lucan writings set forth in Luke 1:4, at the end of the prologue: that Theophilus may recognize the secure basis *(asphaleia)* of the matters in which he had been instructed. For the author of Luke was at pains to show that what the church of his day was teaching was rooted in the teaching of Jesus himself. A Lucan theologoumenon is involved here, and it says more about Luke and his church of the late first century than about Jesus himself or about earlier generations of the Christian community. Security is Luke's concern, and it is a security about instruction. It is not, as is sometimes maintained, that Luke is offering to guarantee the Christian kerygma. He knows that the Spirit guarantees that. It is rather his concern to root what the church of his day was

teaching in the teaching of Jesus himself, linked through the preordained witnesses from Galilee trained by Jesus.

(2) A Matthean passage presently embedded in an account of Jesus' controversies with the scribes and Pharisees discusses the role of teacher. Matthew 23 has parallels with Mark 12:37-40 and with some material derived from "Q," but there is some that is exclusively Matthean. Among the latter is 23:8-10, which reads:

> But you are not to be called rabbi, for you have one teacher (*didaskalos*),[48] and you are all brethren. And call no man your father on earth, for you have one Father, who is in heaven. Neither be called masters (*kathēgētai*), for you have one master (*kathegētēs*), the Christ.

This difficult passage, as it now stands in Matthew, is an explanation offered by Jesus to "the crowds and to his disciples" about the scribes and Pharisees. *Prima facie*, it is a rejection of titles used among them, *rabbî*, *'abbā'*, and possibly *môreh*.[49] The reasons given for the rejection of the first two allude clearly to the Father; but in the case of *kathēgētēs*, the Messiah (*ho Christos*) is introduced. Because of the latter, many commentators think the verses reflect a situation in the Matthean church (ca. A.D. 85) much more than an issue in Jesus' own day.[50] After all, these sayings are exclusively Matthean, and there is no question how *ho Christos* is to be understood (whether as "the Messiah," as in Matt. 2:4; or as "Christ," as in Matt. 1:17). Moreover, *kathēgētēs* denotes someone engaged in instruction; but is it a mere synonym of *didaskalos*? Finally, what sort of a function is implied when this title is given to a Jewish messiah? As a result, the question before us is the bearing of this saying of Jesus, if it were authentic, on the life of the Christian community.[51] Is it to be understood as a prohibition of teachers within the community; does it imply the prohibition of a teaching office? If one were to answer yes, then one would further have to ask how such a prohibition, apparently emanating from the Matthean church, is to be understood in the light of Paul's recognition of the charismatic function (*or* office) of teachers. Finally, one would have to ask how this passage is understood in the light of the next Matthean passage, to which we now turn.

(3) The most crucial synoptic passage is that found at the end of Matthew, where the risen Christ issues a commission to eleven disciples (28:18-20):

"All authority in heaven and on earth has been given to me. Go therefore and make disciples of all nations, baptizing them in the name of the Father and of the Son and of the Holy Spirit, teaching them to observe all that I have commanded you *(didaskontes autous tērein panta hosa eneteilamēn hymin);* and lo, I am with you always, to the close of the age."

This commission given to eleven disciples, based on the authority of the risen Christ, is obviously one to proclaim the gospel, for that is what is meant by making disciples of all the nations. However, it is juxtaposed with two other activities, baptizing and teaching. The response of discipleship might seem to be limited to faith and Baptism, but this Matthean text adds another, the observance of all that Jesus had commanded them, now as *taught* by the eleven. Three things are therefore expected of the nations to be evangelized: discipleship, Baptism, and observance of what is taught as based on Jesus' own teaching. The "you" is directed to the eleven disciples (28:16), and it implies the *Gegenüber,* the basis of an office within the Christian community but also over against the community of believers. The parallelism of participles *(baptizontes* and *didaskontes)* seems to express parallel aspects of the making of disciples. I find no basis for Rengstorf's contention that teaching is the presupposition of *Baptism* and disciple-making.[52] Unfortunately, the object of the teaching is very vaguely expressed: "all that I have commanded you." Even though it is no more definite than the Pauline "ways in Christ" (1 Cor. 4:17) and may in the Matthean context refer to the teaching of Jesus in the five great discourses, the conclusion sounds more like an attempt to base the authority of the teaching office in the Matthean church precisely in a commission from Jesus himself. The least that one can say is that the commission is not unrelated to the gospel, but it would be difficult to restrict the teaching to the gospel. But the commission is related here to a promise of the risen Christ that he will be with them to the end of the age. Like Jesus' promise to Peter in the same Gospel that the gates of hell would not prevail against the Church founded on him as rock (16:18), the continued presence of Christ with his disciples would imply a guarantee of their preaching (making disciples) and their teaching (which could mean the reformulation of the essential kerygma to meet new problems).

IV. Teaching in the Acts of the Apostles

The few details that were singled out in the Lucan Gospel now find an amplification in the story of the early Christian community's growth and development as presented in Acts. Luke sums up his first volume as a narrative of "all that Jesus began to do and *teach*" (Acts 1:1). Now the teaching of Jesus gives way to the teaching of the apostles, and he who preached becomes the object of the preaching and teaching.

In the first major summary of Acts (2:42-46),[53] the four items that characterize early Christian communal life begin precisely with *hē didachē tōn apostolōn:* "the apostles' teaching, fellowship, the breaking of bread, and the prayers." Once again we are unfortunately not told what the *didachē* consisted of or what its object was. Within the community it was scarcely restricted to kerygmatic preaching or evangelization, but how was its content related to the gospel? The scope of it is not clear, and to consider it merely as a body of teaching may be going beyond the meaning of the text, since *didachē* here may connote the activity rather than the content, since *koinōnia, klasis,* and *proseuchai* seem to connote more of the former than the latter.[54]

Later in Acts we read of a local church in which there was a group of teachers, along with prophets (reminding one of 1 Cor. 12:28; Rom. 12:7; and Eph. 4:11): "In the church at Antioch there were prophets and teachers" (13:1). Among them five are named (Barnabas, Simeon Niger, Lucius of Cyrene, Manaen, and Saul), but no attempt is made to identify which were the prophets and which the teachers. According to P. Parker, there is here "some hint of official position."[55]

More numerous, however, are the passages in which various apostles and others are depicted as teaching; thus, Peter and John (4:2), "the apostles" (5:21, 42), Saul and

Barnabas (11:26; 15:35), Paul (18:11; 20:20; 21:21; 28:31), and Apollos (18:25). In connection with such passages, three things must be pointed out: (1) the teaching was often done *epi tō onomati tou Iesou,* "in the name of Jesus," i.e., implicitly on a commission from him (see Luke 24:47). But in 4:18; 5:28 it is said that such an activity of teaching was prohibited to the apostles by Jewish authorities. (2) Teaching and preaching/proclaiming are not infrequently juxtaposed, so that one wonders about the distinction between them. Thus Peter and John in the temple annoyed the temple officials by teaching the people and proclaiming the resurrection of the dead in Jesus (*dia to didaskein autous ton logon kai katangellein en tō Iesou tēn anastasin tēn ek nekrōn,* 4:2). In 5:43 the juxtaposed verbs are actually coordinated and govern the same object: *ouk epauonto didaskontes kai euangelizomenoi ton Christon Iēsoun,* "they did not cease teaching and preaching Jesus as the Christ." Similarly Paul and Barnabas remained in Antioch, *didaskontes kai euangelizomenoi . . . ton logon tou Kyriou,* "teaching and preaching the word of the Lord" (15:35). In Corinth Paul is described as remaining for 18 months, *didaskōn ton logon tou Theou,* "teaching the word of God" (18:11). And Luke finally ends his narrative with the description of Paul welcoming all who would come to him, *kēryssōn tēn basileian tou theou kai didaskōn ta peri tou Kyriou Iēsou Christou,* "preaching the kingdom of God and teaching about the Lord Jesus Christ. . . ." (28:31). In these Lucan passages one sees the juxtaposition of preaching and teaching, even the coordination of them with the same object; indeed, in two places *ho logos,* which means for Luke the Christian message, is explicitly the object of *didaskein* (4:2; 15:35).

This does not mean that *didaskein* is restricted to exegesis of the OT or to instruction in the new interpretation given by Jesus to the Law. Here again the whole complex of Scripture is only a starting-point and background. In the light of it the teaching of the early Church culminates in the call to repentance which is accompanied by *kērygma* about Jesus by the offer of *aphesis hamartiōn* (cf. Ac. 5:31, but also 20:21) . . . . From the standpoint of the history of early Christian proclamation, therefore, there takes place in the *didaskein* of the early community the unconscious transmission and sifting of traditional sayings, while in the *kērygma* we have the beginning of a collection of the narrative material, both under the comprehensive challenge which stands at the head of the Christian message generally: *metanoeite kai pisteuete en tō euangeliō* (Mk 1:15).[56]

(3) The object of the teaching has already been touched on in point 2, but it should be commented on more specifically. In 5:42 the object of both teaching and preaching is "Christ Jesus." In 28:31, whereas the object of the preaching is the kingdom of God, that of teaching is *ta peri tou Kyriou*, "things concerning the Lord" (cf. 18:25, *ta peri tou Iēsou*; also 20:20). Though Rengstorf thinks that the *ta peri . . .* expression "includes proving from Scripture that Jesus is the promised Messiah,"[57] it cannot be restricted to that, for it seems to imply the application of the preached word to new contingencies.

In the material from Luke-Acts it is clear that Luke knows of teachers in the Christian community and thinks of the main activities of the apostles as preaching and teaching in such a way that it is not easy to distinguish between them; they are "the ministry of the word" (Acts 6:4. He is also aware of correct Christian preaching when he depicts Paul addressing the elders of Ephesus at Miletus and recalling how he has gone about "preaching the kingdom" (20:25), knowing that fierce wolves would come in and not spare the flock, warning that "from among your own selves will arise men speaking *(lalountes)* perverse things, to draw away the disciples after them" (20:30). Here one sees an authoritative preacher (Paul) warning other church authorities about deviations from correct teaching. As already indicated, Luke was concerned to show that what the church of his day was preaching and teaching was actually rooted in what Jesus "began to do and teach" (1:1). The concern for authoritative teaching is there, but it is not as clearly expressed as the "sound doctrine" in the next body of literature to which we turn.

V. Teaching in the Deutero-Pauline Letters

Though some scholars are inclined to relate the Deutero-Pauline letters (1 Timothy, Titus, and 2 Timothy) to the second century A.D.,[58] I prefer to keep them in the first century,[59] toward the end of it, preferably about the time of the composition of Matthew and the Lucan writings. When we look at these NT writings which emerged from Pauline circles, especially in their attitude toward teaching, we see the clear emergence of official teaching, even related to an office in the church. The term *didaskalia* is very common in these writings, occurring here 15 out of 21 times in the NT. This is not surprising in view of other developments beyond the genuine Pauline teaching regarding faith and the Church that are found in these letters.

In particular, the emphasis in the Pastoral Letters is on *pistos ho logos*, "the saying is sure" (1 Timothy 1:15; 3:1; 4:9; Titus 3:8; 2 Timothy 2:11). It makes the treatment of teaching in these letters quite definite; just as definite is the view of the church—or some Minister of the church (e.g., Timothy himself)—as "the pillar and bulwark of truth" (1 Timothy 3:15). Here too we find *hē hygiainousa didaskalia*, "sound doctrine" (1 Timothy 1:10;[60] Titus 1:9; 2:1; 2 Timothy 4:3),[61] not only related to the *pistos ho logos* phrase but clearly connoting an official teaching. Rengstorf calls the adjective well adapted to "emphasize the binding character of the historical proclamation." [62] Moreover, the two are closely connected in the expression *ho kata tēn didachēn pistos logos*, "the sure word as taught" (Titus 1:9). The "sound doctrine" is correct teaching in contrast to perverted doctrine, and although obviously meant to be an interpretation of the gospel it is undoubtedly more comprehensive in its scope. It is "the traditional teaching which is established and validated by the apostles and preserved by the office to which Timothy and Titus are called." [63] For Timothy is told: "Till I come, attend to the (public) reading (of scripture),[64] to preaching, to teaching" (1 Timothy 4:13).[65] One may wonder which is the more important in this threesome, whether the scale is ascending or descending. I think its climax is the last-mentioned, teaching, so that even reading is made to serve it; but this may be debatable. Elsewhere the author writes: "All scripture is inspired by God and profitable for teaching, for reproof, for correction, and for training in righteousness. . . ." (2 Timothy 3:16). The uses to which Scripture was being put are expressed here.

Timothy and Titus, who are depicted as delegates of the apostle Paul, are repeatedly told to teach or reminded of their obligation to teach: [66] "preach the word *(kēryxon ton logon)* . . . convince, rebuke, and exhort, be unfailing in patience and in teaching" (2 Timothy 4:2); "Command and teach these things *(parangelle tauta kai didaske,* 1 Timothy 4:11; cf. 6:2); "But as for you, teach what befits sound doctrine" (Titus 2:1 *[sy de lalei ha prepei . . .]*); "Take heed to yourself and to your teaching" (1 Timothy 4:16); "in your teaching show integrity" (Titus 2:7).

The function of teaching is related to one of the offices in the Christian Church that emerges in the Deutero-Pauline letters, for Timothy and Titus are commissioned to set up *episkopoi/presbyteroi* in local churches [67] and are instructed to look for certain qualifications in the *men* [68] they choose for these posts, among which is the quality of a teacher. An *episkopos* must be *didaktikos,* which the *RSV,* following one line of interpretation,[69] translates "an apt teacher" (1 Timothy 3:2), but which other interpreters understand to mean "able to learn." [70] Furthermore, Titus is told that an *episkopos* must "hold firm to the sure word as taught, so that he may be able to give instruction in sound doctrine and also to confute those who contradict it" (1:9). Here the function of the teacher is clearly predicated of the delegates of the apostle and of those whom they appoint as *episkopoi.*[71] It echoes, in effect, the gifts given to the Church in Eph. 4:11, which may reflect something of the same tendency.[72] This does not mean, of course, that such officials are the only teachers in the (local) Christian community, but the Deutero-Pauline letters suggest that concern and wariness for sound doctrine rest with such appointees.[73]

The reason for such instructions is that the author of these letters is aware of false teachers, of those who "teach otherwise" (1 Timothy 6:3; cf. 4:1; 2 Timothy 4:3-4). He feels the obligation to judge their teaching and to warn Christians about their misleading teaching. (The same concern was manifest in Acts 20:30, as mentioned above, and is found again in 2 Peter 2:1, which mentions explicitly "false teachers" *[pseudodidaskaloi]).*

Finally, one should note how Paul, the reputed author of these letters, is made to speak about himself: "You have observed my teaching (*mou tē didaskalia*), my conduct, my aim in life, my faith . . ." (2 Timothy 3:10). He is made to play the role not only of an apostle (which he claimed in his genuine letters) but also of the herald (*or* preacher) and of the teacher: "For there is one God, and there is one mediator between God and men, the man Christ Jesus, who gave himself as a ransom for all, the testimony to which was borne at the proper time. For this I was appointed a preacher (*kēryx*) and apostle (I am telling the truth, I am not lying), a teacher of the Gentiles (*didaskalos ethnōn*) in faith and truth" (1 Timothy 2:5-7). "For this gospel I was appointed a preacher and apostle and teacher" (2 Timothy 1:11). Again one can ask in which direction the climactic order goes.

In the Deutero-Pauline letters, then, we have a clear picture of a number of emergent details regarding the function of teaching in different local churches. The author himself clearly writes as a *didaskalos* guaranteeing the "sound doctrine," [74] and he relates the teaching of it to the office of *episkopos,* who is to be concerned for it and for the judgment and confutation of what is opposed to it. Moreover there emerges in these letters the implication of a succession of doctrine, allegedly from Paul to Timothy and Titus, and from them to the *episkopoi.* Whatever may be said about the full scope of such teaching, it is clearly rooted in the gospel (see 2 Timothy 1:10-11), but the impression is also given that the *kērygma* is now accompanied by other things (e.g., a "teaching which accords with godliness [*tē kat' eusebeian didaskalia*] 1 Timothy 6:3). And herein lies the problem in defining the object of teaching in the Deutero-Pauline letters.

VI. Teaching in the Letter of James

Though the dating of the letter of James is somewhat disputed, I cannot go along with the view that seeks to make it an early letter.[75] It might be debated, of course, whether it should be considered prior to the Deutero-Pauline letters, but this is in reality a minor issue here. The only passage in James that bears on the topic under discussion is 3:1-2: "Let not many of you become teachers, my brethren, for you know that we who teach shall be judged with greater strictness. For we all make many mistakes, and if any one makes no mistakes in what he says he is a perfect man, able to bridle the whole body also." Here the author acknowledges that he is a teacher, or at least poses James as one; moreover, he cautions against too many teachers in the Christian community. Whereas a certain *Gegenüber* in the Christian community is recognized here, there is no way to tell whether the teachers are all in official positions. Much more important, however, is the admission that "we all make many mistakes." This might, of course, be restricted in his thinking to those who teach, but it seems to have a broader scope (not excluding, to be sure, the teachers). One wonders what bearing that statement has on the correctness of the Christian message for which the teacher might be expected to show concern and on the whole later question of infallibility. Finally, his concession that "if any one makes no mistakes in what he says he is a perfect man" may be nothing more than an ironic ideal, which he knows is scarcely to be verified. The data in the letter of James are not abundant, but the slant that it presents may say something about the emergent teachers in the Christian community that one detects elsewhere in the NT writings.[76]

VII. Teaching in the Johannine Literature (John, 1, 2, 3 John)

The last part of the NT writings that we shall interrogate about teaching does not proceed in the same line as the material in Paul's letters from prison or the Pastoral Letters. In fact, it adds an important dimension. In a sense it is similar to the Synoptic material, but it introduces other factors that have to be kept in mind in the discussion of the role of teaching in the Christian Church. Most of the references to teaching in the Johannine literature are found in the Gospel of John, and it says more about the authors' view of Jesus than about a function in the early Christian community.

But one preliminary remark is called for before we look at the data themselves. It is well known that most of the Johannine literature lacks any reference to *ekklēsia* [77] and gives little evidence of a structured community. The extent to which it even hints at a *Gegenüber* within the community similar to that which can be detected elsewhere in the NT is debatable. Moreover, the stress on unity, which is evident in the Johannine gospel (e.g. 17:20) and which may remind one of the emphasis in Ephesians, is nevertheless a stress that is not accompanied by the suggestion of charismatic offices such as that epistle has. Consequently what there is in the Johannine literature about teaching has to be understood in a different way.

In the Fourth Gospel Jesus is again hailed as *rabbi* (explained as *didaskale*),[78] is regarded as *didaskalos*,[79] and acknowledges that he is *didaskalos*;[80] he is also depicted as teaching [81] and as admitting that he has taught.[82] Areas in which the Johannine Gospel differs from the Synoptics have to do with the source of his teaching and its relation to the Spirit.[83] "My teaching is not mine, but his who sent me; if any man's will is to do his will, he shall know whether the teaching is from God or whether I am speaking on my own authority" (John 7:16-17). "I do nothing on my own authority but speak thus as the Father taught me" (8:28). Rengstorf interprets this as "a direct inspiration or revelation," [84] but it is not immediately evident that that is all that is intended. However, if the Father is the source of Jesus' own teaching, the Johannine Gospel makes it clear that whatever the disciples will teach as coming from him will be under the Spirit's guidance: "the Counselor, the Holy Spirit, whom the Father will send in my name, he will teach you all things and bring to your remembrance all that I have said to you" (John 14:26). This teaching of the Spirit, however, has to be understood in the light of the Spirit's role in this Gospel: "When the Spirit of truth comes, he will guide you into all the truth; for he will not speak on his own authority, but whatever he hears he will speak, and he will declare to you the things that are to come" (16:13). This means that the Spirit's role is not the communication of new teaching or new revelation; it is rather the explication of the teaching of Jesus himself. It seems to affirm that the basic rooting of the Christian message, even in its process of developing under the guidance of the Spirit, must be "all that I have said to you" (14:26). It thus implies a twosided understanding of the Christian message; like Janus, it looks back to Jesus, but it looks forward to the future, open for development under guidance from the Spirit. Here then we find the idea of a Spirit-guided teaching within the Christian community, but no indication is given of such teaching resting solely with a group known as teachers.

There are two other aspects of the Johannine view of teaching in the Christian community that must be mentioned. First, in the discourse on the Bread of Life Jesus is made to quote Isa. 54:13 (after a fashion): [85] " 'they shall all be taught by God.' Every one who has heard and learned from the Father comes to me" (6:45). From the standpoint of the author (or authors) of the Gospel, believers are all regarded as *didaktoi theou*. Even though this may not be said in the context of a structured community, it cannot be forgotten, for it reflects a Johannine view of Christian discipleship and provides the background of the Spirit's teaching.

Second, a verse in 1 John may be significant in this regard; it seeks to explain why the letter was written: "I write this to you about those who would deceive you; but the anointing *(chrisma)* which you received from him [probably, the Father] abides in you, and you have no need that any one should teach you; as his anointing teaches you about everything, and is true, and is no lie, just as it has taught you, abide in him" (1 John 2:26-27). The *chrisma* is probably to be understood as the endowment of the Spirit.[86] But the verse raises a question: Is this a warning against teachers in the Christian community [87] or merely a warning against false teachers? I take it to be the latter (cf. vs. 26), but there may be a further hint to the Christian "anointed" even about the role of teaching within the community.

Finally, mention should be made of John 9:34, where the author casts the former blind man, who bears witness to Jesus, in a role of teaching Jesus' adversaries who were interrogating him: "and would you teach us?" The irony of the question is unmistakable, but it does not obscure the function of teaching even within the role of witnessing that the disciple of Jesus has.

Conclusion

The foregoing discussion of the main NT passages dealing with teaching in the early Christian community makes it clear that this function did exist and played an important role in the growth of that community. If at times it was difficult to say whether it was regarded as a function distinct from the function of preaching the gospel, the answer undoubtedly lies in the fact that the teaching function was nothing more than a development or extension of the latter. Though one finds in the genuine Pauline letters a greater emphasis on the function of preaching the gospel than on his awareness of himself as a teacher, he nevertheless knows of teachers within the Christian community along with apostles and prophets, and the categories suggest that he regarded them as distinct. On the other hand, the Lucan usage in Acts suggests that one would preach *or* teach the gospel. Since, however, the teaching touched at times on matters that were no mere expressions or reformulations of the kerygma, such as the circumcision of Gentile Christians, dictary regulations, and the observance of Jewish feasts—e.g., decisions at the so-called Council of Jerusalem—one could see that "the truth of the gospel" was invoked as a norm or criterion for such teaching. It was not just the preaching of the gospel that was considered normative, official, and Spirit-guided, but even such teaching as well: "it has seemed good to the Holy Spirit and to us . . . . ." (Acts 15:28). What is at issue here is the authority for such teaching in the early Church. Underlying it is the conviction that it is based on the authority of Jesus as the Christ and the risen Lord, who commissioned the disciples to preach and to teach (Matt. 28:16-20). In later NT writings the teaching function is in time connected with the office of *episkopos/presbyteros*, and it is expressed often in terms of a concern for "sound doctrine." The latter does not exclude a concern that the gospel be rightly preached, but there is more that is affected by it.

There is, however, another attitude toward teaching in the NT writings, where certain cautions (e.g., in Jesus' saying about the presence of people with the title of teachers in the community, or James' caution about the mistakes that everyone makes, affecting even teachers) are expressed. In other words, the teaching itself would have to be scrutinized. This may mean nothing more than what Paul meant when he referred to "the truth of the gospel" as a norm for Peter's conduct. But it may also suggest that what is taught is subject to more problems than the mere proclamation of the gospel itself.

Furthermore, in the Johannine literature one finds the implication that the guidance of the Spirit, leading the community into a more profound understanding of what the kerygmatic message was, rests as much with the community as a whole as with any group within it that may be regarded as teachers. For in the Johannine Gospel one finds no such group. This is understandable in the Fourth Gospel, which comes from a distinct understanding of Jesus and the Christian message, differing from the other Gospels and other NT books.[88]

The modern discussion of infallibility seeks to give expression to a quality of Christian teaching. It is a quality to which the Christian community only adverted after many centuries of meditation on the NT data about the normative, authoritative, and Spirit-guided teaching which became associated in the NT itself with the kerygmatic preaching imposed by the risen Christ on his followers. The word *infallibility* is not in the NT, nor is the concept with all its specifications and conditions, but it may be seen as a quality based ultimately in qualities that the NT writers associated with the teaching of the Church or its officials.

11

TEACHING OFFICE
IN THE NEW TESTAMENT?
A RESPONSE TO
PROFESSOR FITZMYER'S ESSAY

John Reumann

Any reply to Professor Fitzmyer's excellent survey on teaching and teachers in the New Testament not only must deal with the mass of data and the conclusions which he has set forth but also must indicate possible application of the scriptural material to the problem of teaching office in the church and infallibility. This response hopes in addition to note some alternative methods of approach.

After a few initial observations, I shall generally follow his order of presentation, (a) highlighting briefly what I understand him to be saying and (b) indicating points under dispute in New Testament studies and theological dialogue. (This list will be selective, for obviously in a presentation dealing with so many passages, where opinions vary, on any issue divergent scholarly opinions can be cited, most of which are irrelevant for our purposes.) Finally, suggestions about applications and future concerns will be offered. At the outset I record my gratitude for his encyclopedic study, with its clarity, honesty, and thoroughness.

I. Initial Observations

1. There is comparatively little overlap between the passages treated in the essay on "The Office of Teaching" and those listed for the dialogue in an unpublished paper

by Father Jerome Quinn on traditional "Scriptural Loci on Infallibility." Among the verses noted for both topics were Matt. 28:18-20, John 14:26, Acts 2:42-46, Eph. 4:11-15, and 1 Timothy 3:13-15, but each would have to be examined to see if and how the topics really connect. Does this not mean that *infallibility* and *teaching office* are separate terms, each with its own history, occasionally intertwined, or at least that their concatenation is a postbiblical development?

2. Professor Fitzmyer's methodology stresses the word-study approach and tradition history as an avenue to our topic.

a. Application of the tradition-history method leads to treatment of our sources in the New Testament in roughly the presumed chronological order of the documents: genuine letters by Paul, doubtful Pauline epistles, the Synoptic Gospels, Acts, Deutero-Pauline letters, James, and the Johannine literature, with due attention in the Gospels to the *Sitz im Leben Jesu* and *Sitz im Leben der Kirche*.

One may question whether even this careful sequence, akin to that followed in *Peter in the New Testament*, allows full attention to such stages as pre-Pauline Christianity (Jewish Palestinian, Jewish Hellenistic, and Greek Hellenistic) and, in the Gospels, *Sitz im Gemeindeleben* distinguished from *Sitz im Leben des Redakteurs*. Hence it may be helpful to ask, even more than has been done at times, about Paul's connection with those who were "in Christ" before him (especially when he is called "the first Christian theologian"), and about the distinction of redactoral verses in the Gospels from community tradition and genuine "Jesus material."

b. In the essay hope is expressed at the outset for a possible "trajectory" of the teaching office *(Lehramt)* and, more tentatively, of infallibility. More modestly, the goal is to show a New Testament concern for "authoritative teaching, a teaching function, and even traces of a Ministry of authoritative teaching."

The findings, however, are able to sustain as conclusions only that: (1) the teaching function "played an important role in the growth" of the early Church (*not* a steady growth of the teaching office); (2) teachers in the Christian community varied in their situations; and

(3) their function was "nothing more than a development or extension" of preaching the gospel, and "the truth of the gospel" served as the norm. Even so, (4) there are "cautions" in the New Testament about teachers and teachings, and (5) in the Johannine literature it seems the whole community, under the Spirit, rather than any group of teachers, is charged with guiding people "into a more profound understanding of what the kerygmatic message was." Hence it must be allowed that whatever infallibility means as a modern term for "a quality of Christian teaching," the term is not biblical, "nor is the concept with all its specifications and conditions" to be found in the New Testament; Christians "only adverted" to *infallible* as a predicate for their teaching "after many centuries."

The gap between expectations (remembering that traditional views have often claimed far more to be lodged in the New Testament) and actual findings (even assuming all the above conclusions) is, of course, created by our assigned topic, "The Office of Teaching" set in the context of "Teaching Authority and Infallibility in the Church." For the topic in that context is looking in the New Testament for what are *later* concepts. That *infallibility* is not a New Testament term has already been noted; *Lehramt* may also be a cause for difficulties as a term. The German need mean no more than "office of teacher," but it can also carry overtones, which it has developed in Roman Catholic history, of a strongly dogmatized institutionalizing of the original task of witness by Christians into a *magisterium* of the Church, hierachically conceived.

Perhaps a further difficulty lies in the term *trajectory*. Its application in biblical studies stems from the work of Koester and James Robinson.[1] They sought to show that the ancient, biblical world was not simply a matter of "fixed points" with static "backgrounds," but rather movement and development, with dozens of trajectories, like rockets lighting up the sky. At the least, in a topic such as ours, we must look for several possible trajectories, often with ups and downs, not merely evolutional ascent. But the very term suggests a hand which launches the trajectory and controls it—theologically put, God's hand! That begs the question of whether historical developments, often quite ambiguous, were by divine direction *(iure divino)* or from the vicissitudes of history *(iure humano)*. A more neutral term, like "lines of development" is to be preferred. *(Entwicklungslinie* is employed in the German translation of Koester and Robinson.[2])

c. The word-study method is assiduously followed throughout the essay, involving terms for teaching *(didaskō, didachē, didaskalia)* and for preaching (especially *kērussein* and *euangelizesthai);* hence the frequent use of articles from the Kittel *Theological Dictionary of the New Testament,* supplemented by other bibliography and the author's own astute observations.

In pursuit of this method it can be asked whether related and seemingly important terms like *katēcheō/katēchēsis, paradosis,* and even *paideuō* ought not to be included and be further pursued in order to get at the early Christian view of what was taught in the churches and how it was taught.[3]

A bigger question, quite apart from James Barr's overall strictures about the word-study method,[4] is whether this procedure takes us very far. Does it not leave us with many bits and pieces, without grasping the historical development? The word-study approach, by its very nature, may cause us to concentrate on individual terms, of a certain type at that, twigs and trees at the expense of the forest.

d. The role of certain backgrounds or other trajectories might also be noted at this point. One has to do with Old Testament—Jewish antecedents. Granted, the title of the paper is "The Office of Teaching in the Christian Church According to the *New* Testament," but early Christianity derived many of its offices from the Old Testament and Judaism. Granted, too, such backgrounds are brought in at pertinent points. Thus on p. 193 Rengstorf's opinion is set forth that *didaskein* has a Jewish content of "teaching Torah" and Paul worked in a Hellenistic context, so that the term *didaskein* had greatest use in the world of Jesus and the earliest Church rather than in Gentile Christianity.[5] Note 41 does point out the Palestinian-Jewish background of Jesus' teaching (Hebrew *limmēd*).[6] One cannot do everything at once, and any presentation must adopt its own order and limits, but there is need to keep in mind these Jewish and Old Testament roots, both as a positive influence and as something Christianity reacts against, in developing its own teaching offices.[7]

A similar example concerns the Spirit and the "spiritual" *(pneumatika)* or "grace" gifts *(charismata)* granted from God. Father Fitzmyer's presentation must several times refer to this setting for New Testament discussions about *didaskaloi* (1 Cor. 12:28; Eph. 4:11; Luke 12:12; John 14:26). Indeed, we are again and again forced to say, as in John, that the gift of the Spirit to all the members of the Christian community is what makes teaching-witness by believers possible. *Mutatis mutandis,* the same thing could be said of the Church as depicted in Acts, and the Pauline community in Corinth.[8] It would be well to bear in mind the New Testament communities' claim about having received the Spirit as background to any authority posited for their teachers and teaching. Indeed, the *Lehramt* and teaching-trajectories, if there be such, must intersect often with the trajectory of the Spirit, or even commence with it.

3. The matter of difference between preaching and teaching *(kērygma* and *didachē)* frequently appears in the essay. To be sure, the topic is first introduced as a question, and it is asked whether they are adequately distinct. But the New Testament data are said to provide "distinct terms" for two "distinct functions" (p. 187), though then it is allowed that "it is difficult to single out . . . the crucial difference" and "the nuances" in each case. Nonetheless, this does seem an operating distinction in the paper.

The New Testament evidence at times is disquieting, however. In Acts, "teaching and preaching/proclaiming are not infrequently juxtaposed, so that one wonders about the distinction between them" (p. 203); Luke thinks about them "in such a way that it is not easy to distinguish between them" (p. 204). In Colossians (−Ephesians) "the lack of a clear distinction between teaching and preaching is found"; instead, possibly "an extension of the function of proclaiming to teaching" (p. 195). Hence the conclusion on teaching that "at times it was difficult to say whether it was regarded as a function distinct from the function of preaching the gospel" and that "undoubtedly . . . the teaching function was nothing more than a development or extension of the latter" (p. 211).

Such frequent reservations raise questions about the whole *kērygma/didachē* distinction so long and widely accepted in scholarship. The differentiation is one we owe especially to the writings of C. H. Dodd.[9] These give the impression of *kērygma* as the apostolic message about what God has done to deliver us, preached to the world, and of *didachē* as apostolic teaching or ethical instruction, directed within the believing community. (Such an understanding carries with it many implications about what preaching is and for worship; it is also related to, but not to be confused with, the debate over "indicative" and "imperative.") [10] Yet Dodd himself did not always speak in such limiting terms and at times insisted that *didachē* was more than ethical instruction, embracing also apologetic and the exposition of theological doctrines [11]; it is all that happens after the *kērygma* is announced.

There have been many voices dissenting from Dodd's analysis. What if kerygma were not so propositional and unified as Dodd made the apostolic preaching? Even on Dodd's own showing, one ought to speak in the plural of (Pauline and Jerusalem) *kerygmata*.[12] In the opinion of some, the starting point was really a series of confessional formulae and creedal slogans [13]; in that case both preaching and teaching would be the drawing out of the implications from such a credo in a given situation.[14] Another type of conceptual analysis was offered by H. G. Wood [15] against the view of Dodd (and also in Bultmann) [16] that "Apostolic Preaching" and "Apostolic Teaching" were "separate entities"; according to Wood, "Kerygma and Didachē were distilled out of a tradition that included both" and thus "Didachē and Kerygma together make up Euangelion."

More impressive as hard evidence is the kind of analysis done by Robert H. Mounce [17] and others, arguing that Dodd "drew too sharp a picture between *kerygma* and *didachē*," for the New Testament usage is not so clear. The vagaries of the data are apparent enough. At Matthew 4:23 the evangelist says: Jesus "went about all Galilee,

teaching (didaskōn) in their synagogues
and *preaching (kēryssōn)* the gospel of the kingdom
and *healing* every disease and every infirmity among the people.

The Markan parallel on which Matthew draws has simply: "And he went throughout all Galilee,

preaching in their synagogues
and *casting out* demons (1:39).

(Luke 4:44 keeps only: "he was *preaching* in the synagogues of Judea.") Presumably Matthew has made the editorial changes quite intentionally, for he repeats virtually the same wording in 9:35, the two summary statements providing a frame for chapters 5–9. "Teaching" at 4:23 and 9:35 is meant to refer to the type of material in chapters 5–7, the Sermon on the Mount ("And he opened his mouth and taught them . . . " (5:1). "Healing" is described in the miracle stories in chapters 8–9. "Preaching the gospel of the kingdom" has been tersely described at 4:17 (derived from Mark 1:15, but also on the lips of John the Baptist at 3:2). What we seem to have here is a distinction between *kērygma* and *didachē* (or is it between teaching and healing?—cf. Acts 1:1, "all that Jesus began to *do* and *teach*"), but it is plainly *Matthean* theology, not found in Mark or at this point in Luke. It deserves to be followed up in the context of Matthew's thought, where teaching seems "the highest apostolic function" [18] (cf. 28:19). But did Matthew's predecessors make any such distinction?

Mark 1 is instructive here. Verses 14-15 portray Jesus *preaching* a "little kerygma." Then in v. 21 he enters into a synagogue and teaches, but what he taught we are not told. In vv. 23-26 he casts out an unclean spirit. The people exclaim: "What is this? A new teaching! With authority he commands even the unclean spirits. . . . " or (NAB) "What does this mean? A completely new teaching in a spirit of authority! . . . . " Is the *didachē* here some unreported sayings, or the miracle, or his *kērygma*? For this passage Rengstorf's judgment applies: "When the Synoptists speak of the *didachē* of Jesus, . . . they do not mean a particular dogmatics or ethics, but His whole *didaskein*, His proclamation of the will of God as regards both form and content," [19] and apparently his doing of it too, including miraculous deeds.

Akin to such Synoptic passages is Acts 13:12, where the proconsul Sergius Paulus believed when he saw how Bar-

Jesus was miraculously struck blind at Paul's rebuke, "for
he was astonished at the teaching *(didachē)* of the Lord."

More examples might be explored, but my points are
(1) the distinction between *kērygma* and *didachē* is not so
stark in many New Testament writers as Dodd assumed;
(2) *kērygma* and *didachē* blend and overlap, probably in
early sources as well as late ones, and indeed it may be only
a few theological minds (e.g. Matthew) who distinguish
them, and then not in Dodd's way (in Matthew *didaskein*
seems to be the dominant term, really including "to
preach"); (3) in any analysis, the role of miracles and
mighty works must be considered; (4) the real question
in preaching-teaching-healing is that of the authority *(ex-
ousia)* involved; note especially (5) the need for distinguishing redaction from tradition (e.g. in the Synoptics)
and (6) the need for attention to additional terms (e.g.
katēcheō in Gal. 6:6: what is "the word" which "he who
teaches" sets forth?).

My own impression is that *kērygma* and *didachē* are
more holistically conceived in the New Testament than our
modern dichotomies allow. Elsewhere I have argued that
the gospel (in the sense of good news) includes *both* our
"*kērygma*" and "*didachē*";[20] the latter involves, among
other things, reiteration of the basic saving message and
drawing out of its implications—what D. M. Stanley called
"induction into the *sensus plenior* of the kerygma."[21]
I understand *didachē* (for Paul especially) as including
(1) instructional material from Jesus[22] and (2) catechetical materials[23] developed in the believing community from
a variety of sources, presumably, in the opinion of the community, under the aegis of the Spirit.

Such an understanding of *kērygma* and *didachē* as proclamation about what God has done in Jesus and how in turn
believers respond (the material being variable in content
but remarkably fixed in certain persistent formulas) has
implications for the way we understand preaching/teach-
ing. Theologically it means that any teaching office works
from the gospel as its norm. For topics on which the Church
needs to speak, such as modern problems in social ethics,
it means that while there may be data and influences from
the contemporary sciences and from reason, nature, church
traditions and past practices, the gospel stands as norm

over all of these. The Church's imperatives derive from this central *kērygma*.[24]

II. Exegetical Analysis

A. The Pauline Trajectory

Summary of Professor Fitzmyer's paper:

I. *The Genuine Pauline Letters:* Paul does not often describe himself as teacher (but cf. 1 Cor. 4:17), because he was not taught the gospel which serves as the norm (Gal. 1:12) and which is indeed the truth (Gal. 2:5, 14). But he knows of teachers in early Christianity (mentioned in two lists of charismata, 1 Cor. 12:28; Rom. 12:7) and he knows of official teaching (Rom. 6:17) and doctrine (16:17). *Didaskein* is rare as a term in his Hellenistic churches, since it implies a Jewish concept ("to teach Torah").

II. *The Doubtfully Pauline Letters* lay greater emphasis on the subject. "The traditions you were taught by us" (2 Thess. 2:15) as a phrase suggests either gospel-tradition details which had become the object of teaching or a broader post-Pauline sense. Colossians blurs distinctions by relating teaching to admonition, wisdom, and the receipt of kerygmatic tradition. In Ephesians teachers are fourth in a list of functions but still "charismatic"; teaching relates also to conduct.

V. In the *Deutero-Pauline Letters* "official teaching" emerges, related to office *(episkopoi-presbyteroi)*, the holders of which are obliged, in succession from the apostle, to teach sound doctrine *(kērygma*, piety, etc.).

1. For analysis we may take these three sections together as the *Pauline course of development*. Regardless of where we draw the line between what is "authentically by Paul himself" and "the work of his school," we have a continuity which shows definite development and where Paul is on the way to becoming what he is in patristic tradition, "the divine apostle." [25]

2. The *pre-Pauline picture* does not emerge as clearly as it could. Obviously Paul knew of the idea of oral tradition *(paradosis)*, both in the Jewish sense of "the traditions of my fathers" (Gal. 1:14) and with reference to Christian teachings (1 Cor. 11:2; 2 Thess. 2:15; 3:6). He also reflected the rabbinic pattern of transmitting oral tradition (1 Cor. 15:3; 11:23).

Precisely what makes the difference in Paul is not the method of passing on the materials, but (1) the content and (2) the freedom with which Paul handled what he has received; "for Paul tradition is not sacrosanct"; [26] Christ, the Spirit, and the gospel dominate. His fidelity (to Christ and the gospel) and the freedom with which he handled *paradosis* deserve further exploration. Particularly helpful insights may come from exploring his treatment of authoritative citations from the Hebrew scriptures and of the sayings of Jesus.

3. In tracing the rise of Christian *teachers* in the communities Paul knew, if evidence is difficult to come by as to whether *didaskaloi* arose out of a Jewish background (and first appeared in Jewish Christianity) or out of Hellenistic Judaism,[27] a more sound starting point is with the earliest Christian reference to a teacher engaged in oral instruction of "the word," Gal. 6:6 *(ho katēchōn ton logon)* (cf. 1 Cor. 14:19; Acts 18:25; perhaps Luke 1:4; and note 3 above).

The list at 1 Cor. 12:28 may be dated a bit earlier than that at Romans 12. Conzelmann sums up well the issues and opinions on the Corinthians passage, "First apostles, second prophets, third teachers" (v. 28) refers to three charismatic offices for the Church as a whole, traveling from local community to local community (Harnack). Paul did not diminish charismatic and other offices (Kümmel); all community functions are charismatic. And (Greeven) the prophets and teachers did not travel, they were tied to the local congregation (cf. 1 Cor. 14); a similar view is held by Barrett and Wegenast.[28] Does that mean that apostles were the itinerant regional figures and teachers fixed local ones? That teachers are third also in the Romans list (12:6-7) is less impressive when we note the first two are not "apostles, prophets" but functions: "prophecy" and "service" *(diakonia)*. That, incidentally, is one reason why the footnote in *Eucharist and Ministry* [29] puts teachers in the "special Ministry of the church" (1 Corinthians 12) but hedges on "healing and teaching" (which could go either way), while putting "acts of mercy, aid, and helping" (cf. Rom. 12:7-8) under "the ministry of the people of God."

If one has to guess what teaching by such teachers in these brief references encompassed, it presumably concerned the setting forth of the Christian message (in an ever deepening way), with all its implications (especially for life and conduct), drawing in the Hebrew scriptures, thus passing on and applying the gospel tradition.

4. *Prophets* occur ahead of teachers in the Pauline lists at 1 Cor. 12:28; Rom. 12:6-7; cf. Eph. 4:11, and are mentioned in churches like Corinth as exhorting, comforting, edifying, and communicating knowledge and mysteries (1 Cor. 14:3, 24-25, 31; 13:2). Does a teaching function not occur when such Christian prophets deliver a "sentence of holy law" (such as 1 Cor. 3:17; 14:38; 15:51-52; 16:22; Gal. 5:21; 1 Thess. 3:4 have been analyzed to be)? The proposal of Ernst Käsemann, though it has not gone unchallenged,[30] holds that in small (Galilean) Palestinian communities charismatic figures spoke for God or the risen Christ, and statements from them or later prophets appear in Paul's letters and the Synoptic tradition. Such material would be teaching of highest authority, pointing to divine judgment, from a very charismatic teaching office.

5. With regard to *1 Cor. 4:17* (which turned out to be the "one occasion" where Paul did "describe himself as having taught"), the meaning of "my ways in Christ" can be defined more clearly than as "something broader than the gospel, though based on it" or as "something more than merely faith in the preached gospel" or "imitation" (of what?). The reference is not to life-style or idiosyncrasies of Paul himself, but to his catechetical teachings (and thus to his gospel). They are just "as I teach them everywhere in every church" (no need to delete this ecumenical reference, as J. Weiss proposed, for, as Conzelmann notes, such references also appear at 7:17; 14:33; 1:2; 11:16). Possible background may be "the ways of life" in which one walks according to the Old Testament (Pss. 25:4; 18:21; *derek; halakah;* cf. "the Two Ways" in Didache 1-6). It is catechetical material, if not a primitive catechism, that is meant. Old Testament background for imitation of the Christ as a Christian "way" has been argued by E. J. Tinsley.[31] The dissertation by Donald Manly Williams, referred to in note 14 of Professor Fitzmyer's essay, connects the phrase with Paul's personal example as well as his *paradosis* and argues that his teaching on love in 1 Corinthians 13—termed a "way" or *hodos* in 12:31—is one of his *hodoi.*

6. *Romans 6:17* is likely a later gloss, interrupting an antithetical sentence in Paul's letter. Paul wrote, "Thanks be to God, that

you were once slaves of Sin
and, having been set free from Sin, have become slaves of righteousness.

Between the contrast of "slaves of sin" and "slaves of righteousness" someone inserted the comment, "have become obedient from the heart to the standard of teaching to which you were committed." As an insertion it makes the obedience *prior to* the liberation from sin and captivity to God's righteousness. Its content is singular. Normally tradition is handed on to believers; here believers are handed over to a *typos didachēs*. The whole is uncharacteristic of Paul's emphasis on freedom. Whether by Paul or a later hand, it refers, I agree, to the catechetical tradition.[32] There are pre-Pauline formulas of the type envisioned in Romans at 1:3-4; 3:24-26; 14:8; and elsewhere.

7. If Rom. 6:17 is thus bracketed out or is citing a phrase from catechetical paraenesis, if 1 Cor. 4:17 is taken to refer to catechetical teaching, and if Gal. 6:6 (*katēcheō*) and uses of *paradidōmi* are given their due, then attention to how Paul handled tradition in shaping teaching becomes even more imperative. (The standard study is by Wegenast, whose views I am frequently citing; see especially note 26.)

8. There is growing emphasis in the Pauline corpus, chiefly beyond the uncontested letters and above all in the Pastorals, on (right) "doctrine" (*didaskalia*) and the "deposit" of faith "which has been entrusted" (*parathēkē*, 1 Timothy 6:20; 2 Timothy 1:12, 14). The Pastorals no longer feel the pejorative sense common in the Septuagint and Gospels of *didaskalia* as "human doctrines." "No tension is felt between the gospel, constantly preached afresh, and doctrine to be learnt, kept pure and defended against heresies." [33]

B. Jesus and the Synoptics

Summary of Essay

III. Though use of the sources is complicated by the two *Sitze im Leben,* Jesus can be seen historically in his Palestinian setting as a teacher (rabbi?), but as more than an expositor of Torah. Redactorally, *Luke* emphasizes teaching activity on the part of Jesus (to ground securely what his church was doing). *Matthew* rejects "rabbi" or "master" as a title within the community (23:8-10) for christological reasons, and roots teaching (of what?) in a commission from Jesus himself (28:18-20).

1. *Method:* It has already been suggested that we may need to pay more attention to the oral period and sources like Q in order to develop any trajectory here; we may also need to pay more attention to Mark. Redaction might be more consistently distinguished from tradition. Thus for getting at each gospel's picture of Jesus there would be fuller evidence than just the word-study approach affords.

2. As to the *historical Jesus*, clearly he was a teacher. Whether the term "rabbi" was used in his lifetime depends on when it became a *terminus technicus* in Judaism, and whether we insist on its being a technical term when applied to Jesus. I assume he was "rabbi" in that he taught and had pupils (disciples), but not in the (later) sense of having studied formally and been ordained. What distinguished him was his authority, in which the miracles played a part, as well as his radicalizing of the message about God's reign and will. The picture of him as teacher has doubtless been enhanced by later efforts, in the light of Christology, to gather his teachings and depict him as *the* teacher (of wisdom). The recent attempt by Etienne Trocmé [34] to show Jesus as he might have been looked upon by various groups in his day, on the basis of different forms of oral materials, might be noted: Jesus appears, e.g., to us as seen

| by disciples, | in dominical sayings and apophthegms, | as a { prophet and teacher; |
| by middle and lower-class non-Christians, | in parables, | as a moralist. |

3. How do we deal with a possibly nonchristological portrait of Jesus in the *Q source?* Here he seems to appear as one whose authority as teacher (which was considerable) lay in the fact that he was to be the coming judge. [35]

4. *Mark:* The faultiness in distinguishing too sharply between *kērygma* and *didachē* has been noted. What Jesus *preached* (Mark 1:14-15) was the coming kingdom in its imminence and the necessary human response; what he *taught* (*didaskein*, 4:2, and the following chapter of parables) was the coming kingdom in its imminence and the necessary human response. Teaching for Mark apparently encompasses miracles (1:27), controversy with opponents (2:13ff.; 12:35ff.), Old Testament interpretation (12:35-36), and "the way of God" (an Old Testament phrase? 12:14). Indeed, *didaskein* seems a sort of general, redactoral term in Mark to describe Jesus and his message.[36] In the Gospels generally the teacher becomes the teaching, and the content of Mark's message is Jesus himself (Marxsen).[37]

5. *Luke:* The evidence for "the Lucan emphasis on teaching" (pp. 199-200) becomes ambiguous when we are told that references to Jesus as teacher are "almost as great" in (shorter) Mark as in Luke. Use of infancy material and parallels with John the Baptist seem an indirect way to get at the topic. Jerome Murphy-O'Connor concludes rather that "Luke appears to have felt the inadequacy of 'Teacher' as a Christological title"; Glombitza holds that "in the Third Gospel Jesus is a 'teacher' only as far as strangers are concerned (e.g. 10.25 and 22.11)"; "'Teacher' is a title based on superficial observation, and it is never employed by the disciples. . . . "[38] If we wish to see Jesus teaching in Luke, chap. 20–21 (in the Temple!) and 4:14ff. (use of Old Testament) afford examples.

6. In *Matthew,* 28:16-20 is to be regarded as the best interpretative starting point for the gospel (cf. W. Trilling, Peter Ellis). The content of the teaching there ("all that I have commanded you") must have some connection with the five great discourses in Matthew; these are Jesus' *didachē* and commandment (cf. Deut. 5:30-31). The *commission* comes from the *risen Christ;* the *content* of the teaching comes from the *earthly Lord* (in Matthew, the disciples call Jesus *"kyrie"*; "though Matthew frequently uses the title *didaskalos* or alternatively *rabbi,* he never uses it as a mode of address in the mouth of the disciples, with one exception—Judas Iscariot" at 26:49 and 26:25![39]

Matthew 23:8-10 contains many enigmas (well-posed as questions in Father Fitzmyer's essay). In Jewish use, or if spoken by Jesus himself, "teacher" in v. 8 would have referred "clearly to the Father" (see p. 200); but in the redacted form one cannot be sure if it does; it is more likely christological. The *Kyrios* Jesus is the one *didaskalos,* who sends forth followers to teach what he has commanded. Matthew's church may well have eschewed "teachers/ rabbis" in the Jewish sense, out of reaction to "the synagogue down the street." [40] Jesus is *the* Teacher; there are no others.

However, the Matthean community may well have had a "school of scribes" (13:52) as well as "prophets and wise men" (23:34) who immersed themselves in Scripture in light of the gospel and brought out "what is new and what is old." Is that teaching? One need not be concerned if structures here differed from the charismatic teachers in Corinth 30 years before. The lines of development need not be the same, and besides the Matthean community probably had its troubles with, and reasons to avoid, such Hellenistic wonder-working charismatics.[41]

Last of all, is there in Matthew "the prohibition of a teaching office" (p. 200)? Professor Fitzmyer wrestles with this possibility. Wegenast offers the following opinion apposite to the concerns of this dialogue:

. . . for Matt., Jesus is the teacher of the *church* who supersedes the Sinaitic revelation and its rabbinic interpretations ("it was said to men of old") in order to lay a new foundation ("but I say to you"). After the death of Jesus, Peter guarantees this foundation (Matt. 16:18), holding the office of the keys . . . which to the Jews meant the office of a teacher [*das Lehramt*]. The foundation guaranteed by him is no new law but the fulfilment of the old, now freed from rabbinic distortions. Only now does the original intention of the law become clear (Matt. 19:8: "from the beginning"). These two verses (Matt. 16:18; 19:8) throw light on Matt. 5:19: he who lives without the Torah is without righteousness. The follower of Jesus is called not to lawlessness but to a superior righteousness, the foundation of which is the law and Christ's interpretation of it. This is why, after his resurrection, this interpretation must be passed on through teaching (Matt. 28:20).[42]

Wegenast's analysis points to Jesus as *the* Teacher. The disciples were not above their Teacher (10:24-25). Peter (in the particular role noted above) and presumably all the disciples taught what he, the earthly Risen One, had taught—messianic Torah, in Jesus' interpretation. But they were not themselves teachers—even Peter. Indeed, the eleven on the mountain remained "men of little faith" who both worshiped and doubted (28:17).[43]

It is agreed that the commission to the eleven relates to Christ's promise and presence; their preaching/teaching was to announce the kerygma and all that Jesus command- ed, perhaps even to be a "reformulation of the essential kerygma to meet new problems" (p. 202). But is there a *Gegenüber* in Matthew which implies an office of teacher in the Church "overagainst the community of believers" (p. 201). The *Malta Report* (par. 50) admittedly referred *Gegenüber* to the gospel proclamation, not to an office of teaching (the report used the phrase "office of the minis- try"). Again, the exact sense of *Lehramt* may be a cause of confusion. We must be careful (in light of the way Mat- thew uses *didaskein* terms and of his whole view of the Church)[44] not to read in an office of teaching in opposi- tion to church members, without further evidence, on the grounds it is implied by 28:16-20.

C. Acts

Summary of paper:

IV. *Acts* amplifies the picture in Luke's Gospel. The book knows of teachers in the local community (13:10) and stresses the apostles and others, teaching/preaching, on Jesus' commis- sion, with some concern for correct doctrine.

In this helpful sketch, with which I am in general agree- ment, the evidence seems again to point to teaching as reiteration of *kērygma (logos)*, as scriptural development, and as ethical implications of the *kērygma*. It is not con- cerned, as in Matthew, with exposition of Torah in the sense of laws. What is blurred is not Luke's concept but modern distinctions. What is taught seems more important than who teaches it, even given Luke's emphasis on "the Twelve" (or thirteen).

D. James

Summary of paper:

VI. *James 3:1* shows the author to be a teacher, without official position, but with the awareness, under God's judgment, that teachers may err.

Perhaps this passage should be related to the "teacher of wisdom" tradition. The role of teacher is viewed here as not unimportant in the Church, but with modesty, subject to "sins of the tongue" (3:2-12).

E. Johannine Literature

Summary of paper:

VII. The *Fourth Gospel* contains most of the references here, chiefly to Jesus as the teacher whose source of authority is in the Father and whose teachings will be explicated by the Paraclete. Believers are "taught by God" (6:45), have a *chrisma*, the Spirit (1 John 2:27), and must teach as part of their witnessing (9:34). In the Gospel there is no church structure, yet there is an emphasis on unity (from gospel doctrine?).

This Johannine picture is extremely important for grasping New Testament pluralism. It is a different world from Paul or the Synoptics. Jesus is the "apostle"; disciples abide in him. Is witness really directed outward to the world, except in controversy with "the Jews" (the world), or only inward, to development of the community? Clearly the content of the teaching is Jesus himself, as Revealer.

Those Christians who have the anointing need no further teaching (1 John 2:27; cf. 3:24), and have all knowledge, knowing the truth already (2:21). Is a *Lehramt* conceivable here, or only a proclamation (1:3) to remind hearers of what they already are, of implications of their confession (1:1-2; 4:2, for example), and of the need to keep doing the truth? Note also 2 John 9–10, about "abiding in the *didachē tou Christou*," which is in content "nothing else than the message of Jesus in John 7," [45] i.e., about himself, coming from the Father (John 7:16ff.).

III. Concluding Comments and Further Concerns

1. The essay lays a good groundwork for a difficult subject.

2. It is agreed that the teaching function did exist in early Christianity and grew stronger, if not always clearer (but not in an ever-steady, ascending trajectory). It does become connected, at times, with *episkopoi/presbyteroi* in the Pastoral Letters, but here the gospel of Paul the Apostle dominated those who did the subsequent "traditioning" and teaching. Romans 6:17 well expresses this situation: they "were handed over to the *typos didachēs.*" And the "traditions" involved here, whether written or oral (cf. 2 Thess. 2:15), seem to have been already openly known and accepted by the community of faith.

3. The cautions expressed by Father Fitzmyer on p. 212 are well taken: there is only one Teacher, Jesus Christ, according to Matthew; a certain modesty about teachers and their fallibility is noted by James; the community as a whole, rather than any group within it, serves as Spirit-guided teacher, according to the Johannine literature.

4. There are grounds to question any sharp dichotomy between preaching and teaching. The gospel, consisting of both didactic *kērygma* and kerygmatic *didachē,* seems a better way of conceptualizing what is involved in "the Word of God."

5. It seems necessary to trace *several* lines of development: at the least the Pauline line of development, the Synoptic (with bifurcating lines for each Gospel), and the Johannine. Should others be added to those? (e.g. "Jesus as Teacher," "the Spirit as Teacher," and "the wisdom trajectory"?)

6. An overall impression, as so often with the New Testament, is one of the tremendous variety within the early Church—a variety which must, within certain limits, have been "pleasing to God," orthodox, evangelical, and catholic. Apparently all these teaching models in the New Testament "seemed good to the Holy Spirit and to us" (the early Christian Church).

7. One is struck, from the evidence presented in Professor Fitzmyer's essay, with the centrality of the *kērygma* or gospel in explaining New Testament teaching. The latter overlaps with or derives from the former again and again.

The key New Testament phrase is "the truth of the gospel" (Gal. 2:5, 14). The gospel is the truth which serves as the norm for all teaching and conduct, even of apostles in Antioch and Galatia, and of all teachers and teaching ever since.[46]

12

ON THE TERMINOLOGY FOR
FAITH, TRUTH, TEACHING,
AND THE SPIRIT IN
THE PASTORAL EPISTLES:
A SUMMARY

Jerome D. Quinn

The Pastoral Epistles (PE hereafter) took their present form in the second Christian generation, perhaps around A.D. 80-85. The sources for these compositions and the traditions which they utilize go back into the first Christian generation and the Pauline apostolate itself. Though the PE betray some familiarity with the concepts and the vocabulary that occur in the rest of the Pauline collection, they never explicitly cite other Pauline documents. The links with the concepts and the vocabulary of Luke-Acts are notable and still await systematic explanation.[1] In any event this little collection of correspondence as we now have it must have originally appeared in the order Titus, 1 Timothy, 2 Timothy.[2] The following notes summarize conclusions from the exegesis of the PE.[3]

Faith

The terminology for faith in the PE is predominantly adjectival and substantival. "God, who never lies" (Titus 1:2), has spoken and acted through Jesus Christ (2 Timothy 1:9-10), who is "faithful" (*pistos:* 2 Timothy 2:13). He in turn regarded Paul as "faithful" and placed him in his Ministry (1 Timothy 1:12). Paul's own collaborators are to turn to "faithful men" for those who will carry on the apostle's work (see 2 Timothy 2:2). The whole body of Christians whom they serve are the faithful (see 1 Timothy 4:3, 10, 12), so named not because they believe anything and anyone, not because they are credulous, but because they have believed in God (see Titus 3:8) and in the apostolic teaching (see 1 Timothy 4:6), which in its turn can be formulated in words and proposed for belief.[4]

The apostle (Paul), his co-workers (Titus, Timothy), and those with whom they in turn share that work *(presbyteroi, episkopoi, diakonoi)* exist for the sake of the faith (see Titus 1:1-9; 1 Timothy 1:1-7; 4:6-14; 2 Timothy 2:1-2). That faith is in its turn a single, indivisible reality with an inside and an outside, with subjective and objective aspects.[5] It is the faith of the Church (see *koinē pistis*, Titus 1:4), which is conceived of and expressed through a familial (not a democratic or monarchical) model (see 1 Timothy 3:4-5). This paradigm puts a premium on faithfu'ness, trustworthiness, mutual loyalty, and responsibility within a believing and saved people who are served by a believing and saved apostolic Ministry (see 1 Timothy 4:16). Both the Church and the apostolic Ministry are to profess their belief through action (cf. Titus 3:8); both articulate their belief verbally in forms suitable for the common, public worship of believers.[6]

In the PE faith is always understood to inhere in persons, not in things or words, and these are persons who are responding to the person of Jesus Christ. For the PE, faith *qua* subjective response to the revelation in Christ is a collegial and ecclesial faith (Titus 1:4). Faith, insofar as it is the revelation of "God, who never lies" (Titus 1:2), is Christ himself. In the PE to be "in the faith *(en pistei)* is to be "in Christ" (cf. Titus 3:15; 1 Timothy 1:2 with 1 Timothy 3:13; 2 Timothy 1:13).

Truth

For the PE "the truth" refers to the content of belief which bears fruit in the personal history and conduct of those who have come to the "knowledge of truth." [7] That truth, moreover, comes through the oral proclamation and teaching of the Pauline apostolate (see Titus 1:1-3; 1 Timothy 2:6-7) and, on one occasion, is linked with the apostle's writing (1 Timothy 3:14-15). It has its source in "God, who never lies" *(ho apseudēs theos),* who is the Savior-Father (Titus 1:2-4), and its content is Christ Jesus, incarnate, risen, and proclaimed and believed in as Savior, Lord, and God (cf. 1 Timothy 3:16 with Titus 1:4; 2:13-15; 3:4-7; 2 Timothy 1:8-11). The death and resurrection of Jesus are the principal events proclaimed.

How do the PE conceive of the relation between the truth and the Church? First Timothy 3:14-15 understand this apostolic correspondence as instructing the Pauline coworker so that he in his turn can understand "how one ought *(dei)* to behave in the household of God, which is the church *(ekklēsia)* of the living God, the pillar and bulwark of the truth *(stylos kai hedraiōma tēs alētheias)."* The anarthrous *ekklēsia* here may designate a local congregation [8] or the universal assembly of all believers, as the generic directive that is being formulated may imply.[9] It has been customary to understand the anarthrous phrase, "pillar and bulwark of the truth" in relation to the preceding anarthrous *ekklēsia*. It may also be understood of the "Timothy" to whom this letter is written.[10] In either case the truth (i.e. Jesus Christ) is solidly and publicly upheld (by the Church or the apostolic Minister) in the way a fiery pillar *(stylos)* upheld Yahweh, guiding his people to freedom (Sirach 24:4; cf. 36:24).[11] The image suggests not only believers' assurance and certitude in their relationship to their Lord but also the reciprocity and subordination involved in that relationship.

In the PE the truth is to good actions what errors, lies, and myths are to vice (see Titus 1:14-16; 2 Timothy 2:16-19). The latter are ultimately of demonic origin (see 1 Timothy 4:1-4), as truth and virtue are the harvest of the Spirit (see below). Apostolic teaching (see below) aims for conversion and belief as well as for knowledge (i.e. a profound, precise experience) of the truth (see Titus 1:1; 1 Timothy 2:4; 4:3; 2 Timothy 2:25). This knowledge is not demonstrated or demonstrable but simply confessed without argument.[12] Refutation (see Titus 1:9, 13; 2:15; 1 Timothy 5:20; 2 Timothy 4:2) is very close to repudiation. Because action is a function of truth, both Christ and his apostolic Ministers give directions and commands for living to those who listen to their word (see 2 Timothy 2:15; 4:1-4).

Teaching

Faith and truth (as the PE use that term) are ultimately indemonstrable; they are not unreasonable or foolish. They can thus be taught and ought to be taught correctly to all, whether believers or not (cf. Titus 2:1-15). To designate various aspects of this process the PE employ such terms as *kēryssein, legein (logos), parakalein, paraggelein,* and *didaskein.*

The * *dida-* cluster of terms is paradigmatic for the concept of teaching in the PE. The relatively rare verbal forms *(didaskein, heterodidaskalein)* describe the activity of "Timothy" and his appointees (1 Timothy 4:11; 6:2; 2 Timothy 2:2) as well as an opposing cadre of Christian teachers (Titus 1:10-11; 1 Timothy 1:3; 6:3). The assemblies for public prayer appear to be the setting for this normally oral activity (cf. 1 Timothy 2:12 with 4:13).

Paul is the one teacher *(didaskalos)* for the PE (1 Timothy 2:7; 2 Timothy 1:11); the plural *didaskaloi* has a bad sense (2 Timothy 4:3 and cf. 1 Timothy 1:7). The Pauline gospel (cf. 1 Timothy 1:11; 2 Timothy 2:8), expounded incorruptly, openly to all, and objectively (cf. Titus 2:7-8; 11-14), is the key to interpreting the divinely inspired Scriptures of Israel [13] which (along with other written materials) [14] furnish the apostle, his co-workers, and their appointees with suitable content for exhortation, correction, and direction (2 Timothy 3:14-17). Behind the teaching of a Titus or of a Timothy as well as that of their appointees stands the apostolic command [15] of Paul which is ultimately the command of the Savior God (cf. Titus 1:3 and below on the Spirit). The Pauline interpretation of the Old Testament is in no sense in competition with other interpretations. His *didaskalia* (always in the singular) from the one Spirit simply overwhelms the devilish doctrines of his opponents (plural, *didaskaliais daimoniōn,* 1 Timothy 4:1). The wholesome Pauline teaching proceeds from the knowledge of truth; the infected teachings of his opponents do not.[16] The apostolic teaching about the truth is validated by the Spirit (cf. 1 Timothy 1:18 with 2 Timothy 1:14), not by the letter, even "the sacred letters" of Israel's scriptures (2 Timothy 3:15).

The PE are an attempt in the second Christian generation to recover and use the Pauline (and thus apostolic) principles for explaining and applying the truth, the Word of God, to a Christian living in that generation. The author of the PE is already probing the paradox that the apostle and those who shared his Ministry were servants of and subjects to the Word of God while evidently above the letter of the Scriptures and able to transmit their one true sense. For this correspondence the Pauline apostolate has really continued in Paul's co-workers and their teaching. This had occurred without Paul's bodily presence, for all the conviction of the PE that he is the model and source of the teaching now expounded (cf. 1 Timothy 4:6 with 2 Timothy 1:13; 2:1-2). Since this correspondence does not cite the writings that emanated from "the historical Paul," where does it get its evident and adamant certitude that this teaching really is that of Paul?

The Spirit

Faith, truth, and teaching in the PE came from persons, were about persons, and were proposed to persons for personal reception or rejection and for action. In this interpersonal dynamic the objective and subjective aspects of these realities were indissolubly united. A like typology appears in the way in which the PE conceive of the Holy Spirit, the "objective," divine, personal power in whose gift lies the internal rebirth and renewal of all people in holiness for eternal life (Titus 3:5).[17] This Spirit is, subjectively speaking, the believer's spirit (cf. 2 Timothy 4:22) responding in faith, love, godliness, endurance, moderation, etc. (cf. 2 Timothy 1:7). The Scriptures of Israel and the apostolic faith, truth, and teaching have their vitality from the Spirit who has given them (cf. 2 Timothy 3:16) and who enables them to be received (cf. 2 Timothy 1:14). The Spirit laminates together their objective and subjective aspects. The PE aim at transmitting in the Church and for the Church not just the apostolic teaching but the Pauline apostolate itself. Thus the Spirit authorizes and validates not only the Pauline teaching (*didaskalia*) but also the persons of Paul, Timothy, and those whom they and the Spirit have designated to transmit the revelation (cf. 1 Timothy 1:18, 2 Timothy 1:14; 2:1-2). The indwelling Spirit also guards their transmission of that revelation, and Paul's own *language* for articulating and transmitting the truth is submitted as an authentic paradigm of the way in which all of these persons are to teach (cf. 2 Timothy 1:13-14; 2:1-2, 8). For the PE, the Spirit has himself revealed (1 Timothy 4:1-5) that other teachings emanate from other spirits!

For 1 Timothy 4:11-14 and 2 Timothy 1:6-7 the Pauline and presbyteral imposition of hands bestows a *charisma* (i.e. a tangible gift resulting from the divine *charis*)[18] which in its turn gives life and power to the apostolic Minister's conduct and teaching. In fact, through prophetic activity the Spirit has taken the lead in bringing "Timothy" to his task (cf. 1 Timothy 1:18). Thus for the PE the apostolic Ministry and its teaching are set at every turn in that new order of the Spirit (cf. Titus 3:5) who has vindicated the Lord and the apostolate to all the nations (cf. 1 Timothy 3:16). The confident certitude of the author and those who share his apostolic Ministry (cf. 2 Timothy 1:7-8; 3:14-17 with 1:12; 4:17) has its taproot in the Spirit. They accordingly resemble prophets more than teachers in their adamant certitude about the Word of God entrusted to them.

13

SOME ELEMENTS IN
THE PRE-HISTORY OF
PAPAL INFALLIBILITY

Robert B. Eno

Most historical studies of papal infallibility devote little space to the ancient church. This essay attempts to isolate and briefly analyze the significant patristic elements that contributed cumulatively to the view that there was a divinely assisted doctrinal role for the Roman Church. It should be noted at the start that many of these elements are the same ones previously studied in the development of the Roman primacy. This essay does not take the definition of Vatican I nor such related considerations as the circumstances of an *ex cathedra* definition as a starting point in reviewing the patristic period. Rather than infallibility, the basic conviction of the ancient church might best be referred to as a belief in the inerrant fidelity of the Church to the apostolic gospel.

The ancient world as a whole was oriented toward the past. One of the principal difficulties of the early Christian apologists was to explain why, if Christianity was essential to salvation, it had arrived "so late" in world history. As Marcus Aurelius was praised for restoring old laws rather than making new ones, so Pope Leo I spoke of his ideal as "renewing the old, not doing new things." [1] This preoccupation with the past continued even as subtle changes inevitably crept in. Even the simple repetition of the old formulas was no guarantee against change.

How to Resist Innovation?

After the death of the primary witnesses to the preaching of Christ and of the Apostles, concern grew over divergences in the teaching being transmitted. Evidence of such disquietude can be found in the Pastoral Epistles and in the Didache's attempts to develop criteria for the discernment of true and false prophets. In particular, the Gnostics, with their claim to teach a hidden, esoteric message derived from Jesus, posed a real threat.

In response to these dangers, structures developed designed to protect the precious pearl of the gospel. The Church trusted that the message could never be totally lost or destroyed, that the Holy Spirit, sent to guide the Church into all truth (John 16:13), would not fail in his task (e.g. Tertullian, *Prae* 28). Yet despite this basic trust, one finds, for example, the development of a canon of the New Testament to exclude the new horde of apocryphal scriptures. Brief summaries of the apostolic teaching, the *regula fidei*, and the later elaboration of formal creeds testified to a preoccupation with fidelity.

In considering the question of Roman teaching authority, the single most relevant fact was the development of the idea of apostolic succession and its close link with the apostolically founded sees. This line of thought was found embryonically at least in Clement of Rome's appeal to succession and the first clear emergence of the monepiscopate in Ignatius of Antioch. Irenaeus of Lyon and Tertullian connected the two elements in their argumentation against the Gnostics.

In *Adversus Haereses* III, 3, 1f. (an important primacy text that is also clearly significant for the question of Roman teaching authority), Irenaeus argued that the teachings of the Gnostics are totally unlike anything taught by the bishops. He appealed to the succession of bishops in any of the apostolically founded churches. Rome was singled out as the outstanding church in this regard because of its greater *principalitas*, i.e. its founding by Peter and Paul. In the context of his argument, the Roman Church, however glorious, is not unique. It is not the only one of its kind, but it is the outstanding example of its kind, namely the apostolic sees.[2]

It is not, then, a question of some divine guarantee of preservation from error for the Roman Church. The Irenaean concept of the *charisma veritatis certum* (*AH* IV, 26, 2) does not enter this discussion of Rome in a direct fashion. The precise meaning of the phrase, which apparently found little explicit follow-up in the patristic tradition, is much disputed, but it refers, in general, to the ministers of the churches who are entrusted with the preservation of the gospel teaching, not to any one see.[3]

Despite the apparent tendencies of the arguments of Irenaeus and Tertullian, in the early centuries consensus rather than appeal to any one local church was the basic element in decision making. The gathering of councils, especially the larger councils of the Christian empire, was the quintessential method for settling disputes.

With their continuing concern over the preservation of the teaching of the past, the Church Fathers did not see or did not advert to shifts or developments that modern theologians recognize in the patristic era.[4] They envisaged an unbroken historical continuity of the teaching of the apostolic doctrine. This clear, broad stream of orthodoxy could be verified by reference to the bishops and writers of the past. The classic expression of this appeal to historical consensus is seen in Vincent of Lerins and his well-known though problematic canon: catholic doctrine is that which has been believed everywhere, always, by all (*Comm.* 2.3). Just three years before Vincent wrote, the Council of Ephesus under Cyril's leadership had patristic florilegia introduced as evidence (*Comm.* 29.41). Augustine, finding it necessary in his dispute with the Donatists to insist that Cyprian had sometimes been in error, took a somewhat more nuanced view of the past, especially of councils, even apparently allowing for a certain degree of self-correction and improvement. He seems to have put considerable emphasis on current consensus (*De Baptismo* 2.3.4; also *Contra Ep. Fund.* 5.6).[5]

In all this there was unfolding in the Church at large a process which later theological thought would call *reception*. Why over the centuries had certain doctrines been accepted and others not? Why were some councils accepted and others not? Especially during the controversies following the Council of Chalcedon, some explicit thought emerged concerning this retrospective aspect of the consensus argument. For example, it was claimed that the decisions of Chalcedon could not be reconsidered and certainly could not be altered because the whole Church had accepted them and, especially in the West, because the Roman See had approved them. The patristic era believed explicitly in the assistance of the Holy Spirit in conciliar decisions, yet judgment about the presence or absence of the Spirit at a given council was apparently subject to retroactive approval or disapproval depending on whether or not a later generation viewed a council's decisions as compatible with its view of tradition.

The Roman Church and the Past

Within this general picture of concentration on the past, the Roman Church was, if anything, even more adamant than the rest of the Church. Stephen's rebuke to Cyprian set the tone: *Nihil innovetur nisi quod traditum est.* "Whether it be in the rule of faith or the observance of discipline, the norm of antiquity is to be preserved" (Leo). Why should anyone go beyond the decisions of our ancestors? Why are they not good enough for us? Are we wiser than they, asked Gelasius? The Roman synod of 465 under Pope Hilary summed up its viewpoint by this acclamation, shouted seven times: *Ut Antiquitas servetur, rogamus!* [6]

General uniformity, even beyond doctrine, was the Roman ideal: "If there is one faith, one tradition must also stand; if one tradition, then one discipline must also be observed by all the churches." In the view of Innocent I, discipline and practice as well as doctrine were determined by the apostles and handed on. Obviously since they had all agreed on a common discipline, any current differences signaled a departure from the apostolic norm. Since Rome had certainly preserved tradition intact and unchanged, all deviants must reform according to the Roman and therefore apostolic model. Zosimus put it very clearly: "With us antiquity lives on, its roots unshaken. . . ." [7]

In the Roman view the preservation of good order was all important. Disorder followed inevitably from the breakdown of discipline and the neglect of rules. As Gelasius put it: "Let us keep untouched the rules which the Church has received from the same Fathers and there will be peace. Let them remain fixed and there will be no discord." A failure of *sollicitudo* and *cura* on the part of local bishops meant that the old rules would be lost through ignorance and laziness. This breakdown in turn was the greatest menace to the stability of faith and concord among bishops. ". . . Embrace the grace of ancient tradition and stand firm on the unshaken foundation, not changing your hearts with the times." The point is that in the Roman view, doctrinal inerrancy meant basically transmitting intact the teaching of the past. Their claim was that the Roman Church accomplished this task best of all.[8]

At this point it should be noted that many of the statements made both by Rome about itself and by others about Rome speak explicitly of the Roman Church or the faith of the Roman community rather than about the Roman bishop alone. Yet since even in antiquity it was the Roman bishop who was not only the spokesman but the real decision-maker for the Roman Church, it is probably not unreasonable to presume that many of these statements were understood of the Roman bishop. Even in the Middle Ages canonists discussed the Roman Church as a local community, as the universal Church, as the pope, as the *ecclesia virtualis,* and as the papal curia.

The Roman self-image was one of untainted fidelity to the heritage of the past. Replying to the African condemnation of Pelagianism, Innocent compared Roman teachings to uncorrupted waters flowing from the spring (head) throughout the world. An important part of the Roman care for all the churches was the effort to see that the faith of the gospel was preserved intact in the universal Church. It would be a great sacrilege to depart from the apostolic tradition in anything. Similarly, it would be impossible for anyone ever to be able to get the apostolic see to depart from the decisions of Nicaea, since it cannot equivocate about matters which are clearly consonant with Scripture and catholic doctrine. In short, for Leo the faith of Peter, ever active in the Roman See, is ". . . divinely fortified with such great solidity that, as heretical perversity cannot corrupt it, neither can pagan infidelity overcome it." The popes after Leo, in trying to defend the decisions of the council of Chalcedon and the Tome of Leo, continued to stress their fidelity to the past: "We are not being stubborn; we are defending the teachings of our fathers." [9]

After 451 Leo himself felt the pressure from the East for a new council and resisted it on the grounds that a new council would make it seem that Chalcedon's decisions (and his own Tome) were still subject to doubt and discussion. On the contrary, its decisions were dictated by the Holy Spirit and confirmed by the apostolic see. What is perfect should not be reconsidered and what is defined should not be suppressed. The evangelical and apostolic truths of Chalcedon have been fixed by the Spirit. Leo's successors were equally adamant, as can be seen from the length of the Acacian schism. Neither the decisions of the council nor the teachings of Leo were to be reconsidered. [10]

Occasionally one finds explicit reference to the idea that the Roman bishops could not go contrary to the teachings and actions of their predecessors. As far back as the late second century, Tertullian complained that Praxeas had succeeded in "chasing away the Paraclete" by persuading a Roman bishop (Victor?) that he could not go contrary to the actions of his predecessors. Pope Simplicius, in writing to Acacius, was quite clear that continuity must exist in Roman teaching when he spoke of "the teaching of our predecessors against which no dispute can be made." One of the more embarrassing incidents concerning Roman continuity (but not concerning the faith) happened during the time of Pope Symmachus (c. 500). His predecessor Pope Anastasius II had intervened in the troubled waters of southern Gallic church politics, augmenting the rights of Vienne at the expense of Arles. Symmachus, writing to Arles, admitted that Anastasius had gone against the rulings of earlier popes and lamented the evil consequences of thus weakening the hallowed ordinances of antiquity. In writing to Vienne, however, he stated that since Anastasius had gone *beyond* but not *against* the canons, there could be no reconsideration of his predecessor's actions. [11]

In all this, one must keep in mind that there is a distinction between the idea that Rome has not in fact erred vs. the bolder idea that the Roman Church, by divine ordinance and assistance, cannot err. Gelasius came closest to making the latter assertion. On two occasions he stated that God would not allow the See of Peter to err. In the Acacian schism he stated that the pope could not associate himself with the memory of Acacius, otherwise the See of Peter would itself be in need of a remedy rather than offering one, and God would not allow that. If the apostolic See were stained by any contagion, "which we trust could not be," then where would resistance to error and correction for the erring come from? [12]

The Roman Church, Rock and Norm

From this general Roman assurance that it had preserved the teaching of the Apostles we go now to a consideration of the Roman position that its belief and practice are the norm for the rest of the Church. Early on, the Quartodeciman and Rebaptism controversies had manifested this Roman view. Disputed questions, especially the more important ones, were to be sent on for Roman review. This function of Rome as center and norm was most often acknowledged by the Western churches of Italy, Gaul, and Spain. But even in the Eastern view, in times of crisis Rome in particular and the West in general could be appealed to. Most of the doctrinal disputes of antiquity centering on trinitarian and christological questions began and were carried on in the East. On the other hand, in the West it can be said that most of the Roman correspondence concerned disciplinary matters.[13]

Leo expressed very clearly the idea that as Peter was superior to the other apostles, so the bishop of Rome was superior in power to the other bishops, though all were equal in power of orders (*Similitudo honoris-discretio potestatis*). The Roman Church was to be the norm. After speaking of the Tome of Leo, Simplicius wrote to the emperor: "This same norm of apostolic doctrine remains unshaken in us, the successors of him to whom the Lord entrusted the care of the whole flock, from whom he would never be absent till the end of the world, against whom, he promised, the gates of hell would never prevail, by whose decisions, he affirmed, what was bound on earth would never be loosed in heaven." Rome was also a norm for practice, as Innocent assured Bishop Decent of Gubbio, as well as a norm for doctrine from which the truly orthodox would not separate themselves. All the weightier decisions on disputed questions were to come to Rome and all Rome's decisions were to be obeyed.[14]

The Roman vocabulary of supremacy most commonly centered on the word *firmare* or its cognate forms. In his *Ep.* 26, Gelasius wrote that the decisions of each synod approved by the universal Church were also confirmed and safeguarded by the first see. The word *confirm* was made more concrete and telling by its association with the Petrine imagery of the rock. The intended lesson was that Roman confirmation added a degree of unshakable strength and immobility which the decision did not possess previously. "In Peter the strength of all is fortified . . . so that the firmness, which was given to Peter through Christ, might be conferred on the Apostles through Peter." As the rock of Peter strengthens the whole Church, so Roman approval strengthens local decisions, turning doubtful questions into certainties. "We have frequently indeed, with the instruction of God's Spirit, steadied the brethren's hearts when they were tottering on the slippery places of doubtful questions by formulating an answer either out of the teaching of the Holy Scriptures or from the rules of the Fathers. . . . wrote Leo. It was at this point in time that papal letters began to make frequent use of Luke 22:32.[15]

The Roman Church Has the Final Word

Rome was not only the place to seek answers; after they were given, after decisions received the Petrine solidity, no further appeal was possible. The earliest claims that there could be no reconsideration of Roman decisions are found in the early fifth century letters of Popes Zosimus and Boniface I.[16]

The greatest threat to the Church was mutability, but Rome provided stability. In the last half of the fifth century the most ominous threat to stability was the desire of the Eastern emperors to reconsider the decisions of Chalcedon. The papal letters to the East again and again stressed that this must not and could not be done. Just to speak of such reconsideration gave new strength to heresy and undermined true doctrine. In the Acacian schism, one result of this Eastern attempt to revise Chalcedon, the Roman

Church answered Eastern objections that one patriarchal see had no right to excommunicate another without conciliar consultation and action. Gelasius as usual stated the Roman case most forcefully. Earlier Rome alone defended those unjustly persecuted in the East: Athanasius, Chrysostom, Flavian. In these cases the acquittal granted by Rome alone outweighed all the Eastern condemnations. By what right did they call Rome to judgment? Rome could judge the whole Church and none could dispute its judgment. Just as "what the first see did not approve, could not stand, so what it judged, the whole church accepted." [17]

The well-known statement *Prima sedes a nemine judicatur* first appeared at the beginning of the sixth century in connection with legal disputes surrounding the election of Pope Symmachus. Its formulation was actually derived from a forgery of the acts of a nonexistent African council of Sinuessa. At the beginning of the sixth century it had specific reference to civil charges against the bishop of Rome such as those made against Damasus in the fourth century. In later canonical development, however, it had considerably wider ramifications.[18]

The question of the authority of a general council, the reason for its authority, and its relation to the authority of the Roman See are never treated with canonical precision and consistency in antiquity. As a recent commentator remarked about Ambrose's view of councils, there is a great deal of circularity in the patristic judgment of the value of councils. If a council meets to discuss a question of faith, how can one be certain that its decision is compatible with the faith handed down? If a council is accepted because its faith is that of tradition, how can one be sure that that is in fact the case? Eventually the fact of Roman acceptance of a council came to be seen at least as one among several significant criteria. In the late fourth century Damasus rejected the Council of Ariminum out of hand despite the large number of bishops in attendance because the Roman bishop was not represented and, no doubt, because it went against the Nicene faith.[19]

In mid-fifth century Leo was drawn into the dispute involving Eutyches. In writing to Flavian, Leo's initial reaction was that there was no need for a council in the first place because his Tome explained the matter adequately. After the fiasco of II Ephesus (449), he at first demanded another council to set things right. Then when Marcian became emperor Leo turned against the idea of a new council. Was this because he believed that Roman authority was strong enough and his own explanation definitive enough to obviate the need for such a gathering? Or did he, with good reason, fear that such a meeting beyond his control was at best unpredictable? He instructed his legates in 449 that they were to insist that the council accept what the apostolic See had decided. After the happy event of Chalcedon in which his views were accepted and acclaimed, Leo wrote to the bishops of Gaul in such a way as to emphasize his own perspective that his decision had been the basic one and that the council had simply accepted it.[20]

In his later disputes with the Eastern emperors and in his efforts to block any revision of Chalcedon, Leo stressed that acceptance of the council by Rome and the world Church made revision impossible. As time went on, Chalcedon, especially in the West, came to be regarded as essential and as unshakable a pillar of orthodoxy as Nicaea itself because it was accepted by Rome and the universal Church. The apostolic See was the "unfailing executrix of Chalcedon for the Catholic faith." Gelasius specified definite conditions for the validity of a council. An illegitimate, invalid council goes contrary to the Scriptures, the doctrine of the fathers, and the ecclesiastical rules. It is rejected by the Church and, above all, the apostolic See does not approve it. A valid council, of course, has the contrary qualities; above all (*maxime*) the apostolic see must approve it. Such a valid synod can in no way be changed or even reviewed by a later synod. A new synod must conform completely to the former valid ones. Since the debate about whether a council's decisions conform to or go contrary to the Scriptures, the Fathers, and the canons could be endless, and since acceptance by the universal Church was equally difficult to ascertain and agree upon, the last condition—Roman approval—became the more important since it was more obviously verifiable. During the early stages of the Three Chapters controversy, the African champions of the Western tradition, Ferrandus and Facundus, both stressed the irreversibility of Chalcedon on the grounds of ecclesial and Roman acceptance. For Gelasius what the Roman See had confirmed at Chalcedon had to be accepted by all; what the Roman See rejected, even though the emperor himself supported it (canon 28), had no valid existence.[21]

The Roman Role in Doctrinal Disputes

The role of Rome in the earlier doctrinal controversies is not always clear. As has been noted, the deepest and most serious discussions began and were carried on in the East. Frequently, as in the cases of the condemnations of Origen and Apollinaris, it was simply a matter of the Roman bishop and his synod concurring in the actions of Eastern synods. Earlier reports of Roman condemnations, e.g. against Sabellius, are more difficult to assess because of a lack of information, but probably should be interpreted more as local Roman events than as condemnations of immediate and automatic consequence for the universal Church. Other instances which definitely go beyond Italy, such as the Quartodeciman controversy or the affair of Dionysius of Alexandria, are either not doctrinal or lack sufficient detail to make a judgment.

In the Arian outbreak Rome, while apparently having little impact on the formulation of the Nicene faith, later firmly supported the council and Athanasius. It resisted Eastern efforts to depose him and the appeal canons of Sardica (343) played a significant part in the growth of Rome's vision of itself as the court of final appeal. The latter role was strengthened for the West by the imperial decrees of 378 and 445. In many cases when Rome was appealed to the question might be asked whether it would not more accurate to speak of the Roman function as one of adjudicating rather than of teaching. In the middle of the fourth century Western support for Athanasius sagged temporarily under pressure from Constantius II. After an initial period of resistance and exile, Pope Liberius succumbed as well. While precisely what he did remains uncertain, it seems that the formula he signed (First Sirmium) ignored rather than contradicted the Nicene *homoousios*. His condemnation of Athanasius probably caused greater adverse comment, though neither action apparently provoked much opprobrium in antiquity against Roman prestige. Liberius returned to the city and carried on as bishop.[22]

In the christological controversies of the fifth century, again most of the theological discussion was carried on in the East, but in the later stages Roman intervention was significant. As I have shown elsewhere, the Roman outlook of Celestine and Leo implied very strongly that as far as they were concerned their decisions were the significant ones.[23] The councils agreed with Rome. The Eastern view seemed to be rather that the conciliar decisions were the significant ones, and the Eastern bishops were pleased that the popes agreed with the councils. In general the Roman contribution to the theological elaboration of these doctrines was meager. Even the Tome of Leo was a summation of the relatively unsophisticated Western christological development rather than a "doctrinal definition." Looked at from the level of the universal church, it would be difficult to maintain that a Roman decision was the sole decisive factor in any theological dispute of the patristic age.

The one theological controversy of note that originated and ended in the West was Pelagianism. Here Pope Innocent accepted and confirmed the African condemnation issuing from the Councils of Carthage and Milevis (416). He said specifically that since all the theological points had been explained by the Africans, "no testimony is added here by us." Whether Innocent in fact accepted all the presuppositions of the African viewpoint is debated, but the fact that his successor Zosimus apparently was considering reversing the condemnation does not help the view that the Roman condemnation was considered infallible.[24]

The final case to be considered is the celebrated one of Honorius I (625-638). The most recent study of this episode pictures Honorius as a conservative, one not inclined to theological speculation, and without the knowledge of Greek. In other words, he sounds much like most of his predecessors. When presented by Sergius with questions about the teaching of "one energy" in Christ, Honorius replied by emphasizing the need for unity and for preserving Chalcedon as the basis of faith. He dismissed the discussion of "energies" as another instance of Greek logomachy, but he did speak of one will in Christ as well as of one person. As in previous controversies, the theological discussion took place in the East, the difference being that in the seventh century the West was in an even worse position than usual for evaluating it. Later in the century the presence of Maximus the Confessor in the West improved Western perception of the issues. The III Council of Constantinople (680-681) in its condemnation of Monothelitism included Honorius among the anathematized. Pope Leo II concurred.

As a post-factum judgment of the orthodoxy of earlier decades, the council's condemnation may not seem very fair to the modern historical mind, yet it was not unusual in its time. The words of Leo's condemnation coincide with the ancient view of Rome's mission: ". . . *Honorius Romanus, qui immaculatam apostolicae traditionis regulam, quam a praecessoribus suis accepit, maculari consensit.*" [25] In other words, in terms of Rome's own view of its task as preserver of the apostolic teaching, Honorius was a failure, if only by negligence. His *vigilantia* was not what it should have been. The judgment also points out the shortcomings of the ancient view which fails to take adequately into account the necessity of facing new questions and their complexity. Ironically, the case of Honorius, who sinned by inadvertence rather than by false teaching, seems to be the closest thing to an openly admitted blot on the Roman record.

Religio Immaculata

Another noteworthy facet of this development was the outstanding record of the Roman Church in defending orthodoxy during the early doctrinal disputes. This particular characteristic was linked primarily with the Roman Church as a community rather than to the Roman bishop as an individual. Its theoretical elaboration was supported by an adaptation of Romans 1:8, Paul's statement that the faith of the Romans was "proclaimed in all the world." Cyprian, writing in 252, seemed to go well beyond Paul's simple statement when he remarked: "To them (the Roman Christians) faithlessness can have no access." [26]

Starting from the time of Ignatius of Antioch, who spoke of the Roman faith as being "unstained by any foreign color," it is possible to compose a florilegium of patristic texts which praise the faith and orthodoxy of the Roman Church.[27] In reading them one must be wary of the ancient love of rhetorical exaggeration, most obviously with Jerome, not to mention the ubiquitous *captatio benevolentiae*. Sometimes these statements are broad historical generalizations which do not take into consideration all the details. They usually are most concerned with the immediate question at hand. In general it is necessary to avoid making the dubious transference from functional, historical, rhetorical categories of thought and expression to ontological-"infallibilist" categories and conclusions.

As time went on some of the Western letters to Rome began to echo Roman terminology and imagery, e.g. the letter of the Spanish bishops to Pope Hilary (463-464) and the letter of the African bishops to Pope John II (535). This view of the special character of the Roman faith culminated in the famous formula of Hormisdas which stated (515): ". . . *in sede apostolica immaculata est semper catholica servata religio. . . .*" [28]

Various sections of this essay have referred to key New Testament passages, e.g. Romans 1:8 and the faith of the Romans. Another such central passage is Luke 22:31-32: "Simon, Simon, behold, Satan demanded to have you, that he might sift you like wheat, but I have prayed for you that your faith may not fail; and when you have turned again, strengthen your brethren." A complete survey has not been made of this passage, which later centuries would see as especially significant for the idea of papal infallibility. But the general impression is that while the later popes such as Leo and Gelasius began to use the text with some frequency in connection with Roman prerogatives, earlier Roman sources did not use it in the specific context of teaching so much as in reference to the general Roman obligation to be solicitous for the welfare of the whole Church. The letters of the councils of Carthage and Milevis (416), which might be expected to cite such a passage in their appeal for Roman confirmation, did so but not in any papal sense. Ambrose and Ambrosiaster did not use the passage in a Roman sense.

In similar fashion the use of Matt. 16:18b (the "gates of hell") received greater emphasis with later popes in stressing their view of Roman steadfastness. Readers, however, must be circumspect in making similar judgments about non-Roman authors. More often than not they spoke of the faith of Peter as a symbol or type of the faith of the Church and its invincibility in the face of diabolic assault. In the writings of Augustine, Peter was frequently seen as speaking for the Church *(unus pro omnibus)* and the whole Matthaean text was rarely cited in connection with the Roman See. In his treatise on the Incarnation Ambrose wrote:

Faith, then, is the foundation of the church, for it was not said of Peter's flesh but of his faith that "the gates of hell shall not prevail against it." But his confession of faith conquered hell. And this confession did not shut out one heresy, for, since the church like a good ship is often buffeted by many waves, the foundation of the Church should prevail against all heresies.[29]

One element that definitely tended to strengthen Roman authority was the reference, starting with Damasus and Siricius, to a type of mystery presence of Peter with or possibly in the current bishop of Rome. The precise origin of such a notion is not clear. Whatever the exact explanation, the assertion of Peter's ongoing activity in an individual pope would obviously lend greater authority to that pope's decisions, especially in the affirmation of an unbroken and faithful preaching of the apostolic doctrine. While this line of thought was found in the popes of the late fourth and early fifth centuries, reaching a climax in Leo I, it became less frequent later but did not disappear completely. In the reply of Peter Chrysologus to Eutyches is found a non-Roman echo of the idea. The curious suggestion of Ennodius of Pavia that the sanctity of Peter was somehow transferred to each pope probably also reflected a similar inspiration.[30]

The Three Chapters

The cases of Liberius and Honorius have been studied briefly. Here at somewhat greater length we wish to consider the Western reaction to the events in the mid-sixth century involving Pope Vigilius and the II Council of Constantinople. This discussion will not involve a detailed history of the council or of Vigilius, still less the facts of Chalcedon's views of Theodoret of Cyrrhus or of Ibas of

Edessa. It concerns especially the reaction of some Western churches and the efforts of Vigilius and his successors in the sixth century to defend themselves. It is a story of suspicions of Roman orthodoxy accompanying a prolonged schism of some northern Italian churches. At the least it shows that these latter did not have an automatic presumption that Rome's stand must be the correct one.

The unhappy and confused affair of the Three Chapters had its origins in the desire of the emperor Justinian (527-565) to bring the Monophysites back to the unity of the Church and the Empire. He hoped to appease them by issuing a new condemnation of three of their long-dead adversaries and their writings, namely Theodore of Mopsuesta, Theodoret of Cyrrhus, and the letter of Ibas of Edessa to Maris. Vigilius became Pope in 537 apparently because he had indicated that he would show greater flexibility on the question than had his deposed predecessor, Silverius. When Justinian proceeded with his plan and Vigilius proved less tractable than promised, the pope was brought to Constantinople. Arriving in January, 547, Vigilius was to spend the next eight years there in a position of extreme vulnerability.

After a brave beginning in which he refused communion with the patriarch of Constantinople, who had already approved the imperial project, Vigilius soon softened his stand. In April, 548, he issued his first *Judicatum* condemning the Three Chapters. This provoked such a furor in the West, which viewed any condemnation as a threat to the Council of Chalcedon, that he backed down. To give but one example of Western anger, the African bishops broke communion with him in 550. The offending document was formally returned to him by the emperor in 550 but only after he had secretly sworn to aid in the eventual condemnation.

After being subjected to physical violence and escaping for a time across the Bosphorus to Chalcedon, he issued in May, 553, a nuanced document (the *Constitutum*) which, while denouncing the old christological errors, refused to condemn personages. At almost the same moment the Second (ecumenical) Council of Constantinople was meeting at the emperor's command. It approved his condemnation of the Three Chapters, even using the terms of Justinian's edict of 551. Vigilius was not present; his *Constitutum* was rejected by the council (June, 553). Ultimately, at the end of the same year, Vigilius was prevailed upon to accept the condemnation issued by the council. His second *Judicatum* of February, 554, should not, however, be considered as a total approval of every conciliar decision.

Modern Roman Catholic judgments of the Vigilius case (and of the similar case of Liberius) have refused to see in his decisions and statements an exercise of papal infallibility. Even apart from the question of the danger of anachronism in reading the First Vatican Council's conditions for the exercise of papal infallibility back into the distant past, the question of the validity of decisions and statements made under duress is pertinent here. How are we to consider judgments arrived at in an atmosphere of imperial coercion, pressure, and even physical force? In reality Vigilius had been a prisoner of the emperor for years. The questions debated were a tangle of complex historical and theological issues. Better men than Vigilius would have been sorely tried. Even under these difficult circumstances, Vigilius always insisted that he was not attacking or in any way detracting from Chalcedon. In our eyes he may be faulted for deviousness, for a lack of courage, and especially for the absence of that steadfastness the ancients had come to expect from the rock of Peter. In contrast to the modern viewpoint, the Western judgment of the late sixth century was not so indulgent.

Vigilius himself did not live to reenter Rome. His successor, Pelagius I, after having opposed the condemnation of the Three Chapters, did a turnabout and supported the council in order to gain imperial approval for his election. When Pelagius came back, he was hard put to find any bishop willing to ordain him. He even had a difficult time persuading the Roman people to accept him. Some church leaders at a greater distance did not give in so easily.[31]

With the exception of Letter 11 of Pelagius I and Pelagius II's third letter to the bishops of Istria the papal correspondence of the late sixth century did not deal in any detail with the issues of the Three Chapters, e.g. the orthodoxy of Theodore of Mopsuestia or what the Council of Chalcedon thought of the letter of Ibas of Edessa. These letters dwelt on generalities such as the evil of schism. In so arguing Pelagius I made a new departure, stressing the need for communion with the apostolic sees. (The schismatics of northern Italy were, of course, also out of communion with the Eastern sees.) He quoted a number of otherwise unknown Augustinian texts making the same point. He continually underscored the unanimity of the rest of the Church, giving assurances that the Second (ecumenical) Council of Constantinople did nothing contrary to the faith or the Council of Chalcedon. Pelagius I in particular had to deny the authenticity of certain letters circulated in his name, letters which claimed that the Catholic faith had been corrupted at the Second Council of Constantinople. Pelagius assured Childebert that "his father" Justinian would never have allowed such a thing.[32]

These popes were continually obliged to assert their own orthodoxy, i.e., that they held to the four councils and the doctrine of Leo. Usually little was said about the fifth council. A new "Petrine" text came to prominence, 1 Peter 3:15: "Always be prepared to make a defense to any one who calls you to account for the hope that is in you . . ." Pelagius I, applying this to himself, invited his critics to come to Rome and investigate for themselves, to see that his faith was perfectly orthodox. Admitting that he had earlier opposed Vigilius, Pegalius I asked the significant (and from the traditional Roman point of view more perilous) question: What is so bad about changing? Paul withstood Peter to the face when he was wrong. Did not Augustine write his *Retractationes* in his old age, changing some of the opinions of his youth? [33]

Later Pelagius II was still concerned with the schism in Istria. He alternately argued with the bishops of Istria and sought the aid of the civil power to force unity on them. In his first letter he cited Luke 22:32 to show that the faith of Peter could never be shaken or changed. He also gave assurances of his own orthodoxy, i.e. his own adherence to the four councils and the letters of Leo. The dissidents should come to Rome and satisfy themselves concerning the wholeness of his faith. He even repeated the argument that change is not so bad. Even God changes! [34]

Gregory the Great was still plagued by the same schism and gave many of the same answers. The fifth council did nothing against Chalcedon and against the faith, an assur-

ance he also had to give to the Lombard queen Theode-
linda, who had withdrawn from communion with the
bishop of Milan when the latter reestablished links with
Gregory.[35]

The tarnishing of the Roman image in the eyes of many
Westerners can be seen in the letters of Columban. He
showed great respect and veneration for the Roman See,
yet he could also question its judgment. Writing to Pope
Boniface IV, he spoke of the lasting effects of the Three
Chapters controversy, of the *infamia* of the chair of Peter.
He warned: *Vigila, papa . . . et iterum dico, Vigila quia
forte non bene vigilavit Vigilius quam caput scandali isti
clamant qui vobis culpam iniciunt.*[36]

Evidently, then, despite the strong development of the
papacy in the fourth and fifth centuries, its position was
still not as consolidated as some think, if in the sixth century there could still be so much doubt, questioning, and
criticism of the Roman stand.

Conclusion

The doctrine of papal infallibility as defined at Vatican
I presupposed a long and complex development, most of
which was post-patristic. There was certainly a common
strain of concern—fidelity to the gospel—that could be
traced from first to last. The First Vatican Council declared: The Holy Spirit was promised to the successors of
St. Peter not that they might make known new doctrines by
his revelation, but rather that with his assistance they might
religiously guard and faithfully explain the revelation or
deposit of faith that was handed down through the Apostles" (DS 3070). One difference that comes to mind would
be the greater explicit emphasis and latitude of later times
accorded to the element of "explanation."

The ancient Church spoke simply of handing on unstained and "guarding" the doctrine of the apostles. Its
rhetoric and for the most part its conscious reflection re-
volved around preservation, not expansion. In fact, of
course, the Church was constantly facing change, developments, and expansion. Whether these changes involved
progress or decline is not the question here. Their eyes
remained firmly fixed on the past. There would come a

time when the accumulated changes would force the Church to look at itself and reflect about its path to the present. But that time had not yet come.

Non-Roman Catholic thought has had the most difficulty with the apparent growing autonomy of the papacy/ *magisterium* in relation to the deposit of faith. The early church put such emphasis on being faithful to the past, on a form of historical verification of this continuing fidelity in doctrine, and on an ever-increasing reliance on church office for supervising and insuring this fidelity, that it is not surprising that some of the belief in that divine guarantee should have rubbed off on the officers themselves. Many observers have noticed this development with regret but also with understanding not only of how inevitable it was, given the presuppositions and initial directions, but with some appreciation that it was also at the time a salutary development.

In this essay I have discussed several strands of the evolution of Roman primacy which eventually would become significant threads in the fiber of medieval thinking, namely Rome's position as leader in the West (for it was the church to which questions and problems were brought for answers and solutions) coupled with the Roman idea that its decision was final: the fact that the things it approved gained a special solidity from the rock of Peter; the fact that Roman approbation was necessary for the acceptance of any formulation, even that of an ecumenical council; the fact that, in comparison to the major Eastern sees, Rome's record of supporting orthodoxy (or what eventually turned out to be the orthodox positions) was exceptionally good, though not perfect; finally, related to this last, the evolving tradition that there was some special quality of doctrinal purity in the faith of the Roman community; and all of this was under the seal of Petrine leadership reaching back to the commission of Christ himself.

Most of these elements received some recognition from non-Roman churches, especially those in the West. The East remained much more independent, honoring Rome's position and traditions but not in a subservient way, remaining above all loyal to a more synodal approach to decision making. In later centuries most Western churches would come to accept the Roman version of its place in the

Church, however slow they may have been to do so earlier, even coming to use Rome's own rhetoric in addressing Rome. But in general it was Roman sources that most strongly and consistently urged the Roman position and prerogatives. Embarrassing moments like the Three Chapters affair, which cast a shadow over the tradition of Roman leadership and doctrinal purity alike, however debilitating they might be for a few decades, soon faded from memory as the Roman claims continued to grow and find acceptance.

If we would respect the reality of theological and canonical development, the elements we have listed above should not be equated, singly or collectively, with the definition of 1870. The ancient perspective was different. If the task of the Church as a whole under the guidance of the Spirit was to preserve the gospel, the Roman Church and particularly its bishop claimed that it did this in a peerless way.

14

FALLIBILITY
INSTEAD OF INFALLIBILITY?
A BRIEF HISTORY OF
THE INTERPRETATION OF
GALATIANS 2:11-14

Karlfried Froehlich

The biblical basis for papal primacy has traditionally been found by its advocates in three Petrine texts of the New Testament: Matt. 16:17-19; John 21:15-17; and Luke 22:31-32. These texts have also yielded arguments for papal infallibility when attention is focused on Peter's faith and confession as the divinely inspired presupposition for Jesus' macarism (Matt. 16:17-18) and when Luke 22:32 is combined with John 11:42 and Heb. 5:7 to form a syllogism: Jesus prayed for Peter's faith that it might not fail; Jesus' prayers are always heard; therefore Peter cannot have erred in matters of faith.[1] For such an interpretation Gal. 2:11-14 with its account of the incident between Paul and Peter in Antioch presents an embarrassment. Does this text not suggest that, far from being infallible, Peter did err in a matter of faith? Or are there factors which allow the Antiochian confrontation to be interpreted in a different light? [2]

The earliest echoes of the text in the first centuries do not reflect any embarrassment because the premise of Peter's unerring faith was as yet undeveloped. The great diversity of these echoes, however, indicates that the specific controversies of a particular age have always influenced the exegesis of the passage. On the one hand the text was read as an unfavorable comment on the character of

Paul. In the irreverent attack of a "great" apostle on the one whom Christians claimed to be the prince of the apostles, the writer Porphyry saw an example of the triumph of barbarism in Christianity.[3] No less outspoken in its criticism of Paul is a passage in the pseudo-Clementine *Kerygmata Petrou*, a source which probably dates back to the second century and represents Jewish Christian theology. A strong anti-Paulinism has been identified as an underlying tendency. It is combined with the tradition of Peter's struggle with Simon the Magician, for Paul appears under the name of that arch-heretic. In Homily XVII 19, Peter hectors the Magician (Paul) with a clear reference to the Galatians text.[4] The language is extremely sharp. The author saw the rebuke at Antioch as a diabolic attempt to undermine Peter's preaching of the law, which stood in direct continuity with the Lord's own proclamation. Paul in his presumptuousness offended both God and the Christ who had himself born witness to Peter's divine inspiration in Matt. 16:17-18.

On the other hand Marcion, convinced that the gospel of Jesus had been falsified by Judaizers, claimed that "only Paul, to whom the mystery has been disclosed by revelation, knew the truth."[5] This is a reference to Gal. 1:15, but the Antioch incident must also have played an important role in Marcion's polemics. Tertullian in his refutation devoted two extensive discussions to Marcion's use of the text.[6] It seems that Marcion stressed Peter's guilt and even extended the blame to other apostles. In Peter all who promote judaizing tendencies were rebuked for not "walking according to the truth of the gospel." We find a similar use of the incident in anti-Christian polemics by pagan authors. Porphyry not only criticized Paul's insolence but noted with equal disgust that Peter was caught here in a grave error, an error which made him a hypocrite. The same argument was used by Julian the Apostate in the fourth century.[7]

The situation was quite different where the New Testament canon was accepted in its entirety as the normative apostolic witness. The option of playing up one apostle at the expense of the other then seemed closed. Both apostles commanded respect. But the text itself became a puzzle. Could apostles truly disagree? Could Paul have blamed

Peter falsely? Could Peter have fallen into serious error? In an article published in 1970 Inge Lönning pointed out that the apostolic canon was bound to raise such questions, a fact which made the interpretation of Gal. 2:11-14 a model case of "polemical theology" *(Kontroverstheologie)*.[8]

In view of the dilemma that two apostles were at odds with one another, it is no surprise that the exegesis of this text during the first centuries tended toward apologetic harmonization. Two major lines can be distinguished. One simply tried to eliminate the problem by pretending that the Cephas of Gal. 2:11 was not Simon Peter. We know from Eusebius that Clement of Alexandria favored this opinion and suggested that Cephas was one of the Seventy.[9] The distinction between Cephas and Peter occurs also in some later lists of apostles and later exegetical writings.[10] Jerome described it already as an apologetic theory invented in order to avoid Porphyry's conclusions.[11] The other line—Jerome's own preference—reinterpreted the dispute in terms of an educational event prearranged by the apostles themselves. Chrysostom presented the argument in its fullest form.[12] The incident, he explained, was staged in order to teach the Antiochian Christians the lesson that the time of the observance of the law had passed. Chrysostom found the main support for his simulation theory in Paul's remark that Peter "feared" the circumcision party. Psychologically this seemed impossible. Fear in the heart of the most courageous apostle? The absurdity of such a proposition and the possibility of reading between the lines that both apostles had an educational concern was proof enough that the exchange was an act of *oikonomia,* a "dispensation," as Jerome called it. Chrysostom probably followed Origen in his interpretation. Confirmation for this dependence comes from Jerome, who in his Galatians commentary claimed Origen as his source for the same position.[13] Just as Chrysostom transmitted the argument to all subsequent Eastern exegetes, so Jerome handed it on to the medieval West. It was precisely in the West, however, that this line of argument met with a fundamental challenge, a challenge that led eventually to a third line of apologetic harmonization.

The criticism came from Augustine, bishop of Hippo, whose famous epistolary exchange with Jerome over this

question has often been analyzed.[14] Augustine's first letter
(Epistle 28) already shifted the issue from historical explanation to hermeneutical dilemma. Several of his later
letters come back to it. Augustine was concerned that if the
Antioch incident was just a pious fraud, Paul would be
lying when he called Peter *reprehensibilis*[15] and that the
reliability of all of Scripture was then put in jeopardy.
An apostle may be wrong as a person but never as a writer
of Holy Scripture.[16] This methodological decision paved
the way in the West for a widespread reluctance to accept
the simulation theory. Jerome's explanation was known
throughout the Middle Ages but rarely followed until it
was vigorously reaffirmed under changed circumstances
by Erasmus.[17]

Yet Augustine, precisely because of his insistence on the
integrity of the canon, was unwilling to give up the apologetic postulate of harmony between the apostles. He suggested that historically the scene might be placed before
the Jerusalem Council[18] so that the lack of a clear rule
about the observance of the law might explain Peter's
attitude. Peter was not rebuked for observing the law, for
he was free to do so in the era of the law's "honorable
funeral,"[19] but for compelling the Gentiles to live as Jews
and for his motive, fear. This means that for Augustine
Peter's error was not one of doctrine. Peter knew that the
law was abrogated. His mistake concerned *conversatio,* not
praedicatio.[20] The letters reveal that Jerome was surprised
and offended by the attack, which seemed to him even
more malicious since Augustine's first epistles were published without the author's knowledge before they reached
Jerome. But except for the rightful indignation of his replies, there does not seem to have been much conviction
behind his loquacious self-defense. In fact, in later texts
Jerome seems to have followed more or less in the foot-
steps of Augustine's interpretation.[21] Thus the second
apologetic construct, aimed at eliminating the problem by
means of a simulation theory, was breaking down. What
remained was the Augustinian line which came to dominate
the Latin Middle Ages. It was also an attempt at harmonization, and its harmonistic tendency was now extended
even beyond the dispute of the apostles to the dispute between the two fathers as well. Augustine and Jerome could

no more have seriously disagreed than Peter and Paul. Somehow there was justification for the attitude held by each side. The medieval exegesis of Gal. 2:11-14 was an elaboration of this compromise in several forms.

One form was a compassion theory that would excuse both Peter and Paul by pointing to some higher good for the sake of which minor mistakes can be tolerated even in apostles. Both Peter and Paul made concessions to the Jewish Christians out of love and compassion at various times. It was not different at Antioch. The acts of both were guided by compassion: Peter's for the Jewish Christians, Paul's for the Gentiles. The seemingly disturbing scene was no more than an illustration of most laudable intentions on both sides.[22]

Another form was a psychological theory: the rebuke by Paul was necessary as a means of helping Peter escape a dilemma. Peter wished to eat with the Gentiles but his fear of offending the Jewish converts led him to act against his convictions. Thus he rejoiced at the pub'ic rebuke which gave his true desire the open support of his great colleague.[23]

Most influential, however, was a suggestion made by Augustine himself, who wanted to avoid the charge that his affirmation of a real confrontation at Antioch might lead to an attack on the character of the apostles, since Porphyry and Julian had attacked their character. Peter *was* wrong, but by humbly submitting to the reproach of his "inferior" in the freedom of charity he still could be regarded as an ethical model for posterity.[24] This of course was no longer exegesis but speculation beyond the text. Galatians 2 does not record the outcome of the confrontation, and Peter's humble silence or submission is no more than a hypothesis.[25] Augustine drew here on an older African tradition. In the dispute over the validity of heretical baptism, Cyprian had argued in the same vein; reason, not custom, should decide in a serious controversy. Peter, he said, did not demand obedience to his primacy but yielded to reason and thus "gave an example of concord and patience." [26]

The harmonistic exegesis of the Middle Ages lifted this Cyprianic element out of Augustine's reflections and made it into the very focus of the passage. Aquinas refined the

argument at an important point, introducing the distinction
between venial sin and mortal sin and claiming that the
apostles could not sin mortally after they had received the
Holy Spirit but could commit venial sins on account of
their human weakness.[27] In all the interpretations of this
type the confrontation and the rebuke by Paul remained
real, but rather than lessening Peter's authority, the incident
was turned into the moral example of a prelate's true humility: not relying on superior power, but humbly bowing
to correction from any quarter. Galatians 2:11-14 appeared time and again with ever new variations on the
theme of the "humble prelate." [28] By the 12th century it
could be quoted as the major biblical proof text for the
ethical topos "that evil prelates must be accused and corrected by their subordinates" *(quod praelati mali sunt ar-
guendi et corripiendi a subditis).*[29]

The text found its place in Gratian's *Decretum* under the
same general heading. In C. II q. 7 c. 10ff. Gratian argued
that, as a rule, prelates should *not* be reproved by subordinates. He acknowledged exceptions, however, for which
the exegesis of Gal. 2:11-14 provided the basis: "unless
they leave the realm of faith or force others to do it." [30]
The importance of this text lies in the fact that Gratian
interpreted Peter's error not only as one of *conversatio* but
as one of *praedicatio,* as a deviation from the faith. This
change in the Augustinian basis gave the passage an explosive potential in later discussions about Peter's "error,"
especially when the argument was applied to the office of
Peter's successor, the pope, at a time of growing infallibilist tendencies. Gratian himself made this application in the
famous text of d. 40 c. 6, where he declared the pope to be
exempt from judgment by anybody "except he be found
deviating from the faith." [31] This presupposes that a pope
can err in matters of faith. We know from Brian Tierney's
studies that this clause, after its ramifications had been
explored by the canonists of the 13th and 14th centuries,
shaped much of the conciliarist thinking at the time of the
Great Schism.

Gratian's work coincided with the rise of a new intellectual force in the church: the university teachers, the
"masters." [32] In a climate of increasing papal exercise of
doctrinal authority on the one hand, yet faced with the

canonical possibility of a heretical pope on the other, the theological masters saw their own teaching function as a God-given parallel to that of prelates and popes, a kind of apostolic succession to Paul complementary to that of Peter.[33] Gratian himself made a distinction between the "power to settle disputes" and an authoritative "learning" in matters of the interpretation of Scripture, the former belonging to the prelates, the latter to the masters.[34] At the height of the scholastic period Thomas Aquinas reaffirmed this primacy of prelate over professor. Yet as an academic theologian he also shared the masters' conviction of the authority of their apostolic succession to the Pauline teaching office, including their duty to correct prelates publicly where the truth of the faith is at stake, just as Paul had done at Antioch.[35]

Aquinas did not link Gal. 2:11-14 to the issue of an erring pope. In fact, he may not have seriously envisioned a situation where masters would rebuke a successor of Peter on matters of faith. The 14th century, however, saw several such confrontations in which doubts arose about the faith of the pope. From the writings of such critics as William of Ockham, Marsilius of Padua, Wycliffe, or Huss one gains the impression that the Galatians text played a major role in the masters' argument for their right to challenge the pope in matters of faith.[36]

The case assumed even more serious dimensions with the Great Schism of 1378. It is significant to observe that most conciliarist writers were university masters. They used of course the theme of the "humble prelate" in calling upon the obstinate popes to accept correction. The application of Gal. 2:11-14, however, was now definitely shifting from the moral realm to the more serious issue of an erring pope who must be opposed by the greater authority of the Church in council. It seems that in the development of this latter idea after 1378 the biblical argument from Galatians 2 was and remained a key element. Conrad of Gelnhausen's early tract from 1380, *Epistola Concordiae*,[37] demonstrates its importance as clearly as the mature conciliarist writings of Pierre d'Ailly or Jean Gerson.[38] There may be differences in the details of the passage's interpretation. Pierre d'Ailly, for example, expressly denied that the text gave one the right to accuse Peter of a "heretical" error.[39] But the material reveals a consensus among conciliarist masters in their new appropriation of the older Augustinian line; the reality of Peter's rebuke by Paul was now used to cope with the reality of an erring pope and the need to correct him by the action of a council of prelates and of masters in succession to Paul.

Seen against this background, Luther's interpretation of the text is not as revolutionary as Karl Holl or more recently Inge Lönning have suggested.[40] It is true that Luther's exegesis was part of a new mood which was ready to abandon harmonistic apologetics. Rather than presenting a "problem," Gal. 2:11-14 was a liberating text for Luther. He saw it as part of a total argument in Galatians 1-2 which for him became the most important warrant for his polemical stance on the sole authority of the gospel over against all human authority. But the new focus, i.e., the discovery of the context, and the new radicality in the application of exegetical insights could not obscure the basic continuity with the late medieval tradition. This continuity included not only elements of the conciliarist interpretation but perhaps more importantly Luther's self-image as an academic theologian and thus as a participant in the Pauline succession of "doctors" whose teaching office, in analogy to the encounter at Antioch, had its own dignity and authority even in opposition to the pope.[41]

Holl as well as Lönning and Feld describe a development in Luther's understanding of the passage. Luther began by rejecting the Thomistic understanding of Peter's sin as venial.[42] Still focusing on the person of Peter, he stressed an Augustinian aspect; the passage shows that God's grace can deal even with the gravest offenses. The first Galatians commentary of 1519, however, already contained the major elements of Luther's distinct polemical use of Gal. 2:11-14 in the argument against the papacy. Abandoning the consideration of Peter's personal status, he focused attention on the consequences of the incident for the Petrine office. Peter's error concerned faith, not conduct. Under the norm of the gospel, in this instance Paul was right and Peter was wrong. For Luther this meant that where the truth of the gospel was at stake, Peter was in no way superior to Paul. He could err and actually did err. The pope therefore can and must be corrected, too, if he is in error, and even the simplest Christian could undertake this correction. The Leipzig disputation applied these insights. Against Eck's insistence on Matt. 16:18-19 as the foundation of papal authority *de iure divino,* Luther stressed Peter's public failure in the faith even after the giving of the Holy Spirit. Against Eck's charge that this was Hussite heresy (i.e. by sinning mortally Peter had disqualified himself for an office having unerring authority), Luther stressed that Paul in Gal. 2:11-14 was not talking about personal sin or purity but about public heresy, which alone could be of concern to the Church as a whole. Peter would have had to have been removed from office as *pastor haereticus* had Paul not resisted him to the face and thus rescued him. Throwing all apologetic caution overboard, Luther thus took the step which d'Ailly had not taken; for him the erring Peter of Galatians was the prototype of the *pastor haereticus* on the papal throne, an apocalyptic possibility inherent in any papacy that claimed Petrine authority in contradiction to the gospel. Galatians 2:11-14 proved that the danger was real, not imaginary, from the very beginning of the Church.

Lönning has made the point that the subsequent shift of Lutheran apologetics to the defense of the scriptural principle had an immediate effect on the use of Gal. 2:11-14 in Protestantism.[43] Apostolic authority has to bear an even greater burden of proof theologically when it is fixed in Scripture alone. Thus the old questions rose again and with them the old solutions. Can an apostle—Peter or Paul —really and fundamentally err if both Peter and Paul are among those to whom we owe Scripture, the only source of God's revealed truth? Rather than picking up Luther's theological emphasis on the nature of the Antiochian confrontation as one of gospel against human authority, Protestant orthodoxy was again interested in finding a basic harmony between the apostles when it tried to cope with the text. The reference to the conflict in the passage became simply part of the standard anti-papal polemics.[44] Lönning finds a similar tendency prominent in the 19th century as well as a strong psychological interest in the protagonists of the scene. The psychological interpretation tended to scale down the importance of the confrontation and make it a matter of difference in temperament, a perhaps unfortunate but inconsequential lapse, or Paul's emotional defense of himself and thus only a preface to the real theological subject matter of Galatians.

The latter was the interpretation by J. C. K. von Hofmann, whose minimizing of the seriousness of the passage betrayed the fact that the new enemy was no longer Rome but the rising tide of historical criticism in one's own camp. For the most influential critic, Ferdinand Christian Baur, Gal. 2:11-14 was a text as crucial historically as it had been for Luther theologically. His thesis of two original forms of early Christianity, i.e., Petrine and Pauline, was not just the fruit of his philosophical Hegelianism. His early study on the "Christ party in Corinth" (1831) established the central place of the Galatians passage for his theory long before he started using Hegel.[45] In Baur's eyes the Antioch encounter was the first open expression of the antagonism between the two major factions after the rise of Stephen in Jerusalem; it was an antagonism which was to spread rapidly over the entire mission field: Galatia, Corinth, Rome. The text has been a keystone for the reconstruction of earliest Christian history wherever Baur's thesis has held sway.[46]

We cannot examine here the history of the passage in recent decades, a history which Lönning finds distressing in terms of his interest in "polemical theology" *(Kontroverstheologie)*. Although he acknowledges that the scholarship in recent historical discussions of the text is excellent, he discovers little theological relevance in either the interpretations derived from Baur or in those of Baur's critics down to Johannes Munck and Oscar Cullmann.

Whatever the case may be, the passage seems to have acquired new theological actuality in Roman Catholic discussions of teaching authority after Vatican II. Helmut Feld's studies are indicative of this trend. Feld finds a model for the Church in Gal. 2:11-14; it is one in which apostolic office and apostolic charisma complement each other.[47] There must be room for both in the Church. Karl Rahner makes a similar point when he declares in his commentary on *Lumen gentium* 22 that, while there may be no legal recourse against valid papal teaching, "there can certainly occur in the Church the charismatic and prophetic 'resisting to the face' (Gal. 2:11)."[48] The point seems clear and ecumenically significant. After all, wherever papal "tyranny" was denounced in the history of the Church this passage provided prophets and reformers with an apparently solid biblical basis for their protest. But is this enough? In the history of exegesis the presence of the Augustinian interpretation has first of all served as a reminder of the limits of papal infallibility. We found that the entire trajectory of papal infallibility based on Luke 22:32 and the other Petrine passages has been accompanied in the West by a trajectory of Petrine (and papal) fallibility deduced from Gal. 2:11-14. The Augustinian interpretation, however, also freed the text from being looked at solely in terms of the Petrine office. The focus is on two apostles. The Paul of Galatians 2 is not just a charismatic figure engaged in an occasional protest; he speaks as an apostle to an apostle and assumes that both their offices stand under the judgment of the same gospel. Where can the succession of his teaching office be realized today alongside a *magisterium* [49] in the Petrine succession? In our ecumenical situation this is not only a matter of collegiality among bishops. Does the medieval model of a double magisterial succession of prelate and theologian have a chance today? [50] If the exegesis of Gal. 2:11-14 always reminds the Church of the limits of papal infallibility, it raises with even greater urgency the issues of its wider context.

15

INFALLIBILITY AS
CHARISM AT VATICAN I

Kilian McDonnell

One could ask whether since 1870 the focus of the discussion has not been too much on infallibility with insufficient attention given to the concept of truth. Bishop Gasser, who is rightly considered the most authoritative interpreter of Vatican I, touched indirectly on the question in his *relatio* of July 11, 1870, on the council floor when he posed what he considered to be a somewhat rhetorical question: In what sense is pontifical infallibility absolute? He answered that in no sense is it absolute because "absolute infallibility belongs to God alone, for he is the first and essential truth, who can never in any manner deceive us or be deceived." [1] All other infallibility "has its limits and conditions." [2] When authors in antiquity spoke of the trust believing Christians could invest in the teaching of the Church, they spoke of the truth of the Church. Ostensibly the question of the irreformability of doctrine was not posed in antiquity. In a more general context, when the question was addressed in antiquity, it was that of the truth of tradition received in the baptismal catechesis.[3] Irenaeus had spoken of the bishops as possessing "the charism of truth." [4] It is possible that the charism of truth in Irenaeus is not to be distinguished either from, the truth of the Church or from the tradition of the Church insofar as it mediates the truth by means of apostolic succession.[5] Truth was the point of departure for many of the fathers of Vatican I, especially when speaking of the biblical foundations of infallibility. For instance, Bishop Legat of Trieste explained that the Church cannot fail in its faith because it is directed by the Holy Spirit: "The truth, consequently, is the object from which inerrancy is derived, and the assent given to the truth is a subjective act, which gives birth to faith in the believer." [6]

The bishop added a condition for an infallible pronouncement by the pope: "The sovereign pontiff can proclaim his faith as founded on the divinely revealed truth only if it is attested by the universal magisterium of the entire Church that the truth of this doctrine is contained in the Word of God, either written or traditioned." [7] The doctrine of infallibility has to be placed in the larger context of Christian truth. "Infallibility is at the service of truth, for it is the truth—not changing theories (Eph. 4:14)—which is the source of salvation." [8] The extraordinary *magisterium* of the Church is not the daily life of the Church.

In its earliest form *Pastor aeternus* spoke of the Roman pontiff defining by virtue "of divine assistance" (*diviniam assistentiam*). In the many written responses to the proposed text one finds a fusion of various formulas, usually including the one in the proposed text (*per divinam assistentiam*),[9] but also "by virtue of the divine promises" (*promissionum divinarum virtute*) [10] "through the singular assistance of the Holy Spirit" (*per singularem assistentiam Spiritus sancti*),[11] by the "uninterrupted assistance of the Holy Spirit" (*Spiritus sancti non interrupta assistentia praeditam esse debere*).[12] When Bishop Pie of Poitiers presented the *caput addendum* (to become chapter IV of *Pastor aeternus*), he took up what was the most commonly accepted source of infallibility, namely the promise of Christ (together with the prayer of Christ) which constitutes the meritorious or imperative cause of infallibility, while the efficient cause is the divine assistance of Christ and the Holy Spirit.[13] To this list of causes Cardinal Guidi added formal causality, saying that the assistance of the Holy Spirit is the "efficient and formal cause of infallibility." [14] Guidi held that the pope had the charism of inerrancy in virtue of "the habitual promise" of the Holy Spirit made to him in the person of Peter. Some of the language of the fathers of the council lends itself to being interpreted as the vocabulary of power, if not of domination. Some speak —less frequently, to be sure—of a "privilege" [15] and others of a "prerogative," [16] terms which have less theological content and are more easily misinterpreted.

The link between the Holy Spirit and infallibility was expressed in more general terms, such as saying that the reason the Church cannot fail is because it is "directed by the Holy Spirit." [17] But the fathers attempted to speak in more specific language. Sometimes *donum* (gift) is used, as when a father said that "the gifts of God are given gratuitously and are not to be measured by philosophical principles." [18] *Dos* (gift, endowment, property, quality) was also used.[19] Very frequently *charisma* was used. Archbishop (later Cardinal) Manning, who laid special emphasis on the charismatic quality of infallibility, said that "the inerrancy of the pontiff is a charism given for the good of the Church" (therefore not simply for the good of the individual).[20] He also insisted that "the charism of primacy does not inhere in the person of the pope." [21]

In the decisive *definit* passage, reference is made to the "divine assistance" *(per divinam assistentiam)* but this is preceded by a reference to "the Holy Spirit promised to the successors of Peter" *(Petri successoribus Spiritus sanctus promissus est)* and to the "charism of truth and never-failing faith" *(veritatis et fidei numquam deficientis charisma)* which was promised to Peter.[22] There can be little doubt in the minds of the fathers of the council that the source and cause of infallibility was the Holy Spirit [23] and that one of the preferred ways of speaking of that source and cause was the category of *charism.* Vatican II took up the same vocabulary.

The *Constitution on the Church* speaks five times of the role of the Holy Spirit in article 25, once with regard to "the authentic teachers," the bishops ("by the light of the Holy Spirit they make that faith clear"), twice with regard to the infallibility of the pope ("they [definitions] are pronounced with the assistance of the Holy Spirit, an assistance promised to him in blessed Peter"; "as one in whom the charism of the infallibility of the Church itself is individually present"), and twice with regard to the infallibility of the body of bishops in union with the pope ("on account of the activity of that same Holy Spirit"; "under the guiding light of the Spirit of truth").[24]

The larger context of the section which uses the word *charisma* is an explanation of the famous *ex sese* clause. The *Constitution on the Church* defends the *ex sese* by linking the exercise of papal infallibility to a function of the whole Church. This passage reads: "For then the Roman pontiff is not pronouncing judgment as a private person. Rather, as the supreme teacher of the universal Church, as one in whom the charism of the infallibility of the Church itself is individually present, he is expounding or defending a doctrine of catholic faith." [25] It should be noted that not only does the *Constitution* follow *Pastor aeternus* in repeating the *ex sese*, but also in noting the ecclesial character of papal infallibility. *Pastor aeternus* says that the Roman pontiff "by the divine assistance promised to him in blessed Peter is possessed of that infallibility with which the divine Redeemer willed that his Church should be endowed for defining doctrine regarding faith or morals." [26] In his famous *relatio*, which took four hours to deliver, Bishop Gasser touched on the relationship of the infallibility of the pope to that of the Church. Gasser remarked with sorrow that from the podium on which he was then speaking the doctrine of infallibility was several times (*aliquoties*) formulated "as if all infallibility resided in the pope alone, and from the pope it flowed into the Church and was communicated to her." [27] Then he proceeded to explain the "true reason" why even the bishops united in council are not infallible in matters of faith and morals without the pope: "Because Christ promised this infallibility to the whole *magisterium* of the church, that is, to the apostles together with Peter" (*apostolis simul cum Petro*).[28] What Gasser rejected was the *absolute* necessity of an approbation by the Church, as a *conditio sine qua non*. This was done in opposition to the Gallican theories of that period. It was necessary, said Gasser, to recall that those who objected to the doctrine as formulated in the council demanded a "strict and absolute necessity of consultation and the help of the bishops in any doctrinal, infallible judgment of the Roman pontiff, in a manner that [this condition] would have to have its place in the definition [of *Pastor aeternus*]." Both Gasser and Vatican II lute necessity which constitutes the whole difference between us, and not the matter of opportuneness or a relative necessity which is entirely something for the Roman pontiff to judge according to the circumstances. For this reason this [condition] cannot have a place in the dogmatic definition [of *Pastor aeternus*]." [29] Both Gasser and Vatican II (when speaking of "the charism of infallibility" in the context of the *ex sese* clause) are saying negatively what could also be said positively. Gustave Thils would formulate it in this manner: "The previous acquiescence of the Church, or her concomitant or subsequent acquiescence, can be considered as a habitually and relatively necessary condition to the infallible judgments of the popes." [30] This way of viewing necessity is not, contends Thils, contradictory to the decrees of Vatican I and II. It is clear that the *ex sese* has to do with the basic right of the pope (acting in the Holy Spirit) to define infallibility. The *ex sese* is not concerned with the source of knowledge out of which the pope defines.

In attempting to say what infallibility is, the fathers of the council were more successful in saying what it is not. One father of the council wished to have inserted the words *ex ordinaria constituti ordinis providentia* ("by the ordinary providence of the constituted order") in order "to remove all idea of an extraordinary or miraculous intervention from the divine assistance, since the assistance [here spoken of] is intrinsic to the constitution of the Church." [31] Much more frequently one meets the clear declarations that infallibility does not mean a new revelation or a new inspiration. Both W. G. Ward [32] and Louis Veuillot,[33] the former a theologian and philosopher, the latter a journalist, had raised some questions by making infallibility amount to inspiration in a rather literal sense.

It is clear from even the preparatory documents that these views were not held by the fathers of the council. Already in 1867, in the minutes of the Doctrinal Commission, it was stated that in speaking of infallibility the council "must indicate what the difference is between inspiration and simple assistance." [34]

The first draft of *De Ecclesia Christi* declared that the "privilege of infallibility which has been revealed as a perpetual prerogative of the Church of Christ . . . should neither be confused with the charism of inspiration nor be regarded as destined to enrich the Church with new revelations. . . ." [35] Neither did any of the fathers contend that infallibility was a kind of inspiration nor that it was to be an instrument of new revelations. The only mention in the discussions on the floor of the council was that made in refuting that view. It was precisely the fear that the infallibility of the apostles, which accompanied "direct revelation," would be confused with the infallibility of the ecclesiastical *magisterium*, which concerns the conservation of this revelation, that prompted Bishop Ginoulhiac of Grenoble, who was considered the best theologian among the French bishops,[36] to oppose the phrase "assistance of the Holy Spirit." This phrase was too broad and therefore infallibility was open to being interpreted as a new revelation.[37] The final text of *Pastor aeternus* did not retain the reference either to inspiration or to a new revelation as found in the first draft of *De Ecclesia Christi*, but rather restricted itself to excluding a new revelation, saying: "The Holy Spirit was not promised to the successors of Peter in order that by his revelation they might make known new doctrine, but in order that by his assistance they might inviolably keep and faithfully expound the revelation or deposit of faith delivered through the apostles." [38] The Bishop of Grenoble's intentions were faithfully reproduced here. Gasser, whose *relatio* is understood as an authentic interpretation of the text, also said that infallibility should not be confused with revelation.[39] More precisely, he said that "we do not exclude this cooperation of the Church because the infallibility of the Roman pontiff does not come about by means of inspiration or revelation, but by means of divine assistance." [40] It is obvious from the discussions that both inspiration in the narrower sense and new revelations are not included in the definition of papal infallibility.

The category of *charism* was used toward the end of the debates to clarify an area which was hotly debated before the council convened. In this preconciliar debate the Ultramontanists used three words to describe and qualify their position: infallibility was *personalis, absoluta,* and *separata.* The minority, who opposed the definition, fought against the theological position those words were meant to express. Though the three words appeared in none of the schemas proposed to the fathers of the council, they so correctly and precisely indicate what was central to the conciliar debate that Bishop Bartholomew d'Avanzo predicted that just as the fifth ecumenical council (Constantinople, 553) came to be called the council of "the Three Chapters," so Vatican I would be called the council of "the Three Words." [41]

The debate reached something of a climax in the speech made by Phillip Cardinal Guidi, archbishop of Bologna. He was a man of some competence, a Dominican, formerly a professor of Old Testament and systematic theology; he had taught in Rome and at the University of Vienna. Guidi wished to propose a position which would reconcile the majority (for the definition) and the minority (against) and thus avoid a schism. He asserted that the pope is infallible only in his character as doctor of the universal Church and witness of the catholic tradition and in the measure that he has assured that tradition through previous consultation with the bishops, who are also witnesses to that tradition. The necessity of consulting the bishops, said Guidi, finds ample support in tradition, for instance Bellarmine, Perrone, and in the practice of the popes, most especially the recent consultation of bishops in regard to the definition of the Immaculate Conception. [42] The necessity of consultation was a necessity in law and in fact. [43] Such a position would surely win the support of the minority. On the other hand he declared that he had always believed in the disputed doctrine (infallibility) and that he had always taught it, a position which would find favor with the majority. With these assertions as a *captio benevolentiae* for majority and minority, Guidi wished to launch his role as reconciler.

Guidi was concerned to emphasize the dependency of the pope on the Church. The pope was not separated from the church in the act of defining. "The supposition is false and imaginary of those who say that the pope is infallible in speaking *ex cathedra,* or, which is the same thing, that he can define alone questions of faith and morals independent of the antecedent, concomitant or subsequent consent of the Church. This, I say, is an imaginary supposition, manufactured and altogether false." [44] "Is the head separated or independent from the members?" [45] Guidi demonstrated both *de jure* and *de facto* that these "suppositions" were false.[46] To make sure his position was clearly written into the canons of the council, he proposed the following: "If anyone says that the Roman pontiff, when he gives a decree or constitution, acts of his own will and by himself alone *(ex arbitrio et ex se solo),* independently of the Church, that is separately and not with the counsel of the bishops witnessing to the tradition of the churches, let him be anathema." [47] This bold canon was met with what the text of Mansi calls *rumores et voces: Non, Non.*

A second major concern of Guidi was the depersonalizing of infallibility. In a word, he wished to transfer infallibility from the subject (the pope) to the object (the declaration). Theological statements are infallible, the pope is not. All the pope has is the divine assistance which makes it possible for him, in union with the bishops, to give infallible declarations. "The act is therefore infallible. There is an infallible effect produced by the act." [48] "Therefore infallibility is transferred to the object, and infallibility is to be found there, and the subject is granted to have the aid of divine assistance." [49] Doupanloup, the bishop of Orleans, held a position similar to Guidi's. Doupanloup had earlier said that "the person is not infallible but he is helped infallibly." [50] Though this position was not adopted by the council, Guidi was in part responsible for changing the title of Chapter IV from *De Romani Pontificis infallibilitate* ("The Roman Pontiff's Infallibility") to the less personal, more objective formulation, *De Romani Pontificis infallibili magisterio* ("The Roman Pontiff's Infallible *Magisterium*"). In a highly nuanced way this moved in the direction of placing more emphasis on his teaching authority and definitions than on his person.

A further aspect of this depersonalizing of infallibility was Guidi's contention that the aid given to the pope is a transient, passing aid *(auxilium dixi actuale et lux transiens)* which is received in the person of the pope, without there being any change in the person of the pope himself; nor has he suddenly acquired a new property. Finally one cannot call the person infallible because he produces an infallible effect. It is the act which is infallible, not the person, "because a person is not dominated by an act but by a habit or property. Thus one is not called a drunkard who once or twice gets drunk, or [gets drunk] a few times *(vel aliquoties)*, nor is he called generous who sometimes gives an alms, even though the giving of the alms is an act of charity, and drunkenness is an act of intemperance." [51] This focus on the transient character of the aid given to the pope (and therefore not a permanent property or *habitus*) made it clear to Guidi that a person who has a passing, temporary, transient power to posit an infallible act is not an infallible person.

These were the main concerns of Guidi. His talk caused a "sensation." [52] For his pains as a reconciler Guidi was heckled during his speech. Further, the majority were clearly disturbed. D'Avanzo, who was asked to take the podium as a member of the Deputation of Faith to respond to Guidi, said that Guidi was more Gallican than the Gallicans themselves.[53] He received a reprimand from Pope Pius IX the evening of the speech.[54] Only a few of the minority embraced him as he descended from the podium, which, given his expectations, must have been lonely comfort.

D'Avanzo answered some of Guidi's contentions. First, d'Avanzo addressed himself to Guidi's assertion that the pope himself is not infallible though he is able to make infallible and irreformable decrees and definitions. To this d'Avanzo responded that "the assistance of the Holy Spirit . . . is a *charisma gratis datum*, that is, for the sake of others." [55] He then cited 1 Corinthians 12, giving Paul's teaching on charisms, namely ministries, which are directed to the good of others. Then he continued: "Therefore just as he who has the charism of the apostolate can be called an apostle, and he who has the charism of knowledge and wisdom can be called a doctor, and he who has the grace of miracles can be called a wonder-worker, etc., so he who through the Holy Spirit has the charism of infallible knowledge, that is infallibility, is called an infallible doctor by virtue of the assistance of the Spirit. The pope therefore, by an act, gives an infallible definition, because he has the charism of inerrancy in virtue of the habitual promise of the Holy Spirit made to him in Peter." [56] Therefore one can correctly say "the pope is infallible."

D'Avanzo objected to Guidi's transference of all infallibility to the defined statement. Theological propositions can be true or false, and a true one can be irreformable.[57]

D'Avanzo doubted that the statement itself can be infallible. If, however, it is said that nothing of the quality of infallibility remains in the person of the pope, he can neither authentically interpret nor apply irreformable pronouncements.

Guidi's attempt to depersonalize infallibility raised the Gallican distinction between *sedes* (the Roman Church) and *sedens* (the series of popes). To this distinction d'Avanzo answered: "If the primacy can be truly called personal without offending anyone, why is it odious to use this word of the *magisterium*, which is part of this primacy? If *personalis* is understood in the sense of a private person (whence we have that odious word *personalitas*), then personal should be rejected. But if the word is understood as a person bearing the Church with him *(pro persona ipsam ecclesiam gestante)*, then [that faculty] is personal. For that reason the word *personal* was diligently omitted, to take away all occasion of misunderstanding. Rather a phrase was added: 'acting in his supreme office as doctor of all Christians.'" [58] The ambiguity of the word *personal* was clearly recognized, though it was just as clearly to be understood that the Deputation of the Faith claimed infallibility was in some sense personal.

No less eager to avoid any separation between the pope and the Church, d'Avanzo declared that "whether the pope acts with the clerics of the Roman Church, or with the bishops and provincial councils, or whether he acts in this general council [of Vatican I], the efficient and formal cause of infallibility is the assistance of the Holy Spirit. For this reason infallibility in the Church is one and identical but its modalities are multiple." [59] D'Avanzo then lectured Guidi on one of the elementary points of scholastic philosophy: "It therefore remains that the pope is never separated from the Church. In the schema we have made a distinction, not a separation. He who distinguishes does not separate." [60] With some indignation d'Avanzo concluded: "We did not even think of a separation between the head and the body." [61]

Bishop Gasser also answered Guidi, and his *relatio* has a weightier character than that of d'Avanzo. Very directly Gasser took up the famous three words, *personalis, separata,* and *absoluta*. In what sense, asked Gasser, can the infallibility of the Roman pontiff be said to be personal? "One must call it personal and thus exclude the distinction between the Roman pontiff and the Roman church. Further, infallibility is called personal so that the distinction between *sedes* and *sedens* is excluded." [62] The distinction between *sedes* and *sedens* was important for Gallican thinking. To counter the possibility of interpreting in a Gallican sense what might issue from Vatican I, Gasser wanted to insist that in some sense infallibility is personal, that is it is not a charism given to the papacy considered abstractly. It is personal in the concrete sense that the pope is the subject. Without doubt the intention of the council, as heard through the words of Gasser, was to bury Gallicanism once and for all. Infallibility is not personal in the sense that the pope speaks as a private person or a private doctor, but it is personal in the sense that "he is the person of the Roman pontiff or a public person, that is, head of the church in his relation to the universal Church. . . . Hence the sentence 'The Roman pontiff is infallible' should not be looked upon as false because Christ promised it to the person of Peter and to the person of his successor. But it alone is incomplete since the pope is only *(solummodo)* infallible when with a solemn judgment he defines for the whole Church matters of faith and morals." [63] Yet there is a hesitancy on the part of Gasser to say without qualification that infallibility is personal. "Although we claim it for the person of the pope, we do not speak of personal infallibility." [64] Finally, he is infallible not simply because of his papal authority but because he is under the influence of divine assistance. If the documents of Vatican I would use the phrase "personal infallibility," it could too easily be understood as belonging to him as an individual person. The definition, as a matter of fact, does not speak of "personal infallibility."

Moving on to *separata,* Gasser firmly rejected it as an accurate description of the pope's relation to the Church. In the Church he has a distinct role founded in the special promise of Christ and in the special assistance of the Holy Spirit, "which is not one and the same with that which the whole body of the teaching Church joined to its head enjoys." [65] Again he took up the special role of Peter and his successors as the "center of ecclesiastical unity, whose task it is to keep the Church in the unity of faith and charity." [66] Because the pope has special functions within the Church, he has a special relation to it. In this rather special sense it is proper to speak of "a separate infallibility of the Roman pontiff." [67] "But on that account we do not separate the pontiff from the Church, to which he is 'ordered' in the most forceful way." [68] For the pope is only (*solummodo*) infallible when, acting in his office as doctor of all Christians and therefore representing the universal Church, he judges and defines what must be believed or rejected by all. The foundation stone of a building which carries the whole edifice can no more be separated from that building than the pope can be separated from the Church. "Again we do not separate from the cooperation and assent of the Church the pope who is defining infallibly, at least in this sense that we do not exclude this cooperation and this assent of the Church." [69] At this juncture Gasser was pointing not to the source of the pope's knowledge, which is the Church, but to the absence of the absolute necessity as a matter of law of the assent of the Church, either antecedent or subsequent, even though this assent will never be lacking. To emphasize this close connection between pope and Church, Gasser later added that there are not two infallibilities, one of the pope and one of the Church: "One must not only say that the pope is infallible in matters of faith and morals when he defines doctrines having to do with faith and morals, but that this infallibility [of the pope] is that which the Church enjoys." [70] Gasser's position has been made more difficult by the invocation of the authority of Saint Antoninus, who said: "It is granted that the pope as an individual person and acting in his own name (*motu proprio agens*) can err . . . however, the pope cannot err using the counsel and requiring the help of the universal Church, according to God's ordinance. . . ." [71] Basing himself on the authority of Antoninus, Bishop Legat wished to introduce a phrase which would say that the pope cannot err in matters of faith and morals when he confirms these matters.[72] Bishop Landriot quoted Bellarmine to the same effect, namely: "Definitions which are *de fide* depend most especially on the apostolic tradition and the consent of the churches." [73] Such opinions were not accepted by Gasser, who saw them as limiting the pope to confirming the decrees of ecumenical councils.[74] The ghost of Gallicanism would not be allowed to rise again. One can ask whether the spectre of Gallicanism was not used to bolster a position.

Earlier in this essay Gasser was quoted as saying that absolute infallibility belongs to God alone and that all other infallibility has its limits. Infallibility is limited in that "the charism of truth" can only be exercised in relation to the Church. "To Peter is promised the gift of inerrancy in his relation to the universal Church." [75] Gasser then quoted Matt. 16:18 and John 21:13-17 and continued: "Outside of this relation to the universal Church Peter in his successors does not enjoy the charism of truth promised most surely by Christ. In the same manner the infallibility of the Roman pontiff is really *(reapse)* restricted by reason of the *subject*, when the pope speaks as constituted universal doctor and supreme judge in the seat of Peter *(in cathedra Petri)*, that is, in the center; infallibility is limited by reason of the *object*, when it concerns matters of faith and morals; infallibility is limited by *act*, that is, when he defines what must be believed or rejected by all followers of Christ." [76] It grieved Gasser that some of the fathers of the council wish to write the conditions into the definition, for they are conditions which are found in the tracts of dogmatic theology and Gasser felt they belonged more to the order of morality than of dogma. "Our Lord Jesus Christ did not wish to make the charism of truth dependent on the conscience of the pontiff, which is a private matter *(res)*, indeed most private, known only to God, but rather he wished to make it dependent on the public relation of the pontiff to the universal Church." [77] With some passion Gasser asked that the fathers not write a moral condition into the definition. The pope has a moral obligation to investigate and consult as to what the faith of the Church is precisely because when he defines he acts in regard to the Church. No one disputes this moral obligation. The request of Gasser was that the obligation not be elevated to the realm of dogma.

Both Vatican I and II were in fact extremely cautious about the way in which they phrased the doctrine of infallibility.[78] *Pastor aeternus* declares: "The Roman pontiff, when he speaks *ex cathedra,* is possessed of infallibility, that is, when in discharge of the office of pastor and doctor of all Christians, by virtue of his supreme apostolic authority, he defines a doctrine regarding faith or morals to be held by the universal Church, by the divine assistance promised with which the divine Redeemer willed that his Church should be endowed for defining doctrine regarding faith or morals; and that therefore such definitions of the Roman pontiff are irreformable of themselves, and not from the consent of the Church." [79] *Pastor aeternus* used the phrase *ea infallibilitate pollere,* translated variously, and too literally, as "he is made strong," or "he is possessed of that infallibility." The text neither wants to transfer all infallibility to the doctrine nor to assert personal infallibility in a way which would be misunderstood. *Pastor aeternus,* therefore, does not say that the pope is infallible but that he enjoys or is made strong by infallibility, or he is possessed of it. Also clear is that the infallibility and divine assistance of which the pope "is possessed" are those given to the Church.

In the *Constitution on the Church* the same careful language is used. "This infallibility with which the divine Redeemer willed his Church to be endowed in defining a doctrine of faith and morals extends as far as the deposit of divine revelation. . . . This is the infallibility which the Roman pontiff, the head of the college of bishops, enjoys. . . ." [80] Vatican II also teaches that the infallibility of the pope is that of the Church and that he "enjoys" *(gaudet)* this infallibility. The *pollere* of Vatican I and the *gaudet* of Vatican II make it possible to say that infallibility is in some sense personal, rooted in the person, but that it is not to be identified with the person of the pope in an atomistic way. Like the context of the definition in *Pastor aeternus,* the *Constitution on the Church* makes it clear that the infallibility which the pope enjoys is that which Christ promised to his Church. The pope acts "as one in whom the charism of the infallibility of the Church itself is present. . . ." [81]

No difference is to be found between Gasser and Guidi on the transient nature of the divine assistance in virtue of which the pope is infallible. The pope is always the supreme judge in matters of faith and morals and is always the father and doctor of all Christians, "but he only enjoys *(gaudet)* the divine assistance in virtue of which he cannot err when by an act he exercises his office of supreme judge in controversies concerning the faith and [only] when he acts as doctor of the universal Church." [82] The sentence: "The pope is infallible" is incomplete because "the pope is infallible only when, by a solemn judgment, he defines for the universal Church in matters of faith and morals." This repetition of *solummodo* (only) makes it clear that for Gasser, too, the divine assistance in virtue of which the pope is infallible is not a permanent habit but a passing grace, i.e. what in the terminology of an earlier theological tradition would be called an actual grace. The pope is, then, infallible only in the act of defining.[83] That the pope is *only* infallible when he defines is not clearly stated in the text and therefore is not defined. After Vatican I some theologians (Vacant, Bellamy, Billot, Hürth) defended the thesis that the pope is infallible in his ordinary *magisterium*. But very likely the fathers of Vatican I intended to define that the pope is infallible *only* when he defines.[84]

Vatican II seems to have taken over Gasser's interpretation and incorporated it into the text of the *Constitution on the Church,* which reads: "The Roman pontiff enjoys infallibility when, in a definitive way, he proclaims a doctrine of faith or morals." Thus the pope is infallible only *quando* (when) he defines.

One could supposedly think of infallibility as the result of God's intervening providence which keeps the pope from error in defining. The doctrine of Vatican I is richer than that. The Holy Spirit is not just the efficient cause but is constitutive of that defining process. The most characteristic expression of this perception is "by the special assistance of the Holy Spirit." Charism is not the dominant category in either the discussions or in *Pastor aeternus,* nor is it a major tool of theological analysis. Nevertheless, it was an important concept frequently used in the speeches on the floor of the Council and once each, in places of decisive importance, in *Pastor aeternus* of Vatican I and in the *Constitution on the Church* of Vatican II. Charism expresses the constitutive role the Spirit plays in the papal ministry, that is, not a power added to a previously existing papal structure but the power of God which constitutes the unique papal Ministry in and for the Church.

Infallibility, according to Vatican I, is not a thing; it is, rather, a manifestation of the Spirit in the person of the pope when he ministers to the whole Church in defining matters of faith and morals. For this reason infallibility should not be "thing-ified," as though the pope were saved from error simply in virtue of the papacy considered as a completed and self-contained religious reality. In defining, his decrees are free from error because he is, in that extended moment, under the influence of the Spirit who is manifesting himself in the service of the whole Church. The reason why the Church can never withhold consent from his irreformable definitions is not because it owes him obedience—a dubious formulation since the pope does not exist separate from or above the Church. Rather that assent cannot be wanting because the same Spirit dwells in both the visible head and the members.

The charism of the infallibility of the Church is present in the pope because of the promise of Christ. Christ's promise of the Spirit does not constitute a new fixed property in the person of the pope but is a *lux transiens* (a passing light) directed to that extended moment which is the defining process. Much less is it a permanent ontological quality which enables the pope to operate under direct and immediate inspiration in a manner similar to that attributed to the authors of the Sacred Scriptures. Nor is it a species of divine revelation. The promise of the Spirit is not magical, even when the Spirit is operative. Diligence in searching out the faith of the Church is not displaced by the charism of infallibility. The unique charism of infallibility is operative in the pope in those unique circumstances when *(quando)* he exercises his ministry of defining.

The special charism he exercises corresponds to the special relation he has to the whole body. In his Ministry he is most forcefully "ordered to" the Church, that is, his Ministry does not exist apart from his place within the Church and his service to the Church. For this reason his infallibility is incomplete, which is to say that he defines infallibly in relation to the Church. Apart from it he has no charism. His role as the center of unity, like his charism of infallibility, is not derivative from the bishops, for it is undelegated, promised to him in Peter by Christ himself.

Quite correctly one can speak of personal infallibility because it does not exist in the abstract but in a believing subject. He in whom the charism of the infallibility of the Church is singularly present can be called infallible. Yet it is the act of defining which is preserved from error, and the result of this extended act (a process) is an irreformable doctrine. For this reason one hesitates to speak in an unguarded way of personal infallibility and uses a circumlocution, such as "is possessed of infallibility" *(pollere)*. Infallibility which results in irreformable doctrine is not an absolute; it does not embrace the daily teaching of the popes but is limited to the pope when he speaks as universal doctor and supreme judge to those matters which have to do with faith and morals and to that act by which, or that extended moment, when he defines what is to be believed or rejected by all the faithful.

16

THE HISTORICAL BACKGROUND
OF VATICAN I

Joseph A. Burgess

Vatican I did not take place in a vacuum. On the other hand, to what extent do historical considerations determine the meaning of a dogma? They cannot finally determine dogma, and as a consequence a "very delicate distinction" must be made between history and dogma; nevertheless Vatican I is "incomprehensible" if one does not understand its setting.[1] But which understanding is valid? Interpretations have varied widely, from the early extremes by the conservative official historian Granderath, and the Old Catholic Friedrich, to the recent extremes represented by Williams, a Protestant who interprets Vatican I from Manning's (and ultimately de Maistre's) point of view, and Hasler, a Roman Catholic whose interpretation at times seems Old Catholic.[2] In this short survey I will attempt to highlight the major issues.

Throughout history the Church has reflected what has happened in contemporary society. The relationship might on occasion be weighted toward the Church, but often the church absolutized certain contemporary political, economic, and sociological structures. In this essay I can only mention the important parallel between the form of government in the Roman Empire and in the early Catholic Church[3] and then discuss how structures such as papal primacy and papal infallibility are related to more recent historical developments, particularly to the French Revolution of 1789.

The French Revolution itself did not take place in a vacuum; it reflected changes which were already taking place, such as rationalism, nationalism, discoveries of other cultures and religions, and the breakdown of established socioeconomic patterns. Reason was made into a goddess; the nation became absolute; the existence of other religions raised questions about the superiority of Christianity; democracy seemed a threat to traditional upper-class support of the church; alliances, however uneasy, which had existed in the past between faith and reason, Church and state, and more broadly, Church and world, were breaking down. Opponents of the French Revolution, such as de Maistre, claimed it was caused by the fact that the Reformation had destroyed the authority of the Church.[4]

Many Roman Catholics were gripped by "an obsessive fear" of the French Revolution.[5] Their traditional religious, intellectual, and social authorities were in full retreat, while it seemed to them that change and anarchy held sway. Roman Catholic history from 1789 to 1870 is dominated by the Roman Catholic reaction to the revolutions of 1789, 1830, and 1848. Disaster was the occasion for retrenchment; one extreme produced its opposite. But disaster was also the occasion for renewal, for the old was swept away and the new made possible—which in this case meant greater centralization in the Roman Catholic Church.

What most do not realize is that when the Roman Catholic reaction began at the start of the 19th century, the infallibility of the pope was generally rejected, except for most of Italy and Spain and isolated figures such as de Maistre.[6] There were very few supporters of the independent infallibility of the pope before 1850 in Germany.[7] That the doctrine of papal infallibility developed within 70 years from being widely rejected to being dogmatized is a unique phenomenon in the history of dogma. It indicates the central importance which this doctrine came to have for the Roman Catholic Church in the 19th century.[8]

"The Pope is never so strong as when in chains," writes Jedin,[9] referring, to be sure, to Clement VII in 1527, but his statement is just as applicable to 1789. Pius VI (1775-1799), Pius VII (1800-1823), and Pius IX (1846-1878) drew sympathy and support because they were seen as martyrs. The more the pope lost his temporal authority, the greater the stress on his spiritual authority.

The loss of the pope's temporal authority looks very different in retrospect. As Congar points out, the temporal disasters of the Roman Catholic Church made it possible for it to attempt to be a unifying spiritual power for the whole world.[10] But already in the eighth century the Roman Catholic Church was convinced that it had to possess land in order to be independent.[11] The disadvantage was that the pope became involved in battles over temporal power, as was the case through the following centuries. The French Revolution did not lead to the separation of Church and state on the European continent, and the fact that both Pius VI and Pius VII were taken into exile reinforced the idea that the spiritual independence of the pope could only be preserved if he had strong temporal power. Pius IX was convinced to the very end of his life that the papal states were necessary for the survival of the Roman Catholic Church. On the other hand, European powers often opposed papal infallibility precisely because they feared it was a device to establish the papal states.

The increasing centralization of power and authority in the pope was aided by a number of external factors. First of all, the French Revolution destroyed the political system which had supported Gallicanism. To be sure, the Roman Catholic Church lost its property and the state took over education; the Civil Constitution of the Clergy in 1790 subordinated the Church to the state. But through the Concordat with Napoleon in 1801 Rome instead of the French episcopacy was made head of the church. The pope was able to replace 50 bishops and thus effectively remake the French church. Bishops were given extensive power by the state and as a consequence the lower clergy began to look to Rome for support against them.[12] A similar development took place in Germany. In 1803 the *Reichsdeputations-hauptschluss* secularized church property and made changes which effectively destroyed the episcopal infrastructure. Many episcopal sees remained vacant. By 1818 only three bishops remained in what had been called the German Reich. Episcopal sees were increased in number, which weakened them, and the number of powerful archbishops was decreased. Most German Roman Catholics were in the minority, and they came to look at Rome and to papal infallibility as support for their freedom over against state domination.[13]

Second, the Congress of Vienna in 1814-1815 seemed to signal both political and Roman Catholic restoration. But to identify with the political restoration was not to identify with success. When the Revolution of 1830 overthrew the restoration, those who had supported the restoration were also overthrown. From Roman Catholic restoration, however, was born Ultramontanism, which dominated Roman Catholic history until 1870. Ultramontanism is a variety of Romanticism, that is, it meant among other things both hope and nostalgia for an idealized past, tradition in place of reason, and a return to the sources instead of science. The pope was thought of as an ideal father and authority. Four French literary figures developed and spread these ideas: Chateaubriand pointed out how cultured and beautiful the Roman Catholic Church had been, de Bonald stressed tradition and external authority over against reason, de Maistre in his book *Du pape* (1819) brought together papal infallibility and absolute political authority, and Lammenais was able to convince many of these ideas by portraying the infallible pope as the defender of freedom both for the Roman Catholic Church and for all who are suppressed.[14]

Third, the world grew smaller. New and better means of transportation, such as the steamboat and the train, meant that it was easier and faster to send messages and make trips; it also meant that Rome could control events more directly and was more accessible.

In addition, the Roman Catholic Church itself took positive steps to centralize power and authority in the pope. First of all, the French theological faculties, which were Gallican, had been disbanded; they were replaced after 1815 by reopening colleges in Rome for foreigners. In 1824 Leo XII revived the Roman College, giving it to the Jesuits, and later more colleges were founded. Since France had no Roman Catholic faculty for advanced theological study, students went to Rome. Moreover, Pius IX encouraged priests and students to study in Rome.[15]

Second, Gregory XVI and Pius IX promoted world missions and founded numerous episcopal Sees.[16] Pius IX also restored the Roman Catholic hierarchies in Holland and England.[17] Since many of these places were poor, they were dependent on Rome for financial support, and Rome knew how to use this influence at Vatican I.[18] Pius IX restored the obligation of periodic episcopal visits to Rome, which helped to keep bishops in the Roman orbit.[19]

Third, modern technology was used to promote the Roman cause. The press was made to play an important role in popularizing the pope's concerns. Modern means of transportation made possible huge pilgrimages to Rome in 1854, 1862, and 1867, which demonstrated both Roman Catholic unity and the importance of the pope.[20]

On the other hand, the Roman Catholic Church took certain repressive measures in order to centralize power and authority in the pope. First of all, there was the attempt to control literature and liturgy. Books were placed more frequently on the *Index Librorum Prohibitorum*. Catechisms were modified to promote the Roman point of view. The same was done with theological textbooks; each edition was made to state the argument for papal infallibility with greater force. The Roman rite was used to replace local liturgies.[21]

Second, discipline became more rigorous. Papal nuncios had been the pope's ambassadors to nation states, but now they took a more active role in the internal life of the Roman Catholic Church. They collected information, promoted opposition against and denounced those who were not Ultramontanists, and thus effectively controlled the bishops.[22] Rome condemned ideas held by Hermes (1835), Günther (1857), and Frohschammer (1862), sometimes to the astonishment of many Roman Catholics. Pius VII restored the Inquisition. As late as 1816 it passed a death sentence at Ravenna; inquisitors were still active in 1856; [23] in Proposition # 24 of the *Syllabus* (1864) the following sentence was condemned: "The church has not the power of using force, nor has she any temporal power, direct or indirect"; and in 1869 Pius IX canonized Pedro Arbues, one of the most notorious of the Spanish inquisitors.

Third, centralization meant the suppression of regional autonomy. Pius IX forbade national councils and at first discouraged national bishops' conferences, for either might tend to be independent of Rome. Provincial councils, since they were under papal control, became the means of promoting official doctrine, particularly the dogma of papal infallibility. Rome even modified those decisions by provincial councils which were considered unsuitable, in spite of those who objected, but fewer objections were raised as time went on. Later at Vatican I the decisions of the provincial councils were used as an important argument for the doctrine of papal infallibility.[24]

Fourth, that which seemed to threaten the authority of the Roman Catholic Church, such as liberalism and laicism, was opposed. The Encyclical *Mirari Vos* (1832) condemned liberalism and freedom of conscience; in it Gregory XVI was concerned about Italy, but in fact he spoke to the whole world. Unfortunately Rome viewed liberalism from a very limited Italian perspective. But liberalism was very different in different places, and its development varied as nationalism varied.[25] Anti-Christian liberalism existed, of course, but there were also genuinely Roman Catholic liberals, such as Montalembert. Roman Catholic liberalism may be defined as the effort to adapt to the new relationship between Church and society brought about by the French Revolution.[26] Symbolic of the fact that Rome wanted to proceed in the opposite direction was the fact that the gas street lights which had been installed in Rome by the French were torn out when Pius VII returned,[27] and gas lighting and trains were forbidden in the Papal States.[28]

The Jesuits were blamed for much that was considered oppressive in the events leading up to Vatican I, and "Jesuit" became an uncomplimentary slogan used against the majority at Vatican I.[29] The Jesuits had been restored as an order in 1814 as part of the Roman Catholic reaction to the French Revolution. Through their journal *Civiltà cattolica*, their influential teaching positions in Rome, and their strong influence over the Roman curia, they became a kind of spiritual army for the pope and thus for papal infallibility.[30]

Two events immediately prior to Vatican I were very important for the history of the definition of papal infallibility. In 1854 Pius IX defined the dogma of the Immaculate Conception of Mary. For the first time in history a pope clearly claimed to decide by himself a matter of faith infallibly. The definition of 1854 was a method of pre-empting, even if only symbolically, the decision of infallibility in 1870.[31]

The *Syllabus of Errors* appeared exactly 10 years later; the symbolic importance of this dating should not be overlooked.[32] In itself it was nothing new, for it was a summary of previous papal pronouncements against the errors of the modern world. "But it seemed at the time, erroneously as posterity sees, less like withdrawal behind the convent wall than as an attempt to dominate." [33] Reaction against the *Syllabus* was immediate. The majority of Roman Catholics were astonished that the pope seemed to be condemning progress and modern civilization.[34] Liberal Roman Catholics were embittered.[35] Many countries forbade its publication, and this reaction was fueled by the fact that it was "very commonly defended as *ex cathedra* by the theologians of the sixties and seventies." [36] These extreme interpretations of the *Syllabus* sharply increased in turn the opposition of the Roman Catholic minority to papal infallibility.[37] Non-Roman Catholics feared that if the *Syllabus* was not already an infallible papal pronouncement, the upcoming council would make it so, for in February, 1869, *Civiltà cattolica* published an article advocating dogmatizing the *Syllabus*.[38]

In addition to these two events, the popes themselves were very important for the history of the definition of papal infallibility. Both Gregory XVI and Pius IX carried out comprehensive programs both to increase Roman Catholic piety and to promote papal infallibility.[39] Pius IX turned in this direction especially after the crisis of 1848.[40] He was very conscious of his authority as pope. If possible, Gregory XVI had been careful to pick only supporters of papal infallibility as bishops,[41] and Pius IX continued this practice. Of the 739 Roman Catholic bishops alive in 1869, he had named all but 81, and all had been selected according to their faithfulness to Rome.[42] He carefully controlled the preparations for Vatican I. During the second part of the council he actively promoted papal infallibility and campaigned against its opponents.

An important factor in Pius IX's success was his personality. He was tremendously popular with Roman Catholics, and his simplicity and charm drew people to him. He held innumerable audiences, which cemented the enthusiasm of the masses of people and helped eliminate any remaining resistance to Ultramontanism. Many idealized him as a martyr because of the attacks on the Papal States. A papal cult developed around him, and it served to rally the faithful to support the "personal" infallibility of the pope.[43] At the council the minority reacted sharply to this extreme view.[44]

Only on the basis of the historical setting presented up to this point is it possible adequately to understand the intellectual setting of Vatican I.[45] "The first Vatican Council of 1869-70 was afterwards seen to be concerned with the theology of faith and ecclesiastical certitude. That was not what was believed at the time, not even perhaps by the pope. At the time it was believed to be concerned with the question of questions, whether liberalism and Catholicism could be reconciled." [46] The intellectual roots of this struggle go back at least as far as the Enlightenment, but there were not always two absolute fronts opposing one another. During the last half of the 18th century Roman Catholic thinkers were very much involved in the Enlightenment, Romanticism, and the intellectual ferment caused by Kant and Hegel.[47] What happened? The historical situation changed; the old authorities in politics and society were gone. The Roman Catholic Church more and more came to feel itself on the defensive. Most Roman Catholic apologists came to stress the importance of reason and the necessity of authority,[48] and the two fronts began to form. With each new crisis, such as 1830 and 1848, the fronts hardened. Gregory XVI and Pius IX continuously preached a crusade against the Enlightenment,[49] but about 1850 the crusade truly began. Neo-Thomism was committed to Ultramontanism, gained the upper hand, and became more militant. For example, in Naples a priest teaching experimental physics was transferred because his superiors held that it is not based on Aristotelian principles.[50] According to this way of thinking, truth tends to be clear and static; there is little place for change and historical thinking. To know God is to know the doctrines which he has revealed. Where can these doctrines be found? The answer is: in Scripture and tradition, and the Roman Catholic Church preserves and teaches these doctrines.[51]

The meaning of *church* in this context has its own intellectual history. It is often forgotten that in the West the first ecclesiological treatises were writen by canon lawyers, who described the Church in terms of *potestas*, which is juridical terminology.[52] Furthermore, faced with powerful medieval kings, Wycliffe and Huss, the Conciliarists, the Reformation, nationalism, and revolution, the Roman Catholic Church reacted by thinking of the Church in terms of power and authority; the Roman Catholic Church even seemed to become a monarchy in the political sense. This in turn contributed to anticlericalism.[53]

During the restoration after 1815 some Roman Catholic thinkers, most notably de Maistre and Lammenais, developed a theory of monarchical authority, a "metaphysics of sovereignty."[54] Frustrated royalists, especially in France, transferred their loyalties to the person of the pope.[55] For de Maistre absolute monarchy was instituted by God. The Roman Catholic hierarchy, particularly as it is focused in papal primacy and infallibility, is the guarantee of all authority. Since authorities are collapsing and false authorities abound, an emergency situation exists; the Church can only survive if the pope has the effective competence to decide whatever is needed for the sake of unity.[56]

The emergency situation gradually became the normative situation. At first de Maistre and those with him had only a small following. Once again, by the middle of the century the tide had turned. The understanding of papal primacy and infallibility held by the majority at Vatican I was juridical and, from an historical point of view, the mirror image of the view of absolutely autonomous authority held by liberals such as Rousseau.[57] The Church is the hierarchy with the pope in the center. What is stressed is the empirical structure of the Church.[58]

Much of the agitation just before and at Vatican I was carried out under the guise of eliminating Gallicanism. Defining Gallicanism, however, is not simple, for it varied with the circumstances.[59] *Gallicanism* had by this time become a "shibboleth" for whatever opposed papal absolutism, just as *papal infallibility* had come to mean the whole program of papal centralization.[60] The minority at Vatican I, however, could not be subsumed under either of these categories, for their understanding of the Church was not juridical, but organic.[61] The Ultramontanists often considered those bishops to be Gallicans who were simply holding to their real episcopal privileges.[62] Even the historic patriarchical system would have been considered Gallican in the last part of the 19th century.[63] Historic Gallicanism had died out and hardly needed the solemn condemnation of a council to give it the coup-de-grace.[64] A sort of moderate Gallicanism had survived for the first third of the century,[65] but then it succumbed to the pressures which Rome brought to bear.

Bishop Dinkel, Newman, and Maret held that Vatican I was a victory for the minority.[66] But that is true only if the majority is thought to be made up only of extremists. As a matter of fact, the majority clearly won, particularly through the restrictions which were added to the decree on infallibility in July, 1870.[67] After Vatican I the ultramontane views continued to be more influential than the limitations which the minority had insisted on.[68]

It is legitimate to ask whether events had to develop the way they did. It was not inevitable that the Roman Catholic Church in the 19th century defend the reactionary developments of the time, for they bear no "necessary relation to the nature of Catholicism." [69] The Roman Catholic Church did not have to use the categories of authority and jurisdiction which dominated the contemporary world. Even at the time many voices warned that this meant the loss of decisive elements in the Christian faith.[70] Present-day theology has the task of pointing out what categories would more adequately express what papal infallibility means. As Pottmeyer puts it, to make the emergency solution developed at Vatican I into a timeless model for church structure is to fail to understand the historical context of Vatican I.[71]

At this point it would have been appropriate to describe the history of the Lutheran reaction to the French Revolution and to the Roman Catholic Church between 1789 and 1870. In many ways Lutheran church history is intertwined with Roman Catholic church history.[72] Yet there are important differences. For example, the Prussian Union of 1817 created huge waves within German Lutheranism but scarcely a ripple within Roman Catholicism. France and Italy, where much of the Roman Catholic history of this period took place, were almost completely Roman Catholic and would seem at first glance to have little to do with Denmark, Norway, and Sweden, which were almost exclusively Lutheran. Thus although important parallels between the Lutheran and Roman Catholic histories of this period exist, the interrelationships are too complex to be pursued in this brief essay.

NOTES

1. Teaching Authority and Infallibility In the Church

1. The previous volumes in this series are described in the list of abbreviations.
2. As noted in L/RC 4:9, "ministry" (lowercase) is used for the task of proclaiming the gospel by the whole Church and "Ministry" for that particular form of service, order, function, or gift *(charism)* within and for the sake of Christ's Church in its mission to the world.
3. DS 3074.
4. A. Vacant, L. Billot, E. Dublanchy, J. Salaverri, and J. C. Fenton, among others, ascribed a fundamental infallibility to the ordinary magisterium of the pope. For a survey of opinions on this point, see F. M. Gallati, *Wenn die Päpste sprechen* (Vienna: Herder, 1960), pp. 41-42, 80-85; also A. Peiffer, *Die Enzykliken und ihr formaler Wert für die dogmatische Methode* (Freiburg [Switz.]: Universitätsverlag, 1968), pp. 72-100. Popular catechisms often made no distinction between the ordinary and extraordinary magisterium of the pope, stating simply that the pope is infallible when he proclaims a doctrine of faith and morals to all. See e.g. *A Catechism of Christian Doctrine Prepared and Enjoined by Order of the Third Plenary Council of Baltimore* (New York: Benziger, 1886), p. 30.
5. DS 3885.

6. *Lumen gentium* 25.
7. *Treatise on the Power and Primacy of the Pope;* Tappert 320-335.
8. DS 1451-1492.
9. *Ap.* 7-10; Tappert 168-180.
10. *Ap.* 7-8; Tappert 168-173.
11. *Ap.* 7-8; 33-34; Tappert 174-175; L/RC 4, pp. 18-19; L/RC 5, pp. 25ff.
12. "The Gospel and the Church" (Malta Report of the Joint Lutheran/Roman Catholic Subcommission), par. 16. German text in *Herder Korrespondenz* 25 (1971): 536-544; Eng. tr. in *Worship* 46 (1972): 326-351, and *Lutheran World* 19 (1972): 259-273.
13. MR, par. 17.
14. On the work of the Holy Spirit, see further in par. 12 below.
15. E.g. his message about the kingdom (Matt. 4:17) and "all that I have commanded you" (28:20), which in Matthew's Gospel refers especially to the discourses in chaps. 5–7, 10, 13, 18, 24–25.
16. Cf. André Benoît, "The Transmission of the Gospel," *The Gospel as History,* ed. by Vilmos Vajta (Philadelphia: Fortress, 1975), p. 147. Note the equation: Christ = the power of God (1 Cor. 1:24) = the word of the cross (message about Christ crucified, 1 Cor. 1:18) = the gospel (Rom. 1:16).
17. Cf. Mark 8:35 and 10:29, where the two expressions are placed in parallel, "for my sake and the gospel's." Cf. Willi Marxsen, *Mark the Evangelist* (Nashville: Abingdon, 1969), pp. 120-121, 136-137; J. A. Fitzmyer, "The Kerygmatic and Normative Character of the Gospel," *Evangelium-Welt-Kirche,* ed. by H. Meyer (Frankfurt: Lembeck-Knecht, 1975), pp. 111-128; G. Strecker, "Literarkritische Überlegungen zum *euangelion*-Begriff im Markusevangelium," *Neues Testament und Geschichte,* Festschrift O. Cullmann (Zürich: Theologischer Verlag, 1972), pp. 91-104.
18. Damien van den Eynde, *Les normes de l'enseignement chrétien dans la littérature patristique des trois premiers siècles* (Gembloux: Duculot, 1933), pp. 32-33.
19. Cf. the Biblical Commission's *Instruction concerning the Historical Truth of the Gospels* (Rome, 1964); see TS 25 (1964): 402-408.
20. 1 Cor. 12:28; Rom. 12:6-8; Eph. 4:11. Cf. L/RC 4, p. 10, n. 6.
21. Mark 3:16-19; Matt. 10:2-4; Luke 6:14-16; Acts 1:13; 6:5.
22. Cf. Acts 2:29 and 4:13, referring to the boldness of Peter and John, who had "been with Jesus." The church in Jerusalem prayed to speak the word with boldness (4:29, cf. 31), and the Book of Acts closes with an emphasis on preaching and teaching "with

boldness" (28:31). Cf. 1 Thess. 2:3; 2 Cor. 4:3; Eph.
3:12; and 1 Timothy 3:13 as examples in the Pauline
corpus.

23. Paul stressed that his gospel was not "man's gospel"
but came through a revelation of Jesus Christ (Gal.
1:11-12). Heb. 6:19 states that God provides "a sure
and steadfast anchor." In Heb. 11:1 ff., faith is viewed
as assurance. Assurance is particularly a concern in
Luke-Acts; cf. Luke 1:4, ". . . that you may know
the truth (assurance) concerning the things of which
you have been informed."

24. *Faith and Order Findings* 2 (Montreal, 1963), sect.
45. *Kerygma* means "proclamation" and here denotes
the apostolic gospel. *Paradosis* is the Greek word for
"transmission" or "that which is transmitted" orally,
and is used in the New Testament in a positive sense
for Christian traditions in 1 Cor. 11:2 and 2 Thess.
2:15; 3:6; cf. 1 Cor. 11:23 and 15:3 for the verbal
form. It was a feature of the Montreal statement to
use "the Tradition" (with a capital) with reference
to the New Testament witnesses and "traditions"
(lower case) for the subsequent individual confessional developments of various churches.

25. 1 Thessalonians is dated around A.D. 50. Most New
Testament books were composed by the end of the
century. Some would date 2 Peter towards the end
of the first half of the second century. Cf. *Peter in
the New Testament*, ed. R. Brown, K. Donfried, and
J. Reumann (Minneapolis and New York: Augsburg
and Paulist, 1973), p. 17.

26. The Catholic and Lutheran traditions agree on the 27
books which comprise the New Testament canon.

27. Representative texts are conveniently gathered in
DS 1-75, and in Philip Schaff, *The Creeds of Christen-
dom* 2 (New York: Funk and Wagnalls, 1890), pp.
11-41. Cf. Irenaeus, *Adversus haereses* 1, 10, 1; 3, 4,
1-2; 4, 33, 7; and further, for his salvation-history
approach, *Proof of the Apostolic Preaching*, tr. J. P.
Smith, in *Ancient Christian Writers* 16 (Westminster,
Md.: Newman, 1952); also Tertullian, *De virginibus
velandis* 1; *Adversus Praxean* 2; *De praescriptione
haereticorum* 13, 36. On development from credal elements in the New Testament via the rule of faith to
the Old Roman Symbol and later creeds, cf. J. N. D.
Kelly, *Early Christian Creeds*, 3rd ed. (London: Longmans, Green, 1972).

28. For the development of a pattern of the threefold Min-
istry of deacon, presbyter (priest), bishop, cf. J. F.
McCue, "Apostles and Apostolic Succession in the
Patristic Era," in L/RC 4, pp. 137-171; cf. also ibid.,
pp. 10, n. 6, and J. D. Quinn, "Ministry in the New
Testament," ibid., pp. 69-100, which has now appeared

in revised form in *Biblical Studies in Contemporary Thought*, ed. by M. Ward (Somerville, Mass.: Greeno, Hadden, 1975), pp. 130-160.

29. Cf. L/RC 4, p. 12; MR, par. 15; *Anglican-Lutheran International Conversations* (London: SPCK, 1973), pp. 17ff., sect. 73-74; *Lutheran-Episcopal Dialogue: A Progress Report* (Cincinnati: Forward Movement Publications, 1973), pp. 20-22.

30. L/RC 5, p. 11; *Peter in the New Testament*, pp. 162 ff.

31. *Peter in the New Testament*, pp. 83 ff.

32. Cf. Luke 22:32 Vulgate, *Ut non deficiat fides tua* ("In order that your (singular) faith may not fail").

33. *Peter in the New Testament*, pp. 95 ff.

34. *Ibid.*, 49-50.

35. *Ibid.*, 157-158.

36. The phrase at 1 Timothy 3:15, "pillar and bulwark of the truth," may be understood as referring to the church, local or universal, or to Timothy as a Minister. It was later applied to the gospel, the Spirit, the four Gospels, and even an individual Christian. For details see J. D. Quinn, "On the Terminology for Faith, Truth, Teaching, and the Spirit in the Pastoral Epistles," L/RC 6, pp. 232-237 below. The history of interpretation of the verse points to places where assurance of the truth has been sought.

37. According to the research of Pierre Batiffol, Stephen I (254-257) was apparently the first bishop of Rome to claim explicitly that he held the *cathedra Petri* by succession, but several years earlier Cyprian had argued that "Rome possessed the church instituted first of all in the person of Peter," i.e., the *ecclesia principalis*, the *cathedra Petri*. See P. Batiffol, *Cathedra Petri: Etudes d'histoire ancienne de l'église* (Paris: Cerf, 1948), pp. 13-14; cf. pp. 135-142, 150, 178-181.

38. Epistle *In requirendis* (DS 217; Mirbt-Aland [6th ed.] no. 403); E. Giles, *Documents Illustrating Papal Authority* (London: SPCK, 1952), p. 201.

39. DS 363; Mirbt-Aland, no. 470.

40. H. Grundmann, "Die Papstprophetien des Mittelalters," *Archiv für Kulturgeschichte* 19 (1929): 77-137; Horst D. Rauh, *Das Bild des Antichrist im Mittelalter*, *Beiträge zur Geschichte der Philosophie und Theologie des Mittelalters*, NF 9 (Münster: Aschendorff, 1973).

41. B. Tierney, *Foundations of the Conciliar Theory* (Cambridge: Cambridge University Press, 1955), pp. 57-67 and passim.

42. Epistles 1, 27, 34; 12, 6. See R. Eno, "Some Elements in the Prehistory of Papal Infallibility," L/RC 6, pp. 238-258 below.

43. See R. Eno, ibid. For the concept of "reception," also Y. Congar, "La réception comme réalité ecclésias-

tique," *Revue des sciences philosophiques et Théologiques* 56 (1972) : 369-403.

44. The earliest instances are found in letters of Pope Zosimus (417-418) and Pope Boniface I (418-422).

45. See A. M. Koeniger, ed., "Prima sedes a nemine judicatur," *Festgabe für Albert Ehrhard* (Bonn and Leipzig: K. Schroeder, 1922; reprint, Amsterdam: Rodopi, 1969), pp. 273-300).

46. *Sum.theol.* 2-2, q. 1, a. 10, corpus. See Y. Congar, "St. Thomas and the Infallibility of the Papal Magisterium (S. Th. II-II, q. 1, a. 10)," *Thomist* 38 (1974) : 81-105.

47. *Quodlib.* 9, q. 7, a. 16.

48. This is the thesis of the book by B. Tierney, *Origins of Papal Infallibility* (Leiden: Brill, 1972).

49. The text was published by Bartholomaeus M. **Xiberta,** O. Carm., under the title *Guidonis Terreni Quaestio de magisterio infallibili Romani pontificis, Opuscula et textus,* Series scholastica et mystica, fasc. 2 (Münster: Aschendorff, 1926). For other instances of this use of the term, see Paul de Vooght, "Esquisse d'une enquête sur le mot 'infaillibilité, durant la période scholastique," in O. Rousseau *et al., L'Infaillibilité de l'Eglise: Journées oecuméniques de Chevetogne,* Sept. 25-29, 1961 (Chevetogne: Editions de Chevetogne, 1963), pp. 99-146.

50. To emphasize the revelation in Christ does not detract from the revelation of God through nature or in the Old Testament.

51. *Mysterium Ecclesiae* (AAS 65 [1973] : 402-403).

52. See Avery Dulles, "Infallibility: The Terminology," L/RC 6, pp. 68-80 below.

53. *Lumen gentium* 4.

54. *Ibid.* 23.

55. *Ibid.* 22.

56. *Ibid.* 18, 22, 23, 25.

57. DS 3074. Cf. M. C. Duchaine, "Vatican I on Primacy and Infallibility," in L/RC 5, p. 148.

58. *Ibid.,* pp. 148-149.

59. *Lumen gentium* 25; Duchaine (n. 57 above), p. 149.

60. *Lumen gentium* 25.

61. *Smalcald Articles,* Part 3, art. 4; Tappert 310.

62. WA 10/1,2:48,5; 7:475, 14-18; cf. WA 10/1,1:17,8; LW 35:123; WA 10/1,1:626,6-9; 12:259,8-15.

63. CA 7; Tappert 32.

64. *Formula of Concord, Epitome* 1; Tappert 464-465; *Formula of Concord, Solid Declaration,* Summary Formulation 1-13; Tappert 503-506.

65. *Ap.* 14; Tappert 214-215.

66. E.g. ecumenical councils and synods.

67. CA 18:21; Tappert 84.

68. See L/RC 5, p. 21.

69. *Lumen gentium* 25.

70. Cf. par. 5 above.
71. MR, par. 17.
72. For an argument in favor of Scripture as final norm *(norma normans non normata)* see Walter Kasper, *Glaube und Geschichte* (Mainz: Matthias-Grünewald, 1970), pp. 188-190. Karl Rahner has repeatedly characterized Scripture as being in practice, for the contemporary believer, the only original, underived source of Christian revelation, e.g. in his *Theological Investigations* 6 (Baltimore: Helicon, 1966), pp. 91-95. In this restricted sense, but without questioning the need for the authoritative testimony of tradition and *magisterium*, Rahner is prepared to defend a Catholic *sola scriptura* principle; see ibid., pp. 98-112.
73. But note the Lutheran World Federation as an international study and service agency.
74. *Lumen gentium* 37; *Gaudium et spes* 62.
75. *Lumen gentium* 25.
76. See L/RC 5, pp. 19-23.
77. *Mysterium Ecclesiae* (AAS 65 [1973]: 402-404).
78. Cf. MR, par. 18; *Dei verbum* 10.
79. *Lumen gentium* 25.
80. Cf. E. Gritsch, "Lutheran Teaching Authority: Past and Present," L/RC 6, pp. 138-148 below. The term emerged in the discussions of the dialogue group at its New Orleans meeting, February 1972.
81. The term was used in the meeting between Pope Paul VI and the Ecumenical Patriarch Athenagoras in Istanbul with reference to the mutual excommunications of 1053. See W. M. Abbott and J. Gallagher, *The Documents of Vatican II* (New York: Guild, 1966), p. 726.
82. Cf. *Katholische Anerkennung des augsburgischen Bekenntnisses, Ökumenische Perspektiven* 9 (Frankfurt: Josef Knecht, 1977).
83. *Smalcald Articles*, Part 2, art. 4; Tappert 298-301. See also the Lutheran Reflections below, par. 21.
84. L/RC 5, pp. 21-22.
85. Whether this ministry should be regarded as of divine institution must be judged in terms of the principles and difficulties stated *ibid.*, pp. 22, 30, 31, 34.
86. In this comprehensive sense the term was used in the Tridentine decree on the canon of Sacred Scripture (DS 1501), where *puritas ipsa evangelii* was used to sum up what was promised in "Sacred Scripture" (= the OT) and promulgated by Christ himself. Compare *Dei verbum* 7.
87. E.g. see Thomas Aquinas, *Sum. theol.* 2-2, q. i, a. 9, sed contra.
88. *Ap.* 7:27; Tappert 173.
89. See Georges Dejaifve, "Ex sese, non autem ex consensu ecclesiae," *Salesianum* 24 (1962): 283-297;

Eng. tr. in *Eastern Churches Quarterly* 14 (1962):
360-378; also Heinrich Fries, "Ex sese, non ex consensu ecclesiae," in *Volk Gottes*, Festgabe J. Höfer,
ed. by R. Bäumer and H. Dolch (Freiburg: Herder,
1967), pp. 480-500.

90. L/RC 5, pp. 35-37.

91. Text in AAS 65 (1973): 396-408; Eng. tr. in *Catholic
Mind* 71, no. 1276 (Oct. 1973): 54-64.

92. AAS 65 (1973): 402; *Catholic Mind* (n. 91 above):
58-59.

93. "Tunc enim Romanus Pontifex non ut persona privata
sententiam profert, sed ut universalis ecclesiae magis-
ter supremus, in quo charisma infallibilis ipsius ecclesiae singulariter inest, doctrinam fidei catholicae ex-
ponit vel tuetur" (*Lumen gentium* 25). See J. D.
Quinn, " 'Charisma veritatis certum': Irenaeus, *Adversus haereses* 4, 26, 2," TS 39 (1978): 520-525; also
Kilian McDonnell, "Infallibility as Charism at Vatican I," L/RC 6, pp. 270-286 below.

94. This insight of Vatican II, of course, was not entirely
new. It recalls the famous definition of an article of
faith, used by Thomas Aquinas and many other
Scholastic theologians, as a "glimpse of the divine
truth toward which it tends" *(perceptio divinae veritatis tendens in ipsam)*; see *Sum. theol.* 2-2, q.1, a. 6,
sed contra.

95. See K. Rahner and K. Lehmann, *Kerygma and Dogma*
(New York: Herder and Herder, 1969), pp. 87-88.

96. On this point see G. A. Lindbeck, *Infallibility* (Milwaukee: Marquette University Press, 1972), pp. 21-22
and 60, with references to the work of R. P. McBrien.

97. MR, par. 50.

98. On the problems of interpreting the phrase "pillar and
bulwark of the truth" (1 Timothy 3:15), see above,
"Common Statement," par. 16, n. 36. There are also
several passages in the Fourth Gospel which could be
examined further in this connection.

99. See end of n. 24 above.

100. See e.g. A. Cotter, *Theologia fundamentalis*, 2nd ed.
(Weston, Mass.: Weston College, 1947), p. 681. Cf.
A. Durand, "Exégèse," *Dictionnaire apologétique de
la foi catholique* 1:1838; E. Mangenot and J. Rivière,
"Interprétation de l'écriture," DTC 7:2318.

101. U. Betti, a historian who has devoted much study to
Vatican I and its Decree *Pastor aeternus*, has written: "The interpretation of these two texts (Matt.
16:16-19 and John 21:15-17) as proof of the two
dogmas mentioned does not fall *per se* under the dogmatic definition, not only because there is no mention
of them in the canon, but also because there is not a
trace that the Council wanted to give an authentic
interpretation of them in this sense" *(La costituzione*

dommatica "Pastor aeternus" del Concilio Vaticano I)
(Rome: Antonianum, 1961), p. 592. Similarly, apropos
of Luke 22:32: ". . . the Council abstained from wanting to give an authentic interpretation . . . of that
particular text . . . , although the request had been
made in this sense by someone in the preparatory
phase of the Decree and again during the concilar discussion of the Decree" (p. 628).

102. See Robert Eno, "Some Elements in the Prehistory of
Papal Infallibility," L/RC 6, pp. 238-258 below.

103. See G. Tavard, "The Bull *Unam sanctam* of Boniface
VIII," L/RC 5, pp. 105-119.

104. For John XXII's earlier position, see Marc Dykmans,
Les sermons de Jean XXII sur la vision béautifique
(Rome: Gregorian University, 1973), p. 96. For John
XXII's subsequent retraction and the correction pub-
lished by Benedict XII, see DS 990-991 and 1000-1001.

105. In his controversy with Hans Küng, Karl Rahner
asserted: "All Küng's examples for such erroneous
propositions seem to me either not to have been definitions or else there is question of propositions which
Küng can reject as erroneous only if they are interpreted in a very definite manner which does not un-
ambiguously impose itself" (*"Mysterium Ecclesiae:
Zur Erklärung der Glaubenskongregation über die
Lehre der Kirche," Stimmen der Zeit* 191 [1973]:
587). Cf. Y. Congar, in *Revue des sciences philosophiques et théologiques* 62 (1978) : 87.

106. These definitions, contained in apostolic constitutions
published in the form of bulls, are phrased in unmistakably solemn language (DS 2803, 3903) and clearly
claim to be infallibly uttered.

107. In favor of the infallibility of canonizations, see I
Salaverri, *De ecclesia Christi*, 2nd ed. (Madrid:
B.A.C., 1952), nos. 724-725, pp. 723-725; L. Lercher,
Institutiones theologiae dogmaticae 1, 4th ed., rev. by
F. Schlagenhaufen (Barcelona: Herder, 1945), n.
511b, p. 305; P. Molinari and A. E. Green, "Canoni-
zation of Saints," *New Catholic Encyclopedia* 3:55-61,
esp. 59 and 61.

108. See M. Schenck, *Die Unfehlbarkeit des Papstes in der
Heiligsprechung* (Freiburg: [Switz.]: Paulusverlag,
1965). This is an extended commentary on Thomas
Acquinas, *Quodlib.* 9, a. 16.

109. P. Chirico, *Infallibility: The Crossroads of Doctrine*
(Kansas City: Sheed, Andrews, and McMeel, 1977),
p. 287.

110. The view that *Exsurge Domine* is an infallible document is represented by J. B. Franzelin, *Tractatus de
divina traditione et scriptura* (Rome: Propaganda
Fide, 1870), pp. 112-113. This view is not reflected in
recent textbooks. The question whether Pius IX's

Syllabus of Errors represents infallible teaching has been debated both pro and con by manualists.

111. *Casti connubii* (1930), which is held by F. Cappello and A. Vermeersch to contain an *ex cathedra* definition. For references see J. C. Ford and G. Kelly, *Contemporary Moral Theology* (Westminster, Md.: Newman, 1964), 2:263-271. Ford and Kelly, while holding that the Encyclical contains infallible doctrine, attribute its infallibility to the ordinary and constant teaching of the *magisterium* which this Encyclical confirms. The authority of *Casta connubii* is also discussed by J. Noonan, who inclines toward noninfallibility in his *Contraception* (Cambridge, Mass.: Harvard University, 1965), pp. 427-428.

112. *Humanae vitae* (1968). Some theologians argue that the Encyclical in its prohibition of contraception contains irreformable doctrine because in it "the Pope as supreme teacher in the Church proclaims a truth that has constantly been taught by the Church's teaching office and corresponds to revealed doctrine." These are the words of Cardinal Pericle Felici in *Osservatore romano*, Oct. 3, 1968. Hans Küng, who quotes this in his *Infallible? An Inquiry* (Garden City: Doubleday, 1971), p. 61, also quotes on the preceding page a similar statement by Cardinal Charles Journet. Küng himself, seeking to discredit the doctrine of infallibility, argues that *Humanae vitae*, which he regards as erroneous, engages the claim of infallibility. For an opinion opposing the infallibility of the Encyclical, see K. Rahner, "On the Encyclical 'Humanae vitae,' " *Theological Investigations* 11 (New York: Seabury, 1974), pp. 263-287. See also C. E. Curran, ed., *Contraception: Authority and Dissent* (New York: Herder and Herder, 1969); J. A. Komonchak, *"Humanae vitae* and Its Reception: Ecclesiological Reflections," TS 39 (1978) : 221-257; J. C. Ford and G. Grisez, "Contraception and the Infallibility of the Ordinary Magisterium," TS 39 (1978) : 258-312.

113. In favor of the infallibility of this condemnation, see M. d'Herbigny, *Theologica de ecclesia* 2, 2nd ed. (Paris: Beauchesne, 1921), no. 329, pp. 210-212. For an opposing view, see L. Marchal, "Ordinations anglicaines," DTC 11:1166.

114. According to Paul VI, in an address to the College of Cardinals of June 23, 1964, this teaching of Pius XII still holds good. See AAS 56 (1964) : 588-589.

115. The translation is that of J. A. Komonchak in his article "Ordinary Papal Magisterium and Religious Assent," in Curran, *Contraception*, pp. 101-126, at pp. 102-103.

116. K. Rahner, in H. Vorgrimler, ed., *Commentary on the Documents of Vatican II* (New York: Herder and

Herder, 1967), 1:210. The text of the schema in question is quoted in English translation by Komonchak, "Ordinary Papal Magisterium," pp. 101-102.

117. Besides the article of Komonchak already cited, see A. Dulles, *The Resilient Church* (Garden City: Doubleday, 1977), pp. 107-112, and the various articles of R. A. McCormick there referred to.

118. Quoted by K. Rahner, "Magisterium," *Encyclopedia of Theology: The Concise 'Sacramentum mundi'* (New York: Seabury, 1975), p. 878.

119. Ibid.

120. See *Lumen gentium*, chaps. 3 and 8.

121. Regarding the implicit rather than the explicit faith of many Catholics, see J. H. Newman, *An Essay in Aid of a Grammar of Assent* (London: Longmans, Green, 1888), pp. 146, 153, 211.

122. Vatican II, *Orientalium ecclesiarum* 26-29.

123. Cf. A. Dulles, "A Proposal to Lift Anathemas," *Origins* 4 (1974): 417-421.

124. Whether such sharing is excuded on other grounds is a complicated question that cannot and need not be answered here.

125. In L/RC 1, p. 32, this dialogue already noted: "Different understandings of the movement from kerygma to dogma obtained in the two communities. Full inquiry must therefore be made into two topics: first, the nature and structure of the teaching authority of the Church; and, secondly, the role of Scripture in relation to the teaching office of the Church." The second of these inquiries has not as yet been undertaken by this group.

126. *Ap.* 7-8:27; Tappert 173.

127. "This is a powerful demonstration that the pope is the real Antichrist . . . ;" ". . . we cannot suffer his (i.e., the devil's) apostle, the pope or Antichrist, to govern us" (*Smalcald Articles*, Part 2, art. 4:10 and 1-4; Tappert 300-301. Cf. *Treatise on the Power and Primacy of the Pope* 39-42; Tappert 327-328; *Ap* 7-8:24; Tappert 172; *Ap.* 15:18-19; Tappert 217-218). This historical background is treated in Hans Preuss, *Die Vorstellungen vom Antichrist im späteren Mittelalter, bei Luther und in der konfessionellen Polemik* (Leipzig: Hinrichs, 1906). For more recent echoes, especially in the Lutheran Church–Missouri Synod, see Myron A. Marty, *Lutherans and Roman Catholicism: The Changing Conflict, 1917–1963* (Notre Dame: University of Notre Dame, 1968), pp. 146-170.

128. See the remarks on the definition of Vatican I in such standard works as Karl von Hase, *Handbook of the Controversy with Rome*, vol. 1 (London: Religious Tract Society, 1906), pp. 24-74 and 324-329; W. von Loewenich, *Modern Catholicism* (New York: St. Mar-

tin's, 1959), pp. 49-51; Per E. Persson, *Roman and Evangelical* (Philadelphia: Fortress, 1964), pp. 57-58. For some early reactions cf. Ulrich Nembach, *Die Stellung der evangelischen Kirche und ihrer Presse zum ersten Vatikanischen Konzil* (Zurich: EVZ, 1962).

129. *Munificentissimus Deus,* Nov. 1, 1950 (DS 3900-3904).

130. See the review article by Friedrich Heiler in ThLZ 97 (1954) : 1-48.

131. See e.g., the programmatic essay by Gerhard Ebeling, "The Significance of the Critical Historical Method for Church and Theology" (1950), in *Word and Faith* (Philadelphia: Fortress, 1963), pp. 17-61. An aspect of the historical origins of the historical-critical method is traced by Gottfried Hornig, *Die Anfänge der historisch-kritischen Theologie: Johann Salomo Semlers Schriftverständnis und seine Stellung zu Luther* (Göttingen: Vandenhoeck & Ruprecht, 1961). For a contemporary insistence on inerrancy, see *Crisis in Lutheran Theology: The Validity and Relevance of Historic Lutheranism vs. Its Contemporary Rivals 1: Essays by John Warwick Montgomery,* 2nd ed. (Minneapolis: Bethany Fellowship, 1973).

132. The reference is to theologians such as Matthias Flacius, Martin Chemnitz, and Nikolaus Selnecker, who were prominent in the second half of the 16th century.

133. See Robert D. Preus, *The Inspiration of Scripture: A Study of the Theology of the Seventeenth Century Lutheran Dogmaticians* (London: Oliver & Boyd, 1955); also by the same author, *The Theology of Post-Reformation Lutheranism,* vol. 1 (St. Louis: Concordia, 1970), esp. pp. 339-362.

134. Cf. *Smalcald Articles,* Part 2, art. 1:1; Tappert 292; *Formula of Concord, Solid Declaration* 3:6; Tappert 540.

135. LC, *Lord's Supper* 57; Tappert 444. Similar expressions in the same context include: God's Word cannot "deceive," "cannot err" (ibid.); Scriptures "will not lie to you" (LC, *Lord's Supper* 76; Tappert 455).

136. The "Roman Catholic Reflections" (par. 51) expresses the same sentiment: "Even with regard to infallibility, we have found it increasingly difficult, as our dialogue has proceeded, to specify the exact point at which, in fidelity to our respective traditions, we are bound to disagree."

137. Cf. CA, Preface 13: " . . . we on our part shall not omit doing anything, insofar as God and conscience allow, that may serve the cause of Christian unity" (Tappert 26).

138. "Common Statement," par. 41.

139. "Common Statement," par. 46.

140. Cf. Luther's treatise *Von den Konziliis und Kirchen,*

1539 (WA 50:509-653; LW 41:9-178) and the Common Statement, par. 23.

141. See "Common Statement," par. 28.
142. CA 5:2; Tappert 31.
143. *Book of Concord*, Préface; Tappert 8.
144. See n. 127 above and L/RC 5, p. 25. In making such a recommendation, we are aware that to the best of our knowledge there is no precedent for Lutherans to affirm officially that, in the light of changing historical circumstances, a statement in the Confessions no longer applies. Our churches, however, have long been involved in such historical interpretation of the Confessions.

2. Infallibility: The Terminology

Avery Dulles, S.J.

1. See Vatican II, *Lumen gentium* 12.
2. This seems to be the contention of H. Küng, *Infallible? An Inquiry* (Garden City: Doubleday, 1971), esp. pp. 100-108.
3. Luther himself in his Leipzig Disputation with Johann Eck in 1519 referred to the Bible as "the infallible Word of God," contrasting it with a council, which he called "a creature of that Word" (WA 2:288).
4. Luther in his *Thesen de fide* of 1535 asserted that since the time of the apostles no individual Christian but only the universal Church may claim for itself that it cannot err in faith (see WA 39/1:48, prop. 61; LW 34:113). Melanchthon speaks in similar terms in his *Apology of the Augsburg Confession* 7-8:27; Tappert 173.
5. Luther, *Thesen de fide* (1535) WA 39/1:48, prop. 59; LW 34:113.
6. See the excerpt from the Acts of the Council in *Documents of Vatican II*, ed. by W. M. Abbott (New York: America Press, 1966), pp. 97-98.
7. See J. Ratzinger's observations in H. Vorgrimler, ed., *Commentary on the Documents of Vatican II* (New York: Herder and Herder, 1967), 1:298-299.

3. Moderate Infallibilism

Avery Dulles, S.J.

1. G. Lindbeck, *Infallibility* (Milwaukee: Marquette University Press, 1972).

2. Pages 101-119 in this volume.
3. On the positions of these authors see G. Thils, *L'in-faillibilité pontificale* (Gembloux: Duculot, 1968), pp. 179-185; A. Pfeiffer, *Die Enzykliken und ihr form-aler Wert für die dogmatische Methode* (Freiburg, Switzerland: Universitätsverlag, 1968), pp. 72-100.
4. G. Lindbeck, *Infallibility*, pp. 58-59.
5. M. Luther, *The Bondage of the Will*, WA 18:603; LW 33:21.
6. G. Lindbeck, *Infallibility*, p. 61.
7. According to the summary statement, both Lutherans and Catholics recognize the Nicene dogma as a "definitive reply to an ever-recurring question," L/RC 1, p. 32. G. Lindbeck in L/RC 2, pp. 75-76 acknowledges the Nicene dogma as dogmatically binding because it was required by the scriptural witness in confrontation with new postbiblical questions.
8. Cardinal Newman to Miss Holmes, quoted in Wilfred Ward, *The Life of John Henry Cardinal Newman* (London: Longmans, Green, and Co., 1912), 2:379.
9. H. Küng, *Structures of the Church* (New York: Nelson, 1964), p. 366.
10. M 52:1214A.
11. J. Cardoni, *Elucubratio de dogmatica Romani Pontificus infallibilitate*, 2nd ed. (Rome: De propaganda fide, 1870), p. 189; cf. G. Thils, *L'infaillibilité pontificale*, pp. 101, 194.
12. See M. Bévenot, "Faith and Morals in the Councils of Trent and Vatican I," *Heythrop Journal* 3 (1962): 15-30.
13. M 53:258D; cf. G. Thils, *L'infaillibilité pontificale*, pp. 244-245.
14. Schema of July 1964, p. 93; also in G. Alberigo and F. Magistretti, *Constitutionis dogmaticae Lumen gentium synopsis historica* (Bologna: Istituto per le scienze religiose, 1975), Relationes commissionis doctrinalis (July-Oct. 1964), p. 456. For discussion see K. Rahner's remarks in H. Vorgrimler, ed., *Commentary on the Documents of Vatican II* (New York: Herder and Herder, 1967), 1:202. Similar points were made by the German bishops in their collective declaration in response to Chancellor Bismarck in 1875 (DS 3114-3116).
15. Schema of July, 1964, p. 98; also in Alberigo-Magistretti, p. 459.
16. B. C. Butler, "The Limits of Infallibility—II," *Tablet* (London) 225 (Apr. 24, 1971): 399.
17. G. Tavard, "Theses on Future Forms of the Ministry," *Journal of Ecumenical Studies* 5 (1968): 728; cf. H. McSorley, *The Infallibility Debate* (New York: Paulist, 1971), p. 85.
18. The Declaration of the Sacred Congregation for the

Doctrine of the Faith has pointed out that the teaching office of the pope and bishops "is not reduced merely to ratifying the assent already expressed" by the faithful, but that it "can anticipate and demand that assent," *Mysterium Ecclesiae*, no. 2; text in *Catholic Mind* 71, no. 1276 (Oct. 1973) : 57.

19. Since this article was written, Peter Chirico has published an incisive discussion of the "reception" of papal teaching in his *Infallibility: Crossroads of Doctrine* (Kansas City: Sheed, Andrews, and McMeel, 1977), pp. 239-242.

20. J. Cardoni, *Elucubratio* pp. 207-215; cf. G. Thils, *L'infaillibilité pontificale*, pp. 195-196.

21. M 52:926A; cf. G. Thils, *L'infaillibilité pontificale*, p. 196.

22. *Mysterium Ecclesiae*, no. 3: in *Catholic Mind* 71 (Oct. 1973) : 57.

23. G. Wilson, "The Gift of Infallibility," TS 31 (1970) : 625-643; the quotation is from pp. 639-640.

24. M. 52:1214D.

25. Peter Chirico argues persuasively that for the pope to proclaim effectively what is the faith of the Church, he must in some way find out what that faith is and be gripped by it. For this reason it is a practical necessity for him to consult the Church. (See P. Chirico, *Infallibility*, pp. 231-233, 243-244.)

26. Vatican I certainly did not embrace the extreme opinion of Albert Pighius that the pope could not even as a private person or theologian teach heresy. (See U. Betti, *La constituzione dommatica 'Pastor aeternus' del Concilio Vaticano I* [Rome: Pontificio Ateneo Antonianum, 1961], p. 373.)

27. Since writing this paragraph I have found confirmation in the judgment of Chirico: "Only when the vast numbers of the faithful discover that the meaning of a proclamation resonates with the meaning of the faith within them and, further, make manifest this congruence of meaning explicitly by word or implicitly by action—only then can the Church be assured that its authorities have spoken infallibly" (*Infallibility*, p. 241).

28. The different "thought-forms" in Eastern and Western theology and the inclusive reconciliation of both by the Council of Florence are analyzed by L. Scheffczyk, "Lehramtliche Formulierungen und Dogmengeschichte der Trinität," *Mysterium Salutis*, ed. by J. Feiner and M. Löhrer (Einsiedeln: Benziger, 1967), 2:192-195. For further references on this point see ∴ Dulles, *The Survival of Dogma* (Garden City, N.Y.: Doubleday, 1973), p. 224, n. 25.

29. The question of "reversibly infallible" developments is discussed by G. A. Lindbeck in *The Infallibility De-*

bate, pp. 121-139, and by A. Dulles in *The Resilient Church* (Garden City, N.Y.: Doubleday, 1977), pp. 51-57.

30. The criterion of ecumenicity is discussed by Lindbeck in his *Infallibility,* pp. 21-22, 60, with reference to the previous suggestions of Richard P. McBrien in *The Infallibility Debate,* pp. 49-51.

31. See G. Dejaifve, "Ex sese, non autem ex consensu Ecclesiae," *Eastern Churches Quarterly* 14 (1962): 360-378; G. Thils, *L'infaillibilité pontificale,* pp. 171-175.

32. See H. Küng, *Infallible? An Inquiry* (Garden City, N.Y.: Doubleday, 1971), pp. 152-153.

33. For example, E. Schillebeeckx, "The Problem of Infallibility of the Church's Office," in *Truth and Certainty (Concilium,* vol. 83) (New York: Herder and Herder, 1973), p. 93; see also R. Laurentin, "IV. Peter as the Foundation Stone in the Present Uncertainty," pp. 95-113, and A. Houtepen, "A Hundred Years after Vatican 1: Some Light on the Concept of Infallibility," pp. 117-128, in the same volume for similar suggestions.

34. See Vatican II, *Unitatis redintegratio,* 15; *Orientalium Ecclesiarum,* 26-29.

35. H. Mühlen, "Die Bedeutung der Differenz zwischen Zentraldogmen und Randdogmen für den ökumenischen Dialog," *Freiheit in der Begegnung,* ed. by J. L. Leuba and H. Stirnimann (Frankfurt: Knecht, 1969), pp. 191-227.

36. See A. Dulles, "A Proposal to Lift Anathemas," *Origins* 4 (1974): 417-421.

4. The Reformation and the Infallibility Debate

George Lindbeck

1. The current phase of the debate began with the publication of Hans Küng's *Unfehlbar? Eine Anfrage,* translated into English as *Infallible? An Inquiry* (London: Collins, 1971). When this essay was originally delivered as a paper in 1974, the discussions were considerably livelier than they are now. No substantially new developments have taken place, and I have not attempted to update the documentation. I have dealt with some of the issues treated here more fully in two other places: *The Infallibility Debate,* ed. J. Kirvan (New York: Paulist Press, 1971), pp. 107-152, and *Infallibility,* The Pere Marquette Theology Lecture for 1972 (Milwaukee: Marquette University Press, 1972).

2. LW 40:241, 256-257 (WA 26:155, 167-168; cf. 27:52).
While Luther rarely or never used the word *infallible*
in reference to the Church, he readily employed such
language as this: "Whatever wavers or doubts cannot
be the truth; and what would be the use or need of a
Church of God in the world if it wanted to waver or
be uncertain in its words . . ." (WA 51:511, 6-8;
LW 41:213; cf. WA 18:204 and 207; LW 40:214
and 217, and P. Althaus, *The Theology of Martin
Luther* [Philadelphia: Fortress, 1966], p. 360).
3. Both these theologians have written extensively on
issues related directly and indirectly to the question
of infallibility, but it is in the following essays that
they have most carefully defined their views in relation to those of Hans Küng: K. Rahner, "Replik.
Bemerkungen zu: Hans Küng, Im Interesse der
Sache," *Stimmen der Zeit* 187 (1971) : 145-160; W.
Kasper, "Zur Diskussion um das Problem der Unfehlbarkeit." *Stimmen der Zeit* 188 (1972) : 363-376.
4. Küng expressed his opposition to the term years before his book *Infallible?* See "The Historic Contin-
gency of Conciliar Decrees," *Journal of Ecumenical
Studies* 1 (1964) : 111.
5. This is especially evident in his reproaches to Rahner
in "Im Interesse der Sache. Antwort an Karl Rahner," *Stimmen der Zeit* 187 (1971) : 105-122.
6. See Baum's contribution to *The Infallibility Debate*,
pp. 1-33, esp. 29-30.
7. Even those who are sympathetic to Küng's attack on
papal infallibility sometimes complain that they cannot find in him any clear answer to the question, "Why
stay in the Catholic Church?" See Richard McBrien,
The Infallibility Debate, pp. 35-65, esp. 42-43.
8. Francis Oakley, *Council over Pope?* (New York:
Herder and Herder, 1969) ; Brian Tierney, *Origins of
Papal Infallibility: 1150–1350* (Leiden: Brill, 1972).
9. Nothing "prevents the Pope from single-handedly issuing infallible proclamations, or of course very fallible
ones, whenever and on whatever subject he chooses,
which is exactly what Vatican I wanted and decided"
(*Infallible?*, p. 85). Küng's point is that the restrictions on the papal exercise of infallibility are meaningless because the pope himself is the sole judge of
whether he has adhered to them. "Presumably even
the Roi Soleil would have had no objections to such
theoretical and abstract restrictions of his power"
(*ibid.*, p. 86).
10. Küng develops this argument chiefly in *ibid.*, pp. 129-
158.
11. See note 6 above. I have summarized this view more
fully and accurately in my Pere Marquette Lecture,
Infallibility, pp. 42-45.

12. The arguments of this and the following paragraph are developed at length in my contribution to *The Infallibility Debate*, pp. 107-152.

13. This is part of Luther's rejoinder to Erasmus in *De servio arbitrio*, WA 18:603; LW 33:21.

14. TS 32 (1971) : 205.

15. Karl Rahner, *Theological Investigations*, vol. 6 (Baltimore: Helicon, 1970), p. 308.

16. DS 3074.

17. *The Infallibility Debate*, pp. 49-51.

18. For this reason it seems to him that conciliar infallibility is as objectionable as papal infallibility *(Infallible?*, p. 169).

19. *Ibid.*, p. 153.

20. See note 5 above.

21. This point was made in Bishop Gasser's official commentary at the time of Vatican I. See M 52:1214.

22. The possibility of a heretical pope was widely admitted, not only before Vatican I, but even by conservative canonists afterwards. E.g. F. S. Wernz and P. Vidal, *Jus Canonicum. II. De Personis*, 3rd ed. (Rome: Gregorianum, 1943), pp. 513-521.

23. While I have phrased this description of the situation at Vatican I in my own way, there are those on both sides of the infallibility debate who would agree with its basic accuracy. For Küng, see note 10 above, and for W. Kasper, "Primat und Episkopat nach dem Vatikanum I," *Theologische Quartalschrift* 142 (1962) : 47-83. It should be added, however, that some of the leading supporters of papal absolutism at Vatican I were motivated, at least in part, by the desire to maintain the independence of the church in the face of the growing power of nationalism and of capitalism in 19th century Europe. There was a clear linkage in some cases between concern for the working classes and support for papal infallibility. See George H. Williams, *"Omnium christianorum pastor et doctor.* Vatican I et l'Angleterre victorienne," *Nouvelle Revue Theologique* 96 (1974) : 113-146, 337-365.

24. See note 3 above.

25. I have developed this analogy between law and dogma in "Reform and Infallibility," *Cross Currents* 11 (1961) : 345-356.

26. 2nd ed. (Chicago: Chicago University Press, 1970).

27. To this paper was originally attached an appendix entitled: "Five Speculative Theses on Infallibility." These theses depend on considerations which I have developed not only in the present paper but also elsewhere. For the first two theses see especially my contribution to *The Infallibility Debate* (note 1 above) and "Reform and Infallibility" (note 25 above). For

a fuller statement of the Lutheran criteria for dogma in Thesis 3 (c), see L/RC 2, pp. 75-76.

Thesis 1. In an historical perspective, a dogma is a rule of correct usage expressing a "policy decision" regarding the interpretation in word and action of revelation in a particular situation, rather than a permanently adequate formulation of abiding truth.

Thesis 2. To affirm the "infallibility" or "irreformability" of a dogma, therefore, is to say that it was not a false or wrong decision in the circumstances of its time, and the error it rejected is permanently rejected. Thus at least in its negative import, the decision is irreversible.

Thesis 3. All traditions have dogmas which they treat operationally, even if not officially, as irreversible (and in this sense as infallible), but they differ on the criteria:

(a) for Roman Catholics, one criterion of dogma is *ex cathedra* promulgation by an ecumenical council or pope;

(b) the Orthodox also generally insist on conciliar, but not papal action, and often add the requirement of reception by the universal Church;

(c) for the Reformation, and more specifically the Lutheran tradition, a dogma must be required by Scripture in the sense that it must express a decision that a given position (such as the Arian) is contrary to Scripture's explicit witness to the gospel.

Thesis 4. Given a "hierarchy" of dogmas (to use the expression of Vatican II), it is possible that the churches could reunite on the basis of agreement on the rightness of a limited number of dogmatic decisions defensible by the Reformation scriptural principle combined with mutual acceptance of the theological legitimacy (but not imperativeness) of the dogmas peculiar to each of the reuniting groups.

In order to do this, each party would have to interpret their peculiar dogmas (e.g., the Catholic Marian or papal ones, or the Reformation *sola scriptura*) in such a way as to enable the others to recognize them, even if not as necessarily true, as not opposed to the gospel of Jesus Christ.

Thesis 5. In reference to magisterial infallibility, this latter condition would be fulfilled if

(a) Catholics understood magisterial infallibility as asserting that God in his mercy will see to it that no dogmatic decisions of the *magisterium* accepted by the Church are irreconciliable with the truth of Christ; and if

(b) non-Catholics, while not affirming this as their belief, would hope that it is true—i.e., would not deny the possibility that God has willed to preserve the Church from such errors.

This remaining dogmatic difference between "believing" and "hoping"—between "affirming the reality" and "granting the possibility" of the immunity of an ecumenical *magisterium* (and of the church to which it belongs) from doctrinal decisions so faulty that they should be repudiated rather than reinterpreted— is compatible with mutual recognition of the Christian authenticity of each other's positions. It is not a trivial difference, but it need not constitute a barrier to full communion between the churches.

5. Infallibility Language and the Early Lutheran Tradition

Gerhard O. Forde

1. I leave open for the moment the question of how the term "Word of God" should be more precisely defined, i.e. whether it can simply be equated with "Scripture" or more narrowly (or broadly) with "Christ," "the gospel," "the promises of God," or like expressions. I shall say more about this below.
2. See Georg Hofmann, "Die Frage des Lehramts und der Lehrgewalt im Luthertum," *Zeitschrift für Systematische Theologie* 17 (1940) : 45.
3. A good account of this can be found in Remigius Bäumer, "Luthers Ansichten über die Irrtumsfähigkeit des Konzils und ihre theologiegeschichtlichen Grundlagen," *Wahrheit und Verkündigung*, Festschrift für Michael Schmaus, ed. by Leo Scheffczyk, Werner Dettloff, and Richard Heinzmann (Paderborn: Verlag Ferdinand Schöningh, 1967), 2:987ff.
4. WA 6:411; LW 44:133.
5. Tappert 173.
6. Ibid., p. 330.
7. WA 39/1:185-187. *De potestate concilii*. 10. October 1536? (sic).
8. Paul Althaus, *The Theology of Martin Luther* (Philadelphia, Fortress Press, 1966), pp. 340-341.
9. WA 40/1:132, 17-28; LW 26:66-67. *Commentary on Galatians* (1535). Underscoring added.

10. Cf. WA 38:208, 216; LW 38:161, 170-171; WA 40/
    3:506; LW 13:89. It should be noted, however, that it
    is not in place to ask for forgiveness of sins if one is
    preaching the Word of God. On this see Luther's
    treatise *Against Hanswurst*, WA 51:517-521; LW 41:
    216-218.

11. See, for instance, P. Althaus, *Theology*, p. 337.

12. G. Hofmann, "Die Frage des Lehramts," p. 39.

13. P. Althaus, *Theology*, p. 337.

14. WA 18:606-609, 652-659; LW 33:24-28, 89-100. *The
    Bondage of the Will*, 1525.

15. WA 18:652-653; LW 33:90.

16. WA 7:98, 4-7. *Assertio omnium articulorum M. Lu-
    theri per bullam Leonis X. novissimam damnatorum.*
    1520.

17. WA 2:288, 30-34. *Disputatio I. Eccii et M. Lutheri
    Lipsiae habita.* 1519. It is difficult to determine
    whether Luther was simply quoting Augustine here or
    not. In any case he seemed to approve of the use of
    the term *infallibility* as applied to Scripture. The
    Erlangen Edition of Luther's works (5:107) records
    another instance in which Luther is supposed to have
    quoted Augustine with approval to the effect that the
    Holy Scriptures alone are to be considered *unfehlbar*.
    The sentence, however, does not appear in the *Weimar
    Ausgabe*. It is perhaps significant that the only in-
    stances in which Luther uses the actual term *infal-
    lible* of Scripture are in quotations from Augustine.

18. Tappert, 8. The German has *reinen, unfehlbaren und
    unwandelbaren Wort Gottes;* the Latin *sinceram et
    immotum verbi Dei veritatem;* cf. *Die Bekenntnis-
    schriften der evangelisch-lutherischen Kirche,* 6th re-
    vised ed. (Göttingen: Vandenhoeck and Ruprecht,
    1967), p. 9.

19. For a more conservative view on this question, see M.
    Reu, *Luther and the Scriptures* (Columbus: The
    Wartburg Press, 1944). P. Althaus, *Theology*, and
    Werner Elert, *The Structure of Lutheranism*, trans.
    by W. Hansen (St. Louis: Concordia, 1962), pp. 179-
    191, are representative of a more prevalent position
    among present-day Lutheran theologians.

20. See E. M. Plass, *What Luther Says* (St. Louis: Con-
    cordia, 1959), I:62ff., for a convenient collection of
    such passages.

21. See P. Althaus, *Theology*, pp. 336-337; W. Elert,
    Structure, pp. 179-191.

22. LC 4:57; Tappert 444.

23. LC 5:76; *ibid.* 455.

24. *Ap.* 13:20; *ibid.* 213-214.

25. *Formula of Concord, Epitome* 7:13; *ibid.* 483.

26. *Formula of Concord, Solid Declaration* 11:29; *ibid.*
    p. 621.

27. P. Althaus, *Theology*, p. 336.
28. WA 32:56, 21-27. *Sermons.* 1530.
29. WA 51:4, 8. *Sermons.* 1545.
30. WA 16:113, 5-9. *Sermons on Exodus.* 1524-1527.
31. WA 39/1:47, 19-20; LW 34:112. *Thesen de Fide.* 1535.
32. WA 38:208, 14-21; LW 38:161. *Von der Winkelmesse und Paffenweihe.* 1533.
33. W. Elert, *Structure*, p. 190.
34. WA 18:649-650; LW 33:85. *Bondage of the Will.* 1525.
35. WA 18:653; LW 33:90.
36. WA 18:609; LW 33:28.
37. WA 18:653; LW 33:91.
38. Thus Luther undertook to prove from Scripture itself that it is a clear and sure guide (WA 18:654-656; LW 33:91-94).
39. WA 30/2:420. *Propositiones adversus totam synagogum Sathanae et universas portas inferorum.* 6 Juli 1530.
40. WA 30/2:687ff. *De potestate leges ferendi in ecclesia.* 1530. Translated from the German version.
41. WA 2:409. Cf. W. Elert, *Structure*, p. 183. *Ap.* 4:400; Tappert 168.
42. WA 18:603; LW 33:21. See the addendum to note 10 above.
43. WA 51:518; LW 41:217.
44. WA 18:605; LW 33:24.
45. See the addendum to note 10 above.

6. Lutheran Teaching Authority: Past and Present

Eric W. Gritsch

1. See the convenient summary of texts from the *Book of Concord* by Warren A. Quanbeck, "The Teaching Ministry of the Church in Lutheran Perspective," L/RC 5, pp. 133-139.
2. See *Ap.* 14:1; Tappert 214; *Ap.* 28:13; Tappert 283. On the difference between "human tradition" and "gospel," see CA 7 and 15; Tappert 32 and 36-37. Session 23 of the Council of Trent rejected the Lutheran view and reaffirmed the "sacrament of order" *(Canons and Decrees of the Council of Trent,* ed. and trans. by H. J. Schroeder (St. Louis and London: Herder, 1960), pp. 160-163.
3. See the summary of the Lutheran position by Arthur C. Piepkorn, "*Ius Divinum* and *Adiaphoron* in Relation to Structural Problems in the Church: The Position of the Lutheran Symbolic Books," L/RC 5, pp. 119-127.

4. Edmund Schlink, *The Theology of the Lutheran Confessions*, trans. by P. Koehneke and H. Bouman (Philadelphia: Muhlenberg Press, 1961), p. 267, n. 29.

5. Exemplary for this position are John Headley, *Luther's View of History* (New Haven: Yale University Press, 1963); Wilhelm Maurer, "Die Einheit der Theologie Luthers" and "Die Anfänge von Luthers Theologie" in vol. I of *Kirche und Geschichte*, ed. by Ernst-Wilhelm Kohls (Göttingen: Vandenhoeck and Ruprecht, 1975), pp. 11-37; and Leif Grane, *Modus Loquendi Theologicus* (Leiden: Brill, 1975).

6. *Smalcald Articles*, II, 1:5; Tappert 292. On the Latin phrase see Friedrich Loofs, "Der articulus stantis et cadentis ecclesiae," *Theologische Studien und Kritiken* 90(1917): 323-420.

7. Latin text of CA 5:1; Tappert 31.

8. *Address to the Christian Nobility of the German Nation* (1520). WA 6:407-409; LW 44:128-130.

9. See also Arthur C. Piepkorn, "The Sacred Ministry and Holy Ordination in the Symbolic Books of the Lutheran Church" in L/RC 4, esp. p. 105: "This differentiation (between "office" and "estate") does not, of course carry with it any narrowly clerical or hierarchical implications."

10. *"Superattendent"* was used the first time in the Stralsund *Kirchenordnung* of 1526. See also Bernhard Lohse, "The Development of Offices of Leadership in the German Lutheran Churches: 1517-1918," *Episcopacy in the Lutheran Church?* ed. by Ivar Asheim *et al.* (Philadelphia: Fortress, 1970), p. 52.

11. CA defines episcopacy along these lines (CA 28:8-29; Tappert 82-85). On "emergency bishop" *(Notbischof)*, see Lewis W. Spitz, "Luther's Ecclesiology and His Concept of the Prince as 'Notbischof,'" *Church History* 22 (1953): 113-141.

12. Duke Johann Wilhelm of Saxony's *Visitationsordnung* of 1569, for example, lists "adiaphorist, Anabaptist, Schwenckfeldian, Zwinglian, Antinomian, synergistic and similar sects" as possible errors of faith (See H. Holwein, "Lehrzuchtverfahren," RGG³ 4:281).

13. Especially between "Gnesio-Lutherans" and "Philippists." For evidence see Eric W. Gritsch, "Lutheran Teaching Authority: Historical Dimensions and Ecumenical Implications," *Lutheran Quarterly* 25 (1973): 387.

14. *Epitome* 1-8; Tappert 464-465; *Solid Declaration*, 1-13; Tappert 503-506.

15. CA 5:1; Tappert 31: "To obtain such faith (justification) God instituted the office of Ministry." AC 5 is preceded by AC 4 on "Justification."

16. For a good analysis of the reasons and criteria re-

garding excommunication in the 16th century, see Hans-Werner Gensichen, *Damnamus* (Berlin: Evangelisches Verlagshaus, 1955), esp. pp. 145-146.

17. CA 8:1; Tappert 33. The statement stresses (1) the eschatological dimension of the Church and (2) the efficacy of the sacraments against Donatist errors.

18. See B. Lohse, "Development," pp. 58-68.

19. "The one who was an 'emergency bishop' from Luther's point of view became the proprietor of the episcopal power which had been transferred to him" (*ibid.*, p. 65).

20. See the evidence collected in Wilhelm Maurer, "Lehrverpflichtung," RGG [3] 4:279.

21. *Loci Theologici* XIII (Tübingen: Georg Cottae, 1762-1787), p. 16. This is a significant shift from the position of Luther and the CA according to Werner Elert, *The Structure of Lutheranism*, trans. by Walter A. Hansen (St. Louis: Concordia, 1962), 1:355. Hans E. Weber, *Reformation, Orthodoxie und Rationalismus* (Gütersloh: Gerd Mohn, 1940), 1:2, 359 characterized this shift in terms of the rationalization of the "word" into "doctrine": "Das Wort ist als Lehre rationalisiert; so können Lehre und Ordnung zusammenrücken."

22. Luther regarded the local congregation as a teaching authority which could, under the proper leadership, function as well as conciliar authority. In this context he spoke of "three hierarchies": the home, the government, and the Church. All three are interrelated through the "common priesthood" to which Baptism ordains (see *On the Councils and the Church* [1539], WA 50:652; LW 41:177, and W. Elert, *Structure*, 1:367-379).

23. *Examen theologicum acroamaticum*, 2nd ed. (Lipsiae: Russwormium, 1718). For a detailed discussion see Georg Hoffmann, "Die Frage des Lehramts und der Lehrgewalt im Luthertum," *Zeitschrift für systematische Theologie* 17 (1948): 56-59.

24: This was the proposal of the theologian Nikolaus Hunnius in 1632 (G. Hoffmann, "Frage," p. 59).

25. *On the Councils and the Church.* (1539), WA 50:488-653; LW 41:3-178.

26. Ernst Benz, *Bischofsamt und apostolische Sukzession im deutschen Protestantismus* (Stuttgart: Evangelisches Verlagswerk, 1953) argued—although he was severely criticized—that Zinzendorf's consecration as bishop in apostolic succession should have become the model of Lutheran leadership. Not to have the apostolic succession of bishops constitutes a "charismatic improverization" *(charismatische Verarmung)* of the Reformation!

27. The debate is described in detail by Holsten **Fager-berg,** *Bekenntnis, Kirche und Amt in der deutschen konfessionellen Theologie des 19. Jahrhunderts* (Upssala: Lundequistska Bokhandeln, 1952).

28. *Die Stimme unserer Kirche in der Frage von Kirche und Amt* (Erlangen: A. Deickert, 1852). See also H. Fagerberg, *Bekenntnis,* pp. 111-112.

29. *Acht Bücher von der Kirche* (Schwerin and Rostock: Stiller'sche Buchhandlung, 1854). See also Fagerberg, *Bekenntnis,* pp. 286-299.

30. *Acht Bücher,* p. 461.

31. *Das blinde, undeutliche Wort "Kirche"* (Cologne and Graz: Böhlau Verlag, 1964), p. 694.

32. *Kirchenrecht,* 2 vols. (Leipzig: Dunker and Humbrecht, 1892-1923). Sohm became embroiled with Adolf von Harnack and others in a controversy over the process of institutionalization in the early Church, a process dubbed "Catholization."

33. *Die Grundlagen des evangelischen Kirchenrechts* (Tübingen: Mohr, 1928). This work is usually regarded as a definitive treatment of church law from a Lutheran perspective.

34. The text is found in *Kirchliches Jahrbuch: 1933-1944,* ed. by Joachim Beckmann (Gütersloh: Bertelsmann Verlag, 1948), pp. 63-65. The *Declaration* was published in English in the London Times, June 4, 1934.

35. Art. 4.

36. See Kurt Schmidt-Clausen, "The Development of Offices of Leadership in the German Lutheran Churches: 1918—Present," *Episcopacy in the Lutheran Church?* p. 115. He argues that the *Kirchenkampf* during the Nazi period gave the German churches a new sense of freedom and an awareness of the relativity of law *(ibid.,* pp. 98-99).

37. Martii Parvio, "The Post-Reformation Development of the Episcopacy in Sweden, Finland, and Baltic States," *Episcopacy in the Lutheran Church?* p. 134.

38. "Authority," *The Encyclopedia of the Lutheran Church,* ed. by Julius Bodensieck (Philadelphia: Fortress, 1965), 1:161.

39. For the American scene, see Theodore G. Tappert, "Lutheran Ecclesiastical Government in the United States of America," *Episcopacy in the Lutheran Church?* pp. 155-174. Tappert argues that American Lutherans have rejected any notion of "sacred order." See also Conrad Bergendoff, *The Doctrine of the Church in American Lutheranism,* "Knubel-Miller Foundation Lectures" (Philadelphia: Board of Publication, ULCA, 1956) and Rudolf Schomerus, *Die verfassungsrechtliche Entwicklung der lutherischen Kirche in Nordamerika von 1638 bis 1792* (Göttingen: Kleinert, 1965).

40. Quoted in Tappert, "Lutheran Ecclesiastical Government," p. 172.
41. *Ibid.*, p. 173.
42. LCA, *Constitution and By-Laws*, p. 3.
43. See Vilmos Vajta, "The Confession of the Church as an Ecumenical Concern," *The Church and the Confessions*, ed. by Vilmos Vajta and Hans Weissgerber (Philadelphia: Fortress Press, 1963), pp. 162-188.
44. I use this term to indicate the removal of the historical-critical method from the confessional assertions of churches. The doctrine of verbal inspiration is usually used as the weapon against the historical-critical method. The Lutheran Church–Missouri Synod adopted the doctrine of verbal inspiration in the *Brief Statement* of 1932; the Federation of Evangelical Lutheran Churches in India modified it. See V. Vajta, "Confession," p. 167 and p. 209, n. 24. The 1973 Convention of the Lutheran Church–Missouri Synod reaffirmed the doctrine of verbal inspiration.
45. *Epitome* 1; Tappert 464; *Solid Declaration* 3; Tappert 503-504.
46. See, for example, Peter Brunner, "The LWF as an Ecclesiological Problem," *Lutheran World* 7 (1960): 237-256; Regin Prenter, "Comments on Brunner's Essay," *ibid.*, pp. 257-260.
47. For example, Edmund Schlink has investigated the hermeneutical process by which ordinary piety becomes structured doctrine in "The Structure of Dogmatic Statements as an Ecumenical Problem," *The Coming Christ and the Coming Church* (Philadelphia: Fortress, 1968), pp. 16-84. Gerhard Ebeling has tried to develop an "ecumenical hermeneutic" for an assessment of the history of dogmatic decisions in a collection of essays, *The Word of God and Tradition*, trans. by S. H. Hooke (Philadelphia: Fortress, 1968). George Lindbeck has provided a theological commentary on the dogma of infallibility in *Infallibility* (Milwaukee: Marquette University Theology Department, 1972).
48. A good summary of the discussion, especially with Roman Catholic theologians, is Joachim Rogge, "Zur Frage katholischer und evangelischer Dogmenhermeneutik," ThLZ 98 (1973): 642-655. In relation to Luther see Vilmos Vajta, "Thesen und Antithesen in Luthers Auffassung vom geistlichen Amt in Lichte des Zweiten Vaticanums," *ibid.* 97 (1972): 250-265.
49. I use the term "magisterial mutuality" in order to indicate the move from doctrinal pluriformity (by and large accepted by scholars investigating the hermeneutics of the history of doctrine) to an ecumenical sharing of magisterial authority. L/RC 5 stated this goal in terms of a common call for a "renewal of

papal structures" involving the "principles of legitimate diversity, collegiality and subsidiarity" (L/RC 5, pp. 19-20).

50. Leonard Swidler, "The Ecumenical Problem Today: Papal Infallibility," *Journal of Ecumenical Studies* 8 (1971): 767: "Catholics need to demythologize the Church; they must have the courage to say straight out that the Church, in all of its organs, including the papacy, can err and has erred, and will continue to err. Then they will be able psychologically and theologically to go about their task of being Christians with proper humility, that is, in the truth."

7. The *Magisterium* in the Lutheran Church with Special Reference to Infallibility

Warren A. Quanbeck

1. *Smalcald Articles*, Introduction and Preface; Tappert 287-291.
2. CA 20:13; Tappert 43, and at least 39 other places.
3. CA 21:5; Tappert 50, and 13 other places.
4. CA 21:6; Tappert 50, and 11 other places.
5. *Ap.* 2:19; Tappert 103, *et al.*
6. CA 24:36; Tappert 60, *et al.*
7. CA 26:44; Tappert 70, *et al.*
8. CA 24:35; Tappert 60, *et al.*
9. *Ap.* 2:27; Tappert 104, *et al.*
10. *Ap.* 11:68; Tappert 192, *et al.*
11. *Ap.* 2:21; Tappert 103, *et al.*
12. *Ap.* 4:210; Tappert 136, *et al.*
13. CA 26:13; Tappert 66, *et al.*
14. *Ap.* 12:73-74; Tappert 192, *et al.*
15. *Smalcald Articles*, Preface 3-4; Tappert 289.
16. *Smalcald Articles*, Preface 11,15; Tappert 290-291. It should be noted that the presence of the Turkish army at the gates of Vienna was another factor in the creation of this apocalyptic attitude.
17. Borth, Wilhelm, *Die Luthersache* (Lübeck and Hamburg: Mathiessen Verlag, 1970).
18. *Smalcald Articles*, Preface 2-3; Tappert 288-289.
19. *Ap.* 14:1-5; Tappert 214-215. Cf. L/RC 4, p. 19.
20. For a fuller treatment of the development summarized in this paragraph, cf. Ivar Asheim and Victor R. Gold, eds., *Episcopacy in the Lutheran Church?* (Philadelphia: Fortress Press, 1970).
21. W. Borth, *Die Luthersache.* Cf. Daniel Olivier, *The Trial of Luther* (London and Oxford: Mowbrays, 1971).

22. In the 19th and early 20th centuries Concordia Theological Seminary under C. F. W. Walther and Franz Pieper played a dominant theological role in the Lutheran Church–Missouri Synod. During the same period Luther Seminary under M. O. Bøckman and T. F. Gullixson was only a little less influential among Norwegian-American Lutherans.

23. *Smalcald Articles,* Signatories; Tappert 316-317.

24. Martensen, Daniel F. *The Federation and the World Council of Churches,* LWF Report 3 (Geneva, Switzerland: LWF, December, 1978), pp. 6ff.

25. The LWF Department of Theology and its successor (from 1970), the Department of Studies, have also produced many publications; the volumes listed in notes 20 and 24 are among them.

26. The *Barmen Declaration* appears among the documents assembled in the 1967 Presbyterian *Book of Confessions,* but has not yet been given such status by any Lutheran church.

27. *Proceedings of the Forty-Fourth Regular Convention of the Lutheran Church–Missouri Synod.* San Francisco, California, June 17-26, 1959, p. 191.

28. *Proceedings of the Forty-Fifth Regular Convention of The Lutheran Church–Missouri Synod.* Cleveland, Ohio, June 20-29, 1962, pp. 105-106.

29. *Proceedings of the Fiftieth Regular Convention of the Lutheran Church–Missouri Synod.* New Orleans, Louisiana, July 6-13, 1973. *A Statement of Scriptural and Confessional Principles,* pp. 127-128.

30. Two such documents may be mentioned: *A Brief Statement,* referred to above, note 27. This document, written mainly by Franz Pieper, has been a standard of orthodoxy for many in the Lutheran Church–Missouri Synod. Cf. Carl S. Meyer, "The Historical Background of 'A Brief Statement,'" *Concordia Theological Monthly* 32 (1961): 403-428, 466-482, 526-542. *The Minneapolis Theses* of 1925 is another midwestern Lutheran reaction to theological liberalism. This document had a role in the organization of the American Lutheran Conference (1930) and in the Constitution of The American Lutheran Church (1960). Cf. E. Clifford Nelson, *The Lutheran Church among Norwegian-Americans* (Minneapolis: Augsburg Publishing House, 1960), pp. 285ff.

31. For the years 1959-1965 the member churches of the National Lutheran Council used the Committee on Social Trends for common reflection on such problems as Church and state. After the formation of the Lutheran Council in the U.S.A., the Division for Theological Studies performed similar functions on such questions as the Ministry and the ordination of women.

32. The Lutheran Church in America and the Lutheran Church–Missouri Synod use similar processes in their decision making, especially on ethical questions.

33. Such synodical documents have varying degrees of status or authority. Some are merely "received," some are passed on to congregations for study, and some are adopted.

34. *Handbook of the American Lutheran Church* (Minneapolis: Augsburg, 1968), Constitution, Articles VIII and IX.

35. The decision on the ordination of women, for example, was referred first to the faculty of Luther Theological Seminary in St. Paul. The decision of the faculty was part of the recommendation submitted to the San Antonio, Texas, Convention (1970) by the Church Council of the ALC.

36. CA 7; Tappert 32, German version. The Latin version reads: "one holy church is to continue forever."

37. A third line can be seen in the "high church" theology in Germany, Sweden, or the Buffalo Synod in America. Cf. Eric Gritsch, "Lutheran Teaching Authority: Past and Present," pp. 138-148 above.

38. Schmid, Heinrich, *Doctrinal Theology of the Evangelical Lutheran Church* (Minneapolis: Augsburg, 1961), pp. 38-68.

39. Quoted in H. Schmid, *ibid.*, p. 49.

40. Quoted in H. Schmid, *ibid.*, p. 49.

41. Quoted in H. Schmid, *ibid.*, p. 50.

42. Cf. H. Schmid, *ibid.*, pp. 500-520.

43. Preus, C. K., *Interpreting the Bible* (Minneapolis: Augsburg, 1959). Kierkegaard, S. A., *Concluding Unscientific Postscript*, trans. by D. F. Swenson, completed after his death with introduction and notes by W. Lowrie (Princeton: Princeton University Press, 1941).

44. WA 10/1,2:48, 5; 7:475, 14-18.

8. A Rahner-Küng Debate and Ecumenical Possibilities

Carl J. Peter

1. Hans Küng, "A *Working Agreement* to Disagree," *America* 129, no. 1 (July 7, 1973) : 10.

2. *Ibid.*, p. 11.

3. Karl Rahner, "A *Working Agreement* to Disagree," *ibid.*, p. 11.

4. *Ibid.*
5. *Ibid.*, p. 12.
6. *Declaration in Defense of the Catholic Doctrine on the Church Against Certain Errors of the Present Day* (Washington: U.S.C.C. Publications Office, 1973).
7. Karl Rahner, "A *Working Agreement* to Disagree," p. 11.
8. From another point of view Karl Rahner wonders whether *Mysterium Ecclesiae* actually lives up to its intention of directly challenging Küng's position (cf. *"Mysterium Ecclesiae:* Zur Erklärung der Glaubenskongregation über die Lehre von der Kirche," *Stimmen der Zeit* 191 [1973]: 586-588).
9. *Declaration in Defense of the Catholic Doctrine*, p. 8.
10. For the sense intended, cf. note 3 and corresponding reference in the text.
11. The unfinished character of the *theological* debate about infallibility in Roman Catholic circles is symbolized by the agreement to disagree that was highlighted at the beginning of this paper.
12. Karl Rahner, *"Mysterium Ecclesiae:* Zur Erklärung," pp. 586-588.
13. For Vatican I on truths that were revealed so they might be known without the mingling of error *(nullo errore admixto)*, cf. DS 3005; note as well the dependence on Thomas Aquinas, *Sum. Theol.*, q. 1, a. 1, c.
14. Cf. "Unity of the Faith and Theological Pluralism," *The Tablet* 227 (July 7, 1973): 646-647; "Dogmatic formulations must be considered as responses to precise questions, and it is in this sense that they remain always true. Their permanent interest depends on the lasting relevance of the questions with which they are concerned; at the same time it must not be forgotten that the successive questions which Christians ask themselves about the understanding of the Divine Word, as well as already discovered solutions, grow out of one another so that today's answers always presuppose in some way those of yesterday, although they cannot be reduced to them." See also B. J. F. Lonergan, *Doctrinal Pluralism* (Milwaukee: Marquette, 1971), pp. 11, 12, 70.
15. For further development cf. Carl J. Peter, "Why Catholic Theology Needs Future Talk Today," *Proceedings of the Catholic Theological Society of America* 27 (1972): 163-167.
16. George Lindbeck, *The Infallibility Debate*, ed. by J. J. Kirvan (Paramus: Paulist, 1971), p. 108.
17. George Lindbeck, *Infallibility* (Milwaukee: Marquette University Press, 1972), p. 49.

9. Infallibility: A Structural Analysis

George H. Tavard

1. For an introduction to linguistic and structural methods in theology, see *Recherches de Science Religieuse* 58 (1970): no. 1; 61 (1973): no. 1; 62 (1974): no. 2. The application of such methods to scriptural exegesis has been presented by Daniel Patte, *What Is Structural Exegesis?* (Philadelphia: Fortress, 1976), and to theological methodology by myself, *La Théologie parmi les Sciences Humaines* (Paris: Beauchesne, 1975).

2. Traditional grammars, following the ancient Greek grammarians' analysis of their language, distinguish between subject-verb-predicate, all three being necessary to most sentences. Contemporary linguistics assumes that a sentence is made of a subject (to whom the action is attributed) and a predicate (expressing an action which is described by everything else in the sentence.

3. A. J. Greimas, *Sémantique Structurale* (Paris: Larousse, 1966), pp. 172-191.

4. A. J. Greimas, *Du Sens. Essais Sémiotiques* (Paris: Le Seuil, 1970), pp. 135-166.

5. Louis Hjelmslev, "La Structure Fondamentale de Langage," in *Prolégomènes à une Théorie du Langage* (Paris: Éditions de Minuit, 1969), pp. 185-231.

6. Ferdinand de Saussure, *Course in General Linguistics* (London: Peter Owen, 1960), pp. 65-78.

7. Louis Hjelmslev, *Prologomena to a Theory of Language* (Madison: University of Wisconsin Press, 1969), pp. 47-60; A. Greimas, *Du Sens*, pp. 45-46.

8. "Pope John's Opening Speech to the Council," *The Documents of Vatican II*, ed. by Walter M. Abbott (New York: Guild Press, 1966), p. 715.

9. A Greimas, *Sémantique Structurale*, pp. 69-101.

10. S. T., II II, q. 1, a. 1.

11. De Saussure, *Course*, pp. 67-68; Louis Hjelmslev, *Language: An Introduction* (Madison: U. of Wisconsin Press, 1970), pp. 45-67. Admittedly other linguists have mitigated the element of arbitrariness in linguistic signs.

12. L. Hjelmslev, *Prologomena*, pp. 114-125.

13. *Ibid.*, p. 119.

14. On *parole* and *langue*, see de Saussure, *Course*, pp. 17-20. On myth, see Claude Lévi-Strauss, *Structural Anthropology* (Garden City, New York: Basic Books, 1963), pp. 209-231.

15. See C. Levi-Strauss, *Anthropology*, pp. 206-231; A. Greimas: *Du Sens*, pp. 117-134, 185-230; Dan Sperber, "Le Structuralisme en Anthropologie," *Qu'est-ce que*

le Structuralisme? (Paris: Le Seuil, 1968), pp. 69-238; Noël Mouloud, *Langages et Structures. Essais de Logique et de Sémiologie* (Paris: Payot, 1969), pp. 84-124; Jacques Lacan, "Fonction et Champ de la Parole et du Langage," *Ecrits I* (Paris: Le Seuil, 1971), pp. 111-208.

10. The Office of Teaching in the Christian Church According to the New Testament

Joseph A. Fitzmyer, S.J.

1. Cf. R. E. Brown, K. P. Donfried, J. Reumann, eds.; *Peter in the New Testament* (Minneapolis and New York: Augsburg and Paulist, 1973).

2. Perhaps we should also add *katangellein* to this word-group; see Acts 4:2.

3. The verb *lalein* is sometimes interpreted to mean "teaching"; e.g. Titus 2:1 (RSV).

4. "Report of the Lutheran-Roman Catholic Study Commission on 'The Gospel and the Church,'" *Worship* 46 (1972): 326-351, esp. p. 340, no. (50); "Report of the Joint Lutheran/Roman Catholic Study Commission on 'The Gospel and the Church,'" *Lutheran World* 19 (1972): 259-273, esp. p. 267, no. (50).

5. L/RC 4, p. 11, no. (12).

6. See esp. chap 2, "Presuppositions for the Study," pp. 7-22.

7. Though I personally am rather skeptical about this distinction between seven genuine letters of Paul and three doubtfully genuine ones, I shall honor it here hypothetically, for the sake of a separate discussion of possible differences in the data bearing on the question at hand.

8. The passages chiefly to be considered would be: Heb. 5:12; 6:1-2; 13:9; Rev. 2:14-15, 20, 24; 2 Peter 2:1.

9. J. A. Grassi, *The Teacher in the Primitive Church and the Teacher Today* (Santa Clara: Santa Clara University, 1973), p. 53 ("The person of the teacher lies behind most of the pages of the N.T., especially Paul's letters"). But this is an uncritical massing together of ideas that ought to be kept distinct.

10. Other titles that he used, such as *doulos Iēsou Christou* (Rom. 1:1; Gal. 1:10; Phil. 1:1) or *diakonos kainēs diathēkēs* (2 Cor. 3:6) are of little use to us here.

11. But compare the data in the Deutero-Pauline letters (1 Timothy 2:7; 2 Timothy 1:11); see pp. 206-207 below.

12. See further 1 Cor. 1:23; 9:27; 15:11-12; 2 Cor. 1:19; Gal. 2:2.

13. Cf. 1 Cor. 15:1-2; 2 Cor. 11:7; Gal. 1:11.

14. See W. Michaelis, *"Mimeomai, mimētēs, symmimētēs,"* TWNT 4 (1942): 661-678; TDNT 4 (1967): 659-674; D. M. Stanley, " 'Become Imitators of Me': The Pauline Conception of Apostolic Tradition," *Studia biblica et orientalia,* AnalBib 11 (Rome: Biblical Institute, 1959), 2:291-309, *Biblica* 40 (1959): 859-877; D. M. Williams, *The Imitation of Christ in Paul with Special Reference to Paul as Teacher* (New York: Columbia University dissertation, 1967) [non vidi]. The debate about the understanding of Pauline "imitation" need not engage us here.

15. For instance, see J. Murphy-O'Connor, "Truth: Paul and Qumran," *Paul and Qumran: Studies in the New Testament Exegesis,* ed. by J. Murphy-O'Connor (London: Chapman, 1968), pp. 179-230; I. de la Potterie, "Verità biblica e verità cristiana," *Il Fuoco* 19 (1971): 5-14; "L'arrière-fond du thème johannique de vérité," *Studia Evangelica I, Texte und Untersuchungen* 73 (Berlin: Akademie, 1959): 277-294; Y. Alanen, "Das Wahrheitsproblem in der Bibel und in der griechischen Philosophie," *Kerygma und Dogma* 3 (1957): 230-239; O. Loretz, "Die Wahrheitsfrage in der Exegese: Interpretationen der Konzilskonstitution Dei Verbum," *ThRev* 63 (1967): 4-7; *Die Wahrheit der Bibel* (Freiburg: Herder, 1964).

16. See further *Peter in the New Testament,* p. 30. Cf. R. Bultmann, *"Alētheia, . . . ,"* TDNT 1 (1964: 242: "The truth is the 'valid norm', with perhaps a hint of the Gk. idea of what is 'genuine' or 'proper.' " Cf. TWNT 1 (1933): 242 ("die gültige Norm"); H. Schlier, *Der Brief an die Galater* (Göttingen: Vandenhoeck & Ruprecht, 1965), p. 85.

17. See the *apparatus criticus* for minor variants in some mss.

18. The meaning of the sixth charism is disputed. *Ho proistamenos* may mean both here and in 1 Thess. 5:12, "the one(s) standing at the head," i.e., superior(s). Other interpreters translate it rather "he who gives aid." It is not crucial to this discussion and need not detain us. See H. Greeven, "Propheten, Lehrer, Vorsteher bei Paulus," ZNW 44 (1952-53): 1-43, esp. pp. 31-41, and n. 74 on p. 32.

19. The statement on *Eucharist and Ministry* (L/RC 4, p. 10, n. 6) has already referred to these "varieties of ministering" and has concluded that "everyone would agree that some of these categories belong in the special Ministry of the church (e.g., apostles, prophets, *teachers* [my italics]), and that others reflect the ministry of the people of God (acts of mercy,

aid and helping), and that some are hard to categorize (healing, *teaching* [again, my italics])." The ambiguous status of this sole category in that document reveals perhaps the delicate nature of the topic being discussed here.

20. *"Didaskō, didaskalos,* etc.," TDNT 2 (1964) : 135-165, esp. p. 158; TWNT 2 (1935) : 138-168, esp. p. 160.

21. K. H. Rengstorf (TDNT 2:158; TWNT 2:161) warns against thinking that there is "an order of rank in the lists," for the "order is purely material." He insists that "the activity of the *didaskalos* is needed only when that of the *apostolos* and *prophētēs* has laid the foundation for the construction of a Christian outlook and manner of life" *(ibid.).* Not only does this give more importance to *prophētēs* than Paul suggests, but it plays down something that may not be so meant by him. Rengstorf elsewhere (TDNT 2: 146; TWNT 2: 149) tries to describe the role of *ho didaskōn* (Rom. 12:7) thus: "When Paul . . . summons the *didaskōn* to serve *en tē didaskaliā* of the community, he is not thinking of men who apply the Scriptures to Jesus, but of those who give from Scripture directions for Christian living." And his note reads: "The context demands an interpretation of *didaskein* in relation to the upbuilding of the life of the community rather than its faith" (n. 59).

22. See J. Kürzinger, *"Typos didachēs* und der Sinn von Röm 6,17f," *Biblica* 39 (1958) : 156-176; F. W. Beare, "On the Interpretation of Romans vi. 17," NTS 5 (1958-59) : 206-210; J. A. Fitzmyer, "The Letter to the Romans," JBC 2. no 67 (pp. 310-311) ; O. Kuss, *Der Römerbrief übersetzt und erklärt* (Regensburg: Pustet, 2 (1963), pp. 387-390; E. Käsemann, *An die Römer,* HNT 8a (Tübingen: Mohr, 1973), pp. 171-172.

23. So J. Kürzinger, *"Typos didachēs,"* see n. 22 above.

24. See L. Goppelt, *"Typos,* etc.," TDNT 8 (1972) : 250; TWNT 8 (1969) : 250-251. Cf. F. W. Beare, NTS 5 (1958-59) : 206-210.

25. The destination of Romans 16 is disputed. Was it Rome itself or Ephesus?

26. TDNT 2:146; TWNT 2:149 ("sein Zurücktreten").

27. TDNT 2:138; TWNT 2:141.

28. *Ibid.*

29. See F. Büchsel, *"Didōmi . . . , paradosis,"* TDNT 2 (1964) : 166-173, esp. pp. 172-173 ("In the NT this [word *paradosis*] means 'tradition' . . . only in the sense of what is transmitted, not of transmission." "For Paul Christian teaching is tradition (1 C. 11:2; 2 T. 2:15; 3:6; cf. 1 C. 11:23, 15:1-11), and he demands that the churches should keep to it, since salva-

tion depends on it (1 C. 15:2)." Cf. TWNT 2 (1935):
168-175, esp. pp. 174-175.

30. TDNT 2:146; TWNT 2:149. Cf. E. F. Harrison,
"Some Patterns of the New Testament Didache,"
Bibliotheca sacra 119 (1962): 118-128.

31. TDNT 2:147; TWNT 2:149.

32. As noted by K. H. Rengstorf, TDNT 2:158; TWNT
2:161.

33. Mark 10:17// Matt. 19:16// Luke 18:18; Mark 12:14
// Matt. 22:16 // Luke 20:21; Mark 12:19 // Matt.
22:24; Luke 18:18; also Matt. 22:36//Luke 10:25;
Mark 9:17//Luke 9:38. See further Mark 4:38; 9:38;
10:20, 35; 12:32; 13:1; Matt. 8:19; 12:38; Luke 7:40;
11:45; 12:13; 19:39; 20:39; 21:7. Luke not only uses
epistata in several places for *didaskale* or *rabbi*
(8:24; 9:33, 49), but also employs it in passages
without Synoptic parallels (5:5; 8:45; 17:13).

Mark uses *rabbi* in 9:5; 11:21; 14:45 (cf. Matt.
26:49); Matthew also has it in 23:7-8; 26:25. The
form *rabbouni* may be found in Mark 10:51. That
rabbi equals *didaskalos* can be inferred from Matt.
23:8 (see below, p. 200); John 20:16 equates *didaskalos* and *rabbouni*.

Whether Jesus should be actually thought of as hav-
ing been a rabbi is a matter of debate; see C. H. Dodd,
"Jesus as Teacher and Prophet," *Mysterium Christi:
Christological Studies by British and German Theolo-
gians* ed. by G. K. A. Bell and A. Deissmann (London:
Longmans, Green, 1930), pp. 51-66 (he regards Jesus
as a rabbi); M. Hengel, *Nachfolge und Charisma:
Eine exegetisch-religionsgeschichtliche Studie zu Mt
8 21f. und Jesu Ruf in die Nachfolge*, Beiheft zur
Zeitschrift für die neutestamentliche Wissenschaft
(Berlin: Töpelmann, 1968), pp. 46-54 ("Jesus war
kein 'Rabbi' ").

34. Mark 5:35//Luke 8:49; Matt. 9:11; 17:24.

35. The Synoptics frequently so describe his activity:
Mark 1:21-22//Matt. 7:29//Luke 4:31; Mark 12:14
// Matt. 22:16//Luke 20:21; Mark 6:2//Matt. 13:54;
Mark 6:6b//Matt. 9:35; Matt. 21:23//Luke 20:1. See
further Mark 2:13; 4:1-2; 6:34; 8:31; 9:31; 10:1;
11:17; 12:35; Matt. 4:23; 5:2; 11:1 ("to teach and
preach"); Luke 4:15 (where Mark and Matthew
have *kēryssein* in the parallels); 5:3, 17; 6:6; 13:10,
22, 26; 19:47; 21:37; 23:5.

36. Mark 14:14//Matt. 26:18//Luke 22:11; Mark 14:49
//Matt. 26:55. See further Matt. 23:8.

37. Mark 1:21; 6:2; Matt. 4:23; 13:54; Luke 4:15, 31;
13:10.

38. Mark 12:35; Luke 20:1; 21:37; Matt. 26:55.

39. Luke 5:3.

40. See K. H. Rengstorf, TDNT 2:139; TWNT 2:142.
41. Rengstorf (TDNT 2:135-138; TWNT 2:138-141) contrasts the Hellenistic and Jewish use of *didaskein* (in LXX, Josephus) with the Hebrew *limmēd* (in the later parts of the OT and in rabbinic literature) and stresses the relation of NT religious usage to the latter; "used absolutely, *didaskein* or the corresponding *limmēd* denotes the manner in which, by exposition of the Law as the sum of the revealed will of God, instruction is given for the ordering of the relationship between the individual and God on the one side, and the neighbour on the other, according to the divine will" (p. 137).
42. *Ibid.*, p. 153; cf. TWNT 2:155.
43. *Ibid.*, p. 140; cf. TWNT 2:143.
44. See D. M. Stanley, " 'Become Imitators of Me,' " p. 291: "The notion of collecting a group of disciples around his own person is so foreign to Paul's mind that the word *mathētēs* is found nowhere in his epistles." Instead, according to Stanley, Paul uses the Greek idea of imitation.
45. See K. H. Rengstorf, TDNT 2:139; TWNT 2:142. "He is against estimation of the Law merely for its own sake. . . . He stands in irreconcilable opposition to the lifeless casuistry which does not start with the situation of the one who needs the counsel of experts in the religious sphere but, irrespective of his own questions, subjects him to its own principle and system, bringing about religious separation from those who for practical reasons or for conscience sake cannot allow themselves to be bound by it."
46. *Pace* G. Friedrich (TDNT 3: 713 n. 63; TWNT 3 [1938]: 713 n. 63), who says that "we are never told that John the Baptist taught." Cf. Luke 3:12.
47. For the relation of the Spirit to teaching, see the discussion on the Johannine literature below, p. 209.
48. Consult the *apparatus criticus*, for though *didaskalos* is the reading preferred here by Nestle, Kilpatrick, Bover, Merk, UBS, Souter, important mss. read *kathēgētēs*. This may be a harmonization of the text with the words of v. 10, so that *didaskalos* may seem to be the *lectio difficilior*. But that is not certain, because *didaskalos* as the ordinary equivalent of *rabbi* may also have been secondarily introduced in view of *rabbi* in v. 8.
49. For the equation of *kathēgētēs* with Hebrew *môreh*, see C. Spicq, "Une allusion au Docteur de Justice dans Matthieu, xxiii, 10?" RB 66 (1959): 387-396.
50. See E. Klostermann, *Das Matthäusevangelium*, HNT 4, 2nd ed. (Tübingen: Mohr, 1927), p. 183; W. Grundmann, *Das Evangelium nach Matthäus*, Theo-

logischer Handkommentar zum Neuen Testament 1 (Berlin: Evangelische Verlagsanstalt, 1968), p. 487.

51. The least one can say is that a new nuance has been associated to the Jewish idea of a teacher in that the Christian must remember that all are brothers. See further J. Schniewind, *Das Evanglium nach Matthäus*, NTD 2 (Göttingen: Vandenhoeck & Ruprecht, 1968), p. 227.

52. TDNT 2:145; TWNT 2:147.

53. For the "summary" as a part of the structure and elements of Acts, see R. J. Dillon and J. A. Fitzmyer, "Acts of the Apostles," JBC 2., no. 45:4 (p. 166), and the literature cited there.

54. See J. A. Fitzmyer, "Jewish Christianity in Acts in Light of the Qumran Scrolls," *Studies in Luke-Acts: Essays Presented in Honor of Paul Schubert*, ed. by L. E. Keck and J. L. Martyn (Nashville: Abingdon, 1966), pp. 233-257, esp. pp. 241-242.

55. *Interpreter's Dictionary of the Bible* 4:523. Cf. F. V. Filson, "The Christian Teacher in the First Century," JBL 60 (1941) : 317-328.

56. TDNT 2:145; TWNT 2:147-148.

57. TDNT 2:145; TWNT 2:148.

58. E.g. E. F. Scott, *The Pastoral Epistles*, Moffatt NTC (New York: Harper, 1936), p. xxiii; P. Feine, J. Behm, and W. G. Kümmel, *Introduction to the New Testament* (Nashville: Abingdon, 1965), p. 272.

59. Cf. J. N. D. Kelly, *A Commentary on the Pastoral Epistles: I Timothy, II Timothy, Titus*, Harper's New Testament Commentary (New York: Harper and Row, 1963), pp. 27-36; A. Wikenhauser and J. Schmid, *Einleitung in das Neue Testament*, 6th ed. (Freiburg: Herder, 1973), p. 538.

60. Here a catalog of vices is given among the things that are opposed to such "sound doctrine."

61. Cf. also 1 Timothy 6:3 *hygiainontes logoi;* Titus 2:8, *logos hygiēs*.

62. TDNT 2:162; TWNT 2:165.

63. U. Luck, TDNT 8 (1972) : 312; TWNT 8 (1969) : 312. Luck also points out *(ibid.)* that the expression does not denote "a teaching which makes whole, whose goal is health of soul," and this he maintains against W. Michaelis, *Pastoralbriefe und Gefangenschaftsbriefe* (Gütersloh: Bertelsmann, 1930), pp. 79-80.

64. I have added the parentheses to the RSV translation, since the Greek text has only *tē anagnōsei, tē paraklēsei, tē didaskaliā*.

65. K. H. Rengstorf (TDNT 2:162; TWNT 2:165) understands the teaching here to be closely connected with "the historical revelation of God as attested by Scripture and fulfilled in Jesus."

66. Rengstorf (TDNT 2147; TWNT 2:150) calls it their "privilege and responsibility."

67. I am prescinding from the question of the difference in *episkopoi* and *presbyteroi* in these writings.

68. 1 Timothy 2:12 forbids the role of teaching to women: *didaskein de gynaiki ouk epitrepō*.

69. See further B. Weiss, *Die Briefe Pauli an Timotheus und Titus*, Kritisch-exegetischer Kommentar 11, 7th ed. (Göttingen: Vandenhoeck & Ruprecht, 1902), p. 131 ("bezeichnet die Lehrhaftigkeit [Luther], Lehrtüchigkeit"); M. Dibelius, *Die Pastoralbriefe*, 3rd ed., HNT 13 (Tübingen: Mohr, 1955), pp. 42-43 ("im Lehren geschickt"); J. N. D. Kelly, *Pastoral Epistles*, p. 76 ("a skilled teacher"); Bauer-Arndt-Gingrich, *Lexicon*, p. 190: "skillful in teaching" (only meaning given); also Bauer-Gingrich-Danker, *Lexicon*, p. 191.

70. So K. H. Rengstorf, TDNT 2:165; TWNT 2:168. But cf. B. Weiss, p. 131.

71. Rengstorf *(ibid.)* would phrase it differently; the requirement for the *episkopos* that he be *didaktikos* "belongs to a period when for the sake of spiritual order the free *didaskalos* is merging with the leader of the community." The problem is: When was there a "free *didaskalos*"?

72. The tendency may be traced further in *Didache* 15:1, where *episkopoi* and *diakonoi* are associated with the *prophētai* and *didaskaloi*, without clarity as to which goes with which.

73. Rengstorf (TDNT 2:147; TWNT 2:150) sees a difference between the Deutero-Pauline letters and Colossians in this matter: ". . . what was applied to all Christians in the latter can now be ascribed only to selected Christians, especially the leaders of the congregation. This tallies with the external development of the church noticeable in a comparison between the Past. and Col."

74. Rengstorf (TDNT 2:162; TWNT 2:165) compares this concern with that of the commissioned *apostolos* for the *euangelion tou Christou* (Gal. 1:6-12).

75. See J. A. T. Robinson, *Redating the New Testament* (Philadelphia: Westminster, 1976), pp. 118-139; also my review of this book, *Interpretation* 32 (1978): 309-313; cf. A. H. McNeile, *An Introduction to the Study of the New Testament*, 2nd ed., rev. by C. S. C. Williams (Oxford: Clarendon, 1953), p. 211; P. Feine, J. Behm, and W. G. Kümmel, *Introduction*, p. 291; A. Wikenhauser and J. Schmid, *Einleitung*, pp. 578-579.

76. The verb *ptaiein* means to "stumble, trip" (Bauer-Arndt-Gingrich, *Lexicon*, 734) and hence to "make a mistake, go astray, sin" *(ibid.)*. In the context of

teaching, the first of these derived meanings is appropriate, as the RSV has translated it. The immediately following context mentions another use of the tongue. M. Dibelius, *A Commentary on the Epistle of James*, rev. by H. Greeven, trans. by M. A. Williams (Philadelphia: Fortress, 1976), p. 183: "The interpretation of vv. 1-2 has shown that James does not have in mind the occasional functioning of Christians as teachers, but rather a certain thronging toward the vocation of teacher. If this epistle is not to be transposed into a Jewish context (as Spitta would have it), then his admonition refers not to the rabbinate but to the position of early Christian teacher, and so the author is recognized as being such a teacher also."

77. The word *ekklēsia* does occur in 3 John (vv. 6, 9, 10).
78. John 1:38.
79. John 11:28; 13:13.
80. John 13:13-14.
81. John 6:59; 7:14, 28; 8:2, 20.
82. John 18:19-20.
83. Recall, however, the relation of the Spirit to teaching in Luke 12:12.
84. TDNT 2:143; TWNT 2:146.
85. The quotation is not exact. The MT has *wĕkol bānayik limmûdê Yhwh;* the LXX is closer to the Johannine text, reading *kai pantas tous huious sou didaktous theou.*
86. R. Bultmann *(The Johannine Epistles*, trans. by R. P. O'Hara with L. C. McGaughy and R. W. Funk (Philadelphia: Fortress, 1973), p. 41, n. 31) seems to understand it to refer to Christ. But J. Schneider *(Die Briefe des Jakobus, Petrus, Judas, und Johannes*, NTD 10 [Göttingen: Vandenhoeck & Ruprecht, 1961], p. 159) also understands it to refer to the Spirit.
87. Schneider's further comment is noteworthy: "Would that mean that therefore every kind of teaching authority in the church is excluded? That might be the case, for John has no teaching about offices. For him all members of the congregation are equal bearers of the spirit. He does not distinguish between them" *(ibid.).*
88. Cf. the treatment of the Johannine material on Peter and the Beloved Disciple in *Peter in the New Testament,* pp. 129-147, esp. pp. 137-138, 141, 146.

11. Teaching Office in the New Testament?
A Response to Professor Fitzmyer's Paper

John Reumann

1. Helmut Koester and James M. Robinson, *Trajectories in Early Christianity* (Philadelphia: Fortress, 1971); German, *Entwicklungslinien durch die Welt des frühen Christentums* (Tübingen: J. C. B. Mohr, 1971).
2. For objections to the term *trajectory* see J. Reumann, "Exegetes, Honesty and the Faith," *Currents in Theology and Mission* 5 (1978): 23-25. Compare R. E. Brown, K. P. Donfried, J. A. Fitzmyer, and J. Reumann, *Mary in the New Testament* (Philadelphia and New York: Fortress and Paulist, 1978), p. 25, n. 36.
3. See Klaus Wegenast, "Lehre," in *Theologisches Begriffslexikon zum Neuen Testament*, ed. by L. Coenen et al. (Wupperthal: Brockhaus, 1970), 2:852-867; cited hereafter from the subsequent English trans., "Teach," *The New International Dictionary of New Testament Theology*, ed. by Colin Brown (Grand Rapids: Zondervan, 1978, 3:759-781.

   The verb *katēcheō*, rare in secular Greek and missing in the LXX, may have been introduced by Paul as a term for "the person who teaches the word" (Gal. 6:6), and could thus be "the earliest evidence we have for a 'full-time' teaching office in the early church" (p. 771); cf. also 1 Cor. 14:19; Rom. 2:18; Luke 1:4; Acts 18:25 especially.

   The usual New Testament word for "handing on" a tradition is *paradidōmi*. It is employed not only for Jewish *halakah* (Mark 7:13; Acts 6:14) but also for narratives about Jesus which Christians transmitted (Luke 1:2) and confessions of faith (1 Cor. 11:23; 15:3; cf. 11:2 and Jude 3) and fixed commands (2 Peter 2:21).

   Paideuō/paideia (New International Dictionary of New Testament Theology article by Dieter Fürst) means "teach, instruct, educate," often with a note of discipline or suffering (1 Cor. 11:32; Eph. 6:4, of parents; 2 Timothy 3:16, of Scripture; Titus 2:11-13; Heb. 12:5-9). Inclusion of this term suggests teaching as a work of God includes the development of persons as children of God through agencies other than professional teachers.
4. See especially *The Semantics of Biblical Language* (New York: Oxford University Press, 1961), though there is a considerable subsequent literature.

5. But is it as clear and simple as Rengstorf implies? 2 Thess. (2:15) and the Pastoral Letters, written as much in a Hellenistic context as Paul's unquestioned letters, do have a Jewish sense for *didaskein* as "teaching established traditions." Wegenast, "Teach," p. 764, suggests a more persuasive reason than the Hellenistic context: for Paul, "to teach" implied transmitting "the traditions of the fathers" (Gal. 1:12, 14; Rom. 2:21); therefore he himself avoided it as a term.

6. Wegenast, "Teach," p. 763, after proceeding more redaction-critically, concludes that often in the Synoptics "the rabbinic sense of *didaskō* (i.e., that of the Heb. *limmad*) has been replaced by the meaning 'to proclaim salvation.'"

7. For example, Wegenast points out in connection with *didaskalia* that the LXX avoided the term because "its primary meaning in profane Greek is intellectual training with a view to knowledge, whereas Israel saw teaching as meaning the law of God, to which the only appropriate response was obedience" (p. 769). On the other hand, the Pastoral Letters show no inhibitions about using *didaskalia* (p. 771).

8. First Corinthians 2:13 is a kind of parallel to John 6:45 (about being "taught by the Father," *didaktoi Theou* when it says: "We impart this [God's revelation] in words not taught by human wisdom but taught by the Spirit [*didaktois Pneumatos*], interpreting spiritual truths to those who possess the Spirit."

9. *The Apostolic Preaching and its Developments* (London: Hodder & Stoughton, 1936); *Gospel and Law: the Relation of Faith and Ethics in Early Christianity* (New York: Columbia University Press, 1951).

10. Cf. Victor Paul Furnish, *Theology and Ethics in Paul* (Nashville: Abingdon, 1968), pp. 224-227.

11. *Apostolic Preaching*, p. 7. But cf. *Gospel and Law*, p. 10: *didachē* is "a course of instruction in morals."

12. *Apostolic Preaching*, especially p. 17 for a summary of the *kērygma* recovered from the Pauline epistles, and pp. 21-24 for the Jerusalem *kērygma*; on pp. 25-26 the differences are discussed.

13. Cf. Hans Conzelmann, *An Outline of the Theology of the New Testament*, trans. by John Bowden (New York: Harper and Row, 1969), pp. 62ff., 87ff.

14. So Conzelmann in "On the Analysis of the Confessional Formula in I Corinthians 15:3-5," *Interpretation* 20 (1966): 15-25, and his commentary on the passage in the Kritisch-exegetischer Kommentar series, *Der erste Brief an die Korinther* (Göttingen: Vandenhoeck & Ruprecht, 1969), trans. by J. W. Leitch in Hermeneia, *1 Corinthians* (Philadelphia:

Fortress, 1975). What is at issue between Paul and the Corinthian opponents are the implications of a credo which they both accept.

15. "Didache, Kerygma, and Euangelion," *New Testament Essays: Studies in Memory of Thomas Walter Manson 1893-1958*, ed. by A. J. B. Higgins (Manchester: Manchester University Press, 1959), pp. 306-314. The quotations are from pp. 307, 312.

16. Cf. *Theology of the New Testament*, trans. by Kendrick Grobel (New York: Scribner's, 1951), 1:86: out of the kerygma grew both (1) formulas which crystallized into creeds and (2) the literary form we call the gospel-book, made up of "the kerygma of the death and resurrection of Jesus," visualized by narratives, cult aetiologies, miracle stories, and apophthegms. Bultmann holds that the "sayings of the Lord" were handed down separately from the "christological kerygma" and were combined in "the gospel [book]," first sparingly by Mark, then more by Matthew and Luke. On this view, "Jesus in the role of 'teacher' " (on which, for the "historical Jesus," cf. R. Bultmann, *Jesus and the Word*, trans. by Louise Pettibone Smith and Erminie Huntress [New York: Scribner's, 1934]), now in the gospel-writing stage "had become more important again" (p. 86).

Behind the topic lies the problem posed (but not yet solved) in Robert A. Bartels, *Kerygma or Gospel Tradition—Which Came First?* (Minneapolis: Augsburg, 1961). This monograph raises the perennial question whether there was an authoritative body of teaching material attributed to Jesus in the early Church which was "non-christological," if not "non-kerygmatic"; cf. the debate over a Q source and, more negatively, Howard M. Teeple, "The Oral Tradition That Never Existed," JBL 89 (1970): 56-68, who denies there was "a widespread oral tradition that originated with Jesus' teaching." Such a viewpoint raises the question of "norm" and "canon within the canon" in a way that Lutherans and Catholics alike have not usually had in mind.

17. *The Essential Nature of New Testament Preaching* (Grand Rapids: Eerdmans, 1960). Cf. also Robert C. Worley, *Preaching and Teaching in the Earliest Church* (Philadelphia: Westminster, 1967).

18. Peter F. Ellis, *Matthew: His Mind and His Message* (Collegeville, Minn.: Liturgical Press, 1974), p. 21.

19. TDNT 2:164. Wegenast, "Teach," pp. 762-763, cf. 769, concludes each Synoptic evangelist uses *didaskein* in the senses of "teach" *and* "preach."

20. J. Reumann, "The Kerygma and the Preacher," *Dia-*

log 3 (1964) : 27-35, especially 32-33, where further literature is cited; *Jesus in the Church's Gospels* (Philadelphia: Fortress, 1968), pp. 30-36.

21. *"Didache* as a Constitutive Element of the Gospel-Form," CBQ 17. (1955) : 345.

22. Cf. e.g. W. D. Davies, *Paul and Rabbinic Judaism* (London: SPCK, 1948), pp. 136ff.; C. H. Dodd, "En-nomos Christou," in *Studia Paulina, Festschrift de Zwaan* (Haarlem, Holland: 1953), pp. 96-110, re-printed in *More New Testament Studies* (Grand Rapids: Eerdmans, 1968), pp. 134-148; David L. Dungan, *The Sayings of Jesus in the Churches of Paul: The Use of the Synoptic Tradition in the Regulation of Early Church Life* (Philadelphia: Fortress, 1971).

23. So already Alfred Seeberg, *Der Katechismus der Urchristenheit* (Leipzig: Deichert, 1903, reprinted Munich: Kaiser, 1966) ; Philip Carrington, *The Primitive Christian Catechism* (New York: Cambridge University Press, 1940) ; E. G. Selwyn, *The First Epistle of Peter* (London: Macmillan, 1946), Essay II, pp. 363-466.

24. Examples and discussion in J. Reumann, "Is Writing Confessions Possible Only Where Scripture Speaks?," *The Confession-Making Process*, Studies Series (New York: Lutheran Council in the U.S.A., Division of Theological Studies, 1975) : 25-29. The aim would be neither to restrict church teaching solely to reiteration of scriptural passages nor to allow statements on any basis whatever, but within the scriptural-confessional framework to allow for new insights under the Spirit, but always normed by the New Testament gospel.

25. Maurice F. Wiles, *The Divine Apostle: The Interpretation of St Paul's Epistles in the Early Church* (New York: Cambridge University Press, 1967), especially Chapter II.

26. Wegenast, "Teach," p. 774; cf. 770 (German, p. 860, "Paul always preserves a freedom with the tradition," omitted in the more conservatively oriented English rendering) ; and K. Wegenast's *Das Verständnis der Tradition bei Paulus und in den Deuteropaulinen,* Wissenschaftliche Monographien zum Alten und Neuen Testament 8 (Neukirchen: Neukirchener Verlag, 1962).

27. "The Office of Teaching," p. 193, citing Rengstorf on possible origins in Jewish Christianity. Otherwise H. Greeven, "Propheten, Lehrer, Vorsteher bei Paulus," ZNW 44 (1952-1953) : 1-43 (evidence from Hellenistic Judaism). See also note 5 above.

28. Conzelmann, *1 Corinthians*, p. 215, where references are cited; C. K. Barrett, *The First Epistle to the Corinthians*, Harper/Black's New Testament Com-

mentaries (New York: Harper & Row, 1968), p. 295; Wegenast, "Teach," p. 768.

29. L/RC 4, p. 10, n. 6 ("The Office of Teaching," above, n. 19). See also the "Common Statement" in this volume, p. 17 and note 20.

30. E. Käsemann, "Sentences of Holy Law in the New Testament" (1954), trans. by W. J. Montague in *New Testament Questions of Today* (Philadelphia: Fortress, 1969), pp. 66-81. For criticism of the theory and even the form-critical analysis, see Klaus Berger, "Zu den sogennanten Sätzen Heiligen Rechts," NTS 17 (1970-1971) : 10-40, and David Hill, "On the Evidence for the Creative Role of Christian Prophets," NTS 20 (1973-1974) : 262-274.

31. E. J. Tinsley, *The Imitation of God in Christ* (Philadelphia: Westminster, 1960), pp. 134-165. Some criticism of the Old Testament derivation of the imitation theme is voiced by W. P. De Boer, *The Imitation of Paul* (Grand Rapids: Eerdmans, 1962).

32. R. Bultmann, "Glossen im Römerbrief," ThLZ 72 (1947) : 202, reprinted in his *Exegetica* (Tübingen: Mohr [Siebeck], 1967), p. 283, first spotted the possibility of a later gloss here. The view is followed in the commentaries of Leenhardt (1957) and Michel (1966) and by Wegenast, "Teach," p. 773, and *Verständnis der Tradition*, p. 179 (a mystery-religions concept that *persons* are "handed over" to a form of doctrine). J. C. O'Neill, *Paul's Letter to the Romans*, Pelican New Testament Commentaries (Baltimore: Penguin, 1975), takes all of 6:16-20 as a gloss. On the other hand, the commentaries by Käsemann (1973) and C. E. B. Cranfield (1975, pp. 323-325, but cf. p. 5) accept the phrase as Paul's, from baptismal paraenesis, to stress obedience.

33. Wegenast, "Teach," p. 771. Is it significant that in the Pauline corpus *didaskalia* in the plural has a pejorative sense ("doctrines of demons," 1 Timothy 4:1; cf. Col. 2:22, "human doctrines"), while the singular denotes (Paul's) gospel teaching?

34. *Jesus and His Contemporaries* (London: SCM, 1973), especially chaps. 3, 4, and 6.

35. See Howard Clark Kee, *Jesus in History: An Approach to the Study of the Gospels* (New York: Harcourt, Brace & World, 1970), chap. 3, "Jesus as God's Eschatological Messenger: The Q Document," pp. 62-103; H. E. Tödt, *The Son of Man in the Synoptic Tradition*, trans. by D. M. Barton (Philadelphia: Westminster, 1965), especially pp. 246-269 and 293-296 on how the teaching of Jesus continued after Easter in Q circles with new authority; Siegfried Schulz, *Q. Die Spruchquelle der Evangelisten* (Zurich: Theologischer Verlag, 1972), who divides Q

into earlier and later layers, with the implication
that words spoken by Christian prophets in the period
of post-Easter enthusiasm came to be assigned to the
earthly Jesus prior to his exaltation. In any case,
teaching authority in Q would be charismatic and
based on (future) eschatology. Compare the authoritative statements of Christian prophets noted above
(II.A.4 and note 30).

36. Cf. Wegenast, "Teach," p. 762.
37. *Mark the Evangelist*, trans. by R. A. Harrisville
(Nashville & New York: Abingdon, 1969). Cf. Mark
8:35 and 10:25 with parallels, to see how Mark parallels "Jesus" and "the gospel."
38. *Paul on Preaching* (London: Sheed & Ward, 1964),
p. 68; O. Glombitza, "Die Titel *didaskalos* und *epis-
tatēs* für Jesus bei Lukas," ZNW 49 (1958): 275-
278. Unlike Matthew, who often removes "teacher"
from his sources, Luke simply takes the title over and
adds *didaskalos* four times (7:40; 11:45; 12:13;
19:39); three times he substitutes *epistata* (8:24, 45;
9:49): see Wegenast, "Teach," p. 767.
39. G. Bornkamm, "End-Expectation and Church in Matthew," in G. Bornkamm, G. Barth, and H. J. Held,
Tradition and Interpretation in Matthew, trans. by
Percy Scott (Philadelphia: Westminster, 1963), p. 41.
40. Cf. Krister Stendahl, *The School of St. Matthew*
(1954), 2d ed. (Philadelphia: Fortress, 1968). Wegenast, "Teach," pp. 767-768 (German, p. 858), stresses
Matthew's "Auseinandersetzung mit dem Rabbinat"
as reason for his avoiding the title. On the christological aspects, cf. F. Hahn, *The Titles of Jesus in
Christology*, trans. by H. Knight and G. Ogg (New
York & Cleveland: World, 1969), pp. 75-78; with
Haenchen, he takes 23:8 as formed by the community.
41. G. Barth, *Tradition and Interpretation in Matthew*,
pp. 159-164, "The Antinomians in Matthew."
42. Wegenast, "Teach," p. 763 (cross-references omitted); cf. 767-768.
43. This is to take *kai idontes auton prosekynēsan, hoi
de edistasan*, not in the usual rendering, "And when
they saw him they worshiped him; but *some* doubted" (RSV, emphasis added), leaving it open as to
whether the "some" are a group beyond the twelve
(laity?) who have slipped up to the mountain top
unnoticed, or two or six or whatever out of the eleven
themselves; but rather as "they worshiped and they
doubted," i.e. both reactions came from the same
group. So Benjamin J. Hubbard, *The Matthean Redaction of a Primitive Apostolic Commissioning: An
Exegesis of Matthew 28:16-20*, Society of Biblical Literature Dissertation Series 19 (Missoula, Mont.: SBL
and Scholars' Press, 1974), pp. 75-77.

44. Cf. Eduard Schweitzer, *Church Order in the New Testament*, Studies in Biblical Theology 32, trans. by Frank Clarke (London: SCM, 1961), pp. 51-62.
45. Wegenast, "Teach," p. 770 (more literally translated above from the German, p. 859).
46. On the "gospel function" (truth), which is the norm for even the "Petrine function" (unity of the universal church), cf. L/RC 5, pp. 11, 20-21, especially sections (26) and (28). One finds an exposition of the Galatians 2 theme of "the truth of the gospel" in *Peter in the New Testament*, pp. 24-32, especially p. 30 (on exegesis); see the essay in this volume by Karlfried Froehlich, "Fallibility Instead of Infallibility? A Brief History of the Interpretation of Galatians 2:11-14," pp. 259-269 below, on subsequent interpretations. Further, Peter Stuhlmacher, *Das paulinische Evangelium. I. Vorgeschichte*, Forschungen zur Religion und Literatur des Alten und Neuen Testaments 95 (Göttingen: Vandenhoeck & Ruprecht, 1968), pp. 38, 62-108, especially 70-71: "Paul understands his gospel as revelation itself, that is, he understands it as tradition-affirming but as not bound to what were pre-Pauline normative traditions."

12. On the Terminology for Faith, Truth, Teaching, and the Spirit in the Pastoral Epistles: A Summary

Jerome D. Quinn

1. The author-redactor of the PE knew at least as much about Luke-Acts as he did about the Pauline tradition. For a hypothesis on the relation of Luke-Acts to the PE see my "The Last Volume of Luke" in *Perspectives on Luke-Acts*, ed. by C. H. Talbert (Danville: Assoc. Baptist Professors of Religion, 1978), pp. 62-75.
2. For the evidence, see the study cited in n. 1, pp. 63-64.
3. For the full citation of materials and their analysis see my commentary for the Doubleday Anchor Bible, vol. 35, *I and II Timothy and Titus* (in preparation).
4. See the materials cited with the formula *pistos ho logos* (Titus 3:8; 1 Timothy 1:15; 3:1; 4:9; 2 Timothy 2:11).
5. On the perils of dichotomizing the *fides qua* and *fides quae*, see G. Bornkamm, *Paul* (New York: Harper and Row, 1971), p. 141 and D. Lührmann, *Glaube im Frühen Christentum* (Gütersloh: Mohn, 1976).
6. See the materials cited in n. 4 as well as the hymnic fragments, credal confessions, doxologies, prayers,

homiletic materials from sacramental celebrations, etc. in the PE, *passim*.

7. *Alētheia* occurs 14 times in the PE, usually with the definite article, except in the phrase "knowledge" *(epignōsis)* of truth" in Titus 1:1; 1 Timothy 2:4 (cf. 7) ; 2 Timothy 2:25; 3:7.

8. See 1 Timothy 3:5 as well as U. Wilckens, "stūlos," TDNT 7:736; C. K. Barrett, *The Pastoral Epistles* (Oxford: Clarendon, 1963), p. 63; J. N. D. Kelly, *The Pastoral Epistles* (New York: Harper and Row, 1963) ; pp. 87-88.

9. See E. Stauffer, "hedrāious," TDNT 2:364; M. Dibelius and H. Conzelmann, *The Pastoral Epistles*, trans. by P. Buttolph and A. Yarbro (Philadelphia: Fortress, 1972), pp. 60-61; C. Spicq, *Les épîtres pastorales*, 4th ed. (Paris: Gabalda, 1969), pp. 263 n. 6, 465, 481-482.

10. See A. Jaubert, "l'image de la colonne (1 Timothée 3, 15, *"Studiorum paulinorum congressus internationalis catholicus 1961*, Analecta Biblica 17-18 (Rome: PBI, 1963), 2:101-108; N. Brox, *Die Pastoralbriefe*, 4th ed. (Regensburg: Pustet, 1969), pp. 156-159; J. Murphy-O'Connor, *Paul and Qumran* (London: Chapman, 1968), pp. 219-230. Of historical interest also is the proposal by J. Bengel to put a full stop after "church of the living God" and then read this phrase with 1 Timothy 3:16 and the hymnic confession of Christ cited there.

11. The pillar holding aloft the image of a divinity or an emperor was a not unfamiliar monument in the Roman world, as the columns of Trajan and Marcus Aurelius witness to this day in Rome itself (see Lino Rossi, *Trajan's Column and the Dacian Wars* [Ithaca, N.Y.: Cornell, 1971] not to mention the one for Augustus in Actium (Nicopolis) and the one for Ceres illustrated in the Vienne mosaic calendar (A. Toynbee, ed.; *The Crucible of Christianity* [London: Thames and Hudson, 1969], pp. 128, 359).

12. See Titus 3:9-11; 1 Timothy 6:3-5; and note how the "legitimate teacher" at Qumran and his community do not argue with opponents but know the truth, the mysteries, that the Torah and prophets intended to communicate (see IQS 9:16-19; IQH 10:28-29; and J. Murphy-O'Connor, as cited in n. 10, pp. 213-219).

13. But not vice versa: cf. 1 Timothy 1:8-11.

14. E.g. the midrashic sources behind 1 Timothy 2:13-14; 2 Timothy 2:19-21; 3:8; a collection of dominical logia (cf. 1 Timothy 5:18 with 6:3); even the PE themselves (1 Timothy 3:14).

15. Note at every turn the imperatives with the verbs for teaching in the PE.

16. On the actual force of the health/disease figures in the PE, see A. J. Malherbe, "Medical Imagery in the PE," *Texts and Testaments: Critical Studies in Honor of Stuart D. Currie*, ed. by W. E. March, forthcoming from Trinity University Press, San Antonio, Tex. Professor Malherbe generously shared the ms. of this critical study as I prepared this summary.

17. For more detailed observations, see my essay "The Holy Spirit in the PE," *Sin, Salvation, and the Spirit*, ed. by D. Durken, O.S.B. (Collegeville: Liturgical Press, 1979), pp. 345-368.

18. See H. Conzelmann, "charisma," TDNT 9:402-403, 406.

13. Some Elements in the Pre-History of Papal Infallibility

Robert B. Eno

1. Marcus Antoninus, *Historia Augusta*, XI.10; LCL 1:162; Leo, *Ep.* 10:2; JK 407; PL 54:629.

2. Irenaeus, *Adversus Haereses* III.3.2. "Ad hanc enim Ecclesiam propter potentiorem principalitatem necesse est omnem convenire Ecclesiam, hoc est eos qui sunt undique fideles, in qua semper ab his qui sunt undique conservata est ea quae est ab apostolis traditio."

As most authors note, this text has been the subject of extensive commentary. The fact that the original Greek is no longer extant is a fundamental problem. Without going into detail, it appears that at present the three phrases at the center of the debate are viewed as follows by the majority of scholars:

Ad hanc . . . Ecclesiam: This refers to the local Roman church, not the universal church;

Potentior Principalitas: Not "greater authority" but "more excellent origin," referring to Rome's double apostolic pedigree;

Convenire ad: "agree with," not "come to" in some sense of spatial motion.

I believe the context is decisive for the interpretation of this passage. Irenaeus, disputing the Gnostics, held that the doctrine of Christ was to be found in the churches, not in the conventicles. One recent Roman Catholic commentator, A. Rousseau, takes a conservative position when he interprets the text as maintaining that ". . . the establishment of the apostolic character of the tradition of the Roman Church is enough to establish the apostolic character of the tradition of the whole Church. Rome has an "absolutely unique position" (SC 210:225).

I do not accept this view. It must be asked whether all must agree with Rome because it is Rome or because its doctrine is apostolic. A verbal analysis might lead one to the former conclusion, but an analysis of the context leads to the latter. Irenaeus was stating what he believed to be an historically verifiable fact. In his own time he may have maintained that if something is Roman, it must be apostolic. But he was not asking a question for the future in any clear fashion. It did not occur to him to do so. If one were able to ask Irenaeus about the possibility of aberration on the part of one or several apostolic sees, I think that he would admit that possibility but not the possibility for the whole Church.

Cf. A. Rousseau & L. Doutreleau, eds., *Irénée de Lyon, Contre les Hérésies*, Book III (SC 210-211 (1974); notes by Rousseau, especially pp. 223-236.

See N. Brox, "Probleme einer Frühdatierung des römischen Primats." *Kairos* 18 (1976): 81-99; J. McCue, "The Roman Primacy in the Second Century and the Problem of the Development of Dogma," TS 25 (1964): esp. 175-179.

3. See J. Quinn, "Charisma veritatis certum," TS 39 (1978): 520-525.

4. Lack of historical sense should not be distorted into a complete absence of knowledge of change. Tertullian *(De Corona)* and Basil *(De Spiritu Sancto)* both discussed liturgical customs which were introduced after the apostles. Gregory Nazianzen was aware that the question of the status of the Holy Spirit was a fairly recent one in his own time. *Oratio* 31.27 (SC 250:328 [1978]).

5. On Vincent and Augustine, see Sieben, chaps. 2 and 4. See also R. B. Eno, "Ecclesia Docens. Structures of Doctrinal Authority in Tertullian and Vincent," *Thomist* 40 (1976): 96-115, and "Consensus and Doctrine: three ancient views," *Eglise et Théologie* 9 (1978): 473-483.

6. Cyprian, *Ep.* 74.1, CSEL 3/2:799. Leo, *Ep.* 129.3, JK 505, PL 54:1077. Gelasius, *Ep.* 4.2 (Coll. Avell. 98), JK 625, CSEL 35:438. Hilary, *Ep.* 15:10, Thiel 163.

7. "If there is one faith. . . ." Synod under Damasus included under the letters of Siricius, *Ep.* 10:9, PL 13:1188. Innocent, *Ep.* 17.5,9, JK 303, PL 20:532. Zosimus, *Ep.* 5, JK 334, PL 20:666.

8. Gelasius, *Ep.* 1.19, JK 611, Schwartz 39. This letter, usually attributed to the pontificate of Felix II, was probably authored by Gelasius and will be attributed to him in this essay. "Embrace the grace. . . . " Hormisdas, *Ep.* 17.3, JK 780, Thiel 775. See also *Ep.* 124.4, JK 850, Thiel 929.

9. Innocent, *Ep.* 29.1, JK 321, CSEL 44:702. See also Zosimus, *Ep.* 2.1, JK 329, PL 20:649. "Care for all the churches": Anastasius I, *Ep.* 1.5, JK 282, PL 20:71-72. Innocent, *Ep.* 32, JK 324, PL 20:597. Sixtus III, *Ep.* 1.2, JK 389, PL 50:585. "Great sacrilege," Leo, *Ep.* 157.3, JK 534, PL 54:1133. "No departure from Nicaea," Leo *Ep.* 119.5, JK 495, PL 54:1045. "No equivocation," Leo, *Ep.* 38, JK 432, PL 54:813. Leo, *Ep.* 162.2, JK 539, PL 54:1144. "Divinely fortified," Leo, *Sermo* 3.3, CCL 138:13. "We defend," Felix II, *Ep.* 14.3, JK 613, Thiel 267. Also Gelasius, *Ep.* 14.9, JK 636, Thiel 367. Gelasius, *Tractatus* III.16, Schwartz 95.

10. Leo, *Ep.* 90.2, JK 470, PL 54:933-934. *Ep.* 144, JK 520, PL 54:1113. *Ep.* 162.1, JK 539, PL 54:1144. "Fixed by the Spirit," Leo, *Ep.* 162.3, PL 54:1145. "Leo's successors," Simplicius, *Ep.* 6.4 (Coll. Avell. 60), JK 576, CSEL 35:137-138. Vigilius, *Constitutum de Tribus Capitulis* (Coll. Avell. 83), JK 935, CSEL 35:312.

11. Tertullian, *Adverus Praxean* 1, CCL 2:1159. Simplicius, *Ep.* 2.2 (Coll. Avell. 58), JK 572, CSEL 35:131. Symmachus, *Ep.* 3.1, JK 754, Thiel 655-656; *Ep.* 4, JK 756, Thiel 657. On the Gallic issue, see G. Langgärtner, *Die Gallienpolitik der Päpste* (Bonn: Peter Hanstein, 1964), pp. 105-106; Karl Morrison, *Tradition and Authority in the Western Church* (Princeton: Princeton University Press, 1969), pp. 105-107.

12. Gelasius, *Ep.* 1.27, 34, JK 611, Schwartz 42, 44-45; *Ep.* 12.6, JK 632, Schwartz 21.

13. Rome itself distinguished doctrine and discipline. See the following: Leo, *Ep.* 129.3, JK 505, PL 54:1077. Gelasius *Ep.* 30.7, Thiel 441 (Coll. Avell. 103.14, CSEL 35:479). Roman Council of 495, *"Pro fide catholica vel pro paternis canonibus regulisque."*

14. Leo, *Ep.* 14.11, JK 412, PL 54:676. "Norm," Innocent, *Ep.* 2.1, JK 286, PL 20:469. Simplicius, *Ep.* 3.5 (Coll. Avell. 56), JK 573, CSEL 35:127-128. Innocent, *Ep.* 25, JK 311, Ed. R. Cabié (BRHE 38, 1973). "Norm for the orthodox," Hormisdas, *Ep.* 7.4, JK 774, Thiel 751. "All decisions to Rome," Innocent, *Ep.* 29.1, JK 321, CSEL 44:702-703. Leo, *Ep.* 4.5—6.6, JK 402-404, PL 54:614-620.

15. Gelasius, *Ep.* 26.3 (Coll. Avell. 95), JK 664, CSEL 35:372. "Strength of all is fortified," Leo, *Sermo* 4.3, CCL 138:20. "Adds solidity," Leo, *Ep.* 10.1, JK 407,

PL 54:629. Hormisdas, *Ep*. 80.1, JK 820, Thiel 880. "Strengthens local decisions," Leo, *Ep*. 12.13, JK 408, PL 54:656. Simplicius, *Ep*. 4.1 (Coll. Avell. 59), JK 574, CSEL 35:133-134. "Formulate answers," Leo, *Ep*. 166, JK 543, PL 54:1191-1192. Luke 22:32. See e.g. Gelasius, *Ep*. 4.1 (Coll. Avell. 98), JK 625, CSEL 35:436-437.

16. Zosimus, *Ep*. 12.1, JK 342, PL 20:676. Boniface I, *Ep*. 13.1, JK 363, PL 20.775. *Ep*. 15.5, JK 365, PL 20:781-782.

17. "Stability-Mutability," Leo, *Sermo* 60.4, CCL 138A: 367. "Letters to the East," Simplicius, *Ep*. 3.6 (Coll. Avell. 56), JK 573, CSEL 35:128. Simplicius, *Ep*. 5 (Coll. Avell. 57), JK 575, CSEL 35:130. Simplicius, *Ep*. 7.5, JK 577, Schwartz 122. "No reconsideration," Gelasius, *Ep*. 26.1,6 (Coll. Avell. 95), JK 664, CSEL 35:370, 382. "Rome alone," Gelasius, *Ep*. 1.1, JK 611, Schwartz 33; *Ep*. 26.5, CSEL 35:379-380. "Who dares judge Rome?" Gelasius, *Ep*. 26.5; *Ep*. 10.6,9, JK 622, Schwartz 17-19.

18. "Prima Sedes . . . ," see A. M. Koeniger, *"Prima Sedes a nemine judicatur," Festgabe Albert Ehrhard* 1922 (Reprinted Amsterdam: Hakkert, 1969), pp. 273-300. See also E. Caspar, *Geschichte des Papsttums*. (Tübingen: Mohr [Siebeck], 1933), 2:90ff.

19. On councils, see Sieben and W. de Vries, *Orient et Occident* (Paris: Cerf, 1974). See also R. Eno, "Pope and Council," *Science et Esprit* 28 (1976): 183-211. Damasus, *Ep*. 1.1 (Synod of Rome), JK 232, PL 13:349. Siricius, *Ep*. 1.2, JK 255, PL 13:1133. On "Circularity in Ambrose" see T. Ring, *Auctoritas bei Tertullian, Cyprian und Ambrosius* (Würzburg: Augustinus-Verlag, 1975), pp. 216-217.

20. Leo, *Ep*. 36-37, JK 430-431, PL 54:809-812; *Ep*. 44.1, JK 438, PL 54:829; *Ep*. 103; JK 480; PL 54:992; *Ep*. 139.4, JK 514, PL 54:1107.

21. Leo, *Ep*. 120.1,4, JK 496, PL 54:1046-1048, 1052-1053; *Ep*. 160.2, JK 537, PL 54:1142. *Ep*. 161.2, JK 538, PL 54:1142. "Chalcedon as pillar," Felix II, *Ep*. 17.2, JK 615, Schwartz 79. "Rome executrix," *ibid*. See also Gelasius, *Ep*. 26.9, 14 (Coll. Avell. 95), CSEL 35:386-387, 397; Tractatus IV.9, Schwartz 12; *Ep*. 26.6, CSEL 35:380-381. On Facundus and Ferrandus, see Sieben, part II, chap. 3, pp. 270-305; R. Eno, "Doctrinal Authority in the African Ecclesiology of the Sixth Century: Ferrandus and Facundus," *Revue des Études Augustiniennes* 22 (1976): 95-113. "No Valid Existence," Gelasius, Tractatus IV.1, Schwartz 7-8.

22. On Liberius, see DTC 9/1:631-649 (written c. 1926); *Catholicisme*, 7:601-604 (c. 1972).

23. See note 19.

24. O. Wermelinger, *Rom und Pelagius* (Stuttgart:

Hiersemann, 1975). In the eyes of the African bishops their own decision was an expression of theological truth. Roman approbation lent greater prestige to their own decision in the eyes of the universal Church and thus made it less likely that another regional area like Palestine could cancel out the African judgment.

25. G. Kreuzer, *Die Honoriusfrage im Mittelalter und in der Neuzeit* (Stuttgart: Hiersemann, 1975). Text of Leo II, p. 101, n. 129: *"Nec non et Honorium qui hanc apostolicam ecclesiam non apostolicae traditionis doctrina lustravit, sed persana proditione immaculatam fidem subvertere conatus est";.* For the text cited on p. 15, see P. Conte, *Chiesa e Primato nelle Lettere dei Papi del Secolo VII* (Milan: Vita e Pensiero, 1971), p. 302.

26. Cyprian, *Ep.* 59.14, CSEL 3/2:683. Romans 1:8 is a brief expression of thanksgiving, a conventional part of the greeting. He intimated that Christians around the Roman world were gratified by the knowledge that there were fellow Christians at the very heart of the empire. He was not making any assertion about the orthodoxy of the Roman Christian community.

27. Some non-Roman texts.

Optatus of Milevis (N. Africa, date c. 370) "This Victor of Garba was sent first, I will not say as a stone into a fountain (for he could not ruffle the pure waters of the Catholic people) ... *On the Schism of the Donatists* II.4, CSEL 26:38. Comment: Optatus was discussing the Donatist episcopal succession in Rome. He rejected it as a completely foreign incursion.

The emperor Theodosius I Decree: *Cunctos Populos* (date 380), C.T. 16.1.2, p. 440. "It is our will that all the peoples ... shall practice that religion which the divine Peter the apostle transmitted to the Romans, as the religion which he introduced makes clear even to this day. It is evident that this is the religion that is followed by the pontiff Damasus and by Peter, bishop of Alexandria, a man of apostolic sanctity. ..." Comment: The Roman faith is pointed out as a certain criterion for the orthodoxy which the emperor was espousing and enjoining. However, it is clear that, within this imperial guideline, Rome is not unique, as his recommendation of Peter of Alexander shows.

The Synod of Milan (date 390). Text: Ambrose, *Ep.* 42.5, PL 16:1125. "Let them believe the Apostles' Creed which the Roman Church has always kept undefiled. ..."

Jerome: In his commentary on Galatians (Bk. 2, Preface: date 387) and in *Ep.* 15.1 (c. 376-377), he mentioned Paul's praise of the faith of the Romans. In the latter letter, writing to Damasus he said: "Now that evil children have squandered their patrimony, you alone keep your heritage intact" (CSEL 54:62-63). In this letter, which is filled with effusive praise for Damasus, Jerome, the Roman Christian living in the East, mocked the doctrinal confusion prevailing in the East. One must beware of Jerome's exaggerations. In *Ep.* 127.9 (CSEL 56:152; date after 410), complaining of the "Origenist" wave hitting the West, he wrote: "And the muddy feet of heretics fouled the clear water of the faith of Rome. . . ."

Rufinus of Aquileia, *Commentary on the Apostles' Creed* 3 (date c. 400), CCL 20:136. "No heresy has ever had its origin there" (Rome). Comment: Rufinus is commenting on the fact that in some churches additions have been made to the first article of the creed out of necessity because of heresies. No such additions have been made in Rome.

Augustine Sermo 131.10 (Date: 417), PL 38:734. "For already two councils on this question have been sent to the apostolic see and replies have also come from there. The case is closed; would that the error might be finished!" *Contra duas Epistolas Pelagianorum* II.III.5 (date 420) CSEL 60:464. ". . . The letters of Pope Innocent of blessed memory, by which all doubt concerning this question, was removed. . . ." These statements have to be reviewed in the context of Augustine's eagerness for the successful and rapid overcoming of Pelagianism. In both instances it was to his own advantage to stress Roman authority. In the first, it was Innocent's confirmation of the African that assured widespread respect for the condemnation in the Church at large. In the second case, Augustine wished to eliminate any doubts raised by the vacillations of Zosimus.

Eusebius of Dorylaeum, Appeal to Leo (date: 449). ACO II.2.1, p. 79. ". . . You hold the right meaning and preserve unshaken the faith of Our Lord Jesus Christ."

Theodoret of Cyrrhus, Ep. 116, (date: 449). PG 83:1324-25. "For that holy see has precedence of all churches in the world for many reasons; and above all for this, that it is free of all taint of heresy, and that no bishop of false opinions has ever sat upon its throne, but it has kept the grace of the apostles undefiled." In the cases of Eusebius and Theodoret, we are dealing with the situation after Ephesus II in 449.

Both men had been condemned in the East and hoped Leo's intervention would restore them as well as orthodoxy against Eutyches and Dioscurus. Ignatius of Antioch, *Ep. ad. Romanos:* Prol., LCL 1:226.

28. Bishops of Tarraconensis to Hilary, *Ep.* 13.1, Thiel 155-156. Reparatus of Carthage and African bishops to John II (Coll. Avell. 85.5), CSEL 35:329. Hormisdas, *Ep.* 7.9, JK 774, Thiel 754-755.

29. Non-Roman use of Luke 22:31-32: Augustine *Ep.* 175.4; 176.2; CSEL 44:659, 665-666. These are the letters of the councils of Carthage and Milevis to Pope Innocent I in 416. Ambrose, *De Fide* IV.5.56, PL 16:628. Ambrosiaster, *Quaestiones Novi Testamenti* 79, CSEL 50:135. Roman use of Matt. 16:18b: Leo, *Sermo* 3.3, CCL 138:13. Simplicius, *Ep.* 3.5 (Coll. Avell. 56), JK 573, CSEL 35:127. Gelasius, *Ep.* 3.3, JK 620, Schwartz 50. Ambrose, *De Incarnationis dominicae Sacramento* 5.34, PL 16:827. On Augustine, see A. M. La Bonnardière, *"Tu es Petrus.* La Péricope 'Matthieu 16.13-23' dans l'oeuvre de Saint Augustin," *Irénikon* 34 (1961): 451-499. One Roman Catholic work that tends to take all patristic praise of Peter as testimony supporting the later Roman claims is J. Ludwig, *Die Primatworte Mt 16.18-19 in der altkirchlichen Exegese* (Münster: Aschendorff, 1952).

30. One suggestion that has been put forward as a possible explanation concerns the ancient view of a person's heavenly companion or protector. The Roman view is somewhat different in that it connects Peter's presence with the office and the individuals who hold it successively. On the pagan notion, see S. Mac-Cormack, "Roma, Constantinopolis, the Emperor and his Genius," *Classical Quarterly* 25 (1975): 131-150. Peter Chrysologus, *Ep.* to Eutyches, ACO II.3.1, p. 6. Ennodius, *Libellus pro Synodo*, CSEL 6:295. This is taken up in the *Dictatus Papae* 23, MGH.ES Tome II, Fasc. 1, 207.

31. On the Three Chapters, see E. Amann, DTC 15/2: 1868-1924 (written c. 1950). Pelagius I as a deacon wrote *In Defensione Trium Capitulorum* ed by R. Devreesse (StT 57, 1932).

32. Pelagius I *Ep.* 3.4-5; 10, JK 942; 939; Gasso 8-9, 31.

33. Pelagius I, *Ep.* 10.4; 11:3; JK 939; 938; Gasso 33; 36-37. Citation of 1 Peter 3:15: Vigilius to Justinian, JK 910 (Coll. Avell. 92.12), CSEL 35:352. Pelagius I, *Ep.* 11.10; 7:16, JK 938; 946, Gasso 39; 25. Pelagius II, *Ep.* 1.15 (to the bishops of Istria), JK 1054, ACO IV.2:106. What's wrong with change? Pelagius I, *Ep.* 19.3, JK 978, Gasso 56. Pelagius II, *Ep.* 1.15, JK 1054, ACO IV.2:106. Comment on Augustine and his *Retractationes:* Pelagius I, *Ep.* 19: 12ff., JK 978, Gasso 58-59.

34. Pelagius II, *Ep.* 1.5-6, 15; 3.59-60, JK 1054; 1056, ACO IV.2:105, 106, 119.
35. Gregory I, Reg. II, *Ep.* 49, Reg. IV. *Ep.* 4, JK 1203; 1275, MGH. *Ep.* 1:151; 236.
36. Columban, *Ep.* 1.4, Sancti Columbani Opera, ed. by G. S. M. Walker, SLH II:4-6. Ep. 5.5, SLH II:40 (to Pope Boniface IV).

14. Fallibility Instead of Infallibility?
A Brief History of the Interpretation of Galatians 2:11-14
Karlfried Froehlich

1. See the section on the biblical evidence in E. Dublanchy's article, "Infaillibilité du pape," DTC 7:1639-1655.
2. Two recent summaries of the history of this passage are available: G. H. M. Posthumus Meyjes, *De controverse tussen Petrus en Paulus: Galaten 2, 11 in de historie*, Inaugural Lecture at the University of Leiden (The Hague: Nijhoff, 1967), and H. Feld, "Papst und Apostel in Auseinandersetzung um die rechte Lehre: Die theologische Bedeutung von Gal. 2, 11-14 für das Petrusamt in moderner und alter Auslegung," *Grund und Grenzen des Dogmas*, H. Feld *et al.* (Freiburg: Herder, 1973), pp. 9-26. Still valuable for the patristic period is F. Overbeck, *Über die Auffassung des Streits des Paulus mit dem Petrus in Antiochien bei den Kirchenvätern (Galater 2,11ff)*. (Basel: 1877; reprint Darmstadt: Wissenschaftliche Buchgesellschaft, 1968).
3. The source is Jerome, *Commentary on Galatians*, PL 26:334C-336; 366A-367; cf. *Epistle* 112. 3. 11.
4. "You have in hostility withstood me, who am a firm rock, the foundation stone of the church. If you were not an enemy, then you would not slander me and revile my preaching in order that I may not be believed when I proclaim what I have heard in my own person from the Lord, as if I were undoubtedly condemned and you were acknowledged. And if you call me condemned, then you accuse God, who revealed Christ to me, and disparage him who called me blessed on account of the revelation." E. Hennecke, *New Testament Apocrypha*, ed. by W. Schneemelcher, trans. by R. M. Wilson (Philadelphia: Westminster, 1964), 2:123.
5. Irenaeus, *Adversus Haereses* 3. 13. 1.
6. Tertullian, *Adversus Marcionem* 1. 20 and 4. 3; cf. 5. 3, and *De praescriptione haereticorum* 23-24.

7. A. Harnack, "Petrus im Urteil der Kirchenfeinde des Altertums," *Festgabe für D. Dr. Karl Müller* (Tübingen: Mohr, 1922), pp. 3-4.

8. I. Lönning, "Paulus und Petrus. Gal. 2,11ff als kontroverstheologisches Fundamentalproblem," *Studia Theologica. Scandinavian Journal of Theology* 24 (1970) : 1-69.

9. Eusebius, *Ecclesiastical History* 1. 12. 2.

10. See Th. Schermann, *Propheten- und Apostellegenden nebst Jüngerkatalogen des Dorotheus und verwandter Texte, Texte und Untersuchungen*, 3rd Series, vol. 1, fascicle 3 (Leipzig: Hinrichs, 1907), pp. 302-303.

11. Jerome, *Commentary on Galatians 2*, PL 26:366A-367.

12. Chrysostom, *Commentary on Galatians 2*, PG 61:641-642; *Sermon on Galatians 2:11*, PG 51:371-388; cf. H. Feld, "Papst und Apostel," note 44.

13. Jerome, *Commentary on Galatians 2*, PL 26:363-367; cf. *Epistle* 112. 3. 4. Jerome himself interpreted Peter's action as an accommodation of the kind which Paul also practiced for the sake of the weaker Christians. He cited Paul's vow at Cenchreae (Acts 18:18), the Temple sacrifice (Acts 21:26), the circumcision of Timothy (Acts 16:3), and referred to 1 Cor. 9:20ff.

14. See especially P. Auvray, "Saint Jérôme et saint Augustin: La controverse au sujet de l'incident d'Antioch," *Recherches de Science Religieuse* 29 (1939): 594-610; J. Schmid, "Prolegomena," *S. S. Eusebii Hieronymi et Aurelii Augustini Epistolae Mutuae, Florilegium Patristicum* 22 (Bonn: Hanstein, 1930), pp. 14-22; and in English: W. J. Sparrow-Simpson, *The Letters of St. Augustine* (London: SPCK, 1919), pp. 218-241. An English translation of the pertinent letters may be found in the *Nicene and Post-Nicene Fathers*, ed. by Philip Schaff, First Series, vol. 1 (reprint: Grand Rapids: Eerdmans, 1974) (under Augustine's name: Epistles 28, 40, 67, 68, 73, 75, 82), and Second Series, vol. 6 (reprint, Grand Rapids: Eerdmans, 1954) (under Jerome's name: Epistles 56, 67, 101, 102, 110, 112, 116).

15. Note the imprecision in this translation of the Greek *kategnōsmenos (reprehensus)* in Jerome's Vulgate which steered the later interpretation toward a moral reading.

16. Augustine *Epistle* 82. 2. 16.

17. G. Meyjes, "De controverse," p. 13, assumes a decisive shift towards the Augustinian position in the 12th century only. However there seems to be no evidence for an earlier preference for Jerome. Feld's interpretation of the *Glossa ordinaria* as "preferring" Jerome ("Papst und Apostel," p. 20f.) is unwarranted. For Erasmus see the *Annotations to the New Testament, Des. Erasmi Opera Omnia*, vol. 6, ed. by

J. Clericus (Leiden, 1705; reprint Hildesheim: Olms, 1962), pp. 807-810, and H. Feld, "Papst und Apostel," p. 22.

18. *Epistle* 82. 2. 10.

19. *Epistle* 82. 2. 16; cf. 40. 4. 5.

20. *Epistle* 82. 2. 8. The terms appear already in Tertullian *Adversus Marcionem* 1. 20. For their meaning see F. Overbeck, *Über die Auffassung*, p. 11, n. 5.

21. Jerome, *Dialogue against the Pelagians*, PL 23:575; *Commentary on Philemon*, PL 26:648.

22. E.g., Godfrey of Vendôme, PL 157:220. The text from the *Glossa Ordinaria* (H. Feld, "Papst und Apostel," p. 20) belongs here.

23. Peter Damian, PL 145:709-710.

24. "Peter . . . received with the mildness of a holy and meek humility the reproach advanced by Paul for his good, in the freedom of charity. And thus, by not refusing to be corrected even by his inferior for having accidentally left the path of uprightness, he gave a more precious and holy example to posterity than Paul who demonstrated that those inferior in authority might confidently dare to defend the truth of the gospel by opposing their elders with all due regard to fraternal charity" *(Epistle* 82. 2. 22).

25. On various modern attempts to clarify the outcome see H. Feld, "Christus Diener der Sünde. Zum Ausgang des Streits zwischen Petrus und Paulus," *Theologische Quartalschrift* 153 (1973): 119-131; and "Papst und Apostel," p. 15-17.

26. Cyprian *Epistle* 71. 3. For Cyprian's interpretation and its influence on Augustine, see G. Haendler, "Cyprians Auslegung zu Gal. 2,11ff., ThLZ 97 (1972): 561-567.

27. *S. Thomae Aquinatis Doctoris Angelici super Epistolas S. Pauli Lectura*, ed. R. Cai (Torino: Marietti, 1953), pp. 582-584; an English translation may be found in *Aquinas Scripture Series*, tr. by F. R. Larcher, O.P. (Albany: Magi Books, 1966), 1:46.

28. The thrust in many cases was the justification of a bold rebuke of higher authority—of an emperor (Elipandus of Toledo, PL 96:869) and a pope (Hincmar of Rheims, PL 125:749). Further texts, many of them dependent on Pope Gregory the Great, *Homilies in Ezekiel* (PL 76:1002-1003) and the *Regula Pastoralis* (PL 77:43) in G. Meyjes, "De controverse," pp. 11-12, and n. 34.

29. Alger of Liège, *On Mercy and Justice* 1.34, PL 180:869. On this theme in Aquinas cf. note 35 below.

30. "Paul rebuked Peter who was the prince of the apostles. This suggests the understanding that subordinates may reproach their superiors if the latter are blameworthy. But this is easily refuted when one takes

note of the reason why Peter was rebuked. Peter
forced the Gentiles to judaize and to desert the truth
of the gospel when he associated with the Jews and
withdrew secretly from eating with the Gentiles. Now,
to leave the realm of faith is in itself the same as
luring others away from the faith by word or example. Thus by this example it is not proved that prelates may be rebuked by their subjects unless they
leave the realm of faith or force others to do so."
Decretum C. II q. 7 c. 39 *(Corpus Iuris Canonici,* ed.
by E. Friedberg [Leipzig: Tauchnitz, 1879; reprint
Graz: Akademische Druck- und Verlagsanstalt,
1959], 1:495-496.)

31. Decretum d. 40 c. 6 (ed. by Friedberg, 1:146). For
the history of the text see B. Tierney, *Foundations of
the Conciliar Theory,* Cambridge Studies in Medieval
Life and Thought, n.s. 4 (Cambridge University
Press, 1955), pp. 57-67, and *idem, The Origins of
Papal Infallibility,* Studies in the History of Chris-
tian Thought, ed. by H. A. Oberman, vol. 6 (Leiden:
Brill: 1972), p. 33.

32. For their role in the medieval development of a
teaching office, see Yves Congar, O.P., "Theologians
and the Magisterium in the West: From the Gregorian Reform to the Council of Trent," *Chicago
Studies* 17, no. 2: *The Magisterium, the Theologian,
and the Educator* (summer 1978): 210-224.

33. Meyjes suggests this terminology as an interpretation
of the high medieval preoccupation with Gal. 2:11-14:
"Thus, besides the hierarchical succession symbolized
by Peter, there existed a specific succession of teaching symbolized by Paul" (G. Meyjes, "De controverse," p. 15).

34. *Decretum* d. 20. c. 1 *(Corpus Iuris Canonici,* ed. Friedberg, 1:65). For an English translation and comments
see Congar, "Theologians and the Magisterium," pp.
214-215. Gratian drew on an older tradition which distinguished a "key of power" from a "key of knowledge" or of "discretion." See B. Tierney, *Origins of
Papal Infallibility,* pp. 39-45, and L. Hödl, *Die Geschichte der scholastischen Literatur und der Theologie der Schlüsselgewalt,* part 1. Beiträge zur Geschichte der Philosophie und Theologie des Mittelalters, vol. 38:4 (Münster: Aschendorff, 1960), especially the collections of texts.

35. For texts concerning the distinction between the two
teaching offices see Y. Congar, "Theologians and the
Magisterium," pp. 218-219. Most instructive in terms
of the theme of Pauline succession through the office
of the masters is one of Aquinas' early *Principia,*
"Rigans Montes" *(Sancti Thomae Aquinatis . . .
Opera Omnia, secundum impressionem Petri Fioccar-*

dori, Parmae, 1852-1873 . . . reimpressa. Cum nova introductione generali anglice scripta a Vernon J. Bourke (New York: Musurgia, 1948), 1:xxxvi-xxxi, and his Prologue, "Vas electionis est mihi," to the Commentary on the Pauline Epistles *(ibid.,* 13:1-3). The reference to Gal. 2:11-14 is found in the *Summa Theologiae* IIaIIae q. 33 a. 4 ad 2: "To oppose anyone to his face in public goes beyond the due measure of fraternal correction; and for this reason Paul would not have rebuked Peter if he were not in some way his equal as far as the defence of the faith was concerned. . . . Note, however, that when there is real danger to the faith, subjects must rebuke their superiors even publicly. On this account Paul, who was subject to Peter, publicly rebuked him when there was imminent danger of scandal in a matter of faith" *St. Thomas Aquinas: Summa Theologiae,* Blackfriars Edition (New York: McGraw Hill, 1975), 35:287, 289. As Meyjes, "De controverse," pp. 14-15 correctly notes, the argument has to be seen in the context of the masters' role in the church. Cf. also the otherwise important study by H. Schüssler, *Der Primat der Heiligen Schrift als theologisches und kanonistisches Problem im Spätmittelalter,* Veröffentlichungen des Instituts für Europäische Geschichte Mainz, vol. 86 (Wiesbaden: Steiner, 1977), pp. 53-55, who does not, however, touch on this subject.

36. A full study of the role of Gal. 2:11-14 in the controversies of the 14th century is much needed. In the meantime, cf. for Ockham: Ph. Boehner, *Collected Articles on Ockham,* ed. by E. M. Buytaert (St. Bonaventure, N.Y.: Franciscan Institute, 1958), pp. 447-454; for Marsilius: A. Gewirth, ed., *Marsilius of Padua: The Defender of Peace,* Records of Civilization, vol. 46, part 2 (New York: Columbia University Press, 1956), Discourse II, chaps. 16 (pp. 241-253) and 28 (pp. 371-383); for Huss: P. de Vooght, *Hussiana,* BHRE, vol. 35 (Louvain: Bibliothèque de l'Université, 1960), pp. 193-194.

37. Conrad of Gelnhausen's argument should be mentioned here; it starts with a distinction between the *Ecclesia Romana* as a "particular" church and the *Ecclesia Universalis.* Only the latter can be certain of the unfailing guidance of the Lord promised in Luke 22:32. Claims by any *Ecclesia Particularis* to possess what belongs to the universal Church are blasphemous. Then follows the historical proof; popes of the Roman Church have erred. The standard examples are Pope Marcellinus and Pope Anastasius II. Peter's denial and the Antioch scene belong to the same line of proof. See the text in F. Bliemetzrieder, *Literarische Polemik zu Beginn des grossen abendländischen*

Schismas, Publikationen des österreichischen Historischen Instituts in Rom, vol. 1 (Vienna: F. Tempsky; Leipzig: G. Freytag, 1910; reprint, New York: Johnson Reprint Co., 1967), pp. 122-123, 128-131).

38. A good example is a text from d'Ailly's treatise, *De Materia Concilii Generalis* of 1403: " . . . authority and decision of the council are to be attributed to the Holy Spirit since it says there (Acts 15:28), 'It pleased the Holy Spirit and us.' From this some argue that the general council cannot err in those matters that pertain to faith. This is likewise proved by Jesus' word (Luke 22:32), 'Peter, I have prayed for you that your faith may not fail,' because this is not said of Peter's personal faith, since he himself erred, but of the faith of the universal church which is represented in the general council and about which it is said there, too (Matthew 16:18), 'the gates of the underworld will not prevail against it,' i.e., the church. It does not say, 'against you,' i.e., Peter. It appears therefore that the judgment of the council is preferable to the judgment of the pope since the pope can err in matters pertaining to faith as did Peter about whom Paul says in Galatians 2 that he 'resisted him to his face because he was blameworthy, not walking upright according to the truth of the gospel' " (F. Oakley, *The Political Thought of Pierre d'Ailly* [New Haven: Yale University Press, 1964], p. 306f). For Gerson, cf. the remarks by G. Meyjes, "De controverse," p. 16, and L. Pascoe, *Jean Gerson: Principles of Church Reform,* Studies in Medieval and Reformation Thought, ed. by H. A. Oberman, vol. 7 (Leiden: Brill, 1973), pp. 90-91.

39. F. Oakley, *Political Thought,* p. 310.

40. K. Holl, "Der Streit zwischen Petrus und Paulus zu Antiochien in seiner Bedeutung für Luthers innere Entwicklung," *Gesammelte Aufsätze, III: Der Westen* (Tübingen: Mohr, 1928), pp. 134-146; for Inge Lönning, see note 8 above.

41. For this aspect see especially H. Feld, "Lutherus Apostolus: Kirchliches Amt und apostolische Verantwortung in der Galaterbrief-Auslegung Martin Luthers," *Wort Gottes in der Zeit.* Festschrift K. H. Schelkle, ed. by H. Feld and J. Nolte (Düsseldorf: Patmos, 1973), pp. 288-304. Cf. also H. Feld, "Papst und Apostel," pp. 22-24, and Y. Congar, *Vraie et fausse réforme dans l'Eglise,* Unam Sanctam, vol. 72, 2nd ed. (Paris: Cerf, 1968), pp. 455-463.

42. K. Holl, "Der Streit," p. 138; I. Lönning, "Paulus und Petrus," p. 15; H. Feld, "Lutherus Apostolus," pp. 290-291.

43. I. Lönning, "Paulus und Petrus," pp. 31ff.

44. Lönning discusses Joachim Lange as a representative figure and mentions J. Chr. Schomerus ("Paulus und Petrus," pp. 34-35).
45. On this point see W. G. Kümmel, *The New Testament: The History of the Investigation of Its Problems*, trans. by S. M. Gilmour and H. C. Kee (Nashville: Abingdon Press, 1972), pp. 127-133.
46. I. Lönning, "Paulus und Petrus," pp. 40ff.
47. See H. Feld, "Papst und Apostel," p. 26; "Lutherus Apostolus," pp. 302-304.
48. " . . . so kann es in der Kirche doch durchaus das charismatische und prophetische 'Widerstehen ins Angesicht' (Gal. 2,11) geben" *(Lexikon für Theologie und Kirche. Das zweite Vatikanische Konzil*, H. Vorgrimler, general ed. (Freiburg: Herder, 1966), 1:237). The English translation in H. Vorgrimler, ed., *Commentary on the Documents of Vatican II* (New York: Herder and Herder, 1967), 1:202 obscures the point.
49. Y. Congar has reminded us that the modern use of the term *magisterium* to refer solely to *the* (papal) *magisterium* is of very recent origin: "Pour une histoire sémantique du terme 'Magisterium,' " *Revue des sciences philosophiques et théologiques* 60 (1976) :85-98.
50. This question is raised in a study by A. Dulles, "The Magisterium in History: A Theological Reflection," *Chicago Studies* 17, no. 2: *The Magisterium, the Theologian, and the Educator)* (summer 1978) : 273, 281.

15. Infallibility as Charism at Vatican I

Kilian McDonnell

1. M 54:1214A.
2. *Ibid.*
3. F. Kattenbusch, "Das *somation tais aletheias* bei Irenaeus," ZNW 10 (1909) : 331-332; cf. also B. D. Dupuy, "Le magistère, service de la Parole," *L'Infaillibilité de l'Église* (Chevetogne: Éditions de Chevetogne, 1962), p. 72.
4. Adversus Haereses, IV, 26, 2, (SC 100:718). For a discussion of the different interpretations of texts from Irenaeus, cf. Karl Muller, "Kleine Beiträge zur alten Kirchengeschichte," ZNW 23 (1924) : 214-222. For a bibliography of the discussion of the concept in Irenaeus, cf. Jerome D. Quinn, "Charisma veritatis certum: Irenaeus, Adversus Haereses, IV, 26, 2," TS 39 (1978) : 520-525.
5. Reinhold Seeberg, *Lehrbuch der Dogmengeschichte*,

3rd ed. (Leipzig: A. Deichertschen Verlagsbuch-
handlung, 1922), 1:383.

6. M 52:877A.

7. M 52:878A.

8. Gustave Thils, *L'infaillibilité pontificale: source,
conditions, limites* (Gembloux: Éditions J. Duculot,
S. A. 1969), p. 8. This section of the essay is indebted
to Thils' work.

9. M 51:1001C.

10. *Ibid.*

11. M 51:1031A.

12. M 51:1004B.

13. M 52:36A.

14. M 52:765A.

15. M 51:820D.

16. M 51:821B.

17. M 52:877A.

18. M 52:916D.

19. M 51:821B. Cf. also M 51:820D.

20. M 51:699B.

21. Ibid. Cf. also Manning's pastoral letter to the clergy
published after the council: *The Vatican Council and
its Definitions*, 3rd ed. (New York: D. and J. Sadlier,
1880), pp. 91, 103. In a number of places he refers to
infallibility as a charism, cf. *ibid.*, pp. 91, 97, 103, 147.

22. M 52:1334.

23. Gustave Thils, "La 'Locutio ex Cathedra' et L'Esprit-
Saint," *Ecclesia a Spiritu Sancto edocta: Mélanges
théologiques*, Hommage à Mgr. Gerard Philips (Gembloux: Éditions J. Duculot, S. A., 1970), p. 119.

24. *Lumen Gentium*, 25.

25. *Ibid.*

26. M 52:1334D.

27. M 52:1216B.

28. M 52:1216C.

29. M 52:1215D.

30. *L'infaillibilité pontificale*, p. 175. Thils formulation
is a recasting, indeed a transformation, of a suggestion made in the council by a group of maximalists,
namely "definitiones esse ex sese irreformabiles, quin
sit necessarius consensus episcoporum, sive antece-
dens, sive concomitans, sive subsequens." Cf. Heinrich
Fries, "Ex sese, non ex consensu ecclesiae," *Volk
Gottes*, Festgabe für Josef Höfer (Freiburg: Herder,
1967), p. 489.

31. M 52:1171A. Cf. also Umberto Betti, *La Constituzione
Dommatica "Pastor Aeternus" del Concilio Vaticano I*
(Roma: Pontificio Ateneo Antonianum, 1961), p. 392.

32. *The Dublin Review*, New Series, 13 (1869): 477-480.
Ward is here talking about "dogmatic facts" such as
the Church declaring infallibly that *Augustinus* contains five certain propositions in its legitimate objec-

tive sense. For such an infallible judgment the Church needs a new inspiration. Cf. also Cuthbert Butler, *The Vatican Council* (New York: Longmans, Green, 1930), 1:72-75.

33. *Ibid.*, p. 75.
34. M 49:627C.
35. M 51:542D. Cf. also M 52:746A; M 52:743A. On one occasion, when it was suggested by a speaker in the Council (Guidi) that some fathers might admit that infallibility opens the way to a new and particular revelation, the text indicates that there was a rumble of murmuring (M 52:743A). Guidi did not hold that view.
36. C. Butler, *Vatican Council*, 1:139.
37. M 52:906C.
38. M 52:1334B.
39. M 52:1220B.
40. M 52:1213D.
41. M 52: 761A.
42. M 52:746B-C.
43. M 52:741A; M 52:745B-C.
44. M 52:145B.
45. M 52:744D.
46. M 52:745B-C.
47. M 52:747C.
48. M 52:741D.
49. M 52:742A.
50. M 52:67B.
51. M 52:741D. D'Avanzo showed himself slightly taken aback by the use of the drunkard to argue the point of infallibility (M 52:762B).
52. Roger Aubert, *Le pontificat de Pie IX*, Histoire de Église 21, ed. by A. Fliche and V. Martin (Paris: Bloud and Gay, 1952), p. 353.
53. M 52:763D.
54. In defending his position to the pope, Guidi cited the authorities from tradition. It was at this point that Pius IX said: "La Tradizione son'io!" ("I am tradition!"). Theodor Granderath considers this a piece of curial gossip; see *Geschichte des Vatikanischen Konzils* (Freiburg: Herder, 1906), 3:396, 397. But it seems to be as well established as anything which is said in a private audience (Cf. R. Aubert, *Le pontificat*, p. 354, n. 3).
55. M 52:762B.
56. M 52:762C.
57. *Ibid.*
58. M 52:762D, 763A.
59. M 52:765A.
60. *Ibid.*
61. M 52:765B.
62. M 52:1212D.

63. M 52:1213A.
64. *Ibid.*
65. M 52:1213B.
66. *Ibid.*
67. *Ibid.*
68. M 52:1213C.
69. *Ibid.*
70. M 52:1227A.
71. *Summa Theologica*, III, tit. 22, c. 3 III (Veronae, 1740), p. 118D. Cf. also Umberto Betti, "L'autorita di S. Antonio e la questione dell'infallibilitá pontifica al concilio Vaticano," *Memorie Domenicane* 76(1959) : 173-192.
72. M 52:878D.
73. Robertus Bellarminus, *De Romano Pontifice*, lib. iv, c. 7, *Opera omnia* (Naples: Giuliano, 1857), 1:484B. Cf. M 52:841C.
74. M 52:122A-B.
75. M 52:1214B.
76. M 52:1214C.
77. M 52:1214D.
78. Umberto Betti undoubtedly goes beyond the texts of Vatican I when he says that the council "defined" that the "pontifical prerogative is strictly personal." Rather the council asserted (not defined) that infallibility has a personal quality about it and from the text one would gather that the word *personal* does not adequately express the full character of the prerogative (cf. U. Betti, *La Costituzione Dommatica "Pastor Aeternus" de Concilio Vaticano I*, p. 634).
79. M 52:1334D.
80. *Lumen Gentium* 25.
81. *Ibid.*
82. M 52:1213A.
83. This restriction to the act should not be unduly pushed. The act should include the preparatory development. Cf. G. Thils, "La 'Locutio ex Cathedra, et l'Esprit-Saint," *Ecclesia a Spiritu Sancto edocta*, p. 123.
84. G. Thils, *L'infaillibilité pontificale*, pp. 177, 178.

16. The Historical Background of Vatican I

Joseph A. Burgess

1. Yves Congar, "Bulletin d'ecclésiologie. Église, Conciles, Papauté," *Revue des Sciences Philosophiques et Théologiques* 62 (1978) : 81, 88.
2. Theodor Granderath, S.J., *Geschichte des Vatikanischen Konzils*, 3 vols. (Freiburg: Herdersche Ver-

lagshandlung, 1903-1906); Johann Friedrich, *Geschichte des Vatikanischen Konzils*, 3 vols. (Bonn: Neusser, 1877-1887); George H. Williams, "Omnium christianorum pastor et doctor. Vatican I et l'Angleterre Victorienne," *Nouvelle Revue Theologique* 96 1974) : 113-146, 337-365; August B. Hasler, *Pius IX. (1846-1878), Päpstliche Unfehlbarkeit und 1. Vaticanisches Konzil. Dogmatisierung und Durchsetzung einer Ideologie*, Päpste und Papsttum, vol. 12, 1 and 2 (Stuttgart: Hiersemann, 1977).

3. Kaarlo Jäntere, *Die Römische Weltreichsidee und die Entstehung der Weltlichen Macht des Papstes*, Annales Universitatis Turkuensis, Series B, vol. 21 (Turku: Turun Yliopiston Kustantama, 1936) : Franz Kampers, "Roma aeterna und sancta Dei ecclesia rei publicae Romanorum," *Historisches Jahrbuch*, Bonn 44 (1924) : 240-249; Fedor H. G. H. Schneider, *Rom und Romgedanke im Mittelalter; Die Geistigen Grundlagen der Renaissance* (Munich: Drei Masken Verlag, 1926) : Clemens Bauer, "Bild der Kirche—Abbild der Gesellschaft," *Hochland* 48 (1955-1956) : 519-527.

4. Yves Congar, "L'Ecclésiologie, de la Révolution française au Concile du Vatican, sous le signe de l'affirmation de l'autorité." *L'ecclésiologie au XIXe Siècle*, Unam Sanctam 34 (Paris: Les Éditions du Cerf, 1960), p. 79.

5. Joseph N. Moody, "I. From Old Regime to Democratic Society," *Church and Society: Catholic Social and Political Thought and Movements, 1789-1950*, ed. by J. N. Moody (New York: Arts, Inc., 1953), p. 137.

6. Y. Congar, "L'Ecclésiologie," p. 97; A. Hasler, *Pius IX*, pp. 10-11.

7. Roger Aubert, "La géographie ecclésiologique au XIXe siècle," *L'Ecclésiologie au XIXe Siècle*, Unam Sanctam 34 (Paris: Les Éditions du Cerf, 1960), p. 31.

8. Hermann J. Pottmeyer, *Unfehlbarkeit und Souveränität. Die päpstliche Unfehlbarkeit im System der Ultramontanen Ekklesiologie des 19. Jahrhunderts*, Tübinger Theologische Studien 5 (Mainz: Matthias-Grünewald Verlag, 1975), p. 346.

9. Hubert Jedin, *A History of the Council of Trent*, vol. 1, trans. by Ernest Graf (London: Thomas Nelson and Sons, Ltd., 1957), p. 241.

10. Y. Congar, "L'Ecclésiologie," p. 98.

11. K. Jäntere, *Weltreichsidee*, pp. 295, 350.

12. Roger Aubert, *Le pontificat de Pie IX (1846-1878)*, Histoire de L'Église 21, ed. by A. Fliche and V. Martin (Paris: Bloud and Gay, 1952), pp. 262-263.

13. Fritz Vigener, *Bischofsamt und Papstgewalt*, Kirche und Konfession 6 (Göttingen: Vandenhoeck and Ruprecht, 1964), pp. 46-48; R. Aubert, *Le pontificat*, p. 263.

14. Hermann J. Pottmeyer, " 'Auctoritas suprema ideoque infallibilis,' Das Missverständnis der päpstlichen Unfehlbarkeit als Souveränität und seine historischen Bedingungen," *Konzil und Papst. Historische Beiträge zur Frage der höchsten Gewalt in der Kirche,* Festgabe für Hermann Tüchle, ed. by Georg Schwaiger (Munich, Paderborn, Vienna: Schöningh, 1975), pp. 508-510.

15. R. Aubert, *Le pontificat,* pp. 288-289, 300.

16. Klaus Schatz, S.J., *Kirchenbild und päpstliche Unfehlbarkeit bei den deutschsprachigen Minoritätsbischöfen auf dem 1. Vatikanum,* Miscellanea Historiae Pontificiae 40 (Rome: Università Gregoriana Editrice, 1975), p. 45.

17. Rudolf Lill, "Historische Voraussetzungen des Dogmas vom Universalepiskopat und von der Unfehlbarkeit des Papstes," *Stimmen der Zeit* 186 (1970): 298.

18. A. Hasler, *Pius IX,* pp. 83-84, 115.

19. R. Aubert, *Le pontificat,* p. 287.

20. *Ibid.,* pp. 287, 289.

21. H. Pottmeyer, "Auctoritas," pp. 510, 513; R. Aubert, *Le pontificat,* p. 300; Yves Congar, *L'Église de saint Augustin à l'époque moderne,* Histoire des Dogmas 3 (Paris: Les Éditiones du Cerf, 1970), p. 427.

22. R. Hill, "Voraussetzungen," pp. 297, 300; R. Aubert, *Le pontificat,* p. 288.

23. Karl von Hase, *Handbuch der Protestantischen Polemik gegen die Römisch-Katholische Kirche,* 7th ed. (Leipzig: Breitkopf and Härtel, 1900), p. 232.

24. R. Aubert, *Le Pontificat,* pp. 272, 287; R. Lill, "Voraussetzungen," p. 299; K. Schatz, *Kirchenbild,* p. 77; A. Haseler, *Pius IX,* p. 27.

25. Joseph N. Moody, "The Church and the New Forces in Western Europe and Italy," *Church and Society: Catholic Social and Political Thought and Movements, 1789-1950,* ed. J. N. Moody (New York: Arts, Inc., 1953), pp. 31, 35.

26. Victor Conzemius, "Les foyers internationaux du catholicisme libéral hors de France au XIXe siècle: esquisse d'une géographie historique," *Les catholiques liberaux au XIXᵉ siècle,* Actes du Colloque international d' histoire religieuse de Grenoble des 30 septembre 3 octobre 1971, Collection du Centre d'Histoire du Catholicisme 11 (Grenoble: Presses Universitaires de Grenoble, 1974), p. 50.

27. Carl Mirbt, *Geschichte der katholischen Kirche von der Mitte des 18. Jahrhunderts bis zum Vatikanischen Konzil,* Sammlung Göschen (Berlin and Leipzig: G. J. Göschen'sche Verlagshandlung, 1913), p. 63.

28. Friedrich Heyer, *Die katholische Kirche von 1648 bis*

1870, Die Kirche in ihrer Geschichte, vol. 4, no. 1 (Göttingen: Vandenhoeck and Ruprecht, 1963), p. 123.

29. Ulrich Nembach, *Die Stellung der evangelischen Kirche und ihrer Presse zum ersten vatikanischen Konzil* (Zürich: EVZ-Verlag, 1962), p. 56.

30. R. Aubert, *Le pontificat*, pp. 277, 286; Victor Conzemius, "Das I. Vatikanum im Bannkreis der päpstlichen Autorität," *Die päpstliche Autorität im katholischen Selbstverständnis des 19. und 20. Jahrhunderts*, ed. by Erika Weinzierl, Forschungsgespräche des Internationalen Forschungszentrums für Grundfragen der Wissenschaften Salzburg 11 (Salzburg, Munich: Universitätsverlag Anton Pustet, 1970), pp. 75-76.

31. Manfred Weitlauff, "Die Dogmatisierung der Immaculata Conceptio (1854) und die Stellungnahme der Münchener Theologischen Fakultät," *Konzil und Papst. Historische Beiträge zur Frage der höchsten Gewalt in der Kirche*, Festgabe für Hermann Tüchle, ed. by Georg Schwaiger (Munich, Paderborn, Vienna: Schöningh, 1975), pp. 478-481; for the American point of view, cf. James Hennessy, "A prelude to Vatican I: American bishops and the definition of the Immaculate Conception," TS 25 (1964): 409-419.

32. M. Weitlauff, "Dogmatisierung," p. 483.

33. Owen Chadwick, *The Secularization of the European Mind in the Nineteenth Century* (Cambridge: Cambridge University Press, 1975), pp. 138-139.

34. R. Aubert, *Le pontificat*, p. 225.

35. Friedrich Engel-Janosi, "Liberaler Katholizismus und päpstliche Autorität bis zum Syllabus," *Die päpstliche Autorität im katholischen Selbstverständnis des 19. und 20. Jahrhunderts*, ed. by Erika Weinzierl, Forschungsgespräche des Internationalen Forschungszentrums für Grundfragen der Wissenschaften Salzburg 11 (Salzburg, Munich: Universitätsverlag Anton Pustet, 1970), p. 50.

36. Cuthbert Butler, *The Vatican Council, 1869-1870*, ed. by Christopher Butler, Fontana Library (New York: Collins, 1962), p. 473; Damian McElrath, *The Syllabus of Pius IX. Some Reactions in England*, BRHE 39 (Louvain: Publications Universitaires de Louvain, 1964), pp. 205-206.

37. K. Schatz, *Kirchenbild*, p. 486.

38. Eugene Cecconi, *Histoire du Concil du Vatican d'après les Documents Originaux*, trans. Jules Bonhomme and D. Duvillard (Paris: Librairie Victor Lecoffre, 1887), vol. 3, pp. 202-212, 197; Roger Aubert, *Vaticanum I*, Geschichte der ökumenischen Konzilien 12, ed. by C. Dumiege and H. Bacht (Mainz: Grünewald, 1965), pp. 299-309.

39. R. Lill, "Voraussetzungen," pp. 299, 301; Y. Congar, "Ecclésiologie," p. 104; Y. Congar, "Bulletin," p. 87.

40. R. Aubert, *Le pontificat*, p. 277.
41. A. Hasler, *Pius IX*, pp. 16-18.
42. R. Aubert, *Le pontificat*, pp. 277, 287, 289.
43. *Ibid.*, pp. 289-295. On the extent and implications of the papal cult, see: R. Aubert, *Le pontificat*, pp. 302-303; René Laurentin, "IV. Peter as the foundation Stone in the Present Uncertainty," *Concilium*, N.S. 3, no. 9 (1973) : 102-105; Rudolf Zinnhobler, "Pius IX. in der katholischen Literatur seiner Zeit," *Konzil und Papst. Historische Beiträge zur Frage der höchsten Gewalt in der Kirche*, Festgabe für Hermann Tüchle, ed. Georg Schwaiger (Munich, Paderborn, Vienna: Schöningh, 1975), 387-432; Erika Weinzierl, "Das Selbstverständnis der päpstlichen Autorität bei Pius XII," *Die päpstliche Autorität im katholischen Selbstverständnis des 19. und 20. Jahrhunderts*, ed. by Erika Weinzierl, Forschungsgespräche des Internationalen Forschungszentrums für Grundfragen der Wissenschaften Salzburg 11 (Salzburg, Munich: Universitätsverlag Anton Pustet, 1970), p. 214; E. Weinzierl, "Diskussionen, Pius XII," *ibid.*, pp. 234-237.
44. K. Schatz, *Kirchenbild*, p. 487.
45. Gerald A. McCool, *Catholic Theology in the Nineteenth Century. The Quest for a Unitary Method* (New York: Seabury Press, 1977), a rehabilitation of Neo-Thomism, has described this intellectual setting. His description of the historical setting is, however, too generalized (see esp. pp. 17-36).
46. O. Chadwick, *Secularization*, pp. 112-113.
47. See G. McCool, *Catholic Theology*, and Heinrich Fries and Georg Schwaiger, eds., *Katholische Theologen Deutschlands im 19. Jahrhundert*, 3 vols. (Munich: Kösel, 1975).
48. Y. Congar, "Ecclésiologie," p. 100.
49. R. Lill, "Voraussetzungen," p. 299.
50. Cataline G. Arévalo, S.J., *Some Aspects of the Theology of the Mystical Body of Christ in the Ecclesiology of Giovanni Perrone, Carlo Passaglia and Clemens Schrader. Theologians of the Roman College in the Mid-Nineteenth Century* (Rome: Pontificae Universitatis Gregorianae, 1959), p. 2.
51. K. Blei, *De Onfeilbaarheid von de Kerk* (Kampen: J. H. Kok, 1972), p. 76, cf. 71-77; George Lindbeck, "The Reformation and the Infallibility Debate," see above, p. 113.
52. Victor Conzemius, "Das I. Vatikanum in Bannkreis der päpstlichen Autorität, *Die päpstliche Autorität*, p. 79.
53. Y. Congar, *L'Église*, pp. 428-429.
54. R. Aubert, "La géographie ecclésiologique," p. 18, citing Latreille.

55. Claude Langlois, "Die Unfehlbarkeit—eine neue Idee des 19. Jahrhunderts," *Fehlbar. Eine Bilanz*, ed. by Hans Küng: (Zürich, Einseideln, Cologne: Benziger Verlag, 1973), p. 154.

56. R. Lill, "Voraussetzungen,: p. 295; Y. Congar, *L'Église*, pp. 415-416; H. Pottmeyer, *Unfehlbarkeit*, pp. 395-408, esp. p. 399; cf. Joseph de Maistre, *Oeuvres du Comte J. de Maistre*, publiées par M. L'Abbé Migne (Paris: Chez L'Éditeur, 1841), pp. 243, 496-497.

57. K. Schatz, *Kirchenbild*, pp. 487, 492.

58. K. Blei, *Onfeilbaarheid*, pp. 77-82.

59. Joseph N. Moody, "I. From Old Regime to Democratic Society," *Church and Society*, p. 103.

60. K. Schatz, *Kirchenbild*, pp. 9, 492; cf. Georg Schwaiger, "Der Hintergrund des Konzils: Papsttum und Kirche in der Welt des 19. Jahrhunderts," *Hundert Jahre nach dem Ersten Vatikanum*, ed. by Georg Schwaiger (Regensburg: Pustet, 1970), p. 19; Victor Conzemius, "Liberaler Katholizismus in England," *Kirchen und Liberalismus im 19. Jahrhundert*, Studien zur Theologie und Geistesgeschichte des Neunzehnten Jahrhunderts 19, ed. by Martin Schmidt and Georg Schwaiger (Göttingen: Vandenhoeck and Ruprecht, 1976), p. 176. "Gallicanism is rationalism," wrote Manning in a pastoral letter in 1867 (Y. Congar, "Ecclésiologie," p. 105).

61. K. Schatz, *Kirchenbild*, p. 489.

62. Roger Aubert, "Resumé des discussions," *L'Ecclésiologie au XIXᵉ Siècle*, Unam Sanctam 34 (Paris: Les Éditions du Cerf, 1960), p. 376.

63. O. Rousseau, "Les attitudes de pensée concernant l'unité chrétienne au XIXᵉ siècle," *L'Ecclésiologie au XIXᵉ Siècle*, Unam Sanctam 34 (Paris: Les Éditions du Cerf, 1960), p. 373.

64. Roger Aubert, "L'ecclésiologie au concile du Vatican," *Le Concile et les Conciles* (Paris: Éditiones de Chevetogne and Éditions du Cerf, 1960), p. 280; R. Lill, "Voraussetzungen," p. 300; V. Conzemius, "Das I. Vatikanum im Bannkreis der päpstlichen Autorität," *Die päpstliche Autorität*, p. 72; Robert Aubert, "Motivations théologiques et extra-théologiques des partisans et des adversaires de la définition dogmatique de l'infaillibilité du Pape à Vatican I," *L'Infaillibilité, Son Aspect Philosophique et Théologique*, Actes du Colloque organisé par le Centre International d'Études Humanistes et par l'Institut d'Études Philosophiques de Rome, 5-12 Janvier, 1970, ed. by E. Castelli (Paris: Aubier, 1970), p. 96.

65. A Hasler, *Pius IX*, pp. 12-13.

66. See Harding Meyer, *Das Wort Pius' IX: "Die Tradition bin ich." Päpstliche Unfehlbarkeit und apostol-*

ische Tradition in den Debatten und Dekreten des Vatikanum I, Theologische Existenz Heute, N. F. no. 122 (Munich: Chr. Kaiser Verlag, 1965), p. 17; the same position is held today by Hans Küng, *Strukturen der Kirche,* Quaestiones Disputatae 17 (Freiburg, Basel, Vienna: Herder, 1962), p. 331, and R. Aubert, "Ekklesiologie," p. 315. R. Aubert later modified his opinion, concluding that that is going "too far" (R. Aubert, *Vatikanum I,* p. 284).

67. K. Schatz, *Kirchenbild,* p. 492.
68. H. Pottmeyer, *Unfehlbarkeit,* p. 16; Gustave Thils, *L'infaillibilité pontificale: source - conditions - limites* (Gembloux: Editions J. Duculot, S.A., 1968), p. 254.
69. Joseph N. Moody, "I. From Old Regime to Democratic Society," *Church and Society,* p. 115.
70. H. Pottmeyer, *Unfehlbarkeit,* p. 420; cf. pp. 408 and 416.
71. H. Pottmeyer, "Auctoritas," pp. 519-520.
72. See for example, F. Heyer, *Kirche,* p. 123; Klaus-Martin Beckmann, *Unitas Ecclesiae. Eine systematische Studie zur Theologiegeschichte des 19. Jahrhunderts (Gütersloh: Gütersloher Verlagshaus Gerd Mohn, 1967); Reiner Strunk, *Politische Ekklesiologie im Zeitalter der Revolution,* Gesellschaft und Theologie. Systematische Beiträge 5 (Munich: Kaiser-Grünewald, 1971).

LIST OF PARTICIPANTS

Catholics

The Most Reverend T. Austin Murphy
Auxiliary Bishop of Baltimore, Maryland
The Rev. Maurice C. Duchaine, S.S.
St. Patrick's Seminary, Menlo Park, California
The Rev. Avery Dulles, S.J.
Catholic University of America, Washington, D.C.
The Rev. Robert B. Eno, S.S.
Catholic University of America, Washington, D.C.
The Rev. Joseph A. Fitzmyer, S.J.
Catholic University of America, Washington, D.C.
The Rev. John F. Hotchkin
Director, Bishops' Committee for Ecumenical and Interreligious Affairs, Washington, D.C.
The Rev. Kilian McDonnell, O.S.B.
Executive Director, Institute for Ecumenical and Cultural Research, Collegeville, Minnesota
The Rev. Carl J. Peter
Dean, School of Religious Studies, Catholic University of America, Washington, D.C.
The Rev. Msgr. Jerome D. Quinn
The St. Paul Seminary, St. Paul, Minnesota
The Rev. George H. Tavard, A.A.
Methodist Theological School, Delaware, Ohio

Lutherans

Dr. Paul C. Empie
Former General Secretary, USA National Committee of the Lutheran World Federation, New York, New York

Dr. Eugene L. Brand
Director, Office of Studies, USA National Committee of the Lutheran World Federation, New York, New York

Dr. Joseph A. Burgess
Executive Director, Division of Theological Studies, Lutheran Council in the U.S.A., New York, New York

Dr. Gerhard O. Forde
Professor of Systematic Theology, Luther Theological Seminary, St. Paul, Minnesota

Dr. Karlfried Froehlich
Professor of the History of the Early and Medieval Church, Princeton Theological Seminary, Princeton, New Jersey

Dr. Eric W. Gritsch
Professor of Church History, Lutheran Theological Seminary, Gettysburg, Pennsylvania

Dr. Fred Kramer
Professor of Systematic Theology, Concordia Theological Seminary, Springfield, Illinois

Dr. George A. Lindbeck
Professor of Historical Theology, Yale Divinity School, New Haven, Connecticut

Dr. Warren A. Quanbeck
Professor of Systematic Theology, Luther Theological Seminary, St. Paul, Minnesota

Dr. John Reumann
Professor of New Testament, Lutheran Theological Seminary, Philadelphia, Pennsylvania

Dr. William Rusch
Director for Ecumenical Relations, Lutheran Church in America, New York, New York

Dr. Paul A. Wee
General Secretary, USA National Committee of the Lutheran World Federation, New York, New York